Older Masters

essays and reflections on English and American literature

Also by Donald Davie from Carcanet

POETRY

Collected Poems 1970-1983

Selected Poems

To Scorch or Freeze

Collected Poems

CRITICISM

Under Briggflatts: a history of poetry in Great Britain 1960-1985

Slavic Excursions: essays on Polish and Russian literature

Studies in Ezra Pound

AUTOBIOGRAPHY

These the Companions

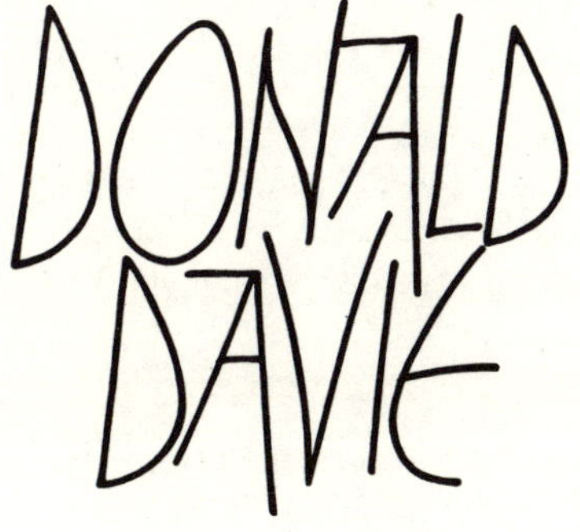

OLDER MASTERS

Essays and reflections on English and American literature

CARCANET

First published in Great Britain in 1992 by
Carcanet Press Limited
208-212 Corn Exchange Buildings
Manchester M4 3BQ

The author and publisher thank Thom Gunn for permission to reprint his poem 'Street Song' (p.35) from *Sunlight* (New York, 1969).

A CIP catalogue record for this book is available from the British Library.
ISBN 0 85635 979 3

The publisher acknowledges financial assistance from the Arts Council of Great Britain

Set in 10pt Bembo by Bryan Williamson, Darwen
Printed and bound in England by SRP Ltd, Exeter

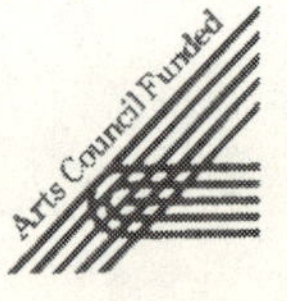

Contents

1 Chaucer and One Idea of Englishness

Before I read Ian Robinson's *Chaucer and the English Tradition*, I had thought that its title meant something like 'The Chaucerian Tradition in English Poetry'. I looked forward to essays which would ask what justification there is, if any, for using the word 'Chaucerian' of later poets so different as George Crabbe and Robert Browning. Such essays, if they were well done, would interest me a great deal. Instead what I found was four pieces on supposedly 'early' Chaucer (*The Book of the Duchess, The House of Fame,* and *The Parliament of Fowls*); then an essay on *Troilus and Criseyde*, followed by six on various parts of *The Canterbury Tales*; and in a last section, an article on *Piers Plowman*, one on *Sir Gawain and the Green Knight*, one on the Scottish Chaucerians, one on Dante, and two last chapters (both very good) called respectively 'Chaucer and criticism' and 'Chaucer the father'. This page of contents certainly takes care of the first half of Ian Robinson's title; but what, I asked myself, had happened to 'the English tradition'? Having read the book, I recognize what has happened to it, and how it has been taken care of – in parenthetical asides and momentary cross-lightings, comparing Chaucer with some of his successors; comparisons which are blankly asserted, provocative at first but later predictable, comparisons asserted or assumed, but not argued for. I see that I was very naïve, not only in looking for names so out of fashion as Crabbe's or Browning's, but also in overlooking the definite article: *the* English tradition – there is only one, and the name that presides over it more insistently than any other is (wait for it!) D.H. Lawrence.

Already I must apologize. When Ian Robinson takes issue with other critics, he does it with burly good humour and hard-hitting but real civility. And I had promised myself that I would observe the same proprieties with him. But it's no good: the part of his book that corresponds to 'the English tradition' seems to me simply outlandish, of an eccentricity that can be acknowledged only by a flurry of astonished exclamation-marks. What else can one do with a comment on 'The Knight's Tale': 'Chaucer may show in this tale a tragic truth that we need to complement Lawrence, or Shakespeare, or Sophocles'? Or – a more sinister example – what but exclamation-marks, less astonished now and more angry, can respond to the admission: 'I do not see how a great English poet could think Dante greater than Chaucer, except in despair of English'?

So that we can be done with the 'English tradition' part of the title, and turn to what is more sensible and useful, Robinson's thoughts about Chaucer, that last admission had better be returned to its context:

> But Chaucer, and Shakespeare, are always trying to find out what they mean: their great and final achievements are the process of discovery – and not the discovery of something pre-existent. I would say that Chaucer creates the idea of patience in English by writing *The Clerk's Tale*. (This does not imply that he could have done so without the aid of other people and the language.) And that is a higher creativity than Dante's.
>
> But I think it would be a bad thing if I could find a cultured Italian to agree with me. These things are bound to look different from different viewpoints: which is not to say that there is no truth in literary criticism. Each national literature is a centre from which to view the rest: I feel at home with Chaucer as I cannot with Dante. If English is one's first language, one naturally takes the greatest kind of poetry to be Shakespeare's – and Dickens's, and D.H. Lawrence's, and Chaucer's. Otherwise one goes against the grain of one's own language, and can be at home nowhere. I do not see how a great English poet could think Dante greater than Chaucer, except in despair of English. And I do say that T.S. Eliot's debts to Dante, so obviously a strength in *The Waste Land* and *Little Gidding*, are in this other way a weakness, and one that it is relevant to think of when considering the peculiarly limited and equivocal nature of Eliot's greatness. If Eliot's endeavour to extend English poetry into our century could have been as daring and English as Chaucer's, if Eliot could have gone back to Chaucer as well as to Dante, English poetry might have survived his death. Eliot's hankering after the Dantesque kind of impersonality and certainty is, at least sometimes, the disguise of an unconfidence in the creative habit of his own language.

The impartial reader may ask: What of Lawrence's writing are we meant to recall, that in prose or what purports to be verse? And: Why is Dante 'a strength' in *The Waste Land* and *Little Gidding*, but not in 'Ash Wednesday'? And: Where is it demonstrated that Eliot's greatness is 'peculiarly limited and equivocal'? And: What does it mean to say that English poetry has not survived Eliot's death? To all of these questions, as to many others, no answer is forthcoming in Ian Robinson's pages; either the answers are in supposedly canonical texts which he does not care to specify, or else he intends by the confidence of his earnest rhetoric to make us take as proven what has not been proved at all.

And yet this, disreputable as it is, is not what one means by calling such a passage 'sinister'. What is so shocking about it is precisely its guilelessness, as appears from the would-be handsome concession to the 'cultured Italian'. Exploded without a second thought is the notion that Dante and Shakespeare, Cervantes and Tolstoy and Goethe, are voices which speak for mankind, or for the mankind of Europe. Shakespeare is *ours*, possessively and exclusively, as Dante is *theirs*; each language-community tends its own hearth, huddling together, turned inward to its own special flame, jealously guarding it against strangers. Anything more self-evidently ostrich-like, in 1972, it is hard to imagine. The self-congratulating insularity which F.R. Leavis's criticism has so often skirted and barely avoided (obeisances are made to him in Robinson's next paragraph) here becomes explicit and ludicrous. 'I feel at home with Chaucer...'; cosily at home is apparently where we should want to be, and where we must make every effort to remain. 'Dante's reputation', Ian Robinson says, 'is unlikely to be touched by any words of mine'. But who cares about 'reputation'? Literary taste and opinion, ignorant and mercurial as we know them to be in Swansea and elsewhere, will be swayed by him out of Europe and into Little England or Little Wales – as he must know, and must intend.

What is peculiarly ludicrous, and lamentable, is that Robinson should anchor this culturally nationalist thesis to that one of the major poets in English who is, by common consent at least since Quiller-Couch, the least insular, the most European. Moreover any one who has tried to write English verse in a narrative or lyrical mode knows that the suave limpidity of Chaucer's verse and the dense multivalence of Shakespeare's present themselves, not as branches off the one stem, but as alternatives that one must choose between. Yet Ian Robinson presents them as parts of one package.

The truth is that despite all the demands that he makes of himself to be a rightly responsive reader (the demands are harsh, and the harshness is what dignifies his best pages), he seldom enters into the processes of composition that have to do with the execution of a poem, rather than its conception. My countervailing instance is less than conclusive because it has to do once again with a body of foreign poetry, the *very* foreign poetry of the troubadours. It so happens that just before I read Ian Robinson's pages on the troubadours, I had read Hugh Kenner's in *The Pound Era*. Kenner quotes two lines of Arnaut Daniel:

Autet e bas entrels prims fuoills
Son nou de flors li ram eil renc...

And he comments:

> A man who begins a song with the phonemes *autet e bas*, or puts *prims* between *entrels* and *fuoills*, expects us to take pleasure in the separation, not the blending, of syllables, and in sound relieving, not prolonging, sound. Tennyson would not have been pleased. Not Daniel but Jaufre Rudel of the fulsome assonances would be the troubadour to interest a Tennyson...

Though I don't know how to pronounce old Provençal (does any one know with certainty?), Kenner's point is surely borne out by his quotation, if orthography gives any clue at all to pronunciation. And his comments are those of a reader who knows, through sympathetic imagination, what it is like to be a writer in the act of writing. When he goes on to explain why Arnaut Daniel mattered to Ezra Pound, and to suggest that 'the moral virtue Blake the engraver attributed to outlines Pound the poet associated with bounded sounds', he may or may not be right; but it is in any case a great leap of the critical imagination, and it is true to the way in which the poet, *any* poet, only half aware what he is doing, makes rapid and momentous choices all the time as his hand moves across the page. By contrast, when Ian Robinson treats of the troubadours (lumping them all together), he talks about nothing but a 'love' which he leaves undefined beyond saying that it isn't copulation; and he briskly dismisses Arnaut and the rest by saying that since theirs was 'a language *only* of love' (his italics), 'they could never rise into the conscious criticism of life that we think of as the typical poetic function.' But of course Kenner's cross-reference to Blake's 'wiry bounding line' suggests precisely a 'criticism of life', one that Blake and Pound and Arnaut concur in (as does Lawrence, incidentally, when he objects to Whitman's 'ghastly merging'). But it is a criticism of life that emerges only when, with Kenner, we attend, not to what the language *says*, but to what it *does*. And that is a rarer kind of responsiveness than the one which Ian Robinson practises.

This is to give to 'criticism of life' a meaning more abstruse than Matthew Arnold's sense of it, or than Ian Robinson's, in whose pages the Arnoldian formula tolls steadily like a lugubrious bell. However, it is precisely the point of the book, and what is of interest in it, that this is a critic who wants to use Arnold's criterion so as to make the highest claims for Chaucer, claims which Arnold himself refused to make or to recognize. What is original and challenging in this view of Chaucer comes out in the chapter on the Scottish makars (a chapter that the Scots will not like), when the critic says of Henryson:

> I think Henryson wrote the fables because they gave him the chance of doing a great many different things in poetry – of bringing in a great range of poetic language – without forcing upon him (comfortable old schoolmaster as he seems to have been, enjoying his grimness in his study) the agony of poetic seriousness.

Is this to say that Chaucer on the other hand agonized over his poems? Yes, it is to say that; so far have we come from what C.S. Lewis called 'Chaucer the cheery dear old man'. The easiest way to displace that caricature is to think of Chaucer as the author of *Troilus and Criseyde*, and one of the surprises is that Ian Robinson judges that poem 'a great failure', as being 'at once a novel and not a novel, with the result that much of it is plain dull.' We may or may not be persuaded; but we must certainly respect the honesty, especially since it turns Robinson back on to the toughest aspect of his assignment – how to find 'the agony of poetic seriousness' in the poetry of a great *comic* imagination. This of course is what defeated Arnold himself, and it remains a central dilemma for all critics of the Arnoldian persuasion, as we see when they address themselves to Jane Austen's novels, or to Lawrence's short stories, or for that matter to Dickens. The beguiling temptation is to applaud as great comedy a work which one's demonstration presents as not comedy at all but satire. And this is another of the pitfalls or evasions which Robinson takes care not to fall into. For him 'The Merchant's Tale' and 'The Miller's Tale' are two of Chaucer's most powerful and serious poems. 'The Merchant's Tale' is not satire or invective or sustained lampoon, but comedy; and 'The Miller's Tale', though it is comedy, is not 'simple comedy' – the description of Alison for instance is winningly lyrical in a way that Robinson's commentary brings out very well.

In any case, of course, the comedy of 'The Miller's Tale' cannot be simple because it is placed inside a frame which has to accommodate also 'The Knight's Tale' and 'The Clerk's Tale', for both of which Robinson argues passionately and with force. He argues for 'The Knight's Tale' as 'tragic', meaning by that something valuably precise. This is the longest chapter in his book, and central to his argument; and it is impressively honest in the way it takes account of how one may be put off the poem, as he admits that he was himself for a long time. We need to acknowledge however that if the proximity of 'The Knight's Tale' ensures that 'The Miller's Tale' is complex, the reverse must also be true and 'The Knight's Tale' must be deflected towards comedy by the neighbours it has to live with. Though Robinson considers 'heroic' as an alternative to 'tragic' for characterizing this tale, he does so only to dismiss it; whereas if it be recognized that the heroic also has its complexities, I suspect that 'heroic' is still the better term.

I must not forget to applaud the last chapter, where Robinson makes sense of the old chestnut about Chaucer 'the father of English'. He does so by arguing eloquently and thinking deeply about what a language is, and what a literature is. This chapter should some day be excerpted and printed separately; it could achieve a sort of classic status.

Essays in Criticism XXII:4 (October 1972).

2 *A Reading of 'The Ocean's Love to Cynthia'*

We can begin by reminding ourselves, in brief and bold strokes, of the personality of Ralegh as it is presented by the biographer. We shall recall that, like Philip Sidney, Ralegh was an amateur in poetry, a many-sided man, already a legend in his own lifetime; but that where Sidney was loved and admired, Ralegh, it seems, was hated and feared, by all but an immediate circle of friends who were devoted to him. And the thing which made him hated, which all his contemporaries record, is his *pride*. The image we get is of a man touchy, insolent, flashy, uncontrollable; a haughty, headstrong exhibitionist.

Something of this can be traced to his origin – significantly different from Sidney's. Ralegh came of the country gentry, of an ancient and honourable family; but he was not born to the highest level of the aristocracy, like the Sidneys, or the Dudleys and Devereux who were later his rivals at court. He could not assume, as Sidney could, that his birth would entitle him from the first to positions of great power. He had to win his way, to force his way to the top by sheer force of personality. And so we may imagine him as a go-getter, a man on the make, a thruster. Everything depended on his pleasing two capricious monarchs. His life and most of his poetry are devoted to this one end. And so there could not be for him, in life or in writing, that ease which is so conspicuous and persuasive in Sidney. Sidney was poet and courtier 'as to the manner born'; Ralegh was poet and courtier because his life depended on it.

It was in 1582, when he was thirty years old, that Ralegh came home from Ireland, an obscure army officer with no backing and no influence. Almost at once he rose to become Elizabeth's favourite. No one knows why – but the story of his laying his cloak on a puddle for the Queen to step on, if it is false in fact, is probably true in spirit. He became the Queen's favourite principally because, in Elizabeth's ceremonious and elaborate and extravagant court, he was the most inventively ceremonious, the most elaborate and extravagant figure of them all. He was in favour from 1582 to 1592.

When, in 1587, Robert Devereux came to court and won Elizabeth's esteem, Ralegh appears for a time to have been under a cloud; but he got back again (and here our interest quickens) by writing to Elizabeth a poem in several books called *Ocean's Love to Cynthia*. Or so we are led to understand by *Colin Clout's Come Home Again*. Spenser's poem seems to say that Ralegh and Spenser, each with a poem in honour of the Queen, went to court together from Ireland. Spenser got little out of it and returned to Ireland; but the trick worked for Ralegh and he was back in high favour.

It seems certain that the poem Spenser refers to is not the poem that we now read. What we have is a continuation of that vanished poem, a further section of *Ocean's Love to Cynthia*, written several years later. For when Ralegh's fall came, in 1592, it came because of a woman. Ralegh had got with child one of Elizabeth's maids of honour, Elizabeth Throckmorton, whom he then married. Elizabeth was annoyed presumably not by his immorality, but because he had dared to look at another woman when she was by. At least – that seems to be the likeliest explanation to us, but really the conventions of Elizabeth's court in these matters appear to us so weird and wonderful that one does not know how to take it. In his poems, of course, Ralegh pretends to be hopelessly in love with the Queen; and the fact that there was now a Lady Ralegh did not prevent her husband from maintaining the fiction of his passion for the elderly and unattractive Queen. Elizabeth must have known that Ralegh's devotion was a convention only, a pretence; then why was she annoyed? Perhaps she was spiteful enough to pretend not to know what she really knew perfectly well. Or else perhaps she took so seriously the principle of ceremonious order that she was determined to maintain the convention for reasons not spiteful at all but, at a deep level, politic.

At any rate Ralegh was recalled (he had departed on an expedition to Panama) and was imprisoned in the Tower:

> To seeke new worlds, for golde, for prayse, for glory,
> To try desire, to try love severed farr,
> When I was gonn shee sent her memory
> More stronge then weare ten thowsand shipps of warr,
>
> To call mee back, to leve great honors thought,
> To leve my frinds, my fortune, my attempte,
> To leve the purpose I so longe had sought
> And holde both cares, and cumforts in contempt.

All things considered, it seems likely that it was now, imprisoned in the Tower, that Ralegh tried the old trick and wrote another book of *Ocean's Love to Cynthia*; and that this is the poem which survives under that title. But if so, the trick did not work this time, or not so well; for it was not until the end of the year that he was released – and then, apparently, because his expedition had returned with the richest prize-ship ever brought to England. Ralegh was released because his sailors had started looting in Dartmouth, and also because he could now buy himself out.

The later chapters of Ralegh's extraordinary career – his restoration to favour in Elizabeth's last years after the failure of Essex's rebellion, his failure from the first to recommend himself to James, the long scandal and agony of his incarceration, his two trials, the harrowing disaster of his last expedition to Guiana – these phases of his life have nothing to do with *Ocean's Love to Cynthia*. It should be interesting to see what we can make of this poem, with no more than this to go upon.

In the first place, the literal sense of the poem is now clear: Ralegh, a favourite out of favour with his sovereign, pretends for the purpose of the poem to be a lover out of favour with his mistress, who writes a poem of expostulation, complaint, flattery, and emotional blackmail, in order to be restored to his former privileges. The reader will recognize the love-convention, and also, in a shadowy and incidental, perfunctory way, another convention, the pastoral. In so far as he is looking for the meaning of the poem, he will recognize these elements only to discard them; though he may recognize also that they are greatly effective as principles of poetic ordering. But what we very properly seek, when we ask for the meaning, is something relevant and interesting not to the peculiar situation of one man at one point in history, but to all men at all times, and in particular to ourselves, in the twentieth century in England.

Looking for this, we may meditate as follows, as we read the poem. Ralegh in disgrace, or at least out of favour, thinks of the cause to which he has devoted all his energies. This cause is Elizabeth; but Elizabeth, for Ralegh here as for Spenser in *The Faerie Queene*, stands for the whole culture of which she was the focus. Ralegh's 'love', therefore, the cause to which he has devoted himself, is the civilization represented by the Renaissance court (in Italy, Spain, or Poland as much as in England). He has been deprived of all opportunities to serve that civilization, to secure it and enrich it; and he asks himself what difference this makes to him.

He finds himself at odds. His reason tells him that the game is not worth the candle; and yet he cannot help but persevere. He is as unreasonable as a lamb, newly weaned, that still returns to the dug; as unnatural as a body that continues to twitch after being killed; as inert as a water-wheel that turns by its own dwindling momentum though the current has changed; as fantastic as a man who mistakes twilight for dawn, and begins at nightfall an enormous task. Indeed, even in his years of power his reason had condemned him:

Twelve yeares intire I wasted in this warr,
Twelve yeares of my most happy younger dayes,
Butt I in them and they now wasted ar,
Of all which past the sorrow only stayes.

So wrate I once, and my mishapp fortolde,
My minde still feelinge sorrowfull success
Yeven as before a storme the marbell colde
Douth by moyste teares tempestious tymes express.

So fealt my hevy minde my harmes att hande
Which my vayne thought in vayne sought to recure;
Att middell day my soonn seemde under land
When any littell cloude did it obscure.

All the more, now that disaster has come upon him, does he see himself as having devoted all his energies to an object discredited by his reason. Even now that the blow has fallen, he finds himself still a divided personality – split between the reasonable mind that watches, afraid and helpless, and the unreasonable will that chooses and drives to action. This is presented most vividly in his recollection of how it was with him when the blow first fell:

Sumetyme I died, sumetyme I was distract,
My sowle the stage of fancies tragedye.
Then furious madness wher trew reason lackt
Wrate what it would, and scurgde myne own consayte.

Oh, hevy hart who cann thee wittnes beare,
What tounge, what penn could thy tormentinge treat
But thyne owne mourning thoughts which present weare, . . . ?

We need not go to the dictionary before we decide that 'distract' is the precise word: the heart running mad is distracted from the reason that watches ('thine own mourning thoughts which present were').

Now that he has had time to accustom himself to his changed fortune, reason should come into her own again; but in fact reason seems as irrelevant, as ineffective as ever. And even as he says so (in what are perhaps the best five stanzas), so his attitude changes and, instead of mourning his reason crippled by his will, he exults in the constancy of his will that can overbear all reasonable injunctions:

And though strong reason holde before myne eyes
The Images, and formes of worlds[1] past
Teachinge the cause why all thos flames that rize
From formes externall, cann no longer last,

Then that thos seeminge bewties hold in pryme
Loves ground, his essence, and his emperye,
All slaves to age, and vassalls unto tyme
Of which repentance writes the tragedye.

But this, my harts desire could not conceve
Whose Love outflew the fastest fliinge tyme;
A bewty that cann easely deseave
Th' arrest of yeares, and creepinge age outclyme,

A springe of bewties which tyme ripeth not
Tyme that butt workes onn frayle mortallety,
A sweetness which woes wronges outwipeth not,
Whom love hath chose for his devinnitye,

A vestall fier that burnes, but never wasteth,
That looseth nought by gevinge light to all
That endless shines eachwher and endless lasteth
Blossumes of pride that cann nor vade nor fall.

If we have read Empson's criticism, we shall soon decide that the ambiguity of this passage is deliberate; in particular it seems to turn on an ambiguity crucial to the Elizabethans in the word 'love', meaning (*a*) the energy towards the object, (*b*) the object of the energy. Here what is spoken of is love (*a*), the energy, for the most part; but 'the vestal fire' suggests Elizabeth, the object, love (*b*). One of the neatest plays on the pun is

A springe of bewties which tyme ripeth not;

for if this were Elizabeth that is spoken of, the phrase would be 'which time *withereth* not'. The word 'ripeth' provides a sardonic surprise and commands immediate assent because it fits Ralegh's situation so well.

[1] Agnes Latham makes the pleasing suggestion that 'worlds' here has to be read as a disyllable because of Ralegh's west-country 'r'. See her edition of *The Poems of Sir Walter Ralegh* (London, 1951).

When Ralegh does go on to the object, Elizabeth, he is more concerned with the flaw in her perfection, her lack of compassion, than with her virtues. Ironically or needlessly, he tells himself to 'leave her praise'; and he elaborates still further on the nature of woman's love and the thankless task of trying to ensure it. This love, woman's love, is subject to mutability, as is emphasized first by beautiful conventional flower-and-fruit images; and at last rammed home by the barest unconventionality:

> The tokens hunge onn brest, and kyndly worne
> Ar now elcewhere disposde, or helde for toyes.

But by this time the reader is huddling or cramming together lines from scattered parts of the poem, and is aware that he is imposing a summary order upon a turbulent flux and reflux of feeling, repeatedly circling back on itself, of which he will admit that he is growing a little weary. So we note in rather summary fashion how a return to pastoral imagery introduces the ploughman, symbol of the man who accustoms himself to mutability by rooting up the old and sowing new. The implication is clear: the lover, if he were reasonable, would do the same. But once again, moving strangely from sorrow to exultation, Ralegh proclaims that for him this is impossible:

> Sorrow was my revendge and wo my hate;
> I pourless was to alter my desire.
> My love is not of tyme, or bound to date.
> My harts internall heat, and livinge fier
>
> Would not, or could be quencht, with suddayn shoures.
> My bound respect was not confinde to dayes
> My vowed fayth not sett to ended houres.
> I love the bearinge and not bearinge sprayes...

And the rest of the poem (though still it ebbs as often as it flows) is a celebration of this 'durable fire', his constancy, which at the end is taken to be the spiritual prize of Ralegh's whole life:

> To God I leve it, who first gave it me,...

And by this time, of course, the mind that began by being so divided against itself is at one, resolved and even calm.

If this is indeed, however roughly, the account of the poem that might be given after an intelligent and sensitive but uninstructed and largely unassisted reading, it would doubtless go along with liking and even enthusiastic admiration for Ralegh's achievement. It is easy to read 'love' as 'dedication' throughout, and any reader will know, from personal experience or else from sympathy with others, those hours in which the dedicated life asks itself if the game is worth the candle, decides that it isn't, and then with bewilderment finds that it will not act upon this decision; this is the subject of Ralegh's poem, and it is one that must strike home to all of us. Moreover, if we have encountered a certain longueur some two-thirds of the way through, we are reconcilded to the poem by some astonishing triumphs in the last pages:

> Butt what of thos, or thes, or what of ought
> Of that which was, or that which is, to treat?
> What I possess is butt the same I sought;
> My love was falce, my labors weare desayte.
>
> Nor less then such they ar esteemde to bee,
> A fraude bought att the prize of many woes,
> A guile, whereof the profitts unto mee –
> Coulde it be thought premeditate for thos?

(The breaking off into the incredulity of the last line comes with the poignancy of unprepared sincerity, but only by contrast with the rhetorical patterning of what has gone before, and of the poem as a whole – an effect contrived elsewhere also, but nowhere so piercingly.) Thus, both in what the poem says and in its ways of saying it, *Ocean's Love to Cynthia* is likely to commend itself to the modern reader. In fact I want to investigate the possibility, not that he won't like the poem enough, but that he will like the poem too much, or at least too promptly, and for the wrong reasons.

We may start by supposing that he likes the poem enough to see what others have said of it. And if the modern reader should turn for instance to an admirable handbook by P. Edwards,[1] he will feel at once that his reading of the poem has been enriched. At line 120, for example, where the poem seems to make a fresh start with 'Twelve yeares intire I wasted in this warr', everyone will relish and endorse Edwards's acute remark, 'But this poem never starts: it is always about to relate the whole great tragedy, but then is pulled aside into a digression. Then we reach a point at which we realise that the whole story has, piecemeal, been related and there is nothing more to do except bring the poem to a close.' The reader will find his moment of tedium acknowledged and in part justified by the comment, 'From line 318, such is the turmoil of the thought –

[1] *Sir Walter Ralegh* (London, 1953).

whether intentional or not – that it is hard to make useful divisions of the poem into sections any further' (though I suspect we are by this time formulating our own ideas about 'whether intentional or not'). And he will be grateful to have his attention returned to the astonishing stanza near the end:

> Shee is gonn, Shee is lost! Shee is found, shee is ever faire!
> Sorrow drawes weakly, wher love drawes not too.
> Woes cries, sound nothinge, butt only in loves eare.
> Do then by Diinge, what life cannot doo...

Because he must have wondered if the sudden exultation of 'she is found, she is ever fair' represented a change of feeling decisive for the poem as a whole, and because he will surely have decided that if so the wrench around is too abrupt to be effective, he will be grateful for Edwards's justified confidence on the point: 'Some have taken this as the turning point of the poem, but it is not so. His denial is a momentary, irresistible ejaculation, expressing the division in his mind that has been present throughout the poem. A coal glows white hot and then dies to an ember and the poem continues with the settled unhappiness that had preceded the outburst.' And finally, our reader should be prepared to revise his too glib idea of how the poem ends, when Edwards says of it, 'It is far better that Ralegh ends his extraordinary poem with a gesture of helplessness than [with] an affirmation – say, of the neo-platonic idea expressed or hinted at in "Do then by dying what life cannot do"'.

But what will our reader make of the observations that emerge from Edwards's examination of the Hatfield MS of the poem, in Ralegh's own hand, the sole manuscript known to exist? Edwards is relying on Agnes Latham's solid authority when he decides, after examining the manuscript, 'Ralegh is transcribing an earlier draft... and he is clearly making changes as he copies, but... the transcript cannot represent the poem in a finished state...' It is on his own authority, however, that he decides in consequence, 'We must clearly make reservations in our criticism, bearing in mind that we have before us poetry being created, and not a finally completed work of art.' It is hereabouts that the modern reader may dig in his heels. For after all it would not be at all surprising if a twentieth-century taste preferred the unfinished state of an Elizabethan poem to its finished state. What offends our modern taste in Elizabethan poetry is precisely that it is, by modern standards, all too 'finished'; it lacks the abruptness of transition, the intriguing gaps that a post-symbolist poet leaves us to fill in for ourselves (or at least he *seems* to leave them). It is true that the poetry of Eliot and Pound is now almost old-fashioned; but at least it will appear that a reader brought up on their poetry, poetry which proceeds by associative not logical linkings, by images merely juxtaposed (the links between them unstated), is likely to like Ralegh's poem precisely because it is unfinished; and to suppose that where Ralegh leaves out logical links, he does so deliberately, as in *The Waste Land*; whereas the manuscript suggests that where this happens, it was as an interim expedient only, an emergency operation to be redressed or concealed in a later working-over.

Yet if we point this out to a modern reader, as Edwards does, he can still impenitently retreat to that metaphysical hinterland of criticism where roam those fabulous beasts, the intentional and the affective fallacies. Certainly he may say, appealing to commonsense, that he has to like or dislike the poem as it stands, since this is all of the poem there is. He may well protest that neither he nor anyone else can be asked, or should be prepared, to read poetry in terms of 'as if' or 'if only'. For Ralegh indeed the poem may have been unfinished (as well as incomplete, lacking as it may an earlier ten or twenty books); but for us as readers the poem must stand as finished and be judged as such.

And from this position (which strikes me as impregnable) he may choose to counter-attack. He may point out that Edwards, like every other commentator on the poem, admits that at least some of the loose ends, the waywardness and abruptness, are deliberate, and would presumably have been retained in any later version. Thus Edwards says, 'The poem is a fevered elegy, obscure, turbulent and erratic, with the incoherence almost of delirium in the flow of its thought. There is nothing like it elsewhere in Elizabethan poetry.' And the modern reader is right to ask how this scholar, with the manuscript before him, decides which of the loose ends would have been tied up later, and which on the contrary are essential to the poem and would have been retained. Edwards has his answer, and it is time to turn to specific cases.

There is line 213:

> But leve her prayse, speak thow of nought but wo, . . .

The uninstructed reader, we remember, remarked that when Ralegh commanded himself to leave her praise, he did so 'ironically or needlessly'. And I think he cannot be allowed to get away with this. Irony is an all too convenient bolt-hole which the twentieth century has been too ready to make use of in such cases. There is nothing ironical elsewhere in the poem, though there is, as Edwards notes, at least one moment of bitter sarcasm. Edwards's case must here be accepted, by which 'But leave her praise' was meant to follow immediately line 192:

> Blossumes of pride that cann nor vade nor fall...,

lines 193-200, and also 200-212, being false starts intended for later deletion or else transference elsewhere. There are marks in the manuscript against both these passages, which may be meant to signify this. And yet even here, even on Edwards's own showing, the illogic of lines 193-212 represent or mime the turbulent flux and reflux of a mind in the act of feeling, rather than the product of feeling tidied up for public consumption. And so how can we reply to the reader who objects that if Ralegh had tidied them up, he would have spoiled them?

Again, there is a similar mark in the MS against line 465:

> My love was falce, my labors weare desayte.

And Edwards suggests that this was marked for alteration because 'love' is there ambiguous. This is a place where the reader has to stick to his post-Empsonian guns. He must maintain that this ambiguity is deliberate, since it is central to the whole argument of the poem as he understands it. If it is pointed out that Ralegh was a pre-Empsonian, to whom it had not occurred that ambiguity was different from muddle, it can be retorted that he was at any rate a contemporary of Shakespeare, whose sonnets provided Empson with his best and most compelling examples of deliberate exploitation of double-meanings. What is more to the point is that one may point to many lines in the poem where this ambiguity appears, such as line 57, 'The honour of her love, Love still devising'. Perhaps the best proof of how Ralegh's mind was exercised continually by love as energy towards an object, played against love as the object drawing the energy, is in lines 37 to 44. Line 37 represents the first of those abrupt transitions which distinguish the whole poem. This is a transition from the hopeless unhappiness and sterility with which the poem starts, to a sudden hymn of adoration; and it is one which Edwards accepts as deliberately intended:

> Oh hopefull love my object, and invention,
> Oh, trew desire the spurr of my consayte,
> Oh, worthiest spirrit, my minds impulsion,
> Oh, eyes transpersant, my affections bayte,
>
> Oh, princely forme, my fancies adamande,
> Devine consayte, my paynes acceptance,
> Oh, all in onn, oh heaven on yearth transparant,
> The seat of joyes, and loves abundance!

The playing off of 'impulsion' against 'adamant' (which *draws*) cannot be unintentional, and it makes manifest the opposite movements which are implicit in the one word 'love', according as it is seen from the man's or from the woman's point of view.

One further example: lines 132-3:

> And as the Isakells in a winters day
> When as the soonn shines with unwounted warme, . . .

If Ralegh was thinking of the poem as written in quatrains (as he surely was, despite occasional five-line stanzas, tercets, and unattached couplets like this one) there can be no doubt that this represents a place where Ralegh knows that smoothing out will be called for. But this is not to say, as Edwards does, that in the re-working, the image of the icicles would be expunged altogether. He takes this as an example of 'images which do not obey the rules of decorum and logical aptness that Ralegh normally adheres to so excellently'. And he goes on to say of this image:

> it involves the suggestion that Ralegh's heart is like an icicle in temperature, and, more important, it relates Cynthia's access of displeasure to the increased *warmth* of the sun. By contrast and much more fitly, Cynthia's displeasure in line 106 is compared to the *setting* of the sun. The 'icicles' image may give an exact sensory impression, but it is out of keeping with the needs of the poem; the metrical and grammatical uneasiness probably indicates Ralegh's dissatisfaction. The marks in the manuscript against line 132 presumably indicate that something was to be changed.

Here surely Edwards wants to tidy up too much. It's true that we have lately and most usefully been made to see how much Elizabethan and Metaphysical poets cared for logical ordering and consonance in their choice of images, how far they were from sharing a modern willingness to let illogical and disordered imagery mime out for the reader an illogical and disordered state of mind. But Edwards has already allowed, as regards *Ocean's Love to Cynthia*, that 'There is nothing like it elsewhere in Elizabethan poetry'. And with that for our warrant, we cannot help but note how, throughout the poem, images are turning over, double-edged; one whole binding sequence of imagery from water, for instance, appears to be deployed with just this in view – no sooner have we grasped an image of the queen as a ruinous inundation flooding the poet's pastures, than we have to adjust ourselves into seeing her as rain which falls too grudgingly upon his thirsty acres. It seems to have been Ralegh's deliberate intention to keep the reader off balance in this way; and therefore I cannot wish the icicles image away.

There is a fine example of this, incidentally, though an unrepresentative one, on the very first page of the poem:

Lost in the mudd of thos hygh flowinge streames
Which through more fayrer feilds ther courses bend,
Slayne with sealf thoughts, amasde in fearfull dreams,
Woes without date, discumforts without end,

From frutfull trees I gather withred leves
And glean the broken eares with misers hands,
Who sumetyme did injoy the waighty sheves
I seeke faire floures amidd the brinish sand.

All in the shade yeven in the faire soon dayes
Under thos healthless trees I sytt alone,
Wher joyfull byrdds singe neather lovely layes
Nor Phillomen recounts her direfull mone.

Here the resolute refusal to indulge the pathetic fallacy, insisting that the birds *were* joyous and the trees *were* fruitful though not to him (how Ruskin would have approved!) induces a sort of vertigo in the reader, never sure which way to take each image as it comes. Perhaps the finest stroke is 'mud', which may be exceptionally fertile (the Nile valley) just as it may be both noisome and sterile.

Surely this is, once again, very much a 'modern' effect. We encounter it, for instance, in *Little Gidding*:

There are three conditions which often look alike
Yet differ completely, flourish in the same hedgerow:
Attachment to self and to things and to persons, detachment
From self and from things and from persons; and, growing
    between them, indifference
Which resembles the others as death resembles life,
Being between two lives – unflowering, between
The live and the dead nettle.

Here, by the enlivening use of a curious English idiom – 'the dead nettle', used of a kind of nettle which is perfectly alive – Eliot plays upon the paradox that death resembles life. And the image which makes of the truly dead because unflowering thing a thrusting weed – this muddles us even further about where life ends and death begins. Add to this the traditional associations of the nettle, stinging and sterility, and the reader experiences a curious vertigo or giddiness every time he re-reads the passage, however firmly at some time or other he may have worked out the prose sense.

We may compare:

> A springe of bewties which tyme ripeth not
> Tyme that butt workes onn frayle mortallety, . . .

It will be recalled that I made the clever but uninstructed reader remark of this that if Elizabeth were the 'spring of beauties', the phrase ought to be 'which time *withereth* not'. To say instead 'ripeth' made it clear that the spring was not the attractiveness of Elizabeth, the loved object, but rather the energy towards the object, the constancy of her lover. What looked like a compliment to her is really the lover complimenting himself. And my reader applauded this as a bold and subtle stroke, affording a sardonic surprise. But this won't do. If we remember Touchstone saying,

> And so, from hour to hour, we ripe and ripe,
> And then, from hour to hour, we rot and rot;

or Malcolm saying,

> Macbeth
> Is ripe for shaking, and the pow'rs above
> Put on their instruments;

or Richard II saying, of the dying John of Gaunt,

> The ripest fruit first falls, and so doth he;

or finally Queen Margaret saying, in *Richard III*,

> So now prosperity begins to mellow
> And drop into the rotten mouth of death;[1]

we realize that to a mind of Shakespeare's generation 'ripe' meant not just the process of maturation in its beneficent and bountiful aspect (which is what it tends to mean for us), but also and equally maturation in its aspect as a stage towards senescence and decomposition. In other words, just as the concept 'ripeness' involves as a corollary the idea of withering, for the Elizabethans the *word* also brought with it this corollary (whereas for us, illogically, on the whole it doesn't). And if so, what emerges from 'ripeth' in Ralegh's lines isn't the fine sardonic stroke we thought we had found there, but a far more complex and ambiguous feeling, playing over a whole gamut of possible tones, of which the sardonic is only one. This induces in us, therefore, nothing so simple as the delighted surprise which wants to slap its thigh at the neatness of the turn, but rather

[1] The citations from Shakespeare are taken from J. V. Cunningham, *Woe or Wonder* (1951), pp. 13, 14. Cunningham uses the citations to show that 'Ripeness is all' in *King Lear* cannot mean what we take it and want it to mean – in his words, 'that maturity of experience is a final good, and that there is a fulness of feeling, an inner and emotional completion in life that is attainable and that will resolve our tragedies'.

once again the sort of giddiness in which we see things turn into their opposites, until our heads swim.

But the passage from Eliot prompts other and more far-reaching reflections. It would not make our heads swim if it were not, as regards syntax, elaborately, even painstakingly, correct. We are baffled not just by the illogicalities and contradictions in terms which lie folded, one within another, in the word 'nettle' as Eliot rings the changes upon it. What really bewilders us as we read is that these illogicalities rise into view from an arrangement of language such as we are used to, an arrangement which is grammatically clear and correct and therefore (so we think, mistakenly) manageable and rational. It is the sinuousness of the sentence which traps us, as much as the double meanings in the words themselves. And this is important. For Edwards, to return to him once more, says of *Ocean's Love to Cynthia*, 'The chaotic syntax must often be the mark of an unfinished poem. Every reader will find passages where sentences are left hanging in the air, verbs without subjects, subjects without verbs, relative clauses with no possible antecedents, all of which can only be loose ends.' And yet, once again, a reader who enjoys the fragmented or aborted syntax of Eliot's *Waste Land* or his 'Ash Wednesday', or of Pound's *Cantos*, will be ready to think that thus to play fast and loose with formal grammar is one of the poet's rights; for only in this way can certain valuable poetic effects be attained. And so, once again, he may take the position that, whatever Ralegh's ultimate intentions, in certain places where syntax is deranged in the poem, the poetry gains thereby; and so he may again refuse to make those allowances which Edwards asks him to make – he won't make allowances for the poem's being unfinished, because he thinks it is all the better for being so.

What he must be told, however, is that he cannot have it both ways. He cannot be stopped from preferring an unfinished Elizabethan poem because it is more like a modern poem than the finished poem would have been. But he can be stopped from making it into two different sorts of modern poem at one and the same time. *Ocean's Love to Cynthia* may, for him, be like 'Ash Wednesday', or it may be like *Little Gidding*; but it cannot be like both at once. In other words he has to decide whether Ralegh is the sort of poet, like Valéry and the later Eliot, who makes elaborately correct syntax serve his purposes, or whether, like Pound and the earlier Eliot, he is the sort of poet who gets his poetic effects by breaking or abrogating syntactical laws. There seems to me no doubt that Ralegh is a poet of the first sort, and therefore that Edwards is perfectly right in his contention that where incomplete or wrenched syntax occurs in the poem, this is a sign of its having been left unfinished.

Perhaps the best example of exceptionally subtle and masterful use of syntax is the single sentence running from line 73 to line 103:

But as a boddy violently slayne
Retayneath warmth although the spirrit be gonn,
And by a poure in nature moves agayne
Till it be layd below the fatall stone;

Or as the yearth yeven in cold winter dayes
Left for a tyme by her life gevinge soonn,
Douth by the poure remayninge of his rayes
Produce sume green, though not as it hath dunn;

Or as a wheele forst by the fallinge streame,
Although the course be turnde sume other way
Douth for a tyme go rounde uppon the beame
Till wantinge strenght to move, it stands att stay;

So my forsaken hart, my withered mind,
Widdow of all the joyes it once possest,
My hopes cleane out of sight, with forced wind
To kyngdomes strange, to lands farr off addrest,

Alone, forsaken, frindless onn the shore
With many wounds, with deaths cold pangs inebrased,
Writes in the dust as onn that could no more
Whom love, and tyme, and fortune had defaced,

Of things so great, so longe, so manefolde
With meanes so weake, the sowle yeven then departing
The weale, the wo, the passages of olde
And worlds of thoughts discribde by onn last sythinge:

As if when after Phebus is dessended
And leves a light mich like the past dayes dawninge,
And every toyle and labor wholy ended
Each livinge creature draweth to his restinge

Wee should beginn by such a partinge light
To write the story of all ages past
And end the same before th'aprochinge night.

Three-quarters of the way through this sentence, there is a patch of very loose construction, the phrase beginning 'the soul even then departing'. But this apart, the control is imperious and magnificent.

First, three images, of the slain but stirring body, of the wintry earth, and of the waterwheel, are presented as it were in parallel, each paralleling both the others but parallel also to an image from the previous sentence, of the lamb weaned but still sucking the dug:

> Mich like the gentell Lamm, though lately waynde,
> Playes with the dug though find no cumfort ther.

So far the syntax is austerely logical, and this is made conspicuous by assigning a quatrain to each image. But the stiffness of the logical parallelism is saved from tedium by the very various affective colouring of the images; the lamb is 'innocent', where the image of the slain body is brutal; the lamb has life before it, the corpse has life behind it; and the images are ranged on a scale from the tender vitality of the lamb through the monstrous life of the murdered body and the exiguous life of wintry nature to the material lifelessness, the mere illusion of life, in the wooden wheel. Moreover, the symmetry is saved from seeming a constraint by the very fact that one of the series of images, the lamb, is carried in a different metrical and grammatical unit from the others. Only now, after twelve lines have already unwound themselves, does the subject of the sentence emerge; and this ('my forsaken hart') has then to wait through no less than nine delays of various kinds (phrases in apposition, an ablative absolute construction, three epithets and three adjectival phrases) before it is allowed to find its verb, 'writes'. Even then, before we learn what is to be written, we are sucked back once again into yet further qualification of this subject so much qualified already:

> as one that could no more,
> Whom love, and time, and fortune had defaced;...

Surely this impetus which so slowly and uncertainly gets the sentence into motion, which, having moved it at last, still rocks back hopelessly upon its starting-point, positively enacts in the reader's mind just what it says, the 'waterwheel inertly turning round / Under a stream that would not fill a jug'. And the crowning triumph remains, when the sentence, having struggled up through its interminable preliminaries to the high point of its verb, rocked back there uncertainly, and at last tumbled over, prolongs itself in a seven-line image of the evening twilight. For this image is parallel once again to the three images, now so distant, from which the sentence started. The day lives on borrowed time after sunset, as the twitching body lived on borrowed time after being slain, and the waterwheel moved on borrowed time after the millstream had been diverted. But what I call the affective colouring is now poignantly different again. Above all (with 'every toil and labour wholly ended') it is wretchedly weary; the day longs for death in nightfall whereas the slain body still struggled for life. And so the speaker longs for release from the faint but nagging compulsion to struggle through how many more sentences as laborious as this one. For the attempt is in any case foredoomed; the weary activity is in any case futile.

Such a sentence is indeed strikingly 'modern'; it *is* what it says, and describes its own creation, like Valéry's *Cimetière Marin*. It provokes a sort of implicated bewilderment in the reader, who asks himself with dizzied anxiety how one supposedly logical because grammatical sentence has led him so far from its own starting-point. His bewilderment continues as he moves on into the next sentence, which slips him before he is aware into just that 'story of all ages past' which he has just heard condemned as futile. This sort of sinuous progression is analogous to some progressions in music; it is in the most striking and effective contrast to the abruptness of the transitions in the first two pages. And just as such abruptness reappears at several points later (as we have seen), so does the insinuating music. It is a music which has more to do with syntax, and so with musical *structure*, than with metre and sound values, musical texture. It shows up again most strikingly perhaps in two passages of extended comparison, lines 221 to 240 (where the syntax is woven bafflingly over the gap between Elizabeth as ruinous flood and Elizabeth as too meagre rainfall), and lines 450 and 461, beginning 'Yet as the eayre in deip caves under ground', where again the simile is illogical so that we emerge from it at a different door from that by which we entered.

It is in this sort of effect, and not in any of the disjointed abruptnesses which may be merely accidents of the poem's unfinished state, that, as I think, Ralegh's 'modernity' is most unexpected, most disturbing, and yet most profoundly satisfying. Let another poet of the present century reveal how far-reaching it is, as a principle. This is Pasternak, in his autobiography, *Safe Conduct*:

> What does an honest man do when he speaks the truth only? Time passes in the telling of truth and in this time life passes onward. His truth lags behind and is deceptive. Should a man speak in this manner everywhere and always?
>
> And in art he has to shut his mouth. In art the man is silent and the image speaks. And it becomes apparent that *only* the image can keep pace with the successes of nature...

This is what one means by saying that one emerges from one of Ralegh's images (not just from his metaphors and similes), or from a train of such images, at a different door from the one we went in by. Time has passed in the deployment of the image, and the image itself takes note of that. It is a perception which poetry shares with the other temporal art, music. And it is therefore no doubt foolish to speak of it as modern; for it is of the nature of the poetic act, and must therefore be available as a resource for the greatly endowed and greatly scrupulous poet of any age. Ralegh was such a poet.

Elizabethan Poetry, Stratford-upon-Avon Studies 2 (London: Edward Arnold, 1960).

3 *Shakespeare and the Practising Poet Today*

There is only one way to start on this topic. And that is by ritually recalling a very famous passage of English criticism, John Dryden's *Essay of Dramatic Poesy*, at the point where Dryden is recalling Shakespeare along with Fletcher and Ben Jonson: 'But it is to raise envy to the living, to compare them with the dead. They are honoured, and almost adored by us, as they deserve; neither do I know any so presumptuous of themselves as to contend with them... We acknowledge them our fathers in wit; but they have ruined their estates themselves before they came to their children's hands....' This is of course the earliest and as it seems to me still the most generous and moving expression of how all subsequent poets of the English language must regard Shakespeare; as a standard so daunting that we cannot afford to be at all constantly aware of it. Shakespeare represents, for all his successors, a vast area of the English language and the English imagination which is as it were 'charged', radioactive: a territory where we dare not travel at all often or at all extensively, for fear of being mortally infected, in the sense of being *overborne*, so that we cease to speak with our own voices and produce only puny echoes of the great voice which long ago took over that whole terrain for its own. If poets today do not constantly frequent Shakespeare, it is because they cannot afford to.

I would set beside this a passage which for writers of my generation was not much less classic than Dryden's, and which points in much the same direction. It is from T.S. Eliot's essay on Dante (1929):

> For the science or art of writing verse, one has learned from the *Inferno* that the greatest poetry can be written with the greatest economy of words, and with the greatest austerity in the use of metaphor, simile, verbal beauty, and elegance. When I affirm that more can be learned about how to write poetry from Dante than from any English poet, I do not at all mean that Dante's way is the only right way, or that Dante is thereby *greater* than Shakespeare or, indeed, any other English poet. I put my meaning

> into other words by saying that Dante can do less *harm* to anyone trying to learn to write verse, than can Shakespeare. Most great English poets are *inimitable* in a way in which Dante was not. If you try to imitate Shakespeare you will certainly produce a series of stilted, forced, and violent distortions of language. The language of each great English poet is his own language; the language of Dante is the perfection of a common language. In a sense, it is more pedestrian than that of Dryden or Pope. If you follow Dante without talent, you will at worst be pedestrian and flat; if you follow Shakespeare or Pope without talent, you will make an utter fool of yourself.

In fact, Eliot was surely excessive and ungenerous when he declared, 'the language of each great English poet is his own language...'. If Ben Jonson is a great poet (and I am sure he is), he seems to me an exception to Eliot's rule; in the present century as in the seventeenth century, poets who are prepared to take the very considerable trouble can learn to write better by attempting to emulate Ben Jonson. Eliot himself rather plainly did not put himself to school to Jonson; and some have thought that he would have been a better poet if he had, as both Yeats and Pound did.

It has been claimed for one of my contemporaries that he has written 'the lines of most near-to-Shakespearian power in twentieth century English or American verse.' This is an astonishing claim to make for anyone, and of its nature a claim that cannot be vindicated conclusively. Yet when I read the recent *Selected Poems* by this poet, my fellow-expatriate Thom Gunn, I found myself persuaded. However, the poems by Gunn which I took to be intended in this claim were, for instance, 'Street Song', which presents the spiel of a San Francisco drug-pusher in a form which in its impassive tone recalls Autolycus the pedlar of *A Winter's Tale*, and in other respects recalls Herrick's 'Cherry Ripe' or Dowland's 'Fine Knacks for Ladies', as well as certain songs from the Shakespeare plays. Or there is the young wino in Gunn's poem called 'Sparrow', where the allusion to pitiful songs from Shakespeare isn't anywhere in the diction but all in the metre and rhyme. This penetration by Thom Gunn to a point where he can make feelingful contact with Shakespeare seems to be the fruit of an admirably single-minded endeavour, sustained over thirty years.

But this, it may be thought, is very much a special case. To emulate, by adapting to twentieth-century subjects and sentiments, the procedures of Shakespeare's songs is not what most people would first have in mind when they wonder about a fruitful relation between a modern poet and the example of Shakespeare. More to the point, it might be thought, would be the Shakespeare of the Sonnets; and as to that possibility I record my sense that the last English language poet who moved into that charged area, and survived (though somewhat mutilated in the process), was George Meredith in *Modern Love*. But surely what we first have in mind when we say 'Shakespeare' is the blank-verse spoken by the characters in the plays. Does this Shakespearean performance in poetry have no immediate and fructifying presence in the poetry of our own time? Undoubtedly, I would say, the great blank-verse passages *are* present in the minds of earnest and dedicated poets of our time; but present in the way that Dryden and Eliot in their different ways indicate – that is to say, as an excellence to be aimed at though never equalled, but never to be aimed at *along the same lines*. The lesson that Shakespeare has for the comtemporary poet is: 'Go thou and do otherwise' – on pains of losing your own identity if you don't.

This is inevitably related to the larger question of the relation between poetry and the theatre in the present century. It seems to me that over my lifetime I have seen a striking change in this respect. The young W.H. Auden, the middle-aged T.S. Eliot, not to speak of Christopher Fry and Ronald Duncan and Archibald MacLeish and (particularly as regards radio-drama) Louis MacNeice – all these poets, active when I was young, showed themselves fascinated, at one point or another in their careers, by the notion of bringing spoken poetry back on to the boards of the theatre; whereas in my generation I believe I am in the majority among serious poets in feeling alienated from the theatre, seldom visiting it, and certainly with no interest in adapting my own writing to theatrical occasions. For this development, if indeed it exists, many reasons could doubtless be found. There is for instance the great development of the public poetry-reading as itself a theatrical performance of a sort, in which the poet does not have to share the limelight with any actors. At a more serious because more technical level, the theatrical career of T.S. Eliot, as he moved from *The Family Reunion* into *The Cocktail Party* and his later plays, seems to many of us to show that in order to reach the theatre audience a poet nowadays must sacrifice so many of the traditional powers and felicities of his language that the game just isn't worth the candle. Or again, some of us have drawn dire conclusions from the appalling vulgarization that the late Robert Lowell perpetrated when he created his *Phaedra* out of the thus mutilated magnificence of Racine. But the root cause of this alienation from the theatre on the part of contemporary poets must, I think, lie deeper. I believe that it is part of our alienation from our societies. For as everyone knows, the theatre exists for enactment of an art that is in some obvious sense social, communal. In the eyes of contemporary poets this tends to mean that it is simply a special province of 'show biz', overlapping in all sorts of ways with that movie and television world which we cannot fail to see as having done us nothing but harm, draining away from us ever more of the readers we might have had.

Contrary to what some people believe, it is only a few bad and fake poets who preen themselves upon their alienation from the society at large, and exult in it. To most of us I think it is a fairly constant source of distress and depression; something we would like to deny, but cannot, because hour by hour we have evidence that all the pressures of our society are directed towards destroying that apprehension which for us is irreplaceable – of our native language as not merely a more or less efficient tool, but as something rare and precious. Accordingly, in this wide perspective we see Shakespeare as representing an organic and mutually enhancing relation between the arts and society, such as we do not have and cannot hope for. In this wistful sense Shakespeare is indeed continually before us as an example of what once was and may yet be again, though certainly not in our lifetime.

It may seem to be a peculiarly modern phenomenon – this too often self-pitying conviction that the present moment in social history not just conditions, but determines and drastically *limits*, the scope of an artist's performance. But on this too we can appeal to that very great and blessedly unpretentious critic, John Dryden. For in the midst of his tribute to Shakespeare and Fletcher and Jonson, Dryden delivers the disconcerting judgement: 'Yet give me leave to say thus much, without injury to their ashes, that not only we shall never equal them, but they could never equal themselves, were they to rise and write again.' Dryden here, if I understand him, judges that English society under Charles II just could not have nourished and sustained the genius of Shakespeare, as did the society of England under Elizabeth I and James I. And if we take that to be a serious and considered judgement on Dryden's part, we cannot help but think that in a society like that of the United States under President Carter, so different from both Shakespeare's England and Dryden's England, a verbal genius of Shakespearean scope might take a wholly unrecognizable form – might, for instance, not be a *theatrical* genius at all. Indeed Dryden forces us to envisage the still more alarming possibility that in a society so hostile to the word, and contemptuously spendthrift of it, as our society is, a verbal genius like Shakespeare might not even *surface*.

This I believe is the standpoint from which to return to what Eliot wrote in 1929. 'For the science or art of writing verse...' so he begins; but all that we know, or can reasonably deduce, about

Shakespeare's way of writing verse is at odds with what we normally associate with either 'science' or 'art'. We do not have to accept the bardolaters' illusions about 'piping his native wood-notes wild' to agree that for Shakespeare, verse-writing must have been something far less premeditated and considered than what we nowadays associate with either 'science' or 'art', if we take either of those words seriously. And this explains why and how we may find Jonson a better exemplar and model for the modern poet than is his greater contemporary. 'Science' and 'art' – yes, these terms apply to Jonson's practice, so far as we can reconstruct it, far more easily than to Shakespeare's. It is as if Jonson, without knowing it, anticipated the phase of history (our own) in which poetry, assailed by a profoundly hostile social environment, would indeed have to close its ranks and declare itself a speciality on a par with other specialities. This explains why the principles that Eliot reads out of Dante – 'the greatest economy of words', 'the greatest austerity in the use of metaphor' – are far more manifestly followed in Jonson's writing than in Shakespeare's. We, twentieth-century poets, live and work in a world where, if poetry is to survive in any form that maintains contact with great poetry of the past, that poetry, beaten back to its last defences, must impose upon itself iron rations such as Jonson (and Eliot) prescribe. How different it was for Shakespeare! Fecundity is what he stands for, not economy or frugality; generosity, not austerity. He represents, for us modern poets, an age of innocence in which the act of verbal creation was so honoured than even its excesses could be indulged, and gloried in. It is not, alas, the world – the *social* world – in which poets of today must somehow work out strategies of survival.

I should like to conclude by reading one of the modern poems I have named, Thom Gunn's 'Street Song'. Think of Autolycus, think of Dowland's pedlar, and Robert Herrick's!

I am too young to grow a beard
But yes man it was me you heard
In dirty denim and dark glasses.
I look through everyone who passes
But ask him clear, I do not plead,
Keys lids acid and speed.

My grass is not oregano.
Some of it grew in Mexico.
You cannot guess the weed I hold,
Clara Green, Acapulco Gold,
Panama Red, you name it man,
Best on the street since I began.

My methedrine, my double-sun,
Will give you two lives in your one,
Five days of power before you crash.
At which time use these lumps of hash
– They burn so sweet, they smoke so smooth,
They make you sharper while they soothe.

Now here, the best I've got to show,
Made by a righteous cat I know.
Pure acid – it will scrape your brain,
And make it something else again.
Call it heaven, call it hell,
Join me and see the world I sell.

Join me, and I will take you there,
Your head will cut out from your hair
Into whichever self you choose.
With Midday Mick man you can't lose,
I'll get you anything you need.
Keys lids acid and speed.

Address to the Shakespeare Association of America, *c.* 1978.

4 *A West-Country Poet: Sidney Godolphin*

Sidney Godolphin is a name to be remembered by every one in the West Country. But outside a small circle of literary scholars, the name is often attached to a nephew of the poet – a later Sidney Godolphin, who was Lord High Treasurer of England. The Sidney Godolphin I am concerned with was born about 1610 and died in 1643. And that may be one reason why he is seldom remembered; because of his early death, he is one of those men famous for their brilliant promise rather than secure achievement, like some of our war poets. And from one point of view that was what he was – a war poet of the seventeenth century.

Yet that is not the whole truth. For from the records we have of him – and they are scanty enough – he seems to have been a sort of man who is great by virtue of what he is, more than by anything he does. And perhaps if Sidney Godolphin had lived longer he would still have been worth remembering, as he is now, as an inspiring and ennobling figure in the background of many enterprises, not as a principal actor in any.

As for what he did with his life, that is soon told. He was the second son of Sir William Godolphin of Godolphin, near Helston in Cornwall, and he was born there, we may presume, shortly before he was baptized at Breage, also in the Duchy, in January 1610. By the time he was three, both parents had died and he was an orphan. From his father he inherited the lease of the Scilly Isles. After that we know nothing of him until he turns up at Oxford, in Exeter College, in 1623; four years later he left without taking a degree. There is some evidence that later he travelled on the continent in the diplomatic service, but all we can be sure of is that he was twice elected member of parliament for Helston, and that in parliament, in the years before the Civil War, he was a staunch supporter of the King. When that war broke out, Godolphin joined the Royalist army in the west, and retreated with it from Sherborne through Minehead to Launceston. Then the Royalists went on the offensive, captured Saltash and crossed the Tamar, splitting into two bodies, one of which remained in Plymouth, while the other went on through Plympton to Kingsbridge and then to Okehampton. Godolphin was with this second body when at Chagford on the 9th of February 1643 he was killed, and buried in Okehampton churchyard the next day.

There is little enough in that record to explain why Godolphin deserves to be remembered more than many another loyal country gentleman who was killed by the Parliamentarians. Moreover, if we want to know the sort of person he was, there is not a lot more to go on – a handful of personal tributes, that's all. It's remarkable, though, that these tributes come from three men who were by common consent among the greatest minds of their age: from Clarendon, its greatest historian, from Hobbes, its greatest philosopher, and Viscount Falkland, arguably its greatest gentleman. Hobbes says:

> I have known cleerness of Judgment, and largeness of Fancy; strength of Reason, and graceful Elocution; a Courage for the War, and a Fear for the Laws, and all eminently in one Man; and that was my most noble and honored friend Mr. *Sidney Godolphin*; who hating no man, nor hated of any, was unfortunately slain in the beginning of the late Civil war, in the publick quarrel, by an undiscerned and an undiscerning hand.

That is a noble tribute in general terms; that is to say, in terms that can be extended to cover many and many a war-hating person who has been killed in war. For a more intimate and informal and vivid picture we can go to Clarendon, who has an uncanny knack for seizing the essential, and in a few words can make us see Godolphin, his striking appearance (he was an exceptionally small man) and some of his tricks of behaviour. But, rather than quote from Clarendon now, we can turn to a still more intimate portrait – the one that Godolphin paints for us himself, in his poems. With a very few exceptions these poems were never published until the twentieth century, but already on the strength of them the discerning recognize Godolphin as one of the best minor poets of his time. What's more, discerning readers will agree that the period when Godolphin wrote produced more good minor poetry than any comparable period in English history; so that to call Godolphin one of the best is saying a great deal. But for the moment we want to use his poetry to find out the sort of person he was. And in doing that, we have to be rather careful; because three hundred years ago people didn't write poetry, as nowadays they mostly do, so as to *express themselves.* At all events they did not 'express themselves' in the ways we are used to; and because people have changed in those three centuries, it seems to us that they don't express themselves at all clearly or directly.

Godolphin, for instance, wrote many love poems. When a love poem is written by a later poet such as Shelley or Browning, we are used to taking it for granted, rightly or wrongly, that the poet felt more or less as he says about a certain woman. From what he says in his poems we can decide what the poet was like when he was 'in love'; whether for instance he idealized women or was cynical about them. It would be idle to make any such inferences about Godolphin, writing at a time when the love poem was highly conventional.

We shall do better to seek out poems where Godolphin expresses something unconventional, something that he shares with none of the poets of his time. And here is such a poem:

> Soft and sweete Aires whose gentle gales
> 	Swell but doe slakely swell our sayles,
> And only such to Heaven convay,
> 	Whom thyr owne Tide doeth waft that way,
>
> Instructing them in happiness
> 	Who weare before in kenn of Blisse.
> Though only saynts doe heare and see
> 	The Angells in your harmony,
>
> Yet even from us ill spirritts Fly
> 	When by such charmes, uncharm'd wee bee.
> The unprepar'd this grace doe Find
> 	Yee coole and doe refresh the Mynde.
>
> But the more peacefull soules and Free
> 	Meete with their owne your Harmony
> Sometimes surpris'd, then doe prevent
> 	The less harmonious Instrument.
>
> Soft ayres yee gently Fan A Fire
> 	Of pure unmixt thoughts which aspire
> Soe of themselves I doe not know
> 	Whither to you they ought can owe.*

This is highly original, whether we take the 'soft and sweete Aires' to be waftings of a light breeze, or musical airs, tunes. I prefer the first alternative. Certainly, in another of his poems Godolphin makes a shepherd sing a song to the air about him:

* The punctuation is uncertain; I have punctuated as seems best.

Thou Joy of my Life
first love of my youth
thou safest of pleasures
and fullest of trueth,
thou purest of Nimphs
and never more fayre
breath this way and coole mee
thou pittying ayre,
come hether and hover
on every parte
thou life of my sense
and joy of my hart.

However it may be with the first poem, in this one there is no doubt that we find expressed a sentiment we could be excused for thinking was unknown before Wordsworth. For the air is said to be not only 'first love of my youth' but also 'fullest of trueth'; it instructs and spiritualizes.

Just here, in an extraordinary way, we find confirmation in Clarendon. We are dealing with a most intimate and tenuous sort of characteristic – a person's peculiar susceptibility to the physical atmosphere. How remarkable that something so hard to pin-point should have been noticed, among such scanty records as we have! How lucky, we might say. But we could just as well say: what genius in Clarendon, what insight into the essential features of an individual! Here is the passage:

> Though every Body loved his Company very well, yet He loved very much to be alone, being in his Constitution inclined somewhat to Melancholy, and to Retirement amongst his Books; and was so far from being active, that He was contented to be reproached by his Friends with Laziness; and was of so nice and tender a Composition, that a little Rain or Wind would disorder him, and divert him from any short Journey, He had most willingly proposed to himself; insomuch, as when he rid abroad with those in whose Company He most delighted, if the Wind chanced to be in his Face, he would (after a little pleasant murmuring) suddenly turn his Horse, and go Home.

We might be there. It is as if on a screen or through a window we saw the little knot of Cavalier horsemen, and then one tiny man turn his horse abruptly for home, while the others look puzzled, or perhaps they call after him a good-humoured joke. It all happened more than three hundred years ago, but we see it happening now. And we cannot but reflect that this man, who could not stand the wind when it was a little raw and blustery, was also the one who appreciated it exquisitely when it was sweet and soft. Those winds were blowing three centuries ago. But we feel them on our faces now. And that is a tribute to Clarendon, but to Sidney Godolphin too.

Take the other part of Clarendon's account, which tells of Godolphin's melancholy, his love of retirement and study, his inactivity. Surely we could have guessed that, too, from his poems. For they are usually argued closely, very concentrated and strenuous. Godolphin certainly makes us feel those 'soft and sweete airs', and he makes us feel his love of them; but he is also arguing about them, asking and answering questions. He asks whether the spirit in Nature (or in music) is felt only by a spiritual sort of person, by people who are already somehow prepared. And he says, No, that the spirit can be experienced by the run of mankind as well as by saintly people, though not perhaps to the same extent. That is a question, incidentally, that I don't think Wordsworth asked. At any rate the point is that this poem could have been written only by a scholar and a thinker, a man given to solitary brooding, the man whom Clarendon describes.

Not all the poets of Godolphin's time were like this. Many of them were 'Laughing Cavaliers' in an obvious sense, like Sir John Suckling, gay, brilliant, sociable and somewhat dissolute. In the poems of these men what we admire is the appearance of ease in the writing. Almost certainly they sweated over their poems, line by line; but what they valued, and what we value them for, is the effect they get of having tossed the poem off, in all its grace and sparkle, in half an hour. It is an effect that Godolphin can contrive sometimes in his love poems, but it is not characteristic of him as it is of Suckling. And Suckling realized this. In his 'Sessions of the Poets', Suckling imagines Apollo, god of poets, presiding at a meeting of the poets of the day, who are mentioned by name; and Godolphin gets a stanza to himself:

> During these troubles in the Court was hid
> One that *Apollo* soon mist, little Cid;
> And having spied him, call'd him out of the throng,
> And advis'd him in his ear not to write so strong.

John Drinkwater was puzzled by this because, he said, what he missed in Godolphin's poetry was 'an occasional transport or vehemence that might have loosened up the whole current'. But this is not what Suckling means by 'strong'. For if we read the poets of that time, we find that 'strength' for them has nothing to do with 'loosening up': it means just the opposite, a *tightening*, a concentration and compression of thoughtful argument. This is what we find in Godolphin's poetry, and it goes with what we learn of his character and his habits.

This can be illustrated by the Godolphin poem most favoured by anthologists, a Christmas poem which brings out his humanity and, in a certain sense, his democracy:

Lord when the wise men came from Farr
Ledd to thy Cradle by A Starr,
Then did the shepheards too rejoyce,
Instructed by thy Angells voyce,
Blest were the wisemen in their skill,
And shepheards in their harmelesse will.

Wisemen in tracing Natures lawes
Ascend unto the highest cause,
Shepheards with humble fearefulnesse
Walke safely, though their light be lesse,
Though wisemen better know the way
It seemes noe honest heart can stray:

Ther is noe merrit in the wise
But love, (the shepheards sacrifice).
Wisemen all wayes of knowledge past,
To 'th shepheards wonder come at last,
To know, can only wonder breede,
And not to know, is wonders seede.

A wiseman at the Alter Bowes
And offers up his studied vowes
And is received, may not the teares,
Which spring too from a shepheards feares,
And sighs upon his fraylty spent,
Though not distinct, be eloquent.

'Tis true, the object sanctifies
All passions which within us rise,
But since no creature comprehends
The cause of causes, end of ends,
Hee who himselfe vouchsafes to know
Best pleases his creator soe.

When then our sorrowes wee applye
To our owne wantes and poverty,

When wee looke up in all distresse
And our owne misery confesse
Sending both thanks and prayers above
Then though wee doe not know, we love.

'To know, can only wonder breede, And not to know, is wonders seede' – there is a whole Aristotelean philosophy in those two lines, and to be able to express so much in so little is what Suckling had in mind when he called Godolphin 'strong'. We need not agree that he is too 'strong', as Suckling implies.

It is surely exciting to be able to sail over three hundred years, buoyed by only a few scraps of paper. It is a sort of detective-story, but what we detect is not just 'whodunit'; it is the very movement and feature of an immortal spirit.

Broadcast for the BBC, Western Region, 1950.

5 *Syntax and Music in* Paradise Lost

I

No lines from *Paradise Lost* are more familiar than those near the beginning of the first Book which describe the fall of Satan from heaven:

> Him the Almighty Power
> Hurld headlong flaming from th' Ethereal Skie,
> With hideous ruin and combustion down
> To bottomless perdition, there to dwell
> In Adamantine Chains and penal Fire,
> Who durst defie th' Omnipotent to Arms.
> (i. 44-9)

'Dramatic' is a poor word for this effect. One wants instead to speak of 'muscularity', using 'muscular', however, in a special sense, different from (because more literal than) the sense in which we can justly speak of other poetry as 'muscular'. The effect is kinetic. The placing of 'Him', 'down' and 'To', in particular, gives us the illusion as we read that our own muscles are tightening in panic as we experience in our own bodies a movement just as headlong and precipitate as the one described. We occupy in ourselves the *gestalt* of the falling, just as we do before a good painting of the same event; it is hardly too much to say that the inversion of word-order (object-subject-verb) has the same effect upon us as seeing the angel's head near the bottom of the painted canvas and his heels near the top.

Because the literally unimaginable nature of his subject prevented Milton from appealing at all often or consistently to our visualizing faculty, he finds an especially valuable compensation for this whenever he can thus appeal to the reader's kinetic sense. Another example of this – again a well-known passage – comes in the course of Satan's flight through Chaos:

> Quencht in a Boggie *Syrtis*, neither Sea
> Nor good dry Land: nigh founderd on he fares,
> Treading the crude consistence, half on foot,
> Half flying; behoves him now both Oar and Sail.

As when a Gryfon through the Wilderness
With winged course ore Hill or moarie Dale,
Persues the *Arimaspian*, who by stelth
Had from his wakeful custody purloind
The guarded Gold: So eagerly the Fiend
Ore bog or steep, through strait, rough, dense or rare,
With head, hands, wings or feet persues his way,
And swims or sinks, or wades, or creeps, or flies.
(ii. 939-50)

From Milton's own day, when some of his contemporaries essayed the same effect before him (with less tact), there have always been those to admire the way in which – with 'strait', rough, dense', and 'head, hands, wings' – Milton crowds stressed syllables together so as to make the vocal exertion in reading image the physical exertion described. It is the reader, too, who flounders, stumbles, pushes doggedly on. Just as skilful, though less conspicuous, is the way in which line-break, punctuation and metre combine to make 'Half flying' act out, in our speaking of the words, the abbreviated and ungainly flap which they describe.

Though dramatic is an inadequate word, it is still the right word for these felicities, because what they do is to force us to participate in the situation and the actions described; we no longer merely observe these, in imagination we suffer them, ourselves embroiled. This point is worth making, because elsewhere Milton uses the same elements – metre played off against syntax and word-order – to quite different effects, no less fine, which I would call rather 'narrative' than 'dramatic'. I have in mind the invocation to Light at the beginning of Book III:

thee I revisit safe,
And feel thy sovran vital Lamp; but thou
Revisitst not these eyes, that roul in vain
To find thy piercing ray, and find no dawn;
So thick a drop serene hath quencht thir Orbs,
Or dim suffusion veild. Yet not the more
Cease I to wander where the Muses haunt
Clear Spring, or shadie Grove, or Sunnie Hill,
Smit with the love of sacred song; but chief
Thee *Sion* and the flowrie Brooks beneath
That wash thy hallowd feet, and warbling flow,
Nightly I visit: nor somtimes forget
Those other two equald with me in Fate,
So were I equald with them in renown,
Blind *Thamyris* and Blind *Maeonides*,

And *Tiresias* and *Phineus* Prophets old.
Then feed on thoughts, that voluntarie move
Harmonious numbers; as the wakeful Bird
Sings darkling, and in shadiest Covert hid,
Tunes her nocturnal Note. Thus with the Year
Seasons return, but not to me returns
Day, or the sweet approach of Ev'n or Morn
Or sight of vernal bloom, or Summers Rose,
Or flocks, or herds, or human face divine;
But cloud in stead, and ever-during dark
Surrounds me, from the cheerful ways of men
Cut off, and for the Book of knowledge fair
Presented with a Universal blanc
Of Natures works to mee expung'd and ras'd,
And wisdom at one entrance quite shut out.
(iii. 21-50)

It seems absurd, in order to illustrate a narrative effect, to take from a narrative poem precisely that passage (an invocation) by which the narrative is interrupted. Yet the distinction of this passage, in all which concerns the manipulation of syntax (and the syntax is profoundly important) is thoroughly a narrative distinction. The language is deployed, just as the episodes are in a story, so as always to provoke the question 'And then?' – to provoke this question and to answer it in unexpected ways. If any arrangement of language is a sequence of verbal events, here syntax is employed so as to make the most of each word's eventfulness, so as to make each key-word, like each new episode in a well told story, at once surprising and just. The eventfulness of language comes out for instance in 'Then feed on thoughts that voluntarie move', where at the line-ending 'move' seems intransitive, and as such wholly satisfying; until the swing on to the next line, 'Harmonious numbers', reveals it (a little surprise, but a wholly fair one) as transitive. This flicker of hesitation about whether the thoughts move only themselves, or something else, makes us see that the numbers aren't really 'something else' but are the very thoughts themselves, seen under a new aspect; the placing of 'move', which produces the momentary uncertainty about its grammar, ties together 'thoughts' and 'numbers' in a relation far closer than cause and effect. Or again, how eventful is 'Day' at the start of line 42! The inversion, 'not to me returns' has forged for the long-awaited subject of 'returns' a link every bit as strong as rhyme, with 'Seasons', in the corresponding place in the line above, and in the same grammatical relation to the identical verb 'return'. Thus, what we expect is a word parallel in meaning, just as it is parallel in metrical placement and grammatical function. We expect 'Spring'. What we get is 'Day'. And this is surprising. Yet the surprise is no cheap or empty one, for the parallel in meaning is in fact better enforced by 'Day' than by 'Spring' which, we now see, would have been lamely predictable. The surprisingness of 'Day' isolates it for our attention so that we take the force of its double meaning as at once a division of time and a synonym for 'light'. Similarly, we might notice how the virtuosity of the grammatical construction 'nor somtimes forget... So were I' works with the metrical arrangement to clamp together 'Fate' and 'renown' in a relationship which is not rhyme but is altogether as close and satisfying as if it were.

Given a syntax as elaborate as Milton's, the variety of effects is endless. Yet all depend equally, at bottom, on provoking and answering the simple narrative question, 'What happens next?' They all become possible only with the recognition, by poet and reader alike, that language and therefore the arts of language operate through and over spans of time, in terms of successive events, each new sentence a new small action with its own sometimes complicated plot. It is a perception about language which much of the most influential modern criticism – working as it does through spatial metaphors, talking of 'the figure in the carpet', of tensions balanced and cancelling out inside structures – seems expressly designed to obscure. This occupying of a duration, of a lapse of time, is what connects the literary arts, but especially poetry, with the art of music, which works through time in the same way. And as, to image the very different effect of the lines on Satan's fall we found an analogy with painting, so to explain effects of this sort our analogies would need to be from music, just because of that central principle of music which Milton himself isolated when he spoke of 'linked sweetness long drawn out'. There is no need to take account of the various sonorities of the invocation to Light, in order to establish that it is exquisitely musical. As in Spenser's marriage-hymns, which may have been Milton's exemplary model for this sort of writing, the music is first and foremost in the structure, metrical and syntactical; it is the way the syntactical units are draped across the line-endings, the playing off of syntactical pause against metrical pause, the varying of word-order and clause-order, which give the centrally musical effect of never stopping but to start again. And all this is logically, as well as (I think) in the experience of reading, prior to the tone-colouring of vowels that are long or short, dark or light, open or closed, and the various combinations of liquid and fricative in consonantal clusters.

II

Reading the note on 'The Verse', prefixed to the *Paradise Lost* of 1668, we learn, of 'true musical delight', that it consists, for Milton, 'only in apt Numbers, fit quantity of syllables, and the sense variously drawn out from one Verse into another'. That last phrase, if we hear it echo 'linked sweetness long drawn out', will have prepared us for just such effects as those of the invocation to Light. What is surprising is that these effects are rather the exception than the rule. Neither kinetic and dramatic effect, as in the lines on Satan's fall, nor narrative and musical effect, as in the invocation to Light, are in evidence at all frequently as we read *Paradise Lost*. For example:

> Others with vast *Typhœan* rage more fell
> Rend up both Rocks and Hills, and ride the Air
> In whirlwind; Hell scarce holds the wild uproar.
> As when *Alcides* from *Œchalia* Crownd
> With conquest, felt th' envenomd robe, and tore
> Through pain up by the roots *Thessalian* Pines,
> And *Lichas* from the top of *Œta* threw
> Into th' *Euboic* Sea.
>
> (ii. 539–46)

Or, more strikingly:

> Th' undaunted Fiend what this might be admir'd,
> Admir'd, not fear'd; God and his Son except,
> Created thing naught valu'd he nor shunnd;
> And with disdainful look thus first began.
>
> (ii. 677–80)

In these passages, the point is not that some of the lines are end-stopped – both 'uproar' in the first, for instance, and 'shunnd' in the second, ending a parenthesis with the end of a line – but that where the line is not end-stopped, the swing of the reading eye or voice around the line-ending is not turned to poetically expressive use. Certainly this happens with lines 539 and 540, where we swing around the line-ending to come hard upon the energetic verb, 'Rend'. But there is no expressive or dramatic reason why 'Air' should be separated in this way from 'In whirlwind' – a phrase which merely dangles limply into the next line. More remarkably, in lines 543 and 544, the interposition of 'Through pain' precludes both of two possible dramatic effects – either the violence of 'Tore' at the beginning of the line, or the even more effective muscularity of having 'tore' separated by the line-ending from 'Up'. Similarly, in the last two lines of the first passage the Latinate inversion of word-order means that as we launch out from 'threw' into the last line, we are asking not '*What* was thrown?' but only the much less interesting question 'thrown where?' In fact, this question is so unexciting that we don't even ask it; so that 'Into th' *Euboic* Sea' hangs superfluous – the sentence could just as well have ended where the line ends, after 'threw'. As for the second passage, the line-endings are so far from being dramatically significant that Milton seems to have gone perversely out of his way to eliminate all that might be suspenseful. Inversion of word-order answers the question of what the Fiend 'admir'd', before we have the chance to ask it. If we had been made to wait for the object of 'admir'd' until after admiration had been distinguished from fear and the distinction elaborated on, a powerful suspense would have been built up. Instead the narrative run is halted while the distinction is laboriously made in a parenthesis which has all the distracting inertness of a footnote.

It's impossible, with this second passage, to think that Milton has simply muffed his chances. We have to suppose that the arrangement is deliberate: that the sort of suspense and eventfulness we are asking for is something that Milton as a general rule won't give; that the expressiveness of the syntax in the invocation to Light is exceptional. And the implication is plain: if the distinction between admiration and fear is, as Milton conveys it, a sort of footnote, then this is a sort of poem in which the footnotes matter more than the text. The story, the narrative, is only a convenient skeleton; its function is to provoke interesting and important speculative questions. Or rather, the story told is centrally important to Milton precisely because it does raise (and, so Milton would claim, it answers) all these questions, all the questions worth asking. But the story told is not important as a story *in the telling*, as narrative, as provoking and then resolving suspense; it does not invite the questions, 'What happened next?' or 'This happened – yes, to whom?'

It would obviously be wrong to say that in *Paradise Lost* there is no element of suspense at all, nothing to keep the mind as well as the ear reaching forward from one paragraph to the next. For instance, a reasonably instructed reader of Satan's encounter at Hell Gate with Sin and Death will note the emblematic, riddling quality in the images of the two mysterious shapes either side of the gate, and will reach forward in an interested suspense to the point at which the riddle is explained and the shapes are named.

Allegory shows how this can become a truly narrative interest, making the emblem reveal its rubric, the riddle its own solution, in one seamless process:

But, full of fire and greedy hardiment,
The youthfull Knight could not for ought be staide;
But forth unto the darksom hole he went,
And looked in: his glistring armour made
A little glooming light, much like a shade;
By which he saw the ugly monster plaine,
Halfe like a serpent horribly displaide,
But th'other halfe did woman's shape retaine
Most lothsom, filthie, foule, and full of vile disdaine.

And, as she lay upon the durtie ground,
Her huge long taile her den all overspred,
Yet was in knots and many boughtes upwound,
Pointed with mortall sting. Of her there bred
A thousand young ones, which she dayly fed,
Sucking upon her poisnous dugs; each one
Of sundrie shapes, yet all ill-favored:
Soone as that uncouth light upon them shone,
Into her mouth they crept, and suddain all were gone.

In the first of these famous stanzas from the first canto of 'The Faerie Queene', the last line ('Most lothsom, filthie, foule, and full of vile disdaine') is the sort of slack wordiness in Spenser, and in the Elizabethans generally, which we cannot justify but have to put up with for the sake of other things. Apart from this, the passage is continuously alive with narrative interest. In the long last line of the second stanza, for instance, the extra foot is turned to brilliant use. It enables Spenser to break the line into equal halves, and then make the second half accelerate away from the first. The line slows to a halt on 'crept', and then, with 'suddain', jumps off rapidly from the comma. 'And suddain all were gone' – the dragon's brood, just now moving sluggishly to their haven, all at once reach it in a flash.

Spenser's passage was certainly in Milton's mind when he created the image of Sin:

Before the Gates there sat
On either side a formidable shape;
The one seemd Woman to the waist, and fair,
But ended foul in many a scaly fold
Voluminous and vast, a Serpent armd
With mortal sting: about her middle round
A cry of Hell Hounds never ceasing barkd
With wide *Cerberean* mouths full loud, and rung
A hideous Peal; yet, when they list, would creep,
If aught disturbd thir noise, into her womb,

And kennel there, yet there still barkd and howld
Within unseen.

(ii. 648-59)

We cannot say that Milton's puppies disappear at a steady pace where Spenser's little reptiles go with a rush. The truth is that the manner of their creeping, the act of it, has not been experienced by Milton, as so clearly it was by Spenser. This is not to say just that Milton hasn't *seen* the incident, though as usual he hasn't, where Spenser plainly has, though his image is just as hard for the mind's eye to grasp. But there are more ways of experiencing than through the eye. Through the ear, for instance; but Milton's hell-hounds just bark and bark unchangingly, from first to last. In Spenser's 'pointed with a mortall sting', the 'point' is not seen but felt. (There's a similar tactile effect in Spenser's 'knots' and 'many boughtes'; Milton's equivalent, 'voluminous and vast' has nothing to recommend it but alliterative sonority.) By contrast, Milton's 'armed / With mortal sting' isn't *experienced* at all; 'armed' represents a high degree of abstraction from any sense-experience. And if the abstractness is confirmed on the one hand by the highly intellectual wit of 'kennel', on the other it produces 'fair' ponderously and needlessly opposed to 'foul'.

Of course this intellectuality of *Paradise Lost*, the absence from it of any immediacy of sense-impression, is an old story. Yet it influences everything else. In the episode at Hell's Gate for instance, as soon as Milton sets one of his Shapes in motion, the shape of Death ('If shape it might be calld that shape had none / Distinguishable in member, joint or limb'), one sees at once how impossible it was for him to enact in syntax across line-division the manner of Death's moving, as Spenser enacts in a slightly later stanza the wreathing leap of his dragon on to the knight's shield. Such enactment cannot take place, since Milton no more than anyone else can explain how Death takes 'horrid strides' when it isn't clear whether Death has legs.

What's most noticeable, however, is how Milton does not avail himself of the narrative interest of allegory. When Spenser describes Error's brood as 'each one / Of sundrie shapes, yet all ill-favored', he is enriching at one and the same time the literal image and the allegorical. The allegorical significance is artfully thus uncovered, gradually, in a way to answer the narrative question 'What next?' Milton, on the other hand, proceeds through two distinct stages – first, the enigmatic image, and then, a hundred lines later, the solution to the enigma, the explanation of how Sin got to be the way she is.

III

There is evidence that in the present age those readers who still take pleasure in *Paradise Lost* sometimes do so by regarding it, not primarily as a narrative (epic or heroic poem), but rather as a poetic encyclopaedia of arcane knowledge, of ardent and curious speculation. This seems to be, for instance, the drift of J.B. Broadbent's insistence:

> Milton's material is not only integrated at every point with his poem's plot, but was a matter of living interest to all educated people at the time of writing. One can only say that to the seventeenth century China, vultures, Ganges, etc., were what the prehistoric past was to the Victorians and what space-satellites and abominable snowmen are to us.[1]

It is doubtless easy to present this sort of reading of *Paradise Lost* as an evasion, by a secularized century, of the theological challenge carried in the myth-story conceived as literally true. And of course it is obvious that to a non-Christian or tepidly Christian reader of the present day some such shift must take place. Yet an examination of the syntax of the poem suggests that this sort of interest was invited by Milton from the first; especially as we read on after the first two books, we encounter more and more cases in which the narrative is quite abruptly halted in order to indulge and invite speculations (often theological, of course, as well as geographical, cosmological and scientific).

For this frustration of the narrative interest can be seen in other ways and on a much larger scale than in the manipulations of syntax by which inverted word-order answers our interesting questions before we have time to ask them. Milton continually disrupts his narrative's present time, by looking into the future. When Satan confronts Death –

> so matcht they stood;
> For never but once more was either like
> To meet so great a foe.
>
> (ii. 720–22)

When he launches out through Chaos –

> So he with difficulty and labour hard
> Mov'd on, with difficulty and labour he;
> But hee once past, soon after when Man fell,

[1] J.B. Broadbent, 'Milton and Arnold', *Essays in Criticism* VI: 4 (October 1956), p.411.

Strange alteration! Sin and Death amain
Following his track, such was the will of Heav'n,
Pav'd after him a broad and beaten way
Over the dark Abyss, whose boiling Gulf
Tamely endur'd a Bridge of wondrous length....
(ii. 1021-28)

(Here the characteristic repetition of 'with difficulty and labour' reveals – as nearly all such cases must – a refusal to profit by syntactical resources, so as to weave the anticipation into the narrative. Milton prefers to halt the narrative and disrupt the narrative time.) Continually, before the Fall has happened, we are made to look forward to what will be when it has. Merely a reference to 'Amarant' is enough to provoke this (iii. 352-59). Or a few lines later, when Satan first alights from Chaos:

So on this windie Sea of Land, the Fiend
Walkd up and down alone bent on his prey,
Alone, for other Creature in this place
Living or liveless to be found was none,
None yet, but store hereafter from the earth...
(iii. 440-44)

And so we are thrust out of the narrative present into this 'hereafter', into what in the story hasn't yet come to pass, to hear a long account of the Paradise of Fools. This sort of thing crops up too consistently, every few pages or so, not to be deliberately contrived. It might be justified as an instance of the so-called 'figural' realism of mediaeval drama, which is similarly lordly about the chronology of sacred events.[1] But because the overt structure of *Paradise Lost* is narrative, and because of the speculative learning encrusted upon its every angle, this consistent disrupting of the present time inevitably distracts the reader's attention from the poem as narrative to the poem as encyclopaedia.

This was the point at issue when John Peter quarrelled with Sir Herbert Grierson about 'Tears such as angels weep'. Sir Herbert had applauded (in his *Milton and Wordsworth*, p.107):

> that tremendous stroke which one might hardly have expected from Milton, Satan shaken with remorse as he surveys the fallen followers of his pride:
>
> 'Thrice he essay'd, and thrice in spite of scorn
> Tears such as angels weep burst forth; at last
> Words interwoven with sighs found out their way'

[1] Erich Auerbach, *Mimesis*, tr. Willard Trask (Princeton, 1953), pp.156-8.

And he asked, 'Is there even in Shakespeare a greater moment?' John Peter, taking up the challenge, set beside these lines a passage from *Coriolanus* and another from *King Lear*, and remarked:

> Someone may indeed point to 'Tears such as angels weep' as being in its way an equivalent for these Shakespearean effects... but will such a claim bear examination? Sir Herbert himself does seem to assume that the phrase is a touch of sublimity and that Milton wants us to feel how precious celestial tears must be. But if we had been through the poem once we should know how frequently Milton strays from his main themes to tell us about the substance and properties of angels and we might well feel that these words contained only a simple prosaic qualification – 'the tears that angels, like men, can weep (for they can)' rather than 'celestial tears'. Thus if in fact we were re-reading the poem we might on the one hand have the advantage of seeing Satan's weeping as a striking variation from his habitual demeanour but on the other hand our reaction to the phrase describing his tears would almost certainly be much cooler and less immediate than Sir Herbert would appear to allow. The definitional sense of the phrase would have shrivelled its connotations of sublimity and we should be able to see how little there is in common between it and the other simile in Coriolanus.[1]

One may believe that Mr Peter read the phrase aright, where Sir Herbert Grierson didn't, and agree that it is indeed used to define. But is this, then, so uninteresting? Mr Peter's 'shrivelled' is a very strong word. Is defining so poor a thing in poetry, as opposed to 'connotations', that words used for denotation can appear only as the shrivelled husk of what could have been, and *should* have been, evocative of reverberations? What we have, Mr Peter says, is 'only a simple prosaic qualification'. But why 'only'? In short, the point is well made that in the past admirers of Milton have often praised him for the wrong reasons. But it is still possible to admire him on quite different grounds, in the way hinted at, for instance, by J.B. Broadbent. Stressing the encyclopaedic interest of the poem, Mr Broadbent speaks also of its 'textural stiffness', and describes its diction as 'stiff, pedantic and exact'. We seem to be in sight of a prosaic *Paradise Lost*, and prepared perhaps to endorse Hazlitt's

[1] John Peter, 'Reflections on the Milton Controversy', *Scrutiny* XIX: I, pp.10-11. The lines from Coriolanus are:

> 'If you have writ your annals true, 'tis there,
> That, like an eagle in a dove-cote, I
> Flutter'd your Volscians in Corioli:
> Alone I did it.'

striking judgement: 'That approximation to the severity of impassioned prose which has been made an objection to Milton's poetry... is one of its greatest excellences.'

To all this, however, there is one great objection. What happens, on this showing, to Milton's notorious 'organ-music'? To come at it another way, the difficulty with any poem that is 'encyclopaedic' is how its encyclopaedic speculations are to be bound together into one whole. Mr Broadbent anticipates this when he says that 'Milton's material is... integrated at every point with his poem's plot'. But we have seen that Milton often deploys his 'plot', the action of his story, in such a way as to frustrate our interest in it. And this means that the developing plot cannot, as we read the poem, hold together the massive and various learning it is made to carry; the unity imposed by the plot is only schematic, it is not felt by the reader as a central interest driving through. What is more, if the unifying structure of the poem is thus not a narrative structure, by the same token it cannot be musical. For music operates, just as narrative does, by provoking and then resolving suspense about 'What next?' And Milton characteristically frustrates this sort of interest, as much in his plotting of the movement through narrated episodes as in his plotting of the movement from word to word, from clause to clause, through a sentence. This means that by and large the famous music cannot be a structural principle, as it is in the invocation to Light, leading on the reader's lively interest from line to line; rather it is a matter of vocal colouring and skilful resonance, leading only the voice and the ear. And this, surely, is what our experience tells us, when we read the poem. The 'musical delight' is all in sonority, not at all in movement forward, through suspense to resolution and a new suspense. Dr Leavis's account of this Miltonic music (there are other musics, in other poems) seems more clearly just on each new reading. And so it appears that the splendidly elaborate syntax, which one could suppose created precisely as a musical resource, which indeed proves itself such a resource in a passage like the invocation to Light, in fact is employed characteristically to check narrative impetus and frustrate musical pleasure. Milton's composition – taken sentence by sentence as well as book by book – may indeed be, in the time-honoured phrase, 'architectural'. From one point of view this is only to emphasize that it cannot be musical; that *Paradise Lost*, in the reading, never or hardly ever profits by what is a fact about it as about any poem – that it exists as a shape cut in time.

The Living Milton, ed. Frank Kermode (London: Routledge & Kegan Paul, 1960).

6 *Edward Taylor and Isaac Watts*

I am very well aware of, and I appreciate very much, the charming anomaly by which, to inaugurate this series of essays to commemorate the Bicentary, the sponsors have invited me, who am not a citizen of the Republic but a subject of Queen Elizabeth. And I'm the more anxious to explain why I've chosen to write of the American poet Edward Taylor not in isolation but in company with his British contemporary, Isaac Watts. My intention is not in the least to minimize Taylor's American-ness; on the contrary I hope to emphasize it and define it, by showing how different the American is from the Englishman, despite the many things that these two had in common – not least, the fact that Edward Taylor passed the first twenty-five years of his life in his native England.

I am not without precedent in this. In particular, my colleague Albert Gelpi, in his book last year, *The Tenth Muse: The Psyche of the American Poet*, introduced the name of Isaac Watts into his discussion of Taylor, being I believe the first historian to do so; and most of what I have to say can be regarded as the teasing out of implications that are pregnantly hinted at by Professor Gelpi, to whom accordingly I am much beholden. And indeed I can appeal further back, to twenty-six years ago, when Louis Martz wrote his Foreword to that splendid monument of American literary scholarship, Donald Stanford's edition of *The Poems of Edward Taylor*. For Professor Martz there and then hazarded the observation that 'poetry with Taylor's peculiar quality could not, I think, have been written at all in England, even by Taylor himself.' I am sure that Louis Martz was right; and insofar as such propositions can be proven, I hope to prove him right. It's with just that end in view that I propose to approach Taylor by way of Watts, a poet of equal seriousness, equally gifted, very similarly placed as regards doctrinal principle and political circumstance, whose poems however are as different as can be conceived from the poems that Taylor was writing at just the same time on the other side of the Atlantic.

Martz's testimony is particularly valuable because of course it was he, the learned author of *The Poetry of Meditation*, who defined conclusively Taylor's relationship with his English predecessors:

> the last heir of the great tradition of English meditative poetry that arose in the latter part of the sixteenth century, with Robert Southwell as its first notable example, continued on through the religious poetry of John Donne (and also in those of his secular poems that have powerful religious elements), reached a fulfillment in the *Temple* of George Herbert, went abroad to include the baroque motifs of Richard Crashaw, found another home in Henry Vaughan's uneven but inspired meditations on the 'creatures,' strengthened the fiber of Andrew Marvell's slender muse, and, so far as England was concerned, died at the death of Thomas Traherne in 1674, with both his prose meditations and their companionate poems unpublished. But as Crashaw had gone abroad to preserve and extend his Catholic allegiance, so, at the end of the line, in 1668, Edward Taylor sailed for New England, and there, surrounded by the rude and dangerous life of the frontier, composed his Puritan and meditative poems.

There may be details here that are worth quarrelling with – I wouldn't myself, for instance, describe Marvell's talent as 'slender' – but it would be rash to dispute that this indeed is the line that Taylor was 'at the end of'. And no reader of Donald Stanford's edition can have failed to notice how constantly George Herbert's *Temple* in particular is in Taylor's mind, and in his inward ear, over most of the more than forty years – from 1682 to 1725 – during which he composed the two series of his *Preparatory Meditations Before My Approach to the Lords Supper.*

On the other hand we are here concerned not with the line of poetic achievement that ends in Taylor, but with another line that we take him to have inaugurated – a line of poetry in English that is distinctively American rather than British. Moreover it is quite wrong to suppose that, just because Taylor's debt to George Herbert is manifest, Herbert is the English poet with whom he must inevitably be compared. On the contrary, the historical contexts are so different that to compare Taylor with Herbert serves rather little purpose. George Herbert, aristocratic scion of an ancient and powerful family of Marcher Lords, Episcopalian, ornament and admired prodigy of the Stuart court until his pastoral calling called him away from it – what has this resplendent figure in common with the obscure provincial Englishman whom the 1662 Act of Uniformity, imposed by the restored Stuart, drove across the Atlantic to Harvard College and thence to the frontier outpost of Westfield? Well! They had something in common after all: Christian piety and pastoral vocation; and also certain trained and temperamental habits of heart and mind which account for the similarities of poetic style. But we must surely beware, as students of literature, of making these similarities conceal from us the unbridgeable gulf created by the events of history. Taylor himself, if we may trust the testimony of his grandson Ezra Stiles, was the last to minimize such historical conditioning. 'He was', says Stiles, 'a vigorous Advocate for Oliver Cromwell, civil and religious Liberty. A Congregationalist in opposition to Presbyterian Church Discipline...[He] greatly detested King James...: gloried in King William and the Revolution of 1688: felt for the dissenters in all their apprehension in Queen Anne's reign.' George Herbert was dead before any of these propositions could have meaning for him; but Isaac Watts, thirty years younger than Taylor, a Dissenting minister as Taylor was, would have concurred in every one of these sentiments and would have understood them to mean precisely what Taylor and Ezra Stiles meant by them. Theologically, politically, socially, above all chronologically, there is so much common ground between Watts and Taylor that it is astonishing how far apart they are in poetic style. And that distance between them *must* be instructive – as instructive about what poetry in English was to become, as the stylistic similarities between Taylor and Herbert are instructive about what that poetry had been.

It is time to remind ourselves what a poem by Watts sounds like. And I give you one that was quoted also by Professor Gelpi:

The Church the Garden of Christ

We are a Garden wall'd around,
Chosen and made peculiar Ground;
A little Spot inclos'd by Grace
Out of the World's wide Wilderness.

Like Trees of Myrrh and Spice we stand,
Planted by God the Father's Hand;
And all his Springs in Sion flow,
To make the young Plantation grow.

Awake, O heavenly Wind, and come,
Blow on this Garden of Perfume;
Spirit Divine, descend and breathe
A gracious Gale on Plants beneath.

Make our best Spices flow abroad
To entertain our Saviour-God:
And faith, and Love, and Joy appear,
And every Grace be active here.

Let my Beloved come, and taste
His pleasant Fruits at his own Feast.
I come, my Spouse, I come, he crys,
With Love and Pleasure in his Eyes.

Our Lord into his Garden comes,
Well pleas'd to smell our poor Perfumes,
And calls us to a Feast divine,
Sweeter than Honey, Milk, or Wine.

Eat of the Tree of Life, my Friends,
The Blessings that my Father sends;
Your Taste shall all my Dainties prove,
And drink abundance of my Love.

Jesus, we will frequent thy Board,
And sing the Bounties of our Lord:
But the rich Food on which we live
Demands more Praise than Tongues can give.

It's easy to mistake just what this poem is saying. For the 'we' of the first line does not mean mankind as a whole, nor Christian mankind as a whole; nor even Christian Englishmen as a whole. 'We' means 'We English Dissenters'. This has to be the case. For what sense would it make to speak of the Church of England as 'A little Spot... Out of the World's wide Wilderness'? How could this be said of a Church whose head is the reigning monarch, whose bishops sit as Lords Spiritual in Parliament? The Church of England is the national Church; that is what is meant by calling it the Established Church. By maintaining the strenuous and transparent fiction that the religious community is coterminous with the national community, the English Anglican, even today, must hope to shame the fiction into becoming fact, thus sanctifying or spiritualizing the entire secular order within the state. Isaac Watts, like Edward Taylor, refused to maintain that fiction or to entertain that hope. And thus the 'we' of Watts's poem includes Taylor and his church in Westfield but not the Archbishop of Canterbury nor the congregation in St Paul's Cathedral. The point is obvious; yet experience tells me that it is best to make it thus explicit.

The history, and the polemics, of post-Revolutionary Russia supply us with two expressions that at this point may be useful – from the point of view of the English crown, if Taylor and his fellow New Englanders were *émigrés*, Watts and his fellow English Dissenters were *internal émigrés*. And once the American colonists began to challenge the Crown, the logic worked itself out as one might have expected: Benjamin Franklin wrote home from England in 1770, 'The Dissenters are all for us'; and when hostilities had started, the English Baptist minister John Collett Ryland (1723-1792) expressed himself, with bloodcurdling ferocity, thus:

> Were I George Washington, I would call together all my brother officers. I would bare my arm and bid every man bare his, that a portion of blood might be extracted and mingled in one bowl, and swear by Him that sitteth on the Throne and liveth for ever and ever not to sheath the consecrated blade till the freedom of this country was achieved.... And if after this any one should turn coward or traitor, I should feel it a duty, a pleasure, a luxury, to plunge my weapon into that man's heart.

However, the situations of the *internal émigré* and of the *émigré* are very different. To be blunt about it, Edward Taylor had no Established Church to contend with; whereas within perhaps half a mile of the meeting-house in London or Southampton where Dissenting congregations sang this hymn by Watts, there stood a parish church celebrating just that nationally instituted Protestant Christianity which Watts and his fellows had repudiated and opted out of – a repudiation which continued to cost them dear, in civil disabilities and often enough in social ostracism, long after the last of the hated Stuarts, Anne, had been succeeded by the princes of the House of Brunswick. Thus the Calvinist 'elect' of Watts's church were necessarily far more immediately aware of the non-elect from which they had been (to use their own word) 'gathered', than the elect of Westfield could be. And it is this, I think, which accounts for the sensation of mutual comfort and compactness, positively of *cosiness*, which breathes from Watts's beautiful quatrains.

The contrast is striking when we look at one of the poems by Taylor that is derived from just the same place in Scripture as Watts's hymn:

> Oh! that my Chilly Fancy, fluttering soe,
> Was Elevated with a dram of Wine
> The Grapes and Pomegranates do yield, that grow
> Upon thy Gardens Appletrees and Vines.
> It shouldst have liquour with a flavour fraight
> To pensil out thy Vines and Pomegranates.
>
> But I, as dry, as is a Chip, scarce get
> A peep hole through thy garden pales at these,
> Thy garden plants. How should I then ere set
> The glory out of its brave Cherry trees?

Then make my fancy, Lord, thy pen t'unfold
Thy Vines and Pomegranates in liquid gold.

Whence came thy garden plants? So brave? So Choice?
They Almugs be'nt from Ophirs golden land:
But Vines and Pomegranates of Paradise
Spicknard, Sweet Cane, and Cynamon plants here stand.
What heavenly aire is breezing in this Coast?
Here blows the Trade winde of the Holy Ghost.

Thy Pomegranates that blushly freckles ware
Under their pleasant jackets spirituall frize,
And Vines, though Feeble, fine, and flourishing are
Not Sibmahs, but Mount Zions here arise.
Here best of Vines, and Pomegranates up hight,
Yea Sharons Rose, and Carmels Lillies White.

These trees are reev'd with Gilliads balm each one
Myrrh trees, and Lign Aloes: Frankincense,
Here planted grow; heres Saffron Cynamon
Spicknard and Calamus with Spice Ensenc'd.
Oh fairest garden: evry bed doth beare
All brave blown flowers whose breath is heavenly aire.

Make me thy Vine and Pomegranate to be
And in thy garden flowrish fruitfully
And in their branches bowre, there then to thee
In sweetend breath shall come sweet melody.
My Spirit then engrapd and pomegranat'de
Shall sweetly sing thee o're thy garden gated.

What we are likely to register first, as something in Taylor to which Watts offers no parallel, may be isolated in the delightful couplet:

What heavenly air is breezing in this Coast?
Here blows the Trade winde of the Holy Ghost.

The 'trade wind of the Holy Ghost' manifests *wit*: the peculiar virtue and felicity of those seventeenth-century poets whom Louis Martz has listed for us, those that we call 'the metaphysicals', whom the present century – instructed by T.S. Eliot – has come to esteem once again, after two hundred years of relative neglect. In Watts, in fact, that 'wit' is to be found. For instance, when he says

And all his Springs in Sion flow,
To make the young Plantation grow,

'plantation' means the gardener's new plantings of trees or shrubs, but it also means – inevitably, given the date and historical context – Plymouth Plantation, or the Plantation of Ulster: a topical and dangerously resonant allusion, which a poet like Donne (or Taylor) would have teased out and made salient, which Watts on the contrary subdues and submerges, particularly by the smooth firmness of his metre. The same wit, deliberately subdued in the same way, is to be found in Watts's great contemporaries, Dryden and Pope; and much might be made of the fact that Taylor left England in 1668, just before the great genius of Dryden had showed itself, drastically modifying the 'metaphysical' tradition so as to make out of it a new style appropriate to the mercantile and scientific and bourgeois England that Dryden sensed as in the offing. Watts, beginning to write in the 1690s, had to take account of Dryden's precedent, as Taylor didn't need to. And Watts's earliest poems in fact, like Dryden's earliest, are exercises in the 'metaphysical' style, from which each of the two poets gradually weaned himself. We may regret that they did so; but in both cases it was deliberate.

Another difference between Taylor and Watts is more far-reaching. In Watts's case, the Church of the elect, conceived of as a garden planted by Christ the gardener, is treated as something that the poet and his hearers are securely *within*, a refuge achieved and occupied, whereas Taylor much more strenuously sees it as something that has to be re-achieved each time that the Sacrament is approached; for at the start of the poem he is *outside* the garden, wistfully peering in:

> But I, as dry, as is a Chip, scarce get
> A peep hole through thy garden pales at these,
> Thy garden plants.

And this surely gives us, all over again, the distinction between what I have called the émigré and the internal émigré. Watts's English Dissenters, *internal émigrés*, form an almost conspiratorial subculture within the national culture, held tautly distinct at every point against the enveloping culture which tolerates but suspects them. And hence 'election' has for them a social dimension, as it could not have for Taylor and his flock at Westfield. For both poets the election of the elect is of course a spiritual state; but over and above that, for Watts it is a social state, embodied as a society within the larger society, whereas for Taylor it is imaginative and psychological, and above all *individual*.

Hence arises a most striking feature of Taylor's *Preliminary Meditations* – the absence, from these poems in and by which the pastor prepares himself for administering the sacrament, of any consideration of the fellow-worshippers to whom he will administer the sacrament, and with whom he will partake of it. The most disconcerting instance of this is not in *Preliminary Meditations* at all, but in a different sequence, *Gods Determinations*, where there is a piece entitled 'The Soul admiring the Grace of the Church Enters into Church Fellowship'. What must be our astonishment, after such a title, to find that 'fellowship' is precisely what the poem does *not* celebrate, any more than the *Meditations* do! One wonders what Taylor's relations with his fellows were, in the Westfield church, and whether indeed there was anyone there whom he would recognize as 'a fellow'. One recalls him writing to Samuel Sewall in 1696 about 'the Foggy damps assaulting my Lodgen in these remotest swamps from the Heliconian quarters, where little save Clonian Rusticity is...' And there can be little doubt that Taylor in Westfield was starved of congenial company, as Isaac Watts in London was not. Nevertheless, congenial company is one thing, union in Christ is something else; and a modern Christian cannot help but find forbidding the way in which Taylor's emphasis on that union takes no notice, or very little, of the several identities of those who are thus united.

Just this indeed may account for the attractiveness to Taylor of that nuptial allegory by which the eroticism of the Book of Canticles – the Song of Solomon, or the Song of Songs, as we more commonly call it – is made to yield the drama of Christ the Bridegroom calling his Bride the Church to sport in His garden. Through the last twelve years of his work on the *Preliminary Meditations* Taylor very rarely meditated on any text that was not from the Book of Canticles, and these include such unpromising texts as 'His belly is as bright ivory overlaid with sapphires', and 'His legs are as pillars of marble, set upon sockets of fine gold' – of which the best we can say is that Taylor's treatment is no worse than that of his English contemporary, the Baptist Joseph Stennett. But in fact all these Meditations toward the end of the Second Series are poor, grotesque, and frigid – all too patently, and pathetically, the work of an old man. Indeed it is fairly plain that what we have in them, very often, is only early and imperfect drafts. (The failure however is not just at the level of technique and taste – see *PM* 2.136, written 1717, where the text 'Turn away thine eyes from me, for they have overcome me' is astonishingly taken as addressed by the Bridegroom Christ to his Bride the Church, rather than the other way round.) By consistently identifying the Church, the body of the Elect, with one being, the Bride, Taylor is saved from ever having to regard the Church as composed of its several members, so many individuals. This is as much as to say that Taylor never envisages the Church as a human *society*; and in nothing else is there so wide a gulf between him and

Watts, who deliberately and consciously subdued or (as he said) 'sank' his style, so that his poems should be sung with full understanding by unlettered congregations, whereas Taylor wrote for no eye but his own and his God's. After 1738, when George Whitefield induced Jonathan Edwards to introduce Watts's hymns to his congregation in Northampton, Watts was sung as widely in New England as in Old, so that more than a century later his hymns made up the body of poetry most insistently and threateningly present to the Amherst spinster, Emily Dickinson. What a difference it would have made, if American congregations had been singing Edward Taylor instead! But the very idea is unthinkable – not just in their form and diction, but in their substance, Taylor's poems are quite unsuited for any sort of communal rendering.

If Taylor's poetry is thus profoundly unsociable, and therefore painfully lacking in any of the feelings that a man may have for his neighbours, on the other hand Taylor is capable of profound fellow-feeling with other and as we think 'lower' forms of life than the human. The example that springs to mind is the justly well-loved, intricate and tender occasional poem, 'Upon a Wasp Child with Cold'. But the same extraordinary sympathy for non-human creatures – insects and birds and even vegetable creatures like nuts – enlivens some of the *Meditations* based on the imagery of the Bridegroom's Garden, out of the Song of Songs. One example out of many is *PM* 2.63, written in 1704:

Oh that I was the Bird of Paradise!
    Then in thy Nutmeg Garden, Lord, thy Bower
Celestiall Musick blossom should my voice
    Enchanted with thy gardens aire and flower.
    This Aromatick aire would so enspire
    My ravisht Soule to sing with angells Quire.

What is thy Church, my Lord, thy Garden which
    Doth gain the best of Soils? Such spots indeed
Are Choicest Plots empalde with Palings rich
    And set with slips, herbs best, and best of seed.
    As th' Hanging Gardens rare of Babylon
    And Palace Garden of King Solomon.

But that which doth excell all gardens here
    Was Edens Garden: Adams Palace bright.
The Tree of Life, and Knowledge too were there
    Sweet herbs and sweetest flowers all sweet Delight
    A Paradise indeed of all Perfume
    That to the Nose, the Eyes and Eares doth tune.

But all these Artificiall Gardens bright
    Enameled with bravest knots of Pincks
And flowers enspangld with black, red and White
    Compar'd with this are truely stincking sincks.
    As Dunghills reech with stinking sents that dish
    Us out, so these, when balanced with this.

For Zions Paradise, Christs Garden Deare
    His Church, enwalld, with Heavenly Crystall fine
Hath every Bed beset with Pearle all Cleare
    And Allies Opald with Gold, and Silver Shrine.
    The shining Angells are its Centinalls
    With flaming Swords Chaunting out Madrigalls.

The Sparkling Plants, Sweet Spices, Herbs and Trees,
    The glorious Shews of aromatick Flowers,
The pleasing beauties soakt in sweet breath lees
    Of Christs rich garden ever upward towers,
    For Christ Sweet Showers of Grace make on it fall.
    It therefore bears the bell away from all.

The Nut of evry kinde is found to grow big,
    With food, and Physick, lodgd within a tower
A Wooden Wall with Husky Coverlid,
    Or Shell flesht ore, or in an Arching bower
    Beech, Hazle, Wallnut, Cocho, Almond brave
    Pistick or Chestnut in its prickly Cave.

These all as meate, and med'cine, emblems choice
    Of Spirituall Food, and Physike are which sport
Up in Christs Garden. Yet the Nutmeg's Spice
    A leathern Coate wares, and a Macie Shirt,
    Doth far excell them all. Aromatize
    My Soule therewith, my Lord, and spirituall wise.

Oh! Sweet Sweet Paradise, Whose Spiced Spring
    Will make the lips of him asleep to tune
Heart ravishing tunes, sweet Musick for our King
    In Aromatick aire of blesst perfume
    Open thy garden doore: mee entrance give
    And in thy Nut tree garden make me live.

If, Lord, thou opst, and in thy garden bring
    Mee, then thy little Linet sweetly Will

Upon thy Nut tree sit and sweetly sing
    Will Crack a Nut and eat the Kirnell still.
    Thou wilt mine Eyes, my Nose, and Palate greet
    With Curious Flowers, Sweet Odors, Viands Sweet.

Thy Gardens Odorif'rous aire mee make
    Suck in, and out t'aromatize my lungs.
That I thy garden, and its Spicie State
    May breath upon with such ensweetned Songs.
    My Lungs and Breath ensweetend thus shall raise
    The Glory of thy garden in its praise.

In the first half of this poem Taylor treats the Bridegroom's Garden in a way that is, for him, characteristic. He was never tempted, as we surmise that Watts must have been, to locate the Garden in the physical actuality of the meetinghouse or in the human actuality of those met there to worship. Instead, as here, he identifies it first with the lost paradise of Eden, and second with the hoped-for paradise of the Heavenly Jerusalem, Zion, the City set upon a Hill. (And incidentally I find that the hard metallic surfaces of the latter – its beds of pearl, its alleys 'opalled' – effectively prevent any of the insistent though ambiguous eroticism of the Song of Songs surviving into Taylor's treatments of it. Watts's softer textures are potentially more erotic; by the 1740s John Wesley was complaining of this, and some years earlier Watts – in a note to his tenth edition – had begun apologizing for having drawn on the Song of Songs so heavily.) However, in this poem, after the walled Zion has been duly invoked, Taylor is led by his text – 'I went down into the garden of nuts to see the fruits of the valley' – into an absorbed sympathy with varieties of nut and their various ways of being, with 'Pistick or Chestnut in its prickly Cave', and with the nutmeg's spice that 'a leathern Coate wares, and a Macie Shirt'. After this astonishing and delightful feat of imagination, Taylor can easily manage the less difficult exertion of sympathizing with a bird, and so he can without any risk of mawkishness identify himself with 'thy little Linet' that 'sweetly will / Upon thy Nut tree sit and sweetly sing'. These imaginative exertions are quite outside Watts's range, and indeed in the long run nothing has so damaged Watts's reputation as his ill-advised attempts, in poems for children, to sympathize with ant and emmet and bee – performances which survived on British and American nursery bookshelves through many generations, until hilariously and lethally parodied by Lewis Carroll.

We need not doubt that there are other points of comparison between these two poets, which it would be instructive to ponder.

But there is no space at my disposal on the present occasion, and I must do the best I can, on the broad contrasts that have so far emerged, to divine, with the advantage of hindsight, what were to be the subsequent developments of American poetry on the one hand, British poetry on the other. And one thing it seems that we might safely prophesy, after looking at Taylor and Watts together: British poetry, we might predict, is thereafter to be social, American poetry is to be unsociable, if not indeed positively anti-social.

This is by no means a novel contention. It may seem to be no more than Louis Martz was saying when, still comparing Taylor with Herbert, he declared: 'the writer in England, wherever he may be living, works within a certain conditioning imposed by the context of that intimate island's culture: he knows the ways of other learned, literary men; he senses the current modes of writing; and even though he believes in freedom of language... the writer is nevertheless tacitly and unconsciously influenced by the accepted conventions of public speech and writing in that culture.' But there is a possible implication here that I find unacceptable. Since it is one that bears more heavily on me than on you, I shall merely notice it and pass on. It is the implication that the British poet can be only as good as the state of British culture allows him to be, that he cannot go against that culture when he perceives it in decline, nor go more than a little in advance of it when he finds it sluggish or stagnant. Whatever we mean by calling British poetry 'social', I hope we do not mean that it can only reflect the state of British society, vigorous at some times, torpid or depraved at others. The British poet may not want to claim as much freedom as the American poet; but he certainly aspires to more freedom than *that*!

Again, Professor Gelpi is plainly saying that British poetry is *social*, when he declares: 'Taylor's poems bespeak a vigorous, passionate, and learned mind shaping its apprehensions and speech without the chastening refinements which a sophisticated society of poets and readers would have bred in him: a society open to and assumed by both Herbert and Watts.' In fact to a Dissenter like Watts that sophisticated society of which Professor Gelpi speaks was 'open' only on very stringent conditions; the door to it was not wide open, but at best ajar, and Watts was the first Dissenting leader to push it open for himself and his fellows, as Dr Johnson realized when in *The Lives of the Poets* he remarked of Watts, 'He was one of the first authors that taught the Dissenters to court attention by the graces of language. Whatever they had among them before, whether of learning or acuteness, was commonly obscured and blunted by coarseness and inelegance of style. He shewed them that zeal and purity might be expressed and enforced by polished diction.' More to the point Watts as we have seen availed himself of his indeed great sophistication only so far as his mostly *un*sophisticated public, his Dissenting congregations, would permit. And this I think is what we should mean when we say that British poetry is social: not that it is sustained by society and social usage, nor that it is inescapably restricted by society and its usages, but that it is *addressed* to society, or rather to some identifiable group within society.

And this, which is plainly not true of Taylor's poetry, seems to be equally untrue of many American poets since Taylor. When I read their poems – I think for the moment of a poet so widely read and widely publicized as Robert Lowell – I get the vivid impression that I am eavesdropping, that the speech I hear is addressed not to me but to someone else, often to the poet's own self or to his God. A generation ago, something similar though not quite the same was said of American prose fiction: that its characteristic mode was not strictly speaking 'the novel' (which is a social form), but 'the romance' (which is not). And the advantage of bringing prose fiction into the discussion is that, ever since Henry James's study of Hawthorne, it has been recognized that the difference between the British and the American developments is rooted in quite definable differences between the structure of British and of American society – which is a great deal better than positing some magically elusive sea-change that transforms the Englishman when he becomes American, as Edward Taylor did. Britain, we are used to saying – and it seems to be as true as any thumping generalization can be – is not a social democracy, but a hierarchy. And when we turn to Watts after looking at Taylor, hierarchy is precisely what we find. The Church of England stands higher in the hierarchy than the Congregationalist Church or the Baptist Church – so it was in Watts's day, so it is in ours. This is not a question of opinion, nor of deserts, still less of fatuous snobbery. The Establishment of the Established Church in England is a fact, political in the first place, a social fact in consequence. I have argued that this is the very substance of Watts's 'We are a garden wall'd around', and that there is not – nor could there be – anything similar or analogous in Taylor. The nearest we can come to an analogy – and it is not very near – is the distinction that Taylor makes between church-members and church-attenders, between, in the terms of his poem, 'The Joy of Church Fellowship rightly attended', the elect who ride to heaven in a coach and the humble members of the congregation who trudge their way on foot. Moreover, since the Episcopal Church in America stands on a level with every other church, what divided the two poets in 1700 must still divide a British from an American poet today.

What's more, addressing everyone is the same as addressing no one. The widest possible audience is no audience at all, precisely because it has no lineaments and no contours. One might as well be speaking to one's self or to one's God, as Taylor did. And that indeed is what happens – or so it must seem to an Englishman: the poet of a social democracy is in effect, since he speaks to so many, speaking only to himself or to his God.

And I hope it is clear that that possibility which I have several times allowed for – 'or to his God' – is something more than a form of words. If the poet in the act of writing cannot believe that he is engaged in a *social* activity, it is hard to see how he can describe that activity except as 'religious'. This will be as true of American poets who are strenuous Unbelievers, as of Edward Taylor who was a strenuous Believer. And I am ready to think that it is very generally true of American poets, or of such of them as need to be remembered: they experience the call to write as a religious calling, a *vocation* in the strictest, most elevating and demanding sense. Rather few British poets, today or for the past three centuries (since John Milton in fact), have regarded their calling as anything so exalted and exacting – though certainly some have, and those among the best.

And yet 'religion', as mere etymology tells us, implies a binding together, a tying up in bundles. How then explain our suspicion that American poetry is not just unsociable but positively anti-social? How should that which is supposed to bind up, in fact cleave apart? Where Edward Taylor is concerned I'm reminded, as Louis Martz was, of William Carlos Williams's perception of what a very special kind of religion it was, that New England fostered: 'its *inhuman* clarity, its steel-like thrust from the heart of each isolate man straight into the tabernacle of Jehovah without embellishment or softening.' 'Each isolate man' – that certainly gives the quality of Taylor's religion. All one needs to add is that, while it certainly isolated the believer from his human fellows, it did not isolate him from – on the contrary, it bound him in with – his non-human fellows like frozen wasps and hard-shelled nuts and piping linnets, just as it bound Jonathan Edwards to his lovingly and intently observed spiders. Even so, the individualism of Taylor is uncompromising, indeed terrifying. And did this die with him, or was it transmitted as a legacy to the American poets, his successors? That is a question that others must answer, not I. I do however remember that we have been led to that question by William Carlos Williams, one American poet whose religious sense of his vocation *did* lead him to celebrate fellowship, a fellowship between suffering human beings, rather than between the human being and the wasp or the spider, the mountain or the wilderness. Did American poetry have to wait for the twentieth century for that to be possible? And is that why devoted American readers love Dr Williams so dearly? These are questions that I am content to leave in the air.

The Yale Review LXV: 4 (June 1976).

7 *Dramatic Poetry: Dryden's Conversation-Piece*

For all the syllabus-makers may say, the *Essay of Dramatic Poesy* is not a masterpiece of our criticism. Its strongest claim on our attention is not as criticism but as conversation-piece – meaning by that, what it has meant to some painters, an idealized picture of ideally civilized social behaviour. And even from that point of view, one may object either that the society is not idealized enough, or else that the society in question does not deserve what Dryden claims for it.

To say that the piece as a whole is not great criticism, not criticism at all, is not to deny, of course, that great criticism is to be found in it. There is, for instance, the examen of *The Silent Woman*, still an excellent introduction to a neglected play; there are the rapid firm delineations of Shakespeare, Beaumont and Fletcher, and Jonson; and there are excellent things in the last few pages, about the use of rhymed verse on the stage. But it can hardly be denied that these are the plums in what is sometimes very suety pudding. No one can be much interested in the issues of Ancient versus Modern drama, or the French tradition versus the English. These questions are 'dated' of course; but that is not the whole of it. Many issues raised in Sidney's *Apologie* are dated; yet a sympathetic reader can re-phrase those issues in terms more suitable to the present day, and can find that they are of living, because perennial, interest. He cannot do this with Dryden's essay. There the issues are dated in another way, more seriously; we are bored not only by the questions themselves, but by the way they are debated. The discussions, as Dryden presents them, are unavoidably inconclusive, because they are so nebulous.

Dryden could have asked, or implied, the questions: Am I, in my next play, to observe the unities? Am I to take Corneille for my model, or Shakespeare? Posed in this fashion, the question of French versus English drama could have come to life; for it would have taken account of the poet's peculiar temperament, his personal aptitudes and limitations, the sort of actors for whom he wrote, the expectations of his audience. And it is obvious that this is how these questions presented themselves to Dryden; but he chose to present them to his reader in a way that drained them of all this vitality. One begins to think that Dryden had not decided what it was he sought to do. If this was to be a conversation-piece, why make the talk about literature? Or else, if Dryden wanted to talk about literature, why do so at the level of the dilettante? As it stands, the essay is neither one thing nor the other. The two halves pull away.

The non-critical aspect of the *Essay* is announced in the Dedication:

> And yet, my Lord, this war of opinions, you well know, has fallen out among the writers of all ages, and sometimes betwixt friends. Only it has been prosecuted by some, like pedants, with violence of words, and managed by others, like gentlemen, with candour and civility.

Dryden intends to show that literary debates can be conducted with candour and civility. It cannot be said that he succeeds. In his endeavours to be a gentleman, he forgets not to be dull. And the experiment worked no better in life than in literature; for Sir Robert Howard, the Crites of the *Essay*, took offence at the only passage where Dryden speaks with a certain warmth and force. And because they could not agree about rhyme in dramatic verse, Howard and Dryden not only argued the point in later writings but were barely civil to each other when they met.

The first pages of the essay show the conversation-piece at its best. Everyone remembers the setting of the scene, as the four gentlemen row out to a place where they can hear the sound of the naval engagement at the river's mouth:

> and then, every one favouring his own curiosity with a strict silence, it was not long ere they perceived the air to break about them like the noise of distant thunder, or of swallows in a chimney: those little undulations of sound, though almost vanishing before they reached them, yet still seeming to retain somewhat of their first horror, which they had betwixt the fleets.

What is less often remembered is that this is not just a setting of the scene, a sort of ornamental frame. This is not just a prelude, announcing a pretty theme not picked up again before the end. One convention governs the whole, or nearly the whole; and if the reader forgets that he is listening to gentlemen conversing on a boating-excursion, the writer does not forget. The prose is as firmly controlled when Eugenius extols the Moderns, as before the talk has started. Dryden never forgets that he can discuss French or Greek drama only in the terms and at the temperature of a gentlemanly relaxation. That is why, when we look for critical penetration, we are for the most part disappointed.

Almost from the start the talk takes a literary turn. This is beautifully handled, and the transition, from the supposed victory to the panegyrics upon it, is admirably smooth. This gives Dryden a chance to comment upon verse in general, before the discussion is narrowed to dramatic verse. The exercise of wit, by Lisideius and Crites, upon the two 'extremities of poetry', illuminates, of course, Dryden's problems in *Annus Mirabilis*, which he was writing at the same time as the *Essay*. All the same, that is just what this is – an exercise of wit, the pleasantry of an intelligent amateur, not the analysis of a practising poet. Already Dryden is in trouble with the convention he has chosen; for what he wants to say about the decadence of the 'metaphysical' tradition is not exhausted by Lisideius's epigrams about Clevelandism. Later in the essay he manœuvres into a position from which he can return to the theme and Eugenius is made to digress from Plautus, so as to compare him with Cleveland, and then wander further into comparing Cleveland with Donne. The digression is anything but natural, and the manœuvre is clumsy. This later passage, in fact, is one of the points where the essay cracks up in the stress of conflicting intentions.

A more obvious, yet more complicated example of this strain occurs early in Crites' speech for the Ancients against the Moderns:

> Dramatic Poesy had time enough, reckoning from Thespis (who first invented it) to Aristophanes, to be born, to grow up, and to flourish in maturity. It has been observed of arts and sciences that in one and the same century they have arrived to great perfection; and no wonder, since every age has a kind of universal genius, which inclines those that live in it to some particular studies: the work then, being pushed on by many hands, must of necessity go forward.
>
> Is it not evident, in these last hundred years, when the study of philosophy has been the business of all the Virtuosi in Christendom, that almost a new Nature has been revealed to us? That more errors of the school have been detected, more useful experiments in philosophy have been made, more noble secrets in optics, medicine, anatomy, astronomy discovered, than in all those credulous and doting ages from Aristotle to us? – so true it is, that nothing spreads more fast than science, when rightly and generally cultivated.

This is flagrant. If Dryden needed or wanted to pay a compliment to the Royal Society, he could have done so more gracefully and plausibly at almost any other point. Crites does not even pursue his observation by evoking the 'universal genius' of Athens, of which literary achievement is only one aspect. The notion of 'universal genius' is pulled in by the ears; it is not merely irrelevant, it is at odds with all that Crites is trying to maintain, and it plays into the hands of his antagonist, as Eugenius is quick to note:

> I deny not what you urge of arts and sciences, that they have flourished in some ages more than others; but your instance in philosophy makes for me: for if natural causes be more known now than in the time of Aristotle, because more studied, it follows that poesy and other arts may, with the same pains, arrive still nearer to perfection...

There is, I conceive, only one explanation of Dryden's clumsiness in giving to Crites such obviously inappropriate sentiments. Feeling the want in the supposed discussion of any cut and thrust, he attempts to supply it by deliberately giving to one speaker an argument which can be turned upon him by another. But he does so most inefficiently, revealing the whole contrivance to the least attentive reader. And if we pursue the question a stage further, and ask why he was so clumsy, the most likely explanation appears to be that he knew he was giving to his conversationalists a disinterested agility that they did not possess. I think he felt uncomfortably that in reality the cut and thrust would not have been verbal only.

In other words, Dryden, in trying to show that gentlemen could argue with candour and civility, was going beyond the pattern that the society of his time could furnish. It is true that there is some evidence for just such urbanity in Charles II himself, who could, it seems, take a joke against himself. But after all the Addisonian reformation of manners had not yet taken place,[1] and there is some reason for supposing that in reality the Buckhursts, Sedleys and Howards modelled themselves on the older pattern of gentility:

> greatly to find quarrel in a straw
> When honour's at the stake.

If this explanation is correct, it explains why all the set discussions in the *Essay* are so dull. For if Sedley and Howard could not brook contradiction, Dryden, when he involved them in argument, had to phrase the argument so vaguely that no one of these touchy gentlemen should ever need to reach for his sword. (He had to do so, that is, if he was to keep in touch with the social reality at all.) It has been pointed out for instance that the only principle all four speakers have in common is that of 'Nature', and yet when they appeal to

[1] See C.S. Lewis: 'Addison', in *Essays on the Eighteenth Century presented to David Nichol Smith* (Oxford, 1945), p.7.

'Nature' they do not all mean the same thing. The point is made by a pair of recent editors:

> It soon becomes apparent in reading these arguments that the chief terms of the disagreement result from two conceptions of the word 'Nature'. The first, which gives Crites and Lisideius their backing, is that Nature teaches restraint, preciseness, that the artist must imitate the generality of Nature, that is to say, he must present aspects which represent the essence or the class of the feature described. Minor variations are not allowed room, for these peculiarities and individual differences are not a part of the eternal truth that the poet must imitate in Nature. The opposite view is supported by Neander, who follows the idea that Nature teaches variety and copiousness. The poet, in this view, must present Nature in all her aspects, her infinite variety on the single pattern.[1]

The editors do more than justice to Crites and Lisideius. The speakers are at all times much further than this would suggest from defining the terms they use. They had to be. If they had offered definitions, disagreement among them would have been sharper than anything Dryden could risk. Only one definition is offered in the essay, and that by Lisideius, who defines a play as *'A just and lively image of human nature, representing its passions and humours, and the changes of fortune to which it is subject, for the delight and instruction of mankind.'* There is a show, but only a show, of disagreement:

> This definition, though Crites raised a logical objection against it – that it was only *genere et fine*, and so not altogether perfect, was yet well received by the rest...

We are left to take the speech as being merely in character, remembering that Crites is 'a person of sharp judgment, and somewhat too delicate a taste in wit, which the world have mistaken in him for ill-nature'. But in fact his objection has substance; since the missing logical term, the *differentia*, is not one that we can do without. Without it, the definition offered by Lisideius comprises the novel no less than the drama. But this is typical of the whole essay; Dryden has to sidestep the crux of any argument. It is only shadow-boxing after all.

It is true enough, however, if we allow ourselves to supply the missing crux (as we have to), that we find it in the notion of 'Nature'. And it is true enough, as the editors say, that the speakers differ in

[1] H.H. Adams and B. Hathaway, *Dramatic Essays of the Neoclassic Age*, (New York, 1950), p.39.

their interpretation of following Nature, according as some take it to mean making Nature stand out in clean unfettered lines, by cleaning her of individual accidents and generalizing the instance, while others, notably Neander-Dryden himself, suppose it to mean preserving as many as possible of such accidents, by copiousness. But this is not the only range of disagreement. The speakers differ, as it were, in another dimension, according as some suppose art more natural the more it seems to be artless, while others, notably Neander-Dryden himself, suppose it more natural the more artificial it is. This last contention, which seems only a tiresome paradox to the modern mind, is of course at the bottom of all Renaissance poetic theory. It seems something more than paradox if one argues as follows: human nature is a part of 'Nature', and indeed a specially important part, since man has potentialities, for good and evil, beyond any other creature; it follows that man is following nature most faithfully, and revering her most, when he does most to realize his nobler potentialities; artistic creation is one of the noblest of his potentialities, since in it he approaches the divine creativity; hence a poet is more natural the more he is creative, the more he can make his creations stand free from himself, elaborate and self-sufficient. This is the Renaissance argument, and it is Dryden's.

As usual the allegiance is nowhere explicit. It is most nearly so in the last pages where Neander-Dryden disputes with Crites-Howard about the use of rhyme. This argument, the third and last, is conducted on a much higher level than the others. Both Crites and Neander, for instance, take into account the expectations of the audience for which they write:

> And this, Sir, calls to my remembrance the beginning of your discourse, where you told us we should never find the audience favourable to this kind of writing, till we could produce as good plays in rhyme as Ben Jonson, Fletcher and Shakespeare had writ out of it. But it is to raise envy to the living, to compare them with the dead. They are honoured, and almost adored by us, as they deserve; neither do I know any so presumptuous of themselves as to contend with them. Yet give me leave to say thus much, without injury to their ashes; that not only we shall never equal them, but they could never equal themselves, were they to rise and write again. We acknowledge them our fathers in wit; but they have ruined their estates themselves, before they came to their children's hands. There is scarce an humour, a character, or any kind of plot, which they have have not used. All comes sullied or wasted to us: and were they to entertain this age, they could not now make so plenteous treatments out of such decayed

> fortunes. This therefore will be a good argument to us, either not to write at all, or to attempt some other way.

The passage is justly famous. It is, on the one hand, a beautiful example of tact and tactics, the most graceful of compliments, the most engaging sort of modesty. This is its appeal in the convention of the conversation-piece, which here, perhaps because this is Dryden speaking, is suddenly impressive. Yet in another way the passage is out of the convention altogether; these are the facts of the case, after all. The argument is not only graceful, but immediate and compelling. This is the voice of the professional, though it speaks with the tact of the amateur. Literary traditions are seen no longer as so many different modes, each with its peculiar pleasure for the discriminating palate, but seen as the poet sees them, pen in hand – as a rich legacy, certainly, but also as a range of treatments no longer practicable, of things that no longer need to be done, that no longer *can* be done, because they have been done consummately well already. Howard and Dryden in fact are criticizing as poets criticize, no longer as dilettanti.

'Nature', accordingly, gets here a more searching scrutiny than anywhere else in the *Essay*. This is seen most clearly perhaps, when Howard replies to one of Dryden's arguments for rhyme:

> But verse, you say, circumscribes a quick and luxuriant fancy, which would extend itself too far on every subject, did not the labour which is required to well-turned and polished rhyme set bounds to it. Yet this argument, if granted, would only prove that we may write better in verse, but not more naturally. Neither is it able to evince that; for he who wants judgment to confine his fancy in blank verse, may want it as much in rhyme: and he who has it will avoid errors in both kinds.

As soon as Howard has allowed himself to distinguish between writing well and writing naturally, he draws back and contradicts himself – 'Neither is it able to evince that.' The distinction seems reasonable enough to the modern mind, but it would not seem so the mind of the Renaissance; for (so Sidney might argue) the better one writes, the more nearly one fulfils the potentialities of human nature, and hence the more 'natural' one is. This is the point at issue between Dryden and Howard – Dryden can agree with Sidney, where Howard cannot.

This does not appear, when Dryden replies to this particular argument. His reply is interesting and impressive for other reasons. It is a good example of what, I tend to think, is Dryden's most enduring contribution to criticism – his practice of using, for the operations of the human mind, a metaphor from corporate human activity. He speaks of the making of a poem as of the mason's building of a house.

And as elsewhere he speaks of it as a hunt, with Invention as the spaniel, so here 'Judgment is indeed the master-workman in a play; but he requires many subordinate hands, many tools to his assistance'. It is a range of metaphor which may be preferred to the mechanical metaphors of Locke or the chemical metaphors of Coleridge, when they cover the same field. Again Dryden's reply is interesting because from it we may infer that in his own estimation, Dryden had himself 'a quick and luxuriant fancy', needing discipline rather than stimulus.

But, to return to 'Nature', Dryden's view of it appears most plainly when he defends rhyming repartee:

> But you tell us, this supplying the last half of a verse, or adjoining a whole second to the former, looks more like the design of two, than the answer of one. Suppose we acknowledge it: how comes this confederacy to be more displeasing to you, than in a dance which is well contrived? You see there the united design of many persons to make up one figure: after they have separated themselves in many petty divisions, they rejoin one by one into a gross: the confederacy is plain amongst them, for chance could never produce anything so beautiful; and yet there is nothing in it that shocks your sight. I acknowledge the hand of art appears in repartee, as of necessity it must in all kind of verse. But there is also the quick and poignant brevity of it (which is an high imitation of Nature in those sudden gusts of passion) to mingle with it; and this, joined with the cadency and sweetness of the rhyme, leaves nothing in the soul of the hearer to desire. 'Tis an art which appears; but it appears only like the shadowings of painture, which being to cause the rounding of it, cannot be absent; but while that is considered, they are lost: so while we attend to the other beauties of the matter, the care and labour of the rhyme is carried from us, or at least drowned in its own sweetness, as bees are sometimes buried in their honey. When a poet has found the repartee, the last perfection he can add to it, is to put it into verse. However good the thought may be, however apt the words in which 'tis couched, yet he finds himself at a little unrest, while rhyme is wanting: he cannot leave it till that comes naturally, and then is at ease, and sits down contented.

Given the fact that Dryden and his contemporaries have to write in rhyme, because Shakespeare has done all that can be done with blank-verse, Dryden has only to point out (as he does) that any convention, however stilted, can be made to serve verisimilitude, so long as it is managed well enough to make the audience accept it. Howard is answered, and the argument is closed – or could be. But Dryden goes beyond this, and in the last two sentences he is arguing not that rhyme can do as well as blank-verse, but that, other things being equal, it will always do better. Ballet is not only as natural as drama; potentially, at any rate, it is more natural, and the more nearly drama approaches the dance, the more natural and better it will be.

It is here that Dryden is most the Elizabethan, and the key to his attitude is in the phrase, 'high imitation of Nature'. The notion that there can be high imitation and low imitation is as queer to the modern reader as it was (presumably) to Howard. Howard is no fool; he does not think, with some late-Romantic critics, that art is more artistic the more artless ('spontaneous') it is. He knows that artifice is always a part of art; he only thinks that the less the artifice appears in the art, the more natural it is. For him it is all a question of degree: and this is how the question is seen today. But Dryden thinks in another dimension altogether, in terms of 'high' and 'low', as well as 'near' and 'far'. So he can say 'heroic rhyme is nearest Nature, as being the noblest kind of modern verse'. Art must be 'wrought up', geared to its highest pitch, to get near to Nature. It is not a question of slackening a convention until it can accommodate a natural untidiness; it is not even true that between a lax convention and a strait one there is nothing to choose; the convention must be made tighter, more exacting, more austere than ever. And if *ars est celare artem*, then the more artificial the art, the more it deserves credit for concealing itself.

In the histories of literature Dryden figures as an innovator; and rightly so. Yet to his contemporaries, as the man who admired the old-fashioned Shakespeare, and found something to say for the old-fashioned Donne, he may well have seemed rather a conservative. It is probable that he spent more time and energy trying to keep in touch with older native traditions than in breaking free of them to adapt his art to novel conditions. His greatness, from one point of view, is in his knowing how far to give way to the pressure of his age, and where to resist it. Because his age was so different in so many ways from what had gone before, he had to make striking innovations; and naturally these are what impress us most forcibly in his work. But no less striking, perhaps, is the extent to which he was able to conserve older procedures and adapt them. In particular Dryden's poetry is usually regarded as the first considerable embodiment in practice of the novel Hobbesian poetic theory; and of course this is right. But in theory as in practice he looked back to masters far older than Hobbes – to Sidney and the Renaissance, from whom he learnt more important things than the Three Unities.

Cambridge Journal V: 9 (June 1952).

8 *The Language of Science and the Language of Literature, 1700-1740*

1

It is generally agreed that in the first half of the eighteenth century, there is an exceptionally close and significant relationship between the two immense fields of human activity so rashly indicated in my title – between science, that is, and literature. And some writers have offered to define this relationship in the roundest, most uncompromising terms. The example I will take is Professor R.L. Brett, on page 14 of his book on *The Third Earl of Shaftesbury. A Study in Eighteenth-Century Literary Theory*.

> The whole movement of philosophy which started with Descartes and which was accompanied by the vast expansion of scientific inquiry and achievement, has been seen, and no doubt rightly, as producing an atmosphere inimical to poetry. The view of the universe its influence had made the generally accepted one, was that of a mechanism run on mathematical principles and devoid of colour, scent, taste and sound. Science had enlarged the size of the universe, but had turned it into a lifeless machine, which worked by forces that could be expressed in mathematical formulae, but not in poetry. What was real was what could be measured, weighed, and expressed in numbers, not what could be made the subject of poetry. Such writers as A.N. Whitehead, Basil Willey and Douglas Bush have all made the point that the mechanical view of the world is one that does not commend itself to the poet. Its declaration that what is "really real" is a world of atoms in motion, devoid of all secondary sense qualities such as colour, scent, taste and sound, ordered by causal laws and explicable only in terms of mathematics, is one that gives little status to the poet. It is one indeed, that gives little status to man himself, since, once the process of scientific explanation had started, it was soon seen that man himself, as part of the natural order, could be explained in similar terms. Poetry was not alone in suffering the effect of the new movement; religion itself was its companion.

The distinguished names which Professor Brett cites as his authorities sufficiently justify my quoting him at such length; his statement is representative – in fact, it is not too much to say that he is here the spokesman of a powerful orthodoxy.

Yet it is surely open to several objections, begs a lot of questions. In the first place it requires us to think in terms of what might have been. It assumes that we are somehow dissatisfied with what poetry we have from this period; for such poetry as we have does its best with the materials and in the conditions Professor Brett thinks so unsuitable. It follows from his argument that there must be something wrong with this poetry; and since this poetry includes the poems of Alexander Pope (to go no farther), this seems a very bold assumption – would certainly have seemed so, for instance, to Dr Johnson. Secondly we may object, with Stéphane Mallarmé, that poetry is written not with ideas but with *words*. We cannot be as confident as Professor Brett that we know what is good for poets and what is bad for them; for poets continue to surprise us by finding themes (which is to say, words) to excite them, where we least expected anything of the sort. The truth is surely that many poets listen to the philosophers, and philosophize about their own activity, much less than many people imagine. There is, it may be thought, a particularly telling example of this in this very period – the case of Pope who, having wavered towards a near-deism in the *Essay on Man*, recanted it in *The Dunciad*.[1] It may be that this represents a change of heart in Pope; but equally well it may witness to a sort of quite legitimate irresponsibility. He believed, in some sense, of course, first the one thing and then the other. But he may have believed as some have held that Yeats 'believed' in the extraordinary farrago he delivered to the world in *A Vision*, as *his* 'philosophy'. These are not, to put it bluntly, the ideas that the poets lived by – those in Pope's case, were, presumably, the precepts of the Roman Church. In both poets, these 'beliefs' sometimes seem no more than a sort of provisional assent or serious make-believe, like the love which Walter Ralegh and some other Elizabethans professed to feel for Queen Elizabeth. When Yeats asked the spirit-medium what it had come for, it replied, 'To give you metaphors for poetry.' Just so may Pope have imagined that the spirits of Bolingbroke and Warburton, Locke and Shaftesbury, came to him. I am not asserting that this is so; I am only pointing out the evidence that the relationship between a poet's poetry and his professed beliefs is by no means so direct as Professor Brett, and thinkers of his school, tend to suppose.

[1] See Arthur Friedman, 'Pope and Deism', in *Pope and his Contemporaries. Essays presented to George Sherburn* (Oxford, 1949).

Historians of ideas are often nowadays solicitous for the poets; and the latter, as often as not, are churlish in their acknowledgements. The truth seems to be that the poet is sturdier, and his attitudes less calculable, than the historians suppose. There is a notion abroad that what is 'organic' is a good thing for poetry; and it follows that what is mechanical isn't. The poet, however, takes his metaphors where he finds them, and may choose to extol the Brooklyn Bridge, no less than the meanest flower that blows. As Hart Crane declared, himself the laureate of the Brooklyn Bridge, 'The familiar contention that science is inimical to poetry is no more tenable than the kindred notion that theology has been proverbially hostile – with the *Commedia* of Dante to prove the contrary.'[1]

It seems, then, that there are sufficient reasons for taking another look at the relations between science and literature at the beginning of the eighteenth century. And we may begin to do so by glancing at some other books which bear upon the matter.

First, there are a number of books by Professor Marjorie Nicolson, of which the most germane to the present purpose is called *Newton Demands the Muse*. This book establishes that some of Sir Isaac Newton's scientific discoveries, particularly those in his *Opticks*, fired the imagination of a number of writers, of whom the most influential in both prose and verse was Addison, and probably the most substantial, in terms of intrinsic merit, was James Thomson, author of *The Seasons*. I am not aware that Professor Nicolson's case has been seriously challenged. And accordingly we find ourselves in the position of having to maintain (if we agree with Professor Brett) that, when certain considerable writers thought themselves imaginatively excited to poetic purpose by the worlds revealed by science, they were self-deluded.

In fact, this self-delusion is something that the orthodox argument requires us to impute to most of the writers of our period. It is notable that Professor Brett (and in this he is typical) says nothing of how the scientific world-view affected the writers of *prose*. And it's easy to see how this comes about. For it is orthodox to suppose that this period, the age of Swift and Berkeley, Addison and Steele, is a great age – perhaps *the* great age – of English prose; and it's orthodox also to think that some of the credit for this goes to the scientists. One may mention here the work of Richard Foster Jones (see *The Seventeenth Century* by R.F. Jones and others, 1951), which substantiates the familiar argument that the scientists had no sooner instituted the Royal Society (for the furtherance of scientific experi-

[1] Quoted by Peter Viereck, *Strike through the Mask!* (New York, 1950), p.68.

ment, and the pooling of its findings), than they began to demand a naked and direct sort of prose appropriate to the lab.-book – a sort of prose handed down as a legacy from Dryden to the prose writers of the age of Queen Anne and the first Hanoverians. Thus we are in the position of congratulating prose writers of this period on their good fortune, at the same time as we commiserate with the poets for their ill luck, living when they did. Yet this is the very opposite of what these writers thought themselves. For if they were poets, they congratulated themselves on inheriting the language from Denham and Waller and Dryden, who, as they said, 'first gave it regular harmony, and discovered its latent powers'; whereas, if they were writers of prose, we find them grumbling about the vicious styles then current and the unstable condition of the language they had to use – as Swift does, for instance, in his *Proposal for correcting . . . the English Tongue*. If we follow Professor Brett, we have to tell the poets that they were living in a fool's paradise, at the same time as we tell the prose writers that they didn't know how lucky they were. Yet perhaps the writers themselves recognized their own situation better than we can. What is more, if we argue in Professor Brett's way, we are obliged to adopt some questionable assumptions about the relation of prose to poetry *at any time*. We are committed to supposing that poetry and prose differ not in degree but radically, in kind; so that the conditions favourable to the one may be death to the other; and the grouping of both sorts of writing under the head of 'literature' is at bottom only misleading. This is the assumption of those Victorian critics who, like Matthew Arnold, defined Dryden and Pope as 'classics of our prose, not of our poetry'. And that, we may hope, is a position no longer respectable.

Another book that may be mentioned here is one that created some stir when it came out some years ago – Miss Kathleen Nott's *The Emperor's Clothes*. This is a work of polemic, not of scholarship; and its lack of scholarship seriously impairs its polemical attacks on Mr Eliot, Professor Lewis, Professor Willey, and others. On the other hand, it asks some of the questions that we have seen to be begged by the orthodox statement of the case. And it asks one other, which is of some importance. In that orthodox view, who are the villains of the piece? Who are these allegedly so powerful enemies of poetry? Are they the practising scientists? Or are they not rather the philosophers who philosophize about what the scientists seem to be doing? These are two distinct classes of people, even when, as in the case of Isaac Newton, they happen to come together in one person. Shall we exonerate the humble and dedicated scientist on the job, like Robert Boyle, the great chemist, while casting all the blame instead on a philosopher like Locke, theorizing *about* science – which is what Miss Nott wants us to do? Or do scientist and philosopher line up in an unholy alliance, as Professor Brett seems to suppose? Or can we exonerate them both?

We get nearer to brass tacks with another American work, a research-thesis by John Arthos, published in 1949, called *The Language of Natural Description in Eighteenth-Century Poetry*. The argument of this massive and learned study is summarized as follows (p.88):

> It may very well be that many poets [i.e. of the eighteenth century] accepted the idea of a conventional language for poetry because they considered the interests of poetry and natural philosophy to be the same in many important respects. Scientific writing required a set vocabulary formed according to set principles, and it must therefore follow that poetry's needs were similar. This is the extreme conclusion. It is, of course, truer of some poets than of others. But its general validity seems proved by the fact that so many of the same terms are found in scientific prose and in the poetry of the eighteenth century.

This brings us to the same point as Marjorie Nicolson's research into the poetic influence of Isaac Newton; *we* have to think that the poets went calamitously wrong precisely where *they* were most hopeful – in supposing 'the interests of poetry and natural philosophy' (that is natural science) 'to be the same in many important respects'. But Arthos is more challenging than Professor Nicolson, because he traces the effect of this assumption or delusion, not in what the poets wrote or what they wrote about, but in their very way of writing, in their vocabulary, in their *words*. Two components of eighteenth-century poetic diction are particularly revealing from this point of view. First there is that characteristic trick of adjectives which are formed by adding the suffix 'y' to nouns – words like 'beamy', 'bloomy', 'moony', 'roofy', 'sluicy'. All these examples are from Dryden, and Arthos gives examples of exactly similar coinings from the prose of late seventeenth-century scientists. (It is worth pausing to see the implications of this – it means that when Wordsworth, objecting to this vocabulary, declared that there was no essential difference between the languages of prose and poetry, he was enunciating a principle from which had come the very vocabulary he objected to.) The second feature of eighteenth-century diction which enforces the point is the periphrasis – locutions like 'bearded product' for 'corn', 'loquacious race' (frogs) and 'scaly locks' (fish). All these, again, are from Dryden, and we can see as soon as Arthos points it out that such expressions are formed on precisely the same principle as the classifications of an eighteenth-century scientist like the great Swedish botanist Linnaeus – the name of the genus together with the distinguishing characteristic which defines the species (e.g., the white water-lily, *Nymphaea alba*). Of course, in so far as we agree with Wordsworth that locutions of this kind are a blemish to poetry – I don't think they are, necessarily – we have not exonerated science, in this case in its aspect of classification, from exerting a bad influence on poetry. But at least we are seeing that influence in unexpected places. A scientific, or scientific-and-philosophical, influence is at work on other features of eighteenth-century poetic diction, as we shall see. Much that we object to in eighteenth-century poetry as florid, excessively 'poetical', too far from prose usage, turns out on the contrary to be, if anything, only too prosaic.

The last book I want to mention is more important than any of these, and takes us at once to the heart of our subject. It is again American (I need not point the moral): W.K. Wimsatt's study of the prose style of Dr Johnson, *Philosophic Words*, published in 1948. This is a brilliant and momentous piece of scholarship. By 'philosophic' in his title, Wimsatt means what Johnson meant by it: that is, as describing whatever pertains to 'natural philosophy' or, as we should say, to the natural sciences. Such words as 'acrimony' and 'volatile' are, in this sense, eminently 'philosophic' words, for they have been adopted into the language at large from the special terminology of chemistry. Wimsatt shows, from a close study of Johnson's *Dictionary*, that as a lexicographer Johnson set out quite deliberately to assist this adoption into the language of the erstwhile specialized terminology of the sciences, attracting such words out of the laboratory into the drawing-room. At the same time, in *The Rambler*, Johnson the essayist was doing the same thing by other means, exemplifying in practice what, in the *Dictionary*, he urged as theory. For, as Wimsatt shows, the prevailingly abstract, Latinate, and sesquipedalian character of Johnson's style, especially in *The Rambler*, is brought about very largely by his consistent use of these words which he called 'philosophic'. Now, the essays in *The Rambler* are moral disquisitions, and have nothing to do with the natural sciences, except occasionally for purposes of illustration. How, then, could Johnson use so many scientific words in a non-scientific context? He could do so only by extending their significations, and giving them a metaphorical as well as a literal bearing. So, when 'acrimony' is used, it still means literally what it meant in the laboratory, 'corrosiveness'; but it means metaphorically, in the context of moral disquisition, 'severity, bitterness of thought or language'. We still speak of a person as having an acrimonious temperament, or of an acrimonious debate. In fact, the adoption of such words has been so complete that, unless we are chemists (and perhaps even if we are), we are unaware, when we use the word, that we are using a metaphor. It is for us a dead metaphor, whereas for Johnson and his predecessors and contemporaries it was a very lively metaphor indeed, daringly far-fetched. It is the very completeness of Johnson's success which obscures, for us, his achievement. As Wimsatt says, Johnson's prose, at any rate in *The Rambler*, is very highly figurative; in fact, it is *poetic* prose. One tends to think that a highly abstract style is a style devoid of images, hence unmetaphorical; but what makes Johnson's style abstract is also what makes it highly metaphorical.

Now, it is unthinkable that a whole vast movement like this, inside the language, should come about by the deliberate manoeuvre of one writer. Johnson assisted the shift, the adoption of scientific terminology by metaphorical extension into common usage. But he cannot have inaugurated this development. He only raised to the level of conscious exploitation a change that was happening in the language itself. Indeed, in the examples of 'beamy', 'moony' and 'sluicy' given by Arthos, we have already seen the shift-over happening more than fifty years before, with Dryden. And an hour or so with the *Oxford English Dictionary* will show that the process was general. I have cited as exemplifying this shift in our period the words 'volatile' and 'acrimony'. Let me give two more, the words 'insipid' and 'astringency'. For 'insipid' as an adjective, the OED gives three senses, as follows (1) 'Without taste, tasteless', of which it gives six examples, ranging between 1620 and 1822; (2) a figurative sense, 'Wanting the qualities which excite interest or emotion; uninteresting, lifeless, dull, flat', the earliest citation being from Evelyn's Diary for 1649, while others include one from Swift, 1710-11; and (3) obsolete sense, 'Devoid of taste, intelligence or judgment; stupid, foolish, dull', exemplified from, among others, Baxter in 1651 and Pepys, 1662-5. It is surely clear that the technical sense 'tasteless' ('Water is an insipid fluid'), which antedates the others, in fact produced those others by metaphorical extension from talking about natural substances to talking about human beings or human products ('an insipid person', 'an insipid book'). And this extension takes place, if we may trust the OED, precisely in the span of years between Dryden and Johnson. The case is clinched when we look further in the OED and find 'insipid' as a substantive (as in *The History of the Insipids*), first used in 1700 and thereafter by Defoe in 1727. A very little reading in the early eighteenth century will establish 'insipid' as a favourite word in the period; and it is easy to see why – it was a newish word even in its literal sense, and very new in its figurative meaning, a lively and daring metaphor taken from technical terminology. As for 'astringency', the earliest example given by the OED of a figurative sense (that is, of the sense we give it today) is John Galt's *Entail* of 1823, just as its earliest example of a figurative sense for 'astringent' comes from Byron's *Don Juan*, Book 5, in 1820. I think I have found what amounts to figurative use of both these words, as of the cognate word 'astringe', in William Law in the 1740s – a matter to which I may return. Otherwise 'astringency', in the eighteenth century, had the sense given to it by Johnson's *Dictionary*: 'The power of contracting the parts of the body; opposed to the power of relaxation.' That is to say, 'astringency' was still a technical term of the science of physiology. And accordingly, its use is exemplified in Johnson's *Dictionary* by a quotation from Arbuthnot's *Essay on Aliments*:

> Acid, acrid, austere, and bitter substances, by their astringency, create horrour, that is, stimulate the fibres.

One could not wish for a more instructive example of how the English of the early eighteenth century is for us a foreign language. Hardly one of the words in this sentence is used as we should use it today. 'Astringency' and, of course, 'bitter', we are accustomed to think of as having both literal and metaphorical senses, but, as we have seen, if 'astringency' had a figurative sense at all in Arbuthnot's day, or Johnson's, that use of it would be daringly novel. 'Acrid' is a word that we *can* use figuratively ('the essay is written in a rather acrid tone', an 'acrid' controversy), but only in its literal sense has it any wide currency. And 'acid' is rather similar, though it is in common use metaphorically on the lower deck of the Royal Navy, to mean 'sarcastic'. But 'austere' and 'horror' are used nowadays only in their figurative senses, so that only with a shock do we realize how they once had literal (i.e. 'philosophic') senses, as part of the technical vocabulary of physic. Arbuthnot's sense for 'horrour' is close to the image carried by the root word in Latin, the image of hair standing up on the head; we see it in poetry when Dryden writes, in a way to us either nonsensical or ludicrous, of a hillside which is 'horrid with fern'.

When we read the English prose of Milton or Sir Thomas Browne, we are ready to recognize that we have to do some translating of their idiom into our own. And similarly, in a later period, with the prose of Johnson or Gibbon – when Johnson in a famous passage declares that pastoral is 'easy, vulgar and therefore disgusting', we are ready to recognize that no one of these words means just what it means today. But with Dryden's prose we seem to leap suddenly into the modern world. And from Dryden through to something later than 1740, the prose, by its familiar colloquial rhythms, deludes us into thinking that no such scrutiny of vocabulary is called for, that the idiom of that day is simply our own idiom. We have found reason to suppose that this isn't so; that semantic changes are going on at least as rapidly in this period as in any other and must be watched at least as closely; above all, that some of these changes have to do with a relation between scientific terminology and common usage. If so, these changes in meaning have everything to do with the question of how, in this period, science and literature are related.

Our subject, therefore, resolves itself from 'Science and Literature' into 'The Language of Science and the Language of Literature', in the first half of the eighteenth century. By thus cutting down at once to the level of language, we shall be working in the spirit of Mallarmé's truism: 'Poetry is written not with ideas but with words.' We shall also be assuming that the history of literature can be accurately studied only as an extension of the history of the language. This is what the historians of the language have been maintaining for a long time, but in practice this principle hardly ever gets applied except in the periods of Old English and Middle English. For the most part we look in vain to the historians of language for any application of the principle to a period as 'modern' as that of the eighteenth century. Instead, it is the critics and literary historians – Arthos and Wimsatt – who can come to our help. To these names I would add one other, that of Professor Empson, who is almost alone among British scholars in turning his attention in this direction. First in some passages of *Some Versions of Pastoral*, and then in his *Structure of Complex Words*, he has done work of the kind we are asking for. And I shall take as my text for the next stage some comments by him on the prose vocabulary of Swift, which I find in *Some Versions of Pastoral*.

2

W.K. Wimsatt, when he establishes how Dr Johnson in *The Rambler* is continually defining human and moral conditions by metaphors drawn from the natural sciences, goes on to show how every such metaphor derives from, and helps to maintain, one philosophical system, that of John Locke. For to bring over into ethics and psychology the terminology of natural science is to imply that the workings of the mind are precisely analogous to the workings of matter; and this was one of the implications, or one of the assumptions, of Locke's philosophy. The point is taken beautifully, later in the century, by William Blake in his notes to Reynolds' *Discourses*. Reynolds writes, 'My notion of nature comprehends not only the forms which nature produces, but also the nature and internal fabrick and organisation . . .

of the human mind and imagination.' This is precisely the assumption which underlies Johnson's metaphorical use of terms from natural science. And Blake pounces at once: 'Here is a Plain Confession that he thinks Mind and Imagination not to be above the Mortal and Perishing Nature. Such is the End of Epicurean or Newtonian Philosophy; it is Atheism.'[1] Hence it is not surprising to find, in Wimsatt's words, that 'Locke was evidently the British philosopher chosen to represent his kind in the Dictionary.' Berkeley, for instance, had challenged the Lockean system; but Johnson, it seems, chose to ignore the challenge. This goes along with Johnson's known dislike of Berkeleyan thought as he understood it; and again it is not surprising that Berkeley is quoted in the *Dictionary* only eight times – a marked contrast to the strongly Berkeleyan cast of Ephraim Chambers' *Cyclopaedia*, a work that in other respects was one of Johnson's main sources.[2]

Already here we come near to answering a question that was raised earlier, that of the role played, in the matter of connections between science and literature, by non-scientists, philosophers like Locke. The case of Johnson shows that such philosophers were essential, as middle-men, as the medium through which scientific terms and conceptions became available to writers for use as metaphors. It suggests further that this sort of deliberately ambiguous vocabulary, a range of effects in which, as we have seen, the language of our period was unusually resourceful, was available only to writers who adopted, consciously or unconsciously, the Lockean or Newtonian 'world-view'.

But this is not so. On the contrary, this range of effects is particularly inviting to writers who are opposed to the Lockean or Newtonian universe. The only difference is that such writers will exploit this vocabulary to comic or satirical effect. And this is a very important point, because a great deal of the finest writing of the period, in verse and prose alike, *is* comic or satirical; just as much of it is produced by men like Swift and Pope, who were bitterly opposed to the whole trend of scientific development in their day.

Berkeley has already been cited as a writer of this kind, an intimate friend of both Pope and Swift, like them a conservative, fighting for a traditional and Christian view of the world in the teeth of the more mechanical and materialist view which a philosopher like Locke was constructing on hints from the scientists. Yet Berkeley's weapon was ridicule, as in the fantasy which he contributed to Steele's *Guardian* (no. 39). This purports to be a visit to the pineal

1 Blake, *Poetry and Prose*, Nonesuch edn. p.807.

2 Wimsatt, *Philosophic Words* (New Haven, 1948), p.96.

gland of a freethinker, the pineal gland in Cartesian philosophy being the seat of the soul. Berkeley visits first the highest part of this structure, the understanding, which he finds 'narrower than ordinary, insomuch that there was not room for a miracle, prophesy, or separate spirit':

> This obliged me to descend a story lower, into the imagination, which I found larger, indeed, but cold and comfortless. I discover'd PREJUDICE in the figure of a woman standing in a corner, with her eyes close shut, and her forefingers stuck in her ears; many words in a confused order, but spoken with great emphasis, issued from her mouth. These being condensed by the coldness of the place, formed a sort of mist...

This is the joke at its broadest. It consists simply in taking the materialists at their word, and trying to visualize psychological processes in mechanical terms. The mock-solemn account of the forming of delusions in terms taken from physics, 'being *condensed* by the coldness of the place', is not much unlike hypotheses that were advanced in all seriousness by some 'mechanical' psychologists. It prepares the reader to see the absurdity when later on in the essay, in a place called 'the store-house of ideas', he is told of 'corporeal spirits'.

Something like this prepares us for the more subtle and powerful treatment of the scientific metaphor as an anti-mechanist joke, where the whole pun is carried in single words. This is what we find all through Swift's *Tale of a Tub*. Empson has argued that Swift's style in this work is determined by the perception that 'Everything spiritual and valuable has a gross and revolting parody, very similar to it, with the same name. Only unremitting judgment can distinguish between them...' And he sees Swift as haunted, throughout this work, by the appalling suspicion that the mechanists were right, that 'everything spiritual is really material; Hobbes and the scientists have proved this; all religion is really a perversion of sexuality.' Whether or not Swift was appalled by this possibility – I prefer to think he was just sardonically amused – Empson is certainly right about the way in which Swift exploited his perception:

> The language plays into his hands here, because the spiritual words are all derived from physical metaphors; as he saw again and again how to do this the pleasure of ingenuity must have become a shock to faith. *Spirit* in English is mixed with the chemical sense – 'the profounder chemists inform us that the strongest spirits may be extracted from human flesh' (the fanatics are lustful), and with its special sense of alcohol (intoxicated with the

> spirit, the fanatics are drunk); and its root derivation is from wind or breath (inspired by the breath of God or the wind of the spirit the fanatics are windbags). In a state of 'enthusiasm' they are possessed by devils or an animal impulse; they ought to possess it. 'Besides themselves' with ecstasy they are mad. When 'profound', being deep, they are low, being dark, they are senseless, or dropping they perform a bathos. When 'sublime', being airy, they are insubstantial (the spiritual is a delusion), being high, they are unsafe or become the mob in the gallery. There was no word with which some such trick could not be played.[1]

With this admirably penetrating and momentous observation, we take a big stride forward. We now see that what we are looking for in the vocabulary of this period is not confined to the new words, like 'acrimony', 'volatile', 'insipid', taken over from the scientists. We have to look just as closely at long-established crucial and familiar words like 'spirit', 'inspiration', 'profundity'. For the process works both ways: if words from physics, chemistry and physiology can be dignified from having a merely material reference into having an immaterial one, words from religion and ethics and aesthetics can be deflated from having a spiritual reference into having a grossly corporeal one. It's easy to see how the perception came about; even as they adopted scientific terms into common usage, by giving them a figurative sense besides their literal sense, the writers were forced to realize that many elevated words in use for centuries had themselves originally been formed in precisely the same way, and the evidence of this was in their etymology, in their Greek and Latin roots. There is another cross-reference here, into poetic diction; for Arthos defines one component of such diction in the eighteenth century as 'words already in good standing in English, but occurring in a construction that is Latin or in a sense that properly belongs to the Latin original', as when Dryden writes 'horrid with fern' or 'the morning dew prevents the sun'. A poet later than Dryden could use this device either to bring his poetic observation into line with scientific observation (as Thomson does, often) or else to ridicule the scientific habit by pressing it to an extreme.

The particular range of puns which Empson isolates accounts for a great deal of the wittiest writing in the anti-mechanist tradition. Take the word 'profundity'. By relying implicitly on the truthfulness of etymology, we get an irrefragable chain of logic: 'Profound' is 'deep'; to go deep is to sink; lead sinks fastest; therefore the most profound thinkers are the most leaden. This is the logic behind that

1 See the passages quoted in the Appendix.

elaborate spoof of the Scriblerus Club, *The Art of Sinking in Poetry, or a Treatise of the Bathos*. 'Bathos' represents an extension of the same logic from Latin etymology into Greek, and comes up with the surprising conclusion that the most profound writers are the most bathetic. Conversely, 'elevation'. 'Elevation' is 'rising high'; what rises high is levity; nothing rises so high as balloons, which are bags of wind; therefore the most elevated writers are the biggest windbags or those who display most levity. Once admit that there is no gulf fixed between the material and the immaterial worlds (which was the admission that Locke demanded), and the reasoning is impregnable.

It is doubtless no accident that a moving spirit behind *The Memoirs of Martinus Scriblerus* was Dr John Arbuthnot, the Queen's physician, whom we have met already as the author of an *Essay on Aliments*. The baffling ambiguity in the terminology of contemporary medicine, an ambiguity which we illustrated from that work, would not be lost on a man like Arbuthnot, who combined the physician and the man of letters. Out of the Scriblerus Club, where Pope and Swift were Arbuthnot's associates, and out of *The Memoirs of Martinus Scriblerus*, came both *Gulliver's Travels* and *The Dunciad*. And so it is no surprise that the pun on 'profundity', for instance, is constantly in evidence in Pope's poem. His dunces, you recall, are led to profundity, that is, to the bottom of the Thames, by the leaden weight of their own stupidity:

> Not so bold Arnall; with a weight of skull,
> Furious he dives, precipitately dull.
> Whirlpool and storms his circling arm invest,
> With all the might of gravitation blest.
> No crab more active in the dirty dance,
> Downward to climb, and backward to advance
> He brings up half the bottom on his head,
> And loudly claims the Journals and the Lead.

This is from Book 2; there is the same pun in Book 4, when the dunces are attracted to their mother-goddess, Dulness, by 'strong impulsive gravity of Head':

> None need a guide, by sure attraction led,
> And strong impulsive gravity of Head;
> None want a place, for all their centre found,
> Hung to the Goddess, and coher'd around.
> Not closer, orb in orb, conglob'd are seen
> The buzzing bees about their dusky Queen.

'Gravity' is a particularly good example. Traditionally used to designate the spiritual quality of certain temperaments and personalities, it is forced back, when Newton with learned propriety adopts it to designate a principle of physics, upon its root meaning in Latin. 'Gravity' becomes 'gravitas', becomes 'weight'. And so, once again, a grave thinker becomes a leaden-footed thinker. His weightiness is all in his lack of buoyancy – one sees how the joke could be extended indefinitely. This is a much better pun than the one in Shakespeare about how, when someone is dead, he'll be a 'grave' man. For Shakespeare's pun is a matter of merely accidental likeness of sound, whereas Pope's feels back along the lines of etymological development to a genuine likeness of meanings. It is used to comic effect, yet the comedy has an edge to it. For it is refusing to take seriously a view, of the relationship of the material to the supposedly immaterial, which was being taken very seriously indeed by many of Pope's contemporaries. It is therefore an extremely serious joke. And incidentally, in an age when physics was trying to explain all phenomena without exception by reference to the laws of motion, 'impulsive', the word that goes with 'gravity', partakes of the same crucial ambiguity.

In a very valuable essay, '*Tristram Shandy* and the Tradition of Learned Wit',[1] D.W. Jefferson has shown that when Sterne adopted Lockean psychology as a structural principle in *Tristram Shandy*, he was exploiting contemporary science in a way not very different from what we have just seen in Pope and Swift. To be sure, Sterne cannot be grouped with these writers in the anti-mechanist camp. On the contrary, he has been called, on the strength of these borrowings, a dsiciple of Locke. But Jefferson shows that this won't do, that Sterne, when he borrowed from Locke, 'exploited his ideas freely as opportunities for wit, playing with them in a manner quite unlike that of their original begetter.' And this is just how one would describe Swift's dealings with the mechanical philosophers in the *Tale of a Tub*, and Pope's in *The Dunciad*.

But Jefferson makes what is for our purposes a more important point when he shows that both Sterne and Swift, when they use science like this, belong in a tradition which goes far back into the sixteenth century. In this 'tradition of learned wit' the most important name is that of Rabelais. We find Rabelais making fun of what Jefferson calls 'intellectual habits belonging to the pre-Enlightenment world of thought'; that is, of such characteristics of medieval thought as the extended catalogue or the appeals to multiple authorities. Jefferson points out that Donne in part belongs to this tradition; for this is the wit we find in Donne's use of Thomist

[1] *Essays in Criticism* I: 3 (July 1951), pp.225-38.

metaphysics in a poem like 'Aire and Angells'. But the crucial point is made when he goes on to point out that 'the ratiocinative ingenuity which writers of the Renaissance and later inherited from the schoolmen was liable to be applied to all kinds of ideas, *even to those of the new science and philosophy*, . . .'[1] As a result, he says, 'although we do not look for jokes among the serious students of Newton and Locke', yet 'a person brought up in the old tradition of wit might well find that some of the ideas of Newton and Locke suited his purpose'. In fact, Jefferson's caution about where we needn't look for these jokes is hardly necessary. For Dr Johnson, as we have seen, was a serious student of Locke, and yet there exists *The Rambler*, no. 117, where Johnson himself makes jokes out of the puns concealed in the idea of 'elevation', arguing that since it's good for an author to have elevated thoughts and style, it is to his advantage to live in a garret, at the top of a house. But the centrally important point remains; that the new philosophy, the new words and ideas which came out of the laboratories of the Royal Society, didn't inaugurate, by reaction, a new tradition of comic writing, but, rather, refreshed and gave new impetus and opportunities to an old tradition. This was the tradition of Rabelais. And Jefferson points out that the English tradition of the later parts of Rabelais did not appear until 1693 and 1694. 'It is noteworthy', he remarks, 'that the completed work was a new book when Swift began to write his early satires.' It is indeed.

We speak of the *Tale of a Tub* and *The Dunciad* as 'satires', yet I have been placing them both, following Jefferson, in a tradition I call 'comic'. But C.S. Lewis has warned us that we tend to underestimate the amount of sheer comedy in a great deal of Augustan writing:

> It is true that they regarded satire as a 'sacred weapon', but we must not so concentrate on that idea as to forget the sheer *vis comica* which brightens so much of their work. *Gulliver* and *The Dunciad* and the whole myth of Scriblerus have missed their point if they do not sometimes make us 'laugh and shake in Rabelais' easy chair.' Even their love of filth is . . . much better understood by schoolboys than by psychoanalysts: if there is something sinister in it, there is also an element of high-spirited rowdiness.[2]

Both Swift and Berkeley were first and foremost devout and militant churchmen; as such, they saw the threat to the Church involved in the doctrines of the mechanic philosophers, and they took care to swim against that current in the thought of their time. But even so,

1 Jefferson, *op. cit.* My italics.

2 C.S. Lewis, 'Addison', in *Essays presented to D. Nichol Smith*, p.1.

they saw this movement as only one among several, all hostile to the cause they were pledged to defend – there were the deists, for instance, vowed to the teachings of Toland and Shaftesbury. And in any case, to the extent that they were both artists, they would feel rather a sort of glee at this weapon put into their hands, the puns uncovered which asked for comic elaboration. The conservative Augustan writers played with the mechanic philosophies, and they amused themselves by drawing upon them, and upon the scientists behind them, for metaphors. Swift and Sterne, of course, and Pope in *The Dunciad*, amused themselves to some purpose; comedy is not irresponsible. But I find little evidence that Hobbes and Descartes and Locke cast a black shadow over them all, as R.L. Brett and William Empson seem to think. The question is how far the poets and prose writers were alarmed and affronted by the mechanical world-view, how far just amused and intrigued. Where they are amused, the punning metaphors go into comedy: where they are alarmed, the mataphors go into satire. And because our sense of humour is less robust than that of the Augustans, we often mistake for satire what in fact is comedy.

But this, for us, is a side issue. If we follow the clue provided by Mallarmé, his reminder that poetry is made not of ideas but of words, we see the creative writer as a marauder, who ransacks the language of his own time and earlier, looking for words which are arresting and suggestive, or for words, dry and inconspicuous in common usage or in the place where he finds them, which can be made remarkable in the different context he envisages for them. When he finds them, he tears them out of the perhaps elaborate structure of meaning in which he finds them, and takes them over for his own purposes. It follows perhaps that the poet is less interested than the prose writer in the 'stability' of the language he uses; indeed, some poets have spoken as if they had a vested interest in instability, conceiving their duty to be the breaking-down of accepted meanings and usual collocations, in order by new combinations to make experience seem once again new and surprising. Swift complained that the language in his time was changing too rapidly, valuable older words continually slipping out of use as new words shouldered their way in. And it is probably true that there are periods when the language is too fluid, even for poets, when they must join forces with the prose writers to arrest the too rapid development of the language. But the poet will tend to welcome fairly rapid change in the language of his time, because the old word slipping out of use can be brought back and used to all the more effect because of the slight tinge of quaintness it has already acquired, and the new word can be acclimatized, while retaining something piquant and surprising.

In *Four Quartets*, T.S. Eliot calls this 'An easy commerce of the old and the new'; and the operative word is 'easy'.

Pope, then, lived at a time when new words were coming into the language in great numbers. Some of these were undoubtedly, as Swift thought, pieces of new-fangled jargon which did not last but were subsequently, by another change of fashion, discarded. But there is the well-known case of the word 'mob', which Swift condemned as a vulgar abbreviation, to show that there was a place in the language for some of the novel words he would have excluded. In his Pelican book, *Our Language*, Simeon Potter remarks 'All those complex changes and developments, all those adoptions and adaptations which had contributed to the making of English over so many centuries, had achieved in the year 1700 a certain balance or equilibrium.'[1] As he goes on to point out, equilibrium in this context is not the same as that 'stability', a condition of impossible stasis, for which Swift yearned. It may be defined, perhaps, as that state of the language in which the old and the new can be brought to consort together with relative ease. And if so, the poets of Pope's age may have been as fortunate as they thought they were, in coming to use the language when they did.

As we have seen, one of the most fruitful sources of new words (and of new senses for old ones) was the writing of those scientists who are often taken to have done so much damage to Augustan poetry. On this showing, it seems, on the contrary, that they helped poets, by opening up new ranges of vocabulary. When we look at Potter's examples of words for which the scientists were responsible ('centrifugal' and 'centripetal', from Newton; 'corpuscle', 'intensity', 'pathological', 'pendulum', from Boyle), we may feel that only one of these, 'intensity', was adopted to any purpose by literature. But as we have seen, not all such words had to wait long before they were adopted. And if we want to know how it was that the poets, for instance, could make sure of this vocabulary so soon, we find that the credit has to go to Brett's other *bête-noire*, the 'mechanic' philosophers. For once Hobbes and Locke had allowed the possibility that man's mind and heart were subject to the same laws as governed the world of physics, the poets were able to use the new words in writing of what was their traditional subject, the emotions and aspirations of man:

> Through clouds of Passion Pulteney's views are clear,
> He foams a Patriot to subside a peer;...

In these lines, which have been ascribed to Pope, the poet is able to

1 Simeon Potter, *Our Language* (London, 1950), p.60.

use the language of the chemical laboratory to describe the character and conduct of a venal politician. He is able to do so because materialistic philosophers have envisaged the possibility that the heart of a politician may function in the same sort of way as a chemical in a retort. It does not matter that the poet may not believe this; whether he believes it or not, the idea (and the words, the words – 'subside') are still there for him to make play with. Even if he is bitterly opposed to all this aspect of the thought of his time, he can, just for that reason, push it to an extreme, to make it look silly. In fact, this pun or this metaphor (the device partakes of both), straddling with one foot in, one out of the laboratory, is a distinctive feature of Augustan writing, in verse and in some sorts of prose; and it is at the bottom of some of the greatest literary achievements of the age. The writers owe it to the scientists and the philosophers.

I shall turn next to some writings in which such devices are used, not to deflating effect in the comic or satiric modes, but affirmatively, seriously, even in the mode that the age itself called 'sublime'. And my examples will centre around, not one of the new words, but the word 'spirit', an ancient aristocrat of the language which became infected, as William Empson has seen, from rubbing shoulders with the *parvenus*.

3

There is a point in *Alice in Wonderland*, where Alice speculates about diet:

> 'When *I'm* a Duchess', she said to herself (not in a very hopeful tone, though), 'I won't have any pepper in my kitchen *at all*. Soup does very well without – Maybe it's always pepper that makes people hot-tempered', she went on, very much pleased at having found out a new kind of rule, 'and vinegar that makes them sour – and camomile that makes them bitter – and – and barley-sugar and such things that make children sweet-tempered. I only wish people knew *that*: then they wouldn't be so stingy about it, you know...'

Alice's 'new kind of rule' isn't new at all, but ancient. And this logic, which for us belongs in Wonderland, or else in childishness, in the past was the logic of science. What is the relation between hot pepper and hot temper, sweet sugar and sweet temper, camomile and a bitter tongue, vinegar and a sour look? We reply, I suppose, that the relationship is metaphorical, or, as we say, *only* metaphorical. But it is indisputable that in the past the relationship was one not of metaphor but of identity, as it is for Alice. What was the relationship for scientists and for laymen, in the early eighteenth century? I shall suggest that if the relationship then was metaphorical, the metaphors were very lively ones, whereas for us they are dead; and that the relationship of identity had been so recently discredited in that period that simple people still believed in it, and more sophisticated people were fairly often trapped by their own metaphors into forgetting that it was metaphors they were using, and so relapsed into the more primitive way of thinking, by which to make yourself sweet-tempered you ate sweet things.

This is only another way of putting Empson's insight about the ambiguity of, for instance, the crucial word 'spirit' in *A Tale of a Tub*. We can see Alice's Wonderland logic operating with the word 'spirit', when we turn to another nineteenth-century example, Charles Lever's novel of 1841, *Charles O'Malley*. Captain Power, a character in the novel, recommends the punch he has prepared:

> 'Eh, doctor? you advise it yourself, to be taken before bedtime; nothing inflammatory in it; nothing pugnacious; a mere circulation of the better juices and more genial spritis of the marly clay, without arousing any of the baser passions; whiskey is the devil for that.'

Whiskey is a spirit; and it raises *your* spirits, if you drink it. What is the relation between that spirit and those spirits? Again we answer: Metaphorical. But Captain Power talks as if they were identical. Also, the spirit of Scotch whisky, is a distillation of the spirit of barley. What is the spirit in barley, and how does it get there? When Captain Power speaks of the 'genial spirits of the marly clay', do we not follow that other ambiguous word 'genial' into thinking of genie or djinns, or into 'the genius of place', so that the spirit becomes at one point an embodied phantom, like a dryad? What do we mean, or what do we think we mean when we say, 'The very spirit of the Highlands is in this whisky'? Can we be absolutely sure that we aren't ourselves trapped by the multiple ambiguities in this word, into envisaging an identity when our rational minds will countenance only a comparison or an analogy?

Only by raising these questions do we put ourselves in the right frame of mind for a passage such as this, from Bernard Mandeville's famous *Fable of the Bees* (1714):

> . . . I shall prove, that, . . . what the greatest Hero differs in from the rankest Coward, is altogether Corporeal, and depends upon the inward make of Man. Whan I mean is call'd Constitution; by which is understood the orderly or disorderly mixture of the

> *Fluids* in our body: That Constitution which favours Courage, consists in the natural Strength, Elasticity, and due Contexture of the finer Spirits, and upon them wholly depends what we call Stedfastness, Resolution and Obstinacy... That some People are very much, others very little frightened at things that are strange and sudden to them, is likewise altogether owing to the firmness or imbecillity in the Tone of the Spirits...
>
> That Resolution depends upon this Tone of the Spirits, appears likewise from the effects of strong Liquors, the fiery Particles whereof crowding into the Brain, strengthen the Spirits; their Operation imitates that of Anger, which I said before was an Ebullition of the Spirits. It is for this reason that most People when they are in Drink, are sooner touch'd and more prone to Anger than at other times, and some raving Mad without any Provocation at all. It is likewise observ'd that Brandy makes Men more Quarrelsome at the same pitch of Drunkenness than Wine; because the Spirits of distill'd Waters have abundance of fiery Particles mixt with them, which the other has not. The Contexture of Spirits is so weak in some, that tho' they have Pride enough, no Art can ever make them fight, or overcome their Fears; but this is a Defect in the Principle of the *Fluids*, as other Deformities are faults of the *Solids*.[1]

You notice here one of the 'philosophic words' like 'insipid'. It is 'imbecillity', still used to refer only to a material condition, not to an immaterial condition, a condition of the mind, as in the modern sense of the word. Thus later in the eighteenth century, the naturalist Gilbert White remarks, 'The imbecility of birds seems not to be the only reason why they shun the rigour of our winters...' And he doesn't mean that birds are weak-minded but that they are weak-bodied. Similarly Mandeville, elsewhere in *The Fable of the Bees* (Remark (N)), declares, 'The firmness and Imbecillity of our Hope depend entirely on the greater or lesser degree of our Confidence, and all Hope includes Doubt...'

Mandeville is a particularly interesting case for our purposes, because, like Arbuthnot, he was a practising physician and published treatises of medicine. That is, like Arbuthnot, he united in his own person the scientist and the man of letters. His modern editor notes that in his *Treatise of the Hypochondriack and Hysterick Passions*, a medical treatise which he published in 1711, Mandeville (edn of 1730, p.163) recognized the physiology of the fluids as perhaps only

[1] *The Fable of the Bees*, Remark (R), in *Works*, ed. F.B. Kaye, (Oxford, 1924) I, pp.211, 212.

a convenient hypothesis. However this may be, in the passage quoted Mandeville is assuming that this physiology is not hypothesis but fact.

Physiology, of course, was one science which had been entirely materialistic since long before Newton and Descartes, Hobbes and Locke, indeed since the time of the ancients. Most readers of literature know vaguely about the role of the four humours in the materialistic physiology of the Elizabethans. No less important to Elizabethan medicine, and no less material, were the 'spirits', which were distinct from the 'humours', though conveyed, like them, in the blood. When Donne writes, 'As our blood labours to beget / Spirits, as like souls as it can', he is referring to the *animal* spirits, which are so called by reference not to the brute creation but to *anima* (soul); thus animal spirits are something very near to soul, though distinct from it – and hence the point of Donne's lines. The animal spirits (located for some authorities in the liver, for others in the head) were distinguished by sixteenth-century physiologists from the *vital* spirits, those again from the *nutrimental* spirits, and those in turn from the *generative* spirit; which last is the 'spirit' of Shakespeare's line, 'The expense of spirit in a waste of shame / Is lust in action'.[1]

While Mandeville may no longer believe in this complicated classification, his talk of 'fluids' and 'spirits' shows him still thinking in Elizabethan terms. And indeed his contemporary John Locke still speaks of 'the animal spirits' quite unmetaphorically. Our emancipation from this world of thought is signalized in the distinction we make between 'spirituous' (used of spirits like alcohol, which are material) and 'spiritual' (used of spirits which are immaterial). But our emancipation is partial, for we haven't two nouns to correspond to these adjectives, but only one, 'spirit'. And what do we mean when we speak of a horse or a young person as 'spirited'? Is the spirit in question material or not? At any rate, our distinction between 'spirituous' and 'spiritual' was unthinkable for the eighteenth century, as this passage of Mandeville shows. It is a distinction – not a very efficient one – designed to cope with the awkwardness of using the same word for alcohol and for the Third Person of the Trinity. We find we need some word to distinguish between those spirits which are methylated and those which are angelic. For Mandeville and his contemporaries no such distinction existed, nor is it clear that they yet felt the need for it. Some of them, indeed, as we shall see, built great hopes and much eloquence on *not* having it, for

1 See Patrick Cruttwell, 'Physiology and Psychology in Shakespeare's Age', *Journal of the History of Ideas*, XII: 1 (January 1951), pp.75-89.

this permitted them to believe in a single principle actuating all forms of life, from the basest to the most ethereal.

One of these, rather surprisingly, was Berkeley. It is surprising because Berkeley, as a friend of Swift and Pope, belongs rather with the men unsympathetic to scientific and materialist thought, who exploited this ambiguous vocabulary to comic or ironical effect. In the sixth dialogue of his *Alciphron, or the Minute Philosopher* (1732), he makes one of his four speakers declare,

> To inspire, is a Word borrowed from the *Latin*, and strictly taken means no more than to breathe or blow in: nothing therefore can be inspired but what can be blown or breathed, and nothing can be so but Wind or Vapour, which indeed may fill or puff up Men with fanatical and hypocondriacal Ravings. This sort of Inspiration I readily admit.

But the speaker here is a representative of the freethinkers whom Berkeley is writing to expose. And he immediately calls on one of his own spokesmen to counter this argument by in the same way reducing the word 'discourse' to its Latin root-meaning, 'running about', thus uncovering the futility of all such arguments from etymology. And in the same Dialogue, when another of the freethinkers manipulates the ambiguity of words like 'spirit', 'unctuous' and 'volatile', to deduce the nature of the human soul from the behaviour of vegetables, Berkeley has his other spokesman retort with the unanswerable question, 'But what relation hath the Soul of Man to Chymic Art?' Yet in his last work, *Siris* (1741), Berkeley, at the end of his life, falls into all these traps which in earlier books he had guarded against so carefully.

It is interesting to see how this comes about. *Siris* is a very peculiar little book, which has for its sub-title, *A Treatise of Tar-Water*. Berkeley, by this time residing in his Irish bishopric, had been concerned about a bad epidemic of cholera in his diocese, and had found, or thought he found, an effective medicine, tar-water. When he tried to account for this and to put it on record, he found himself in the field of pharmacy and botany – in other words, in that scientific area of language where, as we have seen, the ambiguities in a word like 'spirit' were particularly rife and particularly misleading. One other consideration should be taken into account. In the last quotation, one notices the word 'hypocondriacal'. And we have encountered the same word in the title of Mandeville's medical text-book, his *Treatise of the Hypochondriack and Hysterick Passions*. 'Hypochondria' and its derivatives, 'hypochondriac' and 'hypochondriacal', are very common words in this period, just as the peculiar conditions to which they refer were a feature of the life of the time. Ian Watt, in his *Rise of the Novel*, gives evidence of this, and speculates plausibly about the causes of it. 'Hypochondria' was so much in people's minds and mouths that it was abbreviated into 'the hyp'; and I have heard old-fashioned and provincial persons in my own lifetime say, 'Oh, you give me the hyp', where we should say, 'You give me a pain in the neck.' 'The hyp', as the eighteenth century used the term, was sometimes not far from what the present century has learned to call *Angst*. It has even more to do with what we call 'nervous debility'. In other words, it is a malady which belongs bafflingly in a sort of no-man's-land between mind and body; and the eighteenth-century usage represents a first groping towards the territory of psychosomatic medicine. Berkeley is convinced that tar-water is a good medicine for this ailment, as indeed for all others; for it soon appears that for him tar-water is a panacea.

Berkeley's diction, in *Siris*, is based upon a choice of terms which are throughout nicely ambiguous. We speak of a 'mild' purgative as we speak of a 'mild' disposition; and 'mild' therefore can be used so that the reader feels, in the word, an identity of physical and spiritual. Berkeley recommends tar-water (§105) as 'a cordial, not only safe and innocent, but giving health and spirits as surely as other cordials destroy them'. We should not describe a medicine as 'innocent'; for just as we distinguish between 'spirituous' and 'spiritual', so we distinguish between 'innocuous' and 'innocent', keeping 'innocent' to refer (outside of the law courts) exclusively to a spiritual state, immaterial where 'innocuous' is material. But this distinction was unknown to Berkeley, as it was to Donne when he wrote, 'The trepidation of the spheres, / Though greater far, is innocent'; there, both 'trepidation' and 'innocent' have for us the force of learned Latinate puns, though they would not have had that force for Donne's first readers. On the other hand, 'cordial' retains, for us, both its senses, and, as a noun, refers to a medicine having certain properties, while, as an adjective, it describes human temperament and human behaviour. Accordingly this word implies, if we scrutinize it closely, an identity between the world of physical medicine and the world of the human spirit. But of course we do not scrutinize it closely – which only means that the ambiguity of the word can work upon us all the more powerfully.

Again, when we learn (§92) that 'the animal salts of a sound body are of a neutral, bland, and benign nature', it would be wrong to say that the physical properties of the salts are defined by analogy from the moral properties of a virtuous human character. 'Bland' and 'benign' are suspended between the physical order and the moral, partaking equally of both, and implying that the two orders are not ultimately to be distinguished.

We know better than to suppose that this ambiguous vocabulary was Berkeley's creation, any more than it was Johnson's. Some ambiguities were crucial to the thinking of the alchemists, for whom a metal, for instance, could be noble or ignoble, and could have, as plants still have for the herbalist, a specific 'virtue'. (Somewhere hereabouts there is the crucial ambiguity of the one English word, 'virtue', standing for moral worth on the one hand, and on the other for the Renaissance Italian *virtù* – the ambiguity which in our period leads Shaftesbury to say, in his *Advice to an Author*, 'thus the science of virtuosi and that of virtue itself become, in a manner, one and the same.'[1]) But the range of such ambiguities was greatly extended when the scientists of the Royal Society, finding the need of new concepts, with learned propriety constructed their names for these concepts out of Latin roots which had already produced English words, of ethical rather than scientific bearing. The *Shorter Oxford English Dictionary* finds 'bland' first applied to inanimate things in 1667. To call them 'inanimate' begs the question which such words as 'bland' successfully evade. So, too, the dictionary finds 'innocent' first used as opposed to 'malignant' by a pathologist of 1662; and 'benign' used of medicines in 1735.

These usages have an interesting history. Some – 'bland', 'benign' and 'innocent', as applied to medicines – have simply disappeared. Others have been pruned of their ambiguity by dividing into two, as the seventeenth-century 'melancholy' is now shared between 'melancholy' and 'melancholia', having caused many confusions in the process.[2] Others retain their metaphorical power; for what layman, hearing of a person afflicted by a 'malignant' growth, does not feel a tug in the word, towards the idea of possession by evil spirits?

Berkeley, in *Siris*, exploited this field of ambiguity with exceptional thoroughness and consistency:

> The balsam or essential oil of vegetables contains a spirit wherein consist the specific qualities, the smell and taste of the plant. Boerhaave holds the native presiding spirit to be neither oil, salt, earth, or water; but somewhat too fine and subtle to be caught alone and rendered visible to the eye. This, when suffered to fly off, for instance, from the oil of rosemary, leaves it destitute of all flavour. This spark of life, this spirit or soul, if we may so say, of a vegetable departs without any sensible diminution of the oil or water wherein it was lodged.

1 Shaftesbury, *Characteristics*, ed. John M. Robertson, I (London, 1900), p.217.

2 Cf. Amy Reed, *The Background of Gray's Elegy* (New York, 1962).

> It should seem that the forms, souls, or principles of vegetable life subsist in the light or solar emanation; which in respect of the macrocosm is what the animal spirit is to the microcosm – the interior tegument, the subtle instrument and vehicle of power. No wonder, then, that the *ens primum* or *scintilla spirituosa*, as it is called, of plants should be a thing so fine and fugacious as to escape our nicest search. It is evident that nature at the sun's approach vegetates, and languishes at his recess: this terrestrial globe seeming only a matrix disposed and prepared to receive life from his light; when Homer in his Hymns styleth earth the wife of heaven, 'αλοχ' οὐρανοῦ ἀστερόεντος.
>
> The luminous spirit which is the form or life of a plant, from whence its differences and properties flow, is somewhat extremely volatile. It is not the oil, but a thing more subtle, whereof oil is the vehicle, which retains it from flying off, and is lodged in several parts of the plant, particularly in the cells of the bark and in the seeds. This oil, purified and exalted by the organical powers of the plant, and agitated by warmth, becomes a proper receptacle of the spirit: part of which spirit exhales through the leaves and flowers, and part is arrested by this unctuous humour that detains it in the plant. It is to be noted this essential oil, animated, one may say, with the flavour of the plant, is very different from any spirit that can be procured from the same plant by fermentation. [§§ 42, 43, 44.]

Despite the careful disclaimer in the last sentence, it is clear that the 'spirit' named there, which is alcoholic, differs from the 'spirit' of the first sentence only in being fermented. That first 'spirit' is immediately qualified as 'too fine and subtle to be caught alone and rendered visible to the eye'. Yet this is not the immaterial spirit which equals 'soul'; for Berkeley guards against this by explaining, against his normal practice, that this identification is 'only metaphorical' – 'This spark of life, this spirit or soul, *if we may so say*. . .' However, this is an old trick. The writer takes the precaution of 'if I may say so', but he knows very well that that disclaimer hardly weakens the metaphorical force at all; so he has it both ways. And so he is able to move at once to 'forms, souls, or principles' (with no disclaimer this time), to *ens primum* or *scintilla spirituosa*. By this time, the spirit of vegetables is for the reader a spirit as an angel is a spirit; and this is cunningly reinforced by the 'luminous spirit' who soars into the last paragraph. Berkeley is safe. He 'means', logically, the spirit derived from sunlight; but all the force of the locution derives from the disreputable, illogical part of the meaning, by which the 'spirit' is bright and shining as angels are. Finally, in a casual parenthesis, Berkeley returns to the 'spirit', as of wood alcohol. And so, in the end, the reader has been inveigled into accepting an ambiguity as a meaning. The writer is not using the language to think with; he is permitting the language to do his thinking for him.

This is a way of using language which is legitimate in poetry. If it occurs in philosophy more often than philosophers suppose, it isn't anything that they can feel comfortable about. In *Siris* all is metaphorical. What is to be made, for instance, of that nature which 'at the sun's approach vegetates, and languishes at his recess'? Does it 'really' languish? Or is the expression 'figurative'? Truly, we cannot say. For in this world where 'spirit' is something like wood alcohol, yet also a soul, subsisting in the light, we cannot be sure about the languor in nature. Most readers will feel, at any rate, that when Berkeley speaks of nature languishing, he means something less metaphorical, more nearly literal, than a modern speaker would mean; much more literal (for a further example) than if that same speaker were to say of a person that he 'vegetates'. And languor, too, it will be noted, belongs in the ambiguous territory of hypochondria, where a moral and spiritual condition seems open to diagnosis by physicians.

Again and again, tar-water is described in terms which strike the modern reader as applicable only to moral and psychological conditions. It is 'unctuous', 'subtle', 'active'. It is (§49) 'gentle, bland and temperate'. And (§72) 'it is of so just a temperament as to be an enemy of all extremes' – phrasing which one could think to find in Hume, describing a moral man. So too, 'There is a lentor or smoothness in the blood of healthy strong people; there is often an acrimony and solution in that of weakly morbid persons.' And we cannot, perhaps we should not, dismiss the human and moral connotations of 'acrimony' from a passage which purports to be scientific observation. The truth seems to be that for Berkeley here, as for his age in general, the distinction which we make between the scientific and the moral was unnecessary, positively unwanted. For this is what *Siris* is about, at least in its highest reaches – about a divine activity and presence which gloriously informs the whole of created nature, from lowest to highest.

There is an even more rhapsodic treatment of these linguistic muddles in *An Appeal to All that Doubt* (1740), by the famous saint of the English Church, William Law;

> If a delicious, fragrant *Fruit* had a Power of separating itself from that rich *Spirit*, fine *Taste, Smell,* and *Colour* which it receives from the Virtue of the *Sun*, and the Spirit of the *Air*; or if it could in the *Beginning* of its Growth, turn away from the *Sun*, and

> receive no Virtue from it, then it would stand in its own first Birth of *Wrath, Sourness, Bitterness,* and *Astringency*, just as the *Devils* do, who have turned back into their own dark Root, and rejected the *Light* and *Spirit* of God: so that the hellish Nature of a Devil is Nothing else, but its own *first Forms* of Life, withdrawn, or separated from the heavenly Light and Love; just as the *Sourness, Astringency,* and *Bitterness* of a Fruit, are Nothing else but the *first Forms* of its own vegetable Life before it has reached the Virtue of the *Sun*, and the Spirit of the *Air*.[1]

Besides the muddles we are by now familiar with, in the word 'light' and in the 'virtue' which is also *virtù*, we perceive the full range of the bewildering shifts inside the word 'spirit' – from the 'rich Spirit' of a fruit, through 'the Spirit of the *Air*' to 'Spirit of God' and back to 'the Spirit of the *Air*'.

This passage from Law is of peculiar interest because in it, as very often elsewhere, Law is following very closely the doctrines of the German mystic, Jacob Boehme. Now, Isaac Newton himself had read Boehme, and Law asserted most strenuously that it was from Boehme that Newton got the hint for formulating his laws of motion. And Caroline Spurgeon, in the *Cambridge History of English Literature* (vol. 9, p.208), agrees with Law in thinking it 'almost certain that the idea of the three laws of motion reached Newton through his eager study of Boehme'. Others disagree; and the case resolves itself into scrutinizing the ambiguous meanings, in Newton's work, of 'spirit', as well as of some other words like 'attraction' itself (to which Law gives a mystical meaning), and 'tincture' (another ambiguous word, alchemical in origin, very common in the period, in Berkeley, for instance). Stephen Hobhouse, for instance, challenging Spurgeon's assertion, declares, of 'spirit' as used by Newton:

> The conceptions of aether and of aethereal spirit or spirits as used by Gilbert, Descartes, Boyle and other physicists, have a long and varying history. Though the terms have at times theological and mystical, or perhaps we should say animistic, associations, it seems to me clear that in Newton's mind there was nothing properly metaphysical or 'spiritual' (as God and thought are spiritual) about 'aethereal spirit', which was merely an extremely thin, elastic, penetrating, wavelike medium, allied not to thought but to matter, even if apparently different from it in some of its properties.[2]

1 William Law, *An Appeal to All that Doubt*, ch.1, §12.

2 Stephen Hobhouse, 'Isaac Newton and Jacob Boehme: An Enquiry', reprinted as Appendix 4 of his *Selected Mystical Writings* of William Law (1948), pp.416–17.

Hobhouse hedges carefully, putting quotation-marks around 'spiritual', and an explanatory parenthesis after it – 'as God and thought are spiritual'. One respects him for this caginess, as one respects Spurgeon, on the opposite side of the argument, for finding the connection between Boehme and Newton '*almost* certain'. For the truth seems to be that terms like 'spirit', 'tincture', 'attraction' are so slippery in this period that there can be no certainty about their meaning in any context whatever. If so, then the question which Hobhouse and Spurgeon are debating, or (to take another example) the much-debated problem of how to square *Siris* with the rest of Berkeley's thought – these are questions which, in so far as they can be answered at all, can be answered only by the historical semanticist, the student of changing meanings in language. It is my argument that the whole enormous question of the relation between science and literature in this period – perhaps in any period – must be referred to the same authority, and handled only by his tools.

4

As we have seen, the influence of science upon literature in this period is so pervasive and so protean that the only way to grasp and handle it is through close and particular analysis of vocabulary. Moreover, we have seen that we need to look out, not so much for new words borrowed by literature from the sciences (vast and important as that territory is), as for old words which scientific pressure causes to take on new meanings. An easily definable and very important area of the language, in which this process can be observed, is the vocabulary of political theory. And it's from this area that I shall now produce a few examples.

One cannot read Shakespeare or any of his contemporaries without realizing how important for the sixteenth and seventeenth centuries was the habit of regarding the political community of the nation by analogy with the human body. This habit of thought has left indelible traces on our own vocabulary, as when we speak of the National Coal Board or of the House of Commons or of the Privy Council as 'a properly constituted *body*', when we speak of our monarch as 'the *Head* of State', or of whomever it is as the '*head*' of the Coal Board. Sometimes indeed we still speak of the whole bunch of us, in our political aspect, as 'the body politic'. For us these are dead metaphors, which we use (with quite unjustified confidence) as if they were not the highly figurative expressions which they are. For Shakespeare, on the other hand, as we know or must be made to see, they were very lively metaphors indeed; so lively, in fact, that he almost seems to fall, sometimes, into the opposite error from our own, and to regard the analogy between human and political body not as just a manner of speaking, nor even as a manner of thinking, but as a provable fact, on which arguments may be based.

If we ask how the eighteenth century used these metaphors, we should by now be prepared for the answer: Halfway between Shakespeare and ourselves, they think now in his way, now in ours; they start thinking our way and then, without realizing it, relapse into Shakespeare's way; they start thinking his way and then without knowing it slip into our way. The tools they had to use, the vocabulary, were so slippery (because at such a crucial state of transition) that they continually failed them.

Here, for instance, is a good writer we have already considered in other connections, the physician, cynical philosopher and wit, Bernard Mandeville:

> ...I would compare the Body Politick (I confess the Simile is very low) to a Bowl of Punch. Avarice should be the Souring and Prodigality the Sweetning of it. The Water I would call the Ignorance, Folly and Credulity of the floating insipid Multitude; while Wisdom, Honour, Fortitude and the rest of the sublime Qualities of Men which, separated by Art from the Dregs of Nature, the fire of Glory has exalted and refin'd into a Spiritual Essence, should be an Equivalent to Brandy.[1]

It is easy to say that Mandeville, of course, can't be serious. Certainly he isn't serious, in the Shakespearean way, about the metaphor he starts with, that of the body politic. For if the nation is in all seriousness like a human body, how can it at the same time be like a bowl of punch? Plainly at this point 'the body politic' is as much of a dead metaphor for Mandeville as it is for us. But what then, about the alternative analogy, with the bowl of punch? I think it is probably safe to say (I wouldn't like to be any more definite) that Mandeville doesn't *mean* to be serious in this, either. But it's a very dangerous game he is playing. Sooner or later he is sure to cut himself with his own double-edged tools; the slipperiness of his own vocabulary is going to throw him off balance. For his words are ambiguous throughout. Consider, for instance, 'sublime' – that word which was so momentous in the eighteenth century. No less than moralists and poets, and in our day psychoanalysts, chemists can 'sublimate', just as in the eighteenth century they could (and did continually) 'exalt' and 'refine'. We have already noticed 'insipid' as one of the crucial 'philosophic words', taken over from scientific terminology

[1] *The Fable of the Bees*, Remark (K), in *Works*, I, pp. 105-6.

and given a figurative extension. And so, when Mandeville speaks of 'the floating insipid Multitude', we do well to remember a piece of political jargon of our own day, 'the floating vote'. The floating vote stands for those people who Labour and Conservative alike fear may vote Liberal. And alike on the Left and Right we hear of 'milk-and-water Liberalism'. That 'milk-and-water' is our substitute for Mandeville's 'insipid'. Can we be quite sure that we shall at all times remember how this imputed connection between a certain political programme and an infantile diet is no more than figurative? The propagandists and advertisers who put such expressions into circulation are banking on the probability that we shan't remember this. And in the same way we may bank on the probability that Mandeville has forgotten, or will forget, how the connection between the fire of glory and the fire under the chemist's crucible or under the pot with the punch in it, is only a fanciful connection.

Accordingly we cannot be surprised to find Mandeville writing elsewhere:

> Lucre is the best Restorative in the World, in a literal Sense, and works upon the Spirits mechanically; for it is not only a Spur, that excites Men to labour, and makes them in love with it; but it likewise gives Relief in Weariness, and actually supports Men in all Fatigues and Difficulties.[1]

'In a *literal* Sense...', it '*actually* supports...' I do not need to point the moral: the writer is trapped by his own metaphors.

This is to take the metaphor of 'the body politic' all too seriously – to the point of forgetting that a metaphor is what it is. Yet for Mandeville in general, as we have seen, this is a dead and discredited metaphor; and consciously he thinks rather in that mechanical metaphor which was a creation of his own age – that other metaphor for the political community which we use when we speak of 'the balance of power' or of the constitution as 'a system of checks and balances'. There is, for instance, a passage in the sixth dialogue of part II of *The Fable of the Bees*, where there is an elaborate treatment of government precisely as a machine of weights and counter-weights, explicitly compared with, first, a knitting-frame for the weaving of stockings, second, a clock. And yet, had not physiologists advanced the hypothesis that the human body was itself a machine, to be ultimately explained, as knowledge accumulated, in terms of mechanics? Indeed they had:

> Man never exerts himself but when he is rous'd by his Desires: While they lie dormant, and there is nothing to raise them, his

[1] *The Fable of the Bees*, sixth dialogue, in *Works*, II, pp.354-5.

> Excellence and Abilities will be for ever undiscover'd, and the lumpish Machine, without Influence of his Passions, may be justly compared to a huge Wind-mill without a breath of Air.[1]

Here, the air which is to move the sails of the wind-mill is that mere puff or gust to which physics and etymology combined have reduced the idea of 'spirit'. And thus:

> ... the Legislature ought to resolve upon some great Undertakings that must be the Work of Ages as well as vast Labour, and convince the World that they did nothing without an anxious regard to their latest Posterity. This will fix or at least help to settle the volatile Genius and fickle Spirit of the Kingdom...[2]

Here the ambiguity of 'volatile' – that 'philosophic' word – and of 'spirit', is no longer treacherous. For if it be true that 'volatile' can be used literally only in chemistry and biochemistry, and be applied to political behaviour only by figurative extension, still there is no risk in not remembering this, since 'spirit' in both cases operates mechanically.

In other words, in Mandeville and others of his period, the metaphor of 'the body politic' was not at odds with the other metaphor of society as a machine. Both could remain live metaphors and yet be reconciled. For if the human body was itself a machine, then society could preserve its analogy with the human body, at the same time as it worked by checks and balances. So far from being mutually irreconcilable, the two metaphors could seem to support and corroborate each other. Hence, when we seem to find – as we do frequently – a mixed metaphor for political society, when we want to ask, 'Do they conceive of society organically or mechanically?' the writers can only reply with perfect consistency that since for them the organic is mechanical, they never regard society as an organism so thoroughly as when they describe it in terms of mechanics. This is what we find, for instance, in Mandeville (to come back to him for the last time):

> ... Those who immediately lose by the Misfortunes of others are very sorry, complain and make a Noise; but the others who get by them, as there always are such, hold their Tongues, because it is odious to be thought the better for the Losses and Calamities of our Neighbour. The various Ups and Downs compose a Wheel that always turning round give motion to the whole Machine. Philosophers, that dare extend their Thoughts beyond the narrow

[1] *The Fable of the Bees*, Remark (Q), in *Works*, I, p.184.

[2] Mandeville, 'Essay on Charity and Charity Schools', in *Works*, I, p.321.

> compass of what is immediately before them, look on the alternate Changes in the Civil Society no otherwise than they do on the risings and fallings of the Lungs; the latter of which are as much a part of Respiration in the more Perfect Animals as the first; so that the fickle Breath of never-stable Fortune is to the Body Politick, the same as floating Air is to a living Creature.
>
> Avarice then and Prodigality are equally necessary to the Society. That in some Countries, Men are more generally lavish than in others, proceeds from the difference in Circumstances that dispose to either Vice, and arise from the Condition of the Social Body as well as the Temperament of the Natural...[1]

Here Mandeville can adapt or translate into his own materialistic terms a metaphor even more ancient in political thought than that of 'the body politic' – the image of the Wheel of Fortune, turning as there is blown upon it 'the fickle Breath of never-stable Fortune'. And the translation is complete. We may regret the impoverishment of the metaphor in terms of imaginative resonance. We might even feel a sort of wry melancholy at the confidence and buoyancy of this materialism whose hopes or pretensions we have since seen exploded. But we cannot here, as we may elsewhere, point to Mandeville as his own dupe, trapped by metaphors starting to unforeseen life in his own language.

This is so, however, only because we know from the whole tenor of Mandeville's writings that he was – so it appears – a Hobbesian materialistic cynic, by conviction. The case is quite different when we are dealing with a writer whose conscious intention appears to be to refute the whole materialistic thesis. Swift is such a writer. And when we discover in him the image of the body politic and the image of checks and balances used indiscriminately or interchangeably of the political order, we have no recourse but to diagnose a genuine and betraying mixture of metaphors, even to find – dangerous as this is, with a writer such as Swift – a man duped by his own language. We are speaking here not of the ironical Swift of *A Tale of a Tub* or *A Modest Proposal*, but of Swift of *The Conduct of the Allies* or of *A Discourse of the Contests and Dissentions of the Nobles and Commons at Athens and Rome*. One may find Swift's prose much more enjoyable and bracing in such plainly polemical pieces as these, than in the pieces of elaborate irony like the *Argument to prove that the Abolishing of Christianity in England may... be attended with some Inconveniences*. And it is permissible to think that the present age may prefer the squirming ironies chiefly because of our predisposition towards 'complexity', and because, unable ourselves to believe

[1] *The Fable of the Bees*, Remark (Y), in *Works*, I, p.250.

anything with conviction, we cannot sympathize with statements of conviction or with the argument of a straightforward case. Nevertheless it turns out that the irony is a notably effective self-defence – that may indeed be just what is wrong with it – and Swift, shorn of his irony, looks a very vulnerable thinker, shut out by his own intemperance from recognizing the powerful currents of his age (like the revolution of scientific method) and equally incapable therefore of guarding against the intellectual and linguistic quick-sands which those new currents created.

In a commentary which Yeats wrote on his own play about Swift, *The Words on the Window Pane*, Yeats declared that in *A Discourse of the Contests and Dissentions of the Nobles and Commons at Athens and Rome*, Swift's political theory so clearly foreshadows Burke's that between them, he thought, they made of the political philosophy of English conservatism an Anglo-Irish creation. But of course Burke's use of language in political theory is not open to the same objections as Swift's. In particular, he belongs to a later generation when the Christian view of life, and the materialistic or mechanical, are – if still at odds – no longer so overtly and inescapably posed one against the other; Burke's enemies are the radical doctrinaires in politics, who may indeed be the heirs of the materialists, but equally often derive from quite other sources – Deistic rationalism for instance. Burke, because he belongs to a later generation, cannot be fitted into the present scheme. Yet because he is so plainly, by any account, the man in the eighteenth century who most conspicuously combined a genius for language with a genius for political thought, it is worth considering how he avoided or else exploited the ambiguities which, as we have seen, infested the language of political theory for his predecessors. We remember him, of course, as the great champion of the political society conceived as an organism; it is from him, indeed, that we have learned to think of an organic view of society as irreconcilably opposed to a mechanistic view of it. It is his constant contention that a political society grows and changes as a tree grows and changes, according to its own rhythms and its own inherent laws; and that it is dangerous lunacy, therefore, to design for the state a blue-print in the shape of a written Constitution, as one may or must create a blue-print for a machine. It is hardly too much to say, therefore, that Burke spent his lifetime fanning into renewed life the dead or dying metaphor of the state as 'the body politic'. Yet in Burke too, the scientific analogy is never far off:

> When I see the spirit of liberty in action, I see a strong principle at work; and this, for a while, is all I can possibly know of it. The

> wild *gas*, the fixed air, is plainly broke loose: but we ought to suspend our judgment until the first effervescence is a little subsided, till the liquor is cleared, and until we see something deeper than the agitation of a troubled and frothy surface.[1]

This is the old pun extricated by Empson from *The Tale of a Tub*, by which 'spirit' in the language of the divinity school is identified with 'spirit' in the language of the chemist's laboratory. The difference, I suspect, is that the chemistry to which Burke appeals is a chemistry which has asserted its independence of mechanics. M.H. Abrams, in *The Mirror and the Lamp*, has pointed out how the analogy with chemistry recommended itself to Burke's contemporaries who were literary critics, at least one of them – Coleridge – being also a political theorist, and of Burke's organicist persuasion. It seems that of all the natural sciences chemistry was the one which the Romantics embraced as an ally against a mechanistic view of things. But it would need a historian of science, more learned than I am, to confirm my suspicion that this came about because of the changed status of chemistry itself, in relation to the other sciences.

What can be said with some assurance is that when Burke uses the scientific analogy, he does so with a different tone from Swift or Berkeley, Mandeville or William Law, or any of the writers earlier in the century. When Burke writes of 'a sort of flippant, vain discourse, in which, as in an unsavoury fume, several persons suffer the spirit of liberty to evaporate',[2] the metaphor again is the old metaphor of Swift and Berkeley, gone dead in common parlance, into which Burke breathes new life. He remakes the metaphor in a new mould. For the argument of the metaphor in Burke is neither Berkeley's in *Siris* – 'Liberty is a spirit as alcohol is a spirit, for all things are spiritual'; nor Swift's in *A Tale of a Tub* – 'Liberty is a spirit as alcohol is a spirit, for all things are material.' The tone is not exultant, as with Berkeley, nor sardonic, as with Swift. It is sober. The old metaphor is used, but given a new lease of life.

And this, as we have said, is Burke's usual practice: he takes old political metaphors like the Shakespearean metaphor of grafting and gardening[3] and gives them new life:

> Our political system is placed in a just correspondence and symmetry with the order of the world, and with the mode of existence decreed to a permanent body composed of transitory parts; wherein, by the disposition of a stupendous wisdom, moulding

[1] *Reflections on the French Revolution*, pp.6, 7 (Everyman edition).

[2] *Reflections*, p.27.

[3] *Reflections*, p.29.

> together the great and mysterious incorporation of the human race, the whole, at one time, is never old, or middle-aged, or young, but, in a condition of unchangeable constancy, moves on through the varied tenor of perpetual decay, fall, renovation, and progression. Thus, by preserving the method of nature in the conduct of the state, in what we improve, we are never wholly obsolete. By adhering in this manner and on these principles to our forefathers, we are guided not by the superstition of antiquarians, but by the spirit of philosophic analogy. In this choice of inheritance we have given to our frame of polity the image of a relation in blood; binding up the constitution of our country with our dearest domestic ties; adopting our fundamental laws into the bosom of our family affections; keeping inseparable, and cherishing with the warmth of all their combined and mutually reflected charities, our state, our hearths, our sepulchres, and our altars.[1]

This relation which Burke calls 'philosophic analogy' is related to that which Johnson made when he spoke of 'philosophic words'. In both contexts, I think, 'philosophic' means 'of natural philosophy', that is to say, scientific. It was not for nothing that Burke was a younger associate of Johnson and Reynolds. But the analogy with science is now pursued under other patronage than that of John Locke; for it was not for nothing that Burke lived to see Wordsworth's and Coleridge's *Lyrical Ballads*.

But 1798 is a year far outside the limits I have set myself. And for an example which will draw together as many as possible of the threads I have unravelled, I shall do better to withdraw into the period I defined. This, then, is from Berkeley again – not from the elated and innocent Berkeley of *Siris*, but from *Alciphron*, his dialogues of 1732:

> The Wheels of Government go on, though wound up by different Hands: if not in the same Form, yet in some other, perhaps a better. There is an endless Variety in things: weak Men, indeed, are prejudiced towards Rules and Systemes in Life and Government: and think if these are gone, all is gone: But a Man of a great Soul and free Spirit, delights in the noble Experiment of blowing up Systemes and dissolving Governments, to mold them anew upon other Principles, and in another Shape. Take my Word for it: there is a plastic Nature in things that seeks its own End. Pull a State to pieces, jumble, confound, and shake together the Particles of Humane Society, and then let them stand a while,

[1] *Reflections*, pp.31, 32.

> and you shall soon see them settle of themselves in some convenient Order, where heavy Heads are lowest, and Men of Genius uppermost.[1]

The speaker is Lysicles, one of the freethinkers; and so, of course, these are not the views of Berkeley himself. On the contrary, the passage is heavy with irony, as Lysicles damns himself out of his own mouth. It is this that gives the writing such a Swiftian note. Moreover, the style is much more figurative than is usual with Berkeley; and just for that reason it would be hard to find elsewhere, in such short compass, so many of the characteristic and crucial Augustan metaphors. There is first the image of society as a machine ('the Wheels of Government'). Then there is science seen by the Tory, Berkeley, as disruptive and irresponsible ('the noble Experiment of blowing up Systemes...'). 'Plastic Nature' is a concealed gibe at Shaftesbury and the Cambridge Platonists behind him; Brett quotes examples of the phrase used by Cudworth and Norris.[2] Science is narrowed to the specific science of chemistry (the 'particles' are left to 'stand' and 'settle'). And finally comes the old joke of the bathos ('where heavy Heads are lowest'). By implication (since Lysicles is a fool) there is present another, Burkean image of the State as something which, if blown up, dissolved, remoulded, pulled to pieces, jumbled, confounded, shaken together, and allowed to stand, will be harder to replace than the speaker realizes.

This other society, present by implication, may be in the image of 'the body politic'; we shall tend to think so, if we pick up the echoes (unintended, I am sure) to two famous passages of Shakespeare:

> though the treasure
> Of Nature's germens tumble all together
> Even till destruction sicken; answer me...[3]

and

> Smite flat the thick rotundity o' the world!
> Crack Nature's moulds, all germens spill at once...[4]

But it won't do. Berkeley is sincerely appalled at the thought that one should 'jumble, confound, and shake together the Particles of Humane Society'. But his vision of what happens if one does, is not

1 *Aciphron*, dialogue II.

2 R.L. Brett, *The Third Earl of Shaftesbury* (London, 1951), pp.25, 26.

3 *Macbeth* IV, i. 58-60.

4 *King Lear*, III. ii. 7-8.

so precise as Shakespeare's,[1] nor so appalled. His metaphors for doing violence to nature in this way are snatched right and left from various fields of activity, which are not co-ordinated into one total picture; when Shakespeare takes an image from science, that image locks into place, not only in that one field but in one impressive structure of human thought over all.

Thus it is time to admit that the role of the metaphor in Augustan writing, whether of verse or prose, is different from its role in Elizabethan literature. It is not, I think, that there are less metaphors for the Augustans to play with, nor that science and philosophy in their time provided less, or less attractive, metaphors than Elizabethan science and philosophy. But the Augustans are more eclectic. They take their metaphors where they find them, sometimes in Hobbes, sometimes in the alchemists, sometimes in Boyle or Newton, Shakespeare or Milton, Virgil or Homer, often in Latin and Greek etymology. The metaphors of Shakespeare, however apparently diverse, add up to one comprehensive scheme of man's nature and his destiny – this is true at least, by comparison with the Augustans. The Augustan metaphors refer to several 'world-pictures' in turn, the Hobbesian picture among them; and all of these pictures cannot be equally true.

Of this eclecticism it is once again Berkeley's *Alciphron* that provides an example:

> Men are too apt to reduce unknown Things to the Standard of what they know, and bring a Prejudice or Tincture from Things they have been conversant in, to judge thereby of Things in which they have not been conversant. I have known a Fidler gravely teach that the Soul was Harmony; a Geometrician very positive that the Soul must be extended; and a Physician, who having pickled half a Dozen Embryos and dissected as many Rats and Frogs, grew conceited and affirmed there was no Soul at all, and that it was a vulgar Error.

With an unpleasant shock we realize that for Berkeley (this is spoken by Crito, one of his spokesmen against the freethinkers), the idea that the soul is harmony is neither more nor less ridiculous than the idea that it is extended. As he dismisses them together here, so elsewhere he will use them together, or use one or other as he pleases, for metaphors. He can do so because for him a metaphor is merely a figure of speech, not a figure of thought. Here is certainly a contraction not in the field of metaphor, but in man's notions of its

[1] For the meaning of 'germens' see Walter C. Curry, *Shakespeare's Philosophical Patterns* (Baton Rouge, 1959), ch. II; and cf. *Macbeth*, ed. J.D. Wilson, pp. 149-150.

validity. There is some evidence that scientists, and still more, scientific philosophers, are at least partly to blame for this contraction; but to explore this would be another story.

Appendix

'Here it may not be amiss to add a few words upon the laudable practice of wearing quilted caps; which is not a matter of mere custom, humour, or fashion, as some would pretend, but an institution of great sagacity and use; these, when moistened with sweat, stop all perspiration, and by reverberating the heat, prevent the spirit from evaporating any way, but at the mouth; even as a skilful housewife, that covers her still with a wet clout, for the same reason, and finds the same effect.

'. . . upon these, and the like reasons, certain objectors pretended to put it beyond all doubt, that there must be a sort of preternatural spirit possessing the heads of the modern saints; and some will have it to be the heat of zeal working upon the dregs of ignorance, as other spirits are produced from lees by the force of fire.

'. . . I am apt to imagine, that the seed or principle which has ever put men upon visions in things invisible, is of a corporeal nature; for the profounder chemists inform us, that the strongest spirits may be extracted from human flesh. Besides, the spinal marrow, being nothing else but a continuation of the brain, must needs create a very free communication between the superior faculties and those below: and thus the *thorn in the flesh* serves for a spur to the spirit. I think, it is agreed among physicians, that nothing affects the head as much as a tentiginous humour, repelled and elated to the upper region, found, by daily practice, to run frequently up into madness.'

Swift, *A Discourse on the Mechanical Operation of the Spirit* (1704)

The Language of Science and the Language of Literature 1700-1740 (London & New York: Sheed & Ward, 1963).

9 *Berkeley and the Style of Dialogue*

Soon after *The Principles of Human Knowledge* (1710) had appeared, the still youthful Berkeley (1685–1753) wrote to his friend Percival expressing his disappointment that Samuel Clarke had refused to be drawn into discussion of that work:

> That an ingenious and candid person (as I take him to be) should declare I am in an error, and at the same time, out of modesty, refuse to shew me where it lies, is something unaccountable.... I never expected that a gentleman otherwise so well employed should think it worth his while to enter into a dispute with me concerning any notions of mine. But being it was so clear to him that I went on false principles, I hoped he would vouchsafe in a line or two to point them out to me that so I may more closely review and examine them.[1]

We do not always understand what a writer of Berkeley's period meant when he says of some one, as Berkeley says here of Clarke, that he is a candid person. For 'candid' and 'candour' are words of much narrower meaning now than in the eighteenth century. The idea of candour was then relevant in fields of experience where the modern reader, used only to the attenuated notion current today, is not at home with it. And this breadth of meaning seems a characteristic of terms which are crucial to the thinking of man in any given time. It is an interesting question whether the breadth of meaning attached to a word is a consequence of that word's standing for something important, or whether it is not the cause of that importance.

At any rate there is little doubt that an understanding of what 'candour' meant for the Augustans is a key to much that seems odd or elusive in their thought; and this is as true of Berkeley as of the rest. To understand Berkeley's idea of candour leads, by way of profitable surmise, into that part of his thought to which he never gave systematic expression – it leads us to his ethics.

[1] Benjamin Rand, *Berkeley and Percival* (Cambridge, 1914), p.94.

No one claimed more for candour than Blifil in *Tom Jones* (1749), when he was arguing that nowhere in Scripture did 'charity' mean giving things away:

> 'The Christian religion,' he said, 'was instituted for much nobler purposes than to enforce a lesson which many heathen philosophers had taught us long before, and which, though it might perhaps be called a moral virtue, savoured but little of that sublime, Christian-like disposition – that vast elevation of thought, in purity approaching to angelic perfection – to be attained, expressed, and felt only by grace. Those,' he said, 'came nearer to the Scripture meaning who understood by it candour, or the forming of a benevolent opinion of our brethren, and passing a favourable judgment on their actions; a virtue much higher and more extensive in its nature than a pitiful distribution of alms, which, though we would never so much prejudice or even ruin our families, could never reach many; whereas charity, in the other and truer sense, might be extended to all mankind.' (II, v)

Berkeley never makes candour mean as much as this. Nor indeed does Fielding; for Blifil of course is a scoundrel, and here he is damning himself out of his own mouth – the passage is heavily ironical. Yet there would be no point to the irony if claims as large as this were not indeed made for candour in the society which Fielding wrote for. And sure enough, the biblical scholar Edward Harwood, reading in the First Epistle to the Corinthians how charity (which he called 'benevolence') 'beareth all things, believeth all things, hopeth all things, endureth all things', translated this by: 'It throws a vail of candour over all things...'[1] When Berkeley gave Clarke the credit of thinking him a candid person, he was expecting him to do more than just speak his mind. And similarly Dryden was asking a great deal of the speakers in his conversation-piece *Of Dramatic Poesy* (1668), when, in his prefatory epistle to Buckhurst, he promised that they would dispute 'like gentlemen, with candour and civility', and not 'like pedants, with violence of words'.

When Berkeley calls Clarke 'candid' he does not mean only what we should mean, that Clarke speaks his mind without fear or favour. He means that and he means more – that Clarke is so concerned to arrive at the truth that he lets nothing stand in the way of helping others to do so. He means even (in the manner of Captain Blifil) that Clarke is prepared to give any man the benefit of the doubt and

[1] *A Liberal Translation of the New Testament*, 2 vols. (London, 1768); quoted by James Sutherland, 'Some Aspects of Eighteenth-Century Prose', in *Essays on the Eighteenth Century Presented to David Nichol Smith* (Oxford, 1945), p.109.

think him an earnest seeker after truth rather than a whipper-snapper eager to make his mark by dint of outrageous novelty. For I do not think there is anything ironical in Berkeley's letter. If it raises a smile, it is at Berkeley's simplicity, in thinking Clarke could set him right without entering into a dispute with him. And yet perhaps this is not simplicity at all. It takes two to make a quarrel, and perhaps Berkeley was confident of restraining himself even if he found Clarke's objections of no weight. That would be candid; and Berkeley took candour seriously.

Candour, in any sense, is a virtue that shows itself most plainly in intelligent conversation. And unless we realize the presence of candour in the background, we are at a loss to explain the importance that the Augustans gave to 'polite conversation'. Herbert Davis has pointed out how important this was to Swift.[1] How can we explain that the value of good conversation is one of the few positive values to be found in the writings of that supremely negative and destructive mind? It seems to argue in Swift a disastrous lack of proportion – unless we remember that for the Augustans conversation was the chief opportunity for the exercise of candour, and that candour was to them a virtue sometimes hard to distinguish from charity itself.

Herbert Davis appropriately ends his essay with a tribute to Berkeley for introducing 'qualities of good conversation' into philosophical writing, as Addison had introduced them into the *Spectator*'s 'Satuday sermons'. This is nothing new, of course; it is a tribute often paid to Berkeley in particular as to the Augustans in general. But if we take 'candour' into account, then the tribute has an added force. Besides, the qualities of good conversation have an obvious and immediate relevance to a literary form that Berkeley made his own – the dialogue or the conversation-piece. Professor Davis makes his point about Berkeley by quoting from his preface to *Three Dialogues between Hylas and Philonous* (1713). It would have been more elaborate, but also more telling, to illustrate 'qualities of good conversation' from the dialogues themselves, from something that is, however trimmed and elevated, at bottom conversation exemplified.

Berkeley, as a writer of dialogues, has been compared with Plato and Leopardi, and contrasted with Landor, because 'his dialogues embody ideas instead of exhibiting characters'[2]; and the same biographers have endorsed Sir Herbert Read's judgement that in

1 Herbert Davis, 'The Conversation of the Augustans', in *The Seventeenth Century: Studies in the History of English Thought and Literature from Bacon to Pope, by Richard Foster Jones and Others Writing in his Honor* (Palo Alto, 1951).

2 J.M. Hone and M.M. Rossi, *Bishop Berkeley* (London, 1931), pp.79-80.

Berkeley's hands, as in Plato's, 'the dialogue has been purged of its dramatic nature....' But this turns out to rest upon a quibble, for 'if the essential of drama is the portrayal of action, then the essential of dialogue is the creative activity of ideas – ideas in action, one might say'. Indeed one might; and if one did, then, on Sir Herbert's definition of drama, the dialogues of Berkeley would be as dramatic as Landor's.

Berkeley's later dialogues in *Alciphron* (1732) are very different from the *Three Dialogues*, and part of the difference is that there is more 'character' in *Alciphron*. But this does not mean that *Alciphron* is more dramatic. The essential difference between the two works is stated conclusively by Hone and Rossi: 'In the *Dialogues between Hylas and Philonous*, both interlocutors are well disposed persons and lovers of truth; and if there is conflict, it is the conflict of the slow intelligence and the lively one.'[1] In other words, Hylas is as wrong as Alciphron is; but he is candid, where Alciphron is not. It is in the *Three Dialogues* that we see candour, as it were, in action.

Before showing this by example, it will be well to recall what a large undertaking it was. There is a famous work of literature where the same thing is attempted without much success – and this is Dryden's *Of Dramatic Poesy*. E.M.W. Tillyard once made the point: 'Dryden did not reach perfection of tone at once. There is something rather set and formal about they way he treats Ancients, French, and English in the *Essay of Dramatic Poesy*, as if he were arguing for freedom and impartiality, not taking them serenely for granted.'[2] And Tillyard goes on to show that in later critical writings Dryden deals freely and impartially, with less fuss than in the Essay. But it is surely necessary to take into account, in this connexion, the form of the Essay. By throwing it into the form of a conversation-piece Dryden is trying to fulfil the promise he makes in his prefatory Epistle, to show that controversial subjects can be handled 'with candour and civility' in the society for which he writes. As I have argued elsewhere,[3] and as Tillyard obliquely confirms, Dryden was unsuccessful in this. Who or what is to blame for this, whether Dryden in particular or Restoration society at large, is something we cannot determine; if the society failed its poet, the poet too was at fault in mistaking the temper of his society, and looking to it for models which it could not provide. And if we think that Berkeley in the *Three Dialogues* succeeded where Dryden failed, we should

[1] Hone and Rossi, *loc. cit.*

[2] E.M.W. Tillyard, 'A Note on Dryden's Criticism', in *The Seventeenth Century*, *op. cit.*, pp.334–5.

[3] See Chapter 7 above.

be chary of taking the credit for this from Berkeley himself so as to argue that society under Queen Anne was more civilized than it had been under Charles II.

Oddly enough (yet is it so strange?) the words 'candour' and 'candid' do not appear in the *Three Dialogues*. At times 'ingenuous' is used where it seems that 'candid' is meant:

> *Phil*.... But, can you think it no more than a philosophical paradox, to say that *real sounds are never heard*, and that the idea of them is obtained by some other sense? And is there nothing in this contrary to nature and the truth of things?
>
> *Hyl*. To deal ingenuously, I do not like it. And, after the concessions already made, I had as well grant that sounds too have no real being without the mind.
>
> *Phil*. And I hope you will make no difficulty to acknowledge the same of *colours*.
>
> *Hyl*. Pardon me: the case of colours is very different....[1]

There is a sense in which this is thoroughly theatrical dialogue. As we read we put ourselves into the posture of the speakers, of Hylas in particular; what Hylas says is said in a certain, though always changing tone, which is conveyed to us. 'To deal ingenuously...' which is rueful; 'I had as well grant...' (reluctant, without being grudging); 'Pardon me:...' (suddenly alert and assured). We even supply appropriate gestures, an unwilling rub of the nose or the jaw, the biting of a lip. Hylas is by far the more engaging and attractive of the speakers; and this is because of his candour. Repeatedly embarrassed, always pressed hard, he admits the points made against him and is never near to losing his temper, or to escaping through a deliberate quibble. And Philonous too, though he is less sympathetic because always on the winning side, is fair, and more than fair, to his opponent, letting him take his time, letting the argument circle and eddy and return upon itself.

In short, the dialogues are, among other things, an example of good manners and disinterested behaviour. Yet (this is the real achievement) the effect is not obtained by emasculating controversy. In Dryden the speakers are so careful, each of the other's *amour propre*, that they dare not push their disagreements to a point. Not so Hylas and Philonous; neither of them need pull his punches:

> *Hyl*. You may draw as many absurd consequences as you please, and endeavour to perplex the plainest things; but you shall

1 'The First Dialogue between Hylas and Philonous'; *Works*, ed. A.C. Fraser, vol. I (Oxford, 1901), p.392. Future references to Berkeley are to this edition.

never persuade me out of my senses. I clearly understand my own meaning.

Phil. I wish you would make me understand it too. . . . (p.393)

Hyl. I know not how to maintain it; and yet I am loath to give up *extension*, I see so many odd consequences following upon such a concession.

Phil. Odd, say you? After the concessions already made, I hope you will stick at nothing for its oddness. (p.400)

Phil. How many shapes is your Matter to take? Or, how often must it be proved not to exist, before you are content to part with it? (p.433)

There is excellent comedy here, not only the drama of a slow mind and a quick one, but the chastening comedy of how the human mind will twist and turn (unconsciously) to evade unpalatable conclusions, to cling to what is familiar. The candour comes with the realization by both speakers that the game has rules which the mind (however unwillingly) must observe. Hence the frequent excursions into logic:

Hyl. You have indeed clearly satisfied me – either that there is no difficulty at bottom in this point; or, if there be, that it makes equally against both opinions.

Phil. But that which makes equally against two contradictory opinions can be a proof against neither.

Hyl. I acknowledge it. (pp.468-9)

Hyl. I own myself entirely satisfied for the present in all respects. But, what security can I have that I shall still continue the same full assent to your opinion, and that no unthought-of objection or difficulty will occur hereafter?

Phil. Pray, Hylas, do you in other cases, when a point is once evidently proved, withhold your consent on account of objections or difficulties it may be liable to?. . . (p.481)

Disputation observes a discipline, an order that the shifty mind continually seeks to evade. To admit the discipline and bring one's own mind into line – this is one aspect of candour.

The sharpest sarcasm is permissible; and at least once the sarcasm becomes something more elaborate, a Swiftian irony:

Phil. But is it not strange the whole world should be thus imposed on, and so foolish as to believe their senses? And yet I know not how it is, but men eat, and drink, and sleep, and perform all the offices of life, as comfortably and conveniently as if they really knew the things they are conversant about.

Hyl. They do so: but you know ordinary practice does not require a nicety of speculative knowledge. Hence the vulgar retain their mistakes, and for all that make a shift to bustle through the affairs of life. But philosophers know better things.

Phil. You mean, they *know* that they *know nothing*.

Hyl. That is the very top and perfection of human knowledge. (p.443)

On the other hand, a plain admission of confusion deserves a helping hand:

Phil. ... This point I thought had been already determined.

Hyl. I own it was; but you will pardon me if I seem a little embarrassed: I know not how to quit my old notions.

Phil. To help you out, do but consider.... (p.401)

Undoubtedly the disputants, and Hylas in particular, are idealized. We can hardly believe that such self-control and compliance was to be found in the conversations of Augustan London, even in the conclave of the Scriblerus Club. On the other hand, we cannot think that the dialogue has no basis in reality; apart from anything else, the vivid movement of authentic speech is there to prove the contrary – 'But the novelty, Philonous, the novelty!...', '... That is not fair, Philonous...'. 'Things! You may pretend what you please;...' In other words, if the conversation is idealized, it is the most useful kind of idealization, near enough to reality to incite men to realize it. And to that extent, the *Three Dialogues* can be thought of as implicitly a treatise in ethics, an exemplification of the virtue of candour.

Ellen Douglass Leyburn, in a valuable essay, has found a striking similarity between what we take to be the ethical views of Berkeley and what we know to be the views of Dr Johnson: 'It is impossible to read *Alciphron* with Johnson in mind without finding there sentiments that almost make us forget relations of time and space and think them echoes of *Rasselas* and *The Rambler*.'[1] However it may displease the Irish admirers of Berkeley, for whom his Irishness is his greatest virtue, I think this comparison is valid and striking. There *is* a similarity between Berkeley's outlook on human conduct and Johnson's. And it seems plain, when we consider Johnson's mostly disparaging comments on Berkeley, that he had probably read none of Berkeley's works, and almost certainly not *Alciphron*.

1 'Bishop Berkeley, Metaphysician as Moralist' in *The Age of Johnson: Essays Presented to Chauncey Brewster Tinker* (New Haven, 1949), p.328.

On the other hand, there is one matter on which they plainly part company. There can be little doubt that Berkeley enjoyed disputation, but hardly in the sense in which it was 'Johnson's favourite sport'.[1] And he would surely have disapproved of a conversationalist who disputed to gain the victory at any cost. Berkeley, I fear, would have found Johnson a not wholly candid man.

Berkeley's achievement in the *Three Dialogues* can be valued at the rate it deserves if that work is compared with Shaftesbury's *The Moralists: a Philosophical Rhapsody*. Despite the ominous sound of 'rhapsody' in the title, *The Moralists* is in fact one of the best things in the *Characteristics* (1711). And – what is more surprising – it is, at its best, genuinely expansive and enlivening, precisely in its rhapsodical passages, where Shaftesbury's optimism builds on a Spinozistic basis with most enthusiasm. Though on scrutiny seldom genuinely eloquent, yet these passages are placed in the economy of the whole – and so, to some extent, 'placed' in another sense, so as to quell our disquiets about them – by rising out of dialogue. For this is Shaftesbury's own experiment in the manner of dialogue which elsewhere in the *Characteristics* he has recommended as a philosophical and literary form, a recommendation which he here repeats. As the sub-title indicates ('a Recital of Certain Conversations on Natural and Moral Subjects'), *The Moralists* is itself a dialogue, though one in which the conversations are for the most part reported instead of being *oratio recta*. As such, it is by no means unattractive. Particularly interesting is the presence of two shadowy figures, named only as an old gentleman and his younger companion, who – though they say very little – considerably enliven the scene for as long as they are present. There is for instance an admirably contrived situation in which Philocles, one of the principal speakers, explicitly speaks as *advocatus diaboli*, on the side of irreligion. This is a convention which Philocles' antagonist, Theocles, can agree to for the sake of discussion, whereas the old gentleman, continually blurring convention into reality, supposes that Philocles must be truly an infidel. This is a far subtler effect than any contrived by Dryden or, to take another instance, by Mandeville; it looks forward to the use of false-naïveté by one of the speakers in Berkeley's second set of conversation-pieces, his *Alciphron* of 1732. Yet as a whole *The Moralists* is best compared with *Three Dialogues*, Berkeley's earlier attempt at the dialogue form. For Shaftesbury

[1] 'Bishop Berkeley, Metaphysician as Moralist', in *The Age of Johnson: Essays Presented to Chauncey Brewster Tinker*, p.321.

had made it very plain that in his view the Dialogue could give only an idealized image of the common pursuit of truth, since in actuality candour and civility were so wholly lacking in the society of his and Berkeley's time. In *The Moralists* he wrote:

> You know too, that in this academic philosophy I am to present you with, there is a certain way of questioning and doubting, which no ways suits the genius of our age. Men love to take party instantly. They cannot bear being kept in suspense. The examination torments them. They want to be rid of it upon the easiest terms. 'Tis as if men fancied themselves drowning whenever they dare trust to the current of reason. They seem hurrying away they know not whither, and are ready to catch the first twig. There they choose afterwards to hang, though ever so insecurely, rather than trust their strength to bear them above water. He who has got hold of an hypothesis, how slight soever, is satisfied. He can presently answer every objection, and with a few terms of art, give an account of everything without trouble.[1]

The image of the current of reason and the twigs of hypothesis is as good as anything Shaftesbury ever achieved. Hardly less admirable is his comparison of these modish thinkers with geometers ('They are all Archimedeses in their way, and can make a world upon easier terms than he offered to move one'). And the same assurance informs his next paragraph:

> In short, there are good reasons for our being thus superficial, and consequently thus dogmatical in philosophy. We are too lazy and effeminate, and withal a little too cowardly, to dare doubt. The decisive way best becomes our manners. It suits as well with our vices as with our superstition. Whichever we are fond of is secured by it. If in favour of religion we have espoused an hypothesis on which our faith, we think, depends, we are superstitiously careful not to be loosened in it. If, by means of our ill morals, we are broken with religion, 'tis the same case still: we are as much afraid of doubting. We must be sure to say, 'It cannot be', and ''tis demonstrable. For otherwise who knows? And not to know is to yield!'

The attack is rounded off which a backward glance at earlier periods 'when not only horsemanship and military arts had their public places of exercise, but philosophy too had its wrestlers in repute' (we may think, justly enough, of the first page of Sidney's *Apologie*),

[1] Shaftesbury, *Characteristics*, ed. John M. Robertson, vol.II (London, 1900), pp.7-8. Future references to Shaftesbury are to this edition.

and the point is made that in such an age as Shaftesbury's the philosophical dialogue could be written only by swimming against the current, by taking few hints from the actual conduct of conversations and disputations and many more from the sense of how they should have been conducted. Accordingly, Shaftesbury's Theocles and Philocles are idealized further than Berkeley's Hylas and Philonous – further, and also less skilfully, less persuasively, for Theocles is pompous and priggish.

Shaftesbury in these passages argues that the difficulty of writing the philosophical dialogue in the early eighteenth century derived from a deep-seated intellectual insecurity in English society of that time – not the sort of thing we are invited to think about the English Augustan Age. Elsewhere, however, and chiefly in the *Advice to an Author*, Shaftesbury finds not psychological but social and historical reasons. *Advice to an Author* is conducted so diffusely, and contains so much of the affected writing which Shaftesbury called 'rhapsody', that it is hard and inconvenient to recognize that what Shaftesbury says about the dialogue is interesting good sense. Though Berkeley was right in *Alciphron* to ridicule the affectation with which Shaftesbury elaborated his idea to begin with, yet his ideal of 'mirror-writing', of the author in dialogue with himself, could be said to contain all Romanticism in embryo. Moreover, Shaftesbury quite justly extends the idea of dialogue to comprehend, as the true end of the noblest literature, the dramatic and the objective. It is thus that he can link together Plato and Homer. And however strangely it may consort with his proto-Romanticism, and still more with the self-regarding affectation of his own style, Shaftesbury's preference for this objective and dramatic manner to the direct wooing of the reader by the writer is a lesson worth learning in an age like the present, when 'tone' in the writer counts perhaps for too much.

As Shaftesbury develops his theme, the dialogue of a writer with himself becomes the dialogue of a writer with his subject, with 'Nature'. It is still opposed to the dialogue of writer with reader:

> An author who writes in his own person has the advantage of being who or what he pleases. He is no certain man, nor has any certain or genuine character; but suits himself on every occasion to the fancy of his reader, whom, as the fashion is nowadays, he constantly caresses and cajoles. All turns upon their two persons. And as in an amour or commerce of love-letters, so here the author has the privilege of talking eternally of himself, dressing and sprucing himself up, whilst he is making diligent court, and working upon the humour of the party to whom he addresses. This is the coquetry of a modern author, whose epistles dedicatory,

> prefaces, and addresses to the reader are so many affected graces, designed to draw the attention from the subject towards himself, and make it be generally observed, not so much what he says, as what he appears, or is, and what figure he already makes, or hopes to make, in the fashionable world. (1, 131)

Shaftesbury's conspicuous refusal to write dedications and prefaces suggest that his other affectations, like his waywardness, his launchings into rhapsody and jerkings out of it, are clumsily derived to make the effect dramatic and objective – as a soliloquy overheard, not a speech addressed to the reader, who on the contrary by these means is continually wrong-footed. The dialogue, Shaftesbury goes on to say, excludes all this 'pretty amour and intercourse of caresses between the author and reader':

> ...here the author is annihilated, and the reader, being no way applied to, stands for nobody. The self-interesting parties both vanish at once. The scene presents itself as by chance and undesigned. You are not only left to judge coolly and with indifference of the sense delivered, but of the character, genius, elocution, and manner of the persons who deliver it.... (1, 132)

Then, after copying the abruptness and lack of ceremony with which at the start of a Platonic dialogue the poor philosopher accords a powerful dignitary, Shaftesbury observes:

> Whilst I am copying this... I see a thousand ridicules arising from the manner, the circumstances and action itself, compared with modern breeding and civility. – Let us therefore mend the matter if possible, and introduce the same philosopher, addressing himself in a more obsequious manner, to *his Grace, his Excellency,* or *his Honour*, without failing in the least title of the ceremonial.... Consider how many bows and simpering faces! how many preludes, excuses, compliments! – Now put compliments, put ceremony into a dialogue, and see what will be the effect!
>
> This is the plain dilemma against that ancient manner of writing which we can neither well imitate nor translate, whatever pleasure or profit we may find in reading those originals. (1, 133-4)

Though Shaftesbury here seems to mistake the symptoms for the disease, he puts his finger on that feature of his society which had distorted Dryden's conversation-piece. And his conclusion – 'Our commerce and manner of conversation, which we think the politest imaginable, is such, it seems, as we ourselves cannot endure to see represented to the life' – brings it home to us why Dryden had to fail, and why Berkeley, in order to succeed with *Three Dialogues*, had to depart from verisimilitude.

If Shaftesbury had lived to read *Alciphron*, he would hardly have admitted that these were dialogues in which 'the self-interesting parties both vanish at once'. For no one will contradict R.L. Brett when he protests that in *Alciphron* Berkeley is unfair to Shaftesbury.[1] He is unfair to Shaftesbury, and to Mandeville too, chiefly because he uses the *argumentum ad hominem*. These arguments are not philosophical; but then, *Alciphron*, though it contains much philosophy, is a work of Christian apologetics, to which the precept which Berkeley observes, 'By their fruits shall ye know them', is appropriate though 'unfair'. And of course there is nothing unfair about his procedures if they are seen as procedures of literature. Berkeley plays the game according to the rules not of the philosopher but the dramatist; and his arguments are no less telling for being embodied in character and situation. For *Alciphron* is an altogether different affair from the *Three Dialogues*. True, the free-thinkers' arguments are rebutted time and again with strict logic; and if this is philosophical, it is also (as Berkeley does it) intensely dramatic. But over and above this there is the point, made by drama in a less abstracted sense, that both the free-thinkers, Lysicles and Alciphron, are uncandid. Berkeley says, in effect, 'These arguments can be demolished, as I show; but, in any case, what sort of person uses them?' And he shows that too. Lysicles is a young puppy; but Alciphron is a more formidable disputant, and a subtler portrait. In many ways he is a model of good breeding; and yet there is something wrong about him. It is hard to define this, except in the way that Berkeley hints at. Briefly, he lacks candour. He is more concerned to score a point than to get at the truth; that is one way of putting it. In any situation he prefers to think the worst; that is another.

Probably a score of readers will enjoy *Alciphron* for every one who will enjoy *Three Dialogues*. For we like in prose what we would not approve in conversation, hard-hitting vigour and vividness, sarcasm, bitterness, eloquence, the full battery of rhetorical resources. What we respond to most immediately in Dryden, for instance, are the places where he is fighting hard and remorselessly, arguing with his back to the wall or else in complete confidence about the rightness of his case, and using all the tricks of argument, candid or uncandid, to make his point. In his preface to *The State of Innocence* (1677), for example, Dryden's apology for poetic licence, however right and timely, is conducted by way of blank assertions, ridicule, sarcasm, all the tricks of the rhetorical trade. We would not tolerate it in conversation; it is *not* candid, it is *not* civil – and if it were we should

[1] R.L. Brett, *The Third Earl of Shaftesbury: a Study in Eighteenth-Century Literary Theory* (London, 1951), p.170.

like it much less. Very often, when candour and civility are achieved in literature, they bore us. To the perfect good manners of Addison, or of Berkeley in the *Three Dialogues*, we prefer the relatively uncandid Swift, or Johnson as Boswell reports him, or the Berkeley of *Alciphron*. It is tempting to say that we are right to feel thus; that what we look for in literature, and rightly, is to have our emotions played upon by the rhetorician, not our reasons satisfied by fair and scrupulous argument. But of course, even if literature is a province of rhetoric, not essentially of logic or dialectic, there is abundant ancient precedent for not absolving the rhetorician, however brilliant and resourceful he may be, from responsibility for the truth of what he is saying as well as for the effect of it upon his readers. And when we read works which are eloquent and candid as well, such as the *Three Dialogues* or Johnson's review of Soame Jenyns,[1] it is hard not to think that the literary pleasure these afford, to just the degree that it is less immediate and vivid, is more elevated, more substantial, and more refined.

If it is true, as Aubrey Williams has argued in his book on *The Dunciad*,[2] that Pope's lifetime saw a crisis in the status and understanding of the traditional discipline of rhetoric, and in particular a general agreement not to require of the orator truth in his matter as well as winningness in his manner, then the development of the dialogue in this period might seem a particular instance of this crisis. After the relative failure of Dryden's conversation-piece had shown that English society did not after all provide models for candour and civility, two courses were open – to use the dialogue as an image of what should be, or of what was. Berkeley followed the first course in *Three Dialogues*; the second in *Alciphron*.

The second course was perhaps easier than the first. But it required great capacities. If *Three Dialogues* should be compared with Shaftesbury, *Alciphron* earns our respect when it is set beside Mandeville's dialogues in Part 2 (1729) of *The Fable of the Bees*. Mandeville there grumbles:

> When partial Men have a mind to demolish an Adversary, and triumph over him with little Expence, it has long been a frequent Practice to attack him with Dialogues, in which the Champion, who is to lose the Battel, appears at the very beginning of the Engagement, to be the Victim, that is to be sacrifised, and seldom makes a better Figure, than Cocks on Shrove-Tuesday, that

[1] *The Literary Magazine*, XIII-XV (1757), reprinted in *Johnson: Prose and Poetry*, ed. Mona Wilson (London, 1950), pp.351-74.

[2] Aubrey L. Williams, *Pope's Dunciad: a Study of its Meaning* (London, 1955).

> receive Blows, but return none, and are visibly set up on purpose to be knock'd down.[1]

This is what Mandeville accuses Berkeley of in *A Letter to Dion* (1732), where he maintains that Lysicles and Alciphron are mere men of straw. Mandeville has a very skilful and amusing parody of Berkeley's style in *Alciphron*. But the very fact that he misses or ignores the sharp distinction between Berkeley's Alciphron and his Lysicles is enough to make Mandeville's criticism wide of the mark. And in Mandeville's own dialogues his Antonio is far more of a man of straw, far less credible, than either Lysicles and Alciphron. Mandeville seems to have grown tired of the dialogue form as he proceeded with it, for the character of Antonio as sketched in the preface, together with some rather clumsy attempts at verisimilitude in the first two dialogues, suggest that Mandeville meant to make of him what Berkeley made of Alciphron, a study in lack of candour; but if that was his original intention he soon wearied of it. Moreover, the colloquialism which the dialogue demands of Mandeville in the second part of *The Fable of the Bees* precludes the eloquence and fanciful imagery which quite often in Part I (1714) dignify his rough and hearty style. Mandeville's Antonio, after a little perfunctory huffing and puffing in the first two dialogues, takes the instructions of Cleomenes even more meekly than Hylas in his dealings with Philonous; and yet, at the same time, at the beginning of each dialogue there is an attempt at tedious and irrelevant verisimilitude which is no more than stage-business. Mandeville's dialogues fall between the two stools of the consciously idealized candour of Hylas and Philonous, and the far more lifelike behaviour of the four speakers in *Alciphron*.

The point of comparing Berkeley with distinguished contemporaries like Mandeville and Shaftesbury is to make it clear that Berkeley, when he wrote his conversation-piece, did not share in a general bounty vouchsafed to all cultivated and energetic men. It was not Augustan society nor 'the spirit of the age' which wrote *Three Dialogues* and *Alciphron*. James Sutherland, in an essay to which all students of eighteenth-century prose are indebted,[2] quotes an admirable passage from Colley Cibber's autobiography, and then observes:

> Nobody taught Cibber to write like this; he learnt to write this admirable prose by having first learnt to write dialogue for his

1 Bernard Mandeville, *The Fable of the Bees*, ed. F.B. Kaye, vol.II (Oxford, 1924), p.8.

2 James Sutherland, 'Some Aspects of Eighteenth-Century Prose', *op. cit.*, p.101.

> comedies, and he learnt to write that partly by imitating Congreve, and partly by listening to the conversation of gentlemen, and so in time acquiring it, or something like it, himself.

As a verdict on Cibber this may well be just. Yet the principle is a dangerous one. The Augustans themselves did not have such a high opinion of the conversation of the gentlemen of their day, as Swift's *Tatler* essay 'On Corruptions of Style' may remind us. In the Augustan age as in any other, to deal candidly with oneself, still more to give a lively and edifying image of candour in others – these achievements were won by the lonely and exacting labour of distinguished individuals who were not carried by the current of their times but strove against it.

The English Mind: Essays Presented to Basil Willey, eds H.S. Davies and G. Watson (Cambridge: CUP, 1964).

10 Yeats, Berkeley and Romanticism

'Romanticism', of course, is by this time quite unmanageable. By itself it gets us nowhere. When a reviewer of Yeats's *Collected Poems* (in *Adelphi*, November 1950) sees the volume as striking a blow for 'the franker, simpler, more intelligible, and often, even to the end, romantic ways of poetry,' there is no way of rebutting him: since, among the unmanageably many meanings that have been given to 'romantic' and 'romanticism', there is doubtless one that does indeed relate it to frankness and simplicity. And I have no doubt that there are other meanings of 'romantic' in terms of which one could quite properly regard all Yeats's poetry, first and last, as romantic. On the other hand I shall argue that there is another sense of 'romantic', by which Yeats can be seen, in the 1920s, to break quite deliberately with the romanticism of his youth. This again is not disputed; no one is likely to deny that in one sense 'Among School Children' is a less romantic poem than 'The Lake Isle of Innisfree'. But I shall argue that this change in the poet goes deep; that the obvious and commonly recognized change in style testifies to a far-reaching and permanent change in a philosophic attitude. And this, I think, is less generally acknowledged.

There is obviously a connection here – or at least the possibility of a connection – with Yeats's interest, at the time he wrote 'Among School Children', in the thought of Berkeley. For Berkeley too, until twenty or thirty years ago, was regarded as a proto-Romantic philosopher, one of the fathers of subjective idealism; and Yeats became interested in him at just about the time when Berkeleyans began to challenge this reading of him, and to take seriously his own claim to be a philosopher of common sense. I shall argue, to buttress my claim for an anti-Romantic Yeats, that the poet's enthusiasm for the philosopher was not just a trailing of his Anglo-Irish coat (such as we find, for instance, in the Berkeleyan stanza of 'Blood and the Moon'), but that it came out of a real grasp of Berkeley's significance as something other than what Coleridge, for instance, supposed.

The romanticism, then, that I am talking about, is the romanticism that Yeats explicitly discards in the last stanza of 'Among School Children':

Labour is blossoming or dancing where
The body is not bruised to pleasure soul,
Nor beauty born out of its own despair,
Nor blear-eyed wisdom out of midnight oil.
O chestnut-tree, great-rooted blossomer,
Are you the leaf, the blossom or the bole?
O body swayed to music, O brightening glance,
How can we know the dancer from the dance?

In the second, third, and fourth lines the poet rejects three kinds of more or less deliberate self-division, willed mutilation or sickness, as ways toward beauty and wisdom. For instance 'the body.. bruised to pleasure soul' is surely a sort of shorthand not just for the flagellations and mortifications of religious asceticism, but also for that Romantic tradition of sexual passion which comes from the Courtly Love of the Middle Ages through the *Vita Nuova* and the Platonism of Sidney's 'Astrophel and Stella'. For to delay carnal consummation indefinitely, or to exclude it altogether, so as to screw up sexual desire into something 'purer', more intellectual and spiritual, is a clear case of mortifying the flesh. And yet this was precisely the traditional spiritual discipline by which Yeats had schooled himself throughout his early life, in his wilfully exacerbated hopeless passion for Maud Gonne (who is, of course, much in evidence in earlier stanzas of this poem).

Again 'beauty born out of its own despair' can refer, not only once again to Maud Gonne (if the poet's love for her had not been despairing, it would not have been beautiful, nor produced beauty in poems), but also to the 'terrible beauty' that was born in 1916 out of the despair of a foredoomed enterprise. It can also be taken to describe the whole of Yeats's earlier practice of quarrelling with himself, in mask and antimask, calling up his own opposite, adopting a pose and then forcing himself to live up to it – in poetry, if not in life.

As for 'blear-eyed wisdom out of midnight oil', the most revealing commentary on this was surely written by a great contemporary, Thomas Hardy, in his portrait of Clym Yeobright in *The Return of the Native*:

> The face was well shaped, even excellently. But the mind within was beginning to use it as a mere waste tablet whereon to trace its idiosyncrasies as they developed themselves. The beauty here visible would in no long time be ruthlessly overrun by its parasite, thought, which might just as well have fed upon a plainer exterior where there was nothing it could harm. Had Heaven preserved Yeobright from a wearing habit of meditation, people would have said, 'A handsome man.' Had his brain unfolded

> under sharper contours they would have said, 'A thoughtful man.' But an inner strenuousness was preying upon an outer symmetry, and they rated his look as singular.
>
> Hence people who began by beholding him ended by perusing him. His countenance was overlaid with legible meanings... He already showed that thought is a disease of flesh, and indirectly bore evidence that ideal physical beauty is incompatible with emotional development and a full recognition of the coil of things. Mental luminousness must be fed with the oil of life, even though there is a physical need for it; and the pitiful sight of two demands on one supply was just showing itself here.
>
> When standing before certain men the philosopher regrets that thinkers are but perishable tissue, the artist that perishable tissue has to think.

Yeats in this place is plainly Hardy's artist who regrets 'that perishable tissue has to think.' And his thought is Hardy's thought – 'thought is a disease of flesh'. Behind them both, as often behind another contemporary, Thomas Mann, lies the conception of the artist or the thinker as an individual carrying the curse of a society, his gifts a sort of sacred sickness; and this is, as a fact of literary history, a conception thrown up by the Romantic movement in Europe.

Yeats in all three lines is probing that aspect of Romanticism misleadingly labelled 'introspection'. It is not Romantic to be capable of self-consciousness and hence of introspection; of making one part of the personality regard what some other part is thinking and feeling, even as it quite 'sincerely' thinks and feels. Romanticism takes the further step from self-regarding to self-manipulating; and by harnessing the will to one half of the divided personality it induces the other half to think and feel as it wants to feel. Hence, ever since *Le Neveu de Rameau*, the Romantic fascination with the hypocrite, the actor, and the double; and its ever more frantic attempts to surprise itself into feeling what it is not prepared to feel. Hence too its search for primitive minds in which the vicious circles of self-consciousness have not yet appeared – the noble savage, the idiot, the naïf, the good and simple peasant. (But all this of course is just a dogmatic aside.)

Where does Berkeley stand in relation to this? Oddly enough he can be detected in at least one place considering the issue in just the homemade, unphilosophical terms I have adopted here. This comes in the fifth dialogue of the relatively late work, *Alciphron*, where Berkeley is attacking Shaftesbury. Berkeley's spokesman, Crito, is made to read from Shaftesbury's *A Soliloquy, or Advice to an Author*, mocking Shaftesbury's Ciceronian style by reading it as if it were loose and irregular dramatic verse. Euphranor, Crito's ally, carries on the joke by pretending that it is a play or a poem that is being read. And the freethinker Alciphron, Shaftesbury's apologist, falls into the trap:

> You are mistaken, it is no Play nor Poetry, replied Alciphron, but a famous modern Critic moralizing in Prose. You must know this great Man hath (to use his own Words) revealed a *Grand Arcanum* to the World, having instructed Mankind in what he calls *Mirrour-writing, Self-discoursing Practice, and Author Practice,* and shew'd 'That by virtue of an intimate Recess, we may discover a certain Duplicity of Soul, and divide our *Self* into two parties, or (as he varies the Phrase) practically form the Dual Number.' In consequence whereof he hath found out that a Man may argue with himself and not only with himself, but also with Notions, Sentiments, and Vices, which by a marvellous Prosopopoeia he converts into so many Ladies: and so converted, he confutes and confounds them in a Divine Strain. Can anything be finer, bolder, or more sublime?

Here Berkeley by implication condemns and derides the attitude behind Yeats's famous dictum that out of quarrels with others the poet makes rhetoric; out of quarrelling with himself, poetry. As I should prefer to say, he stands with the later Yeats against the earlier. Berkeley derides proto-Romanticism in Shaftesbury, in the interests of Augustan common sense; the later Yeats, I think, also rejects Romanticism – and partly at least (in view of his enthusiasm at this period for Anglo-Irish Augustanism) in the interests of the same Berkeleyan ideal.

It would be disingenuous to take this passage of *Alciphron* (relaxed as it is, and wholly directed to scoring off an opponent) as a considered statement of the philosopher's central position. Yet it is thoroughly in line with the bearing of his thought as a whole. Notoriously, Descartes drove a wedge between that part of the personality which knows the world through the senses, and that other part which knows, as he maintains more reliably, by cogitation, deducing which of the reports made by the senses can be trusted. Locke drives the wedge a little deeper, deducing the existence of 'matter', as to which, since it is colourless, scentless, soundless, tasteless, the senses give us no reports at all. The old-fashioned view of Berkeley was that he drove the wedge a little deeper still, and so took his place in the line of succession from Locke through Hume to Kant. But the modern reading is that Berkeley's criticism of Locke was more radical; that he refused as a psychological impossibility the Lockean and Cartesian view that the self which knows through perception and the self which knows through cogitation can be distinct and at variance in their findings. This revised view of his significance seems preferable on many counts – not only because it is, as Dr Luce and others have shown, consonant with the argument of Berkeley's *Principles*; but also because it is consonant with the tone of his writing there, which is the tone of a man who believes himself to be irritably clearing away unnecessary refinements and false subtleties. Moreover this anti-Cartesian conservatism is what one would expect of a friend of Pope and Swift.

It is not easy to determine which view of Berkeley was held by Yeats. When he writes, in 'Blood and the Moon', of 'God-appointed Berkeley that proved all things a dream', he seems to lean towards the older view. Yet Dr Luce himself (*Berkeley's Immaterialism*, Preface p.viii) contends that Yeats had 'met the true Berkeley', when he wrote: 'Descartes, Locke, and Newton, took away the world... Berkeley restored the world. Berkeley has brought back to us the world that only exists because it shines and sounds.'

For our purposes, I believe, Yeats's position is made sufficiently clear by the characteristically wayward but often profound introduction he wrote, in 1931, to Hone's and Rossi's *Bishop Berkeley. His Life, Writings, and Philosophy*. Yeats here declares, 'The romantic movement seems related... to Locke's mechanical philosophy, as simultaneous correspondential dreams are related, not merely where there is some traceable influence but through their whole substance.' This may be to say no more than I have argued, that the split in the Romantic personality, between the part that feels and the part that manipulates itself feeling, is at bottom the split made by Descartes and widened by Locke. Yeats goes on, in a well-known passage,

> The romantic movement with its turbulent heroism, its self-assertion, is over, superseded by a new naturalism that leaves man helpless before the contents of his own mind. One thinks of Joyce's *Anna Livia Plurabelle*, Pound's *Cantos*, works of an heroic sincerity, the man, his active faculties in suspense, one finger beating time to a bell sounding and echoing in the depths of his own mind....

That Yeats was certainly wrong about Pound, and may have been no less wrong about Joyce, is here beside the point. We find him distinguishing his own attitude from theirs, in that he refuses to split himself into two halves, the one part listening to and recording what happens in the other. He claims Berkeleyan authority for this refusal and this claim is vindicated by the view of Berkeley which has gathered ground steadily since Yeats wrote. It is Berkeley he appeals to, along with Swift, Goldsmith, and Burke, when he protests further, 'And why should I, whose ancestors never accepted the anarchic subjectivity of the nineteenth century, accept its recoil; why should men's heads ache that never drank?' We may, if we like, retort that not his ancestors but Yeats himself had joined in the Romantic bottle party; but his attitude now seems to be that his doing so was an aberration, that the Romantic phase was part of the logic of historical events for an English mind, but not for an Irish mind such as his own. At any rate, it seems clear that Yeats in 1931 was so far from considering himself a Romantic, that he thought of his escaping Romanticism (and its consequences) as part of his very Irishry.

And yet it is the poem that must have the last word. I have said that the last stanza of 'Among School Children' rejects the characteristically Romantic ways toward wisdom and beauty. But how should we understand this 'rejection'? What are the alternative ways that are accepted? It is easy to reply: the Berkeleyan, the Anglo-Irish Augustan ways. And no doubt when Yeats asks (rhetorically):

> O chestnut-tree, great-rooted blossomer,
> Are you the leaf, the blossom or the bole?

– he is invoking a way of life in which the self is not divided against itself, in which art and life attain, in his own phrase (again from the introduction to Hone and Rossi), 'swiftness, volume, unity'. But if we put the stanza back in its place at the end of the poem we have to see that the tree is growing, 'Labour is blossoming or dancing', not under any circumstances that man can bring about, but only in some realm of the ideal. For 'Among School Children' is largely a poem about what it is like to grow old. And Yeats in the poem sees that the knowledgeable will, probing to perjure the candid sense ('The body... bruised to pleasure soul'), is not the product of any human perversion, but an inescapable condition of life on any terms. For what is old age but the decrepitude of sense defaced by informed will? – if not by man's will, then by will of that power which set him his course to run, which, in the course of perfecting a few souls, mutilates all bodies. Thus Yeats, like Hardy in the passage I have quoted, saw that the setting up of soul or mind against body was a law of life, whether we like it or not. There remains, I suppose, only the question whether we should adopt this law for ourselves, furthering and hastening the progress, aggravating the sickness to which we are born; or whether we should (however vainly, in the last resort) resist it. Yeats's early thought goes all by contraries: Robartes and Aherne; man and mask; primary and antithetical tinctures. This shows him taking for granted the self-division caused by the introverted will, abetting it and embracing it as a technique for dealing with experience. I have argued that the later Berkeleyan Yeats resented this law and protested against it, as Hardy declares that the artist should.

Irish Writing 31, Yeats special number, ed. S.J. White (Summer 1955); reprinted in *English Literature and British Philosophy*, ed. S.P. Rosenbaum (Chicago, 1971).

11 *Language and Poetry in the English Enlightenment*

There is a trap in my title. For what *was* the English Enlightenment? And when did it happen? English students of English literature seldom ask these questions, let alone answer them. The questions crop up only when, as too seldom happens, we try to see our native literature in the context of foreign literatures; for then we discover that, in any foreign literature we are likely to look at, the term and the concept, 'the Enlightenment', turn out to be natural and indispensable for designating a well-defined phase of that literature, or rather of the whole foreign culture of which the literature is one facet. In the case of English culture and English literature this is not the case; 'the Enlightenment' is for the most part, apparently, a category we can do without when we look at the English past and at the history of the English imagination. And yet not just the Germany of the *Aufklärung* or the France of the *encyclopédistes*, but equally the Russia of Catherine the Great or the Latin America of the Liberators, are in an obvious and necessary sense 'Enlightenment cultures', as the England of George III and George IV is not. More strikingly, the disparity can be brought nearer home; for there are English-speaking cultures that go through an Enlightenment phase as the culture of England does not: not only the North America of the first presidents, but also the Scotland of David Hume and Adam Smith, are normally taken to be Enlightenment cultures. If we look, in the England of the last decades of the eighteenth century and the first decades of the nineteenth, for figures that manifest the ideological traits that we recognize as of the Enlightenment, they turn out to be generally regarded by the English as more or less inspired cranks and oddities, such as Tom Paine, Richard Price, Joseph Priestley, the Boswell of the Hypochondriack essays rather than the biography, Richard Lovell Edgeworth, Thomas Day (the author of *Sandford and Merton*), William Godwin. (And Boswell is a Scot, in any case, and Edgeworth an Irishman.) In narrowly literary terms, the most respected figure to whom the tag 'Enlightenment' might be generally applied as necessary and proper is Maria Edgeworth.

And accordingly it is not altogether surprising that the *Shorter Oxford English Dictionary* gives, for 'Enlightenment' in a figurative sense:

> (after Ger. *Aufklärung*) Shallow and pretentious intellectualism, unreasonable contempt for authority and tradition, etc.; applied *esp.* to the spirit and aims of the French philosophers of the 18th c.

At the date given, 1865, when Idealism was at its height among philosophers, this unambiguously loaded definition would not have been unexpected. But what is remarkable is that the Oxford lexicographers offer it as the sense still current in England at the present day. It is striking evidence of how 'the Enlightenment', a concept and a category still honorific in foreign parts (particularly among Marxists, for instance), in England and to the English connotes shallowness and eccentricity.

The question becomes altogether more complicated as soon as we realize that Enlightenment thinkers outside England habitually revered certain Englishmen – notably Newton and Locke – as the pathfinders and pacemakers of the Enlightenment scheme of things. Acting on this hint, it is thoroughly plausible to decide that England did indeed have its Enlightenment, but that it happened up to a century earlier than anywhere else – say between the years 1680 and 1730. But in that case what shall we say of later figures as different as William Blake and Edward Gibbon? Is there nothing to be gained from asking, as we too seldom do, in what sense and to what extent either Blake or Gibbon is an Enlightenment figure? I suspect, on the contrary, that there is much to be gained from putting this question; for it cannot be without significance that Gibbon was Diderot's contemporary. But whatever way we look at it, the English eighteenth century is intriguingly out of step with the rest of Western Europe and the Americas. And yet this is not something that we customarily bear in mind when we examine English literature of that century.

What we have to do with, when we look at the England of the eighteenth century, is a society that is, and conceives itself to be, in a post-revolutionary situation; whereas every foreign society we are likely to compare it with is, and increasingly conceives itself to be, in a pre-revolutionary phase. For in the Americas, in France, in Germany, and in Russia, what made the Enlightenment so momentous at the time, and what makes it bulk so large in retrospect, is that it was marshalling forces and forging weapons to overthrow an *ancien régime*. Thus the Enlightenment in these cultures was essentially dynamic, forward-looking, and urgent. To the Englishman of the eighteenth century, however, with his 'glorious revolution' behind him, the very concepts – for instance, 'nature' and 'reason' –

that abroad were levers and battering rams and explosive charges, were hoops and rivets to hold together a state of society already achieved, and to prevent it from back-sliding. Hence arises the impression of stasis in English eighteenth-century society. And indeed the most powerful imaginations of that England seem very often to be fascinated by, and in search of, images of fixity and rigidity.

This explains the image that more than any other focused the imaginations of the English in that period, and focused them so generally and so powerfully that it is not excessive or pretentious to call it the myth that informed the entire civilization. This is the image that we rightly isolate when, as Englishmen reviewing our own eighteenth century, we call it not the Age of Enlightenment but the Augustan Age. It is the image, the myth, of Augustan Rome. This had a meaning for the English that, in the very nature of the case, it could not have for Frenchmen or Russians or Americans. For the Roman Empire cannot figure for the imagination as other than an image of order, and by and large very fixed and rigid order. In our post-Darwinian century, just as we always take 'dynamic' to be good and 'static' to be bad, so also we approve the adaptable and condemn the rigid. And so the English eighteenth century, which took 'rigid' to be another word for 'rigorous',[1] applauded in the Roman civic and imperial achievement precisely what we are likely to deplore or condescend to:

> The Western Empire died because the predominant race in the basin of the Mediterranean failed, after the opening of the Christian era, to develop the qualities necessary for survival under the conditions which then prevailed. The struggle for supremacy, among the Phoenicians, the Greeks and the Romans, had lasted for upward of one thousand years. The Phoenicians had succumbed rather early in the conflict; the Greeks, though highly gifted in many directions, lacked the administrative energy which alone creates social cohesion; while the Latins, excelling as administrators and soldiers, were intellectually inflexible.
>
> This rigidity wrought their destruction....

If we set this post-Darwinian and American version, from Brooks Adams's *The New Empire* (1902), against some English eighteenth-century comparisons between Greece and Rome, we get a just sense of the gulf that opens between ourselves and the English Augustans. Take, for instance, two famous couplets from Samuel Johnson's *Vanity of Human Wishes* (1749):

[1] See Susie I. Tucker, *Protean Shape. A Study in Eighteenth-Century Vocabulary and Usage* (London, 1967), p.44.

The senate's thanks, the gazette's pompous tale,
With force resistless o'er the brave prevail.
Such bribes the rapid Greek o'er Asia whirl'd,
For such the steady Roman shook the world....

It is not enough to say that Johnson holds the balance between 'rapid Greek' and 'steady Rome' more evenly than is possible for Brooks Adams or for any of us. For the regular metrical ictus in Johnson's verses, and the rigidity as of a metal box that the rhyming couplet imposes on him, tilts the balance of approval decisively toward 'the steady' and away from 'the rapid'. This is so foreign to our way of thinking and imagining that in other English Augustan versions of this stock comparison we are likely to detect irony where none was intended. This may happen, for instance, with Swift's *Letter to a Young Gentleman Lately Entered into Holy Orders* (1721):

> The two great Orators of Greece and Rome, Demosthenes and Cicero, though each of them a Leader (or as the Greeks called it, a Demagogue) in a popular state, yet seem to differ in their Practice upon this Branch of their Art: The former, who had to deal with a People of much more Politeness, Learning, and Wit, laid the greatest Weight of his Oratory upon the Strength of his Argüments offered to their Understanding and Reason: Whereas Tully considered the Dispositions of a sincere, more ignorant, and less mercurial Nation, by dwelling almost entirely on the pathetick Part.

This is a different case, because Swift undoubtedly wants his young clergyman to follow Demosthenes' Greek model; yet the effect of 'sincere, more ignorant, and less mercurial', by which we are swayed one way by 'more ignorant' only to be swayed back by 'less mercurial', is to produce in us a sort of self-balancing erectness that is rightly taken to be distinctive of eighteenth-century writing at its best, and certainly part of what I characterize as its rigidity. The writing is not 'slanted', except momentarily in a way that is at once corrected; its dynamics are self-cancelling and self-correcting; and the total effect is astringent and chastening. This flavour is too dry for most readers, who accordingly seize rather on Swift's ironical writings, such as *A Tale of a Tub* (*c.* 1698), where the sway from the vertical is much broader and the self-cancellation, though it still goes on, returns us to the vertical feeling giddy, with our heads spinning. The effect is not different, except that it is less elaborate, in Pope's verse to Burlington: 'Thou show'st us Rome was liberal, not profuse.'

Indeed that snip-snap of antithesis and sharp distinction, which everyone recognizes as the characteristic grammar of the heroic couplet, may usefully be seen in just these terms: as one sharp sway or pressure immediately corrected by another, so as to return us continually to the vertical. The erectness is not absolute, the rigidity is not inert: moment by moment the order is lost and at once recovered; it is a feat of balance. The four lines that Sir John Denham addressed to the Thames in *Cooper's Hill* (1642) – verses admired or imitated by one English Augustan after another – are as remarkable for this self-correcting equilibrium as for the compactness of expression that Johnson in his *Life of Denham* applauded as an instance of Denham's famous 'strength':

> O could I flow like thee, and make thy stream
> My great example, as it is my theme!
> Though deep, yet clear; though gentle, yet not dull;
> Strong without rage, without o'erflowing full.

This is distinctive and delightful, as well as profoundly significant in the way I have indicated. But the cost must be counted. Every thrust of meaning, however powerful and even violent, must be contained; no impetus can be other than short-lived and counterbalanced. This means that verse in couplets, although it may be marvellously euphonious (as it often is in Pope), is essentially unmusical. The distrust of the dynamic, the hankering after and faith in the rigid, precludes any possibility of weaving together extended passages by a rhythm that rides over, or rides away from, metre. As Ezra Pound justly complained of 'The Vanity of Human Wishes', 'The cadence comes to an almost dead end so frequently that one doesn't know the poem is going on.'[1] This applies to the unsounded rhythms of syntax as well as to the rhythms that we hear. And yet the model for just such over-riding rhythms, for the musical dynamics of 'linked sweetness long drawn out', was available to English eighteenth-century poets in the epic blank verse of Milton. Of the two greatly gifted poets who essayed this alternative, William Cowper saw the issues the more clearly, but it was James Thomson – a great poet scandalously underrated – who in *The Seasons* (1730) pursued the Miltonic model with most success. The reason is not far to seek: Thomson was the most sanguine and forward-looking of our eighteenth-century poets, the most like an Enlightenment poet in the eager sympathy he felt for the future of commercial and maritime expansion on the one hand, and for Newtonian science on the other. For Cowper, locked into the intricate rigidity of Calvinism, the musical dynamic of blank verse – however much he preferred it and yearned for it on aesthetic grounds – was most of

[1] Ezra Pound, *Guide to Kulchur* (London, 1938), p.180.

the time inapt for conveying his experience of life as he recognized and interpreted it.

In proportion as music was ruled out of court for the English Augustans as a paradigm, they espoused instead the spatial arts of architecture, sculpture, and above all painting. Jean Hagstrum has shown how in their poetic theory this came about by a misunderstanding that they inherited of the Horatian tag *ut pictura poesis.*[1] And it has been pointed out by others that the difficulties of Augustan readers with Shakespeare derived from the same source: because they were so sure that the activity of the imagination was to visualize (in the narrowest sense), because they conceived the poetic image to be in the most literal way a mental picture, they found themselves obliged time and again to censure Shakespeare for using, as they supposed, mixed metaphors. But we have still not sufficiently recognized the implications of C.F. Chapin's study of eighteenth-century personification which shows how the use that the Augustans made of that ancient rhetorical resource depended upon a quite exceptional readiness in the instructed reader to visualize abstractions grouped and posed.[2] We may set beside the striking examples that Chapin gives of this aptitude in British readers, an American instance, the 25-year-old John Adams writing in his diary for 1761:

> October 18. Sunday. Arose at six. Read in Pope's Satires. Nil Admirari. I last night read through both of Dr Donne's Satires versified by Pope. Was most struck with these lines:
>
> "Bear me, some god! Oh! quickly bear me hence,
> To wholesome solitude, the nurse of sense,
> Where contemplation prunes her ruffled wings,
> And the free soul looks down to pity kings."
>
> "Prayer." A posture; hands uplifted, and eyes. A very proper prayer for me to make when I am in Boston. "Solitude" is a personage in a clean, wholesome dress, the "nurse" and nourisher of sense. "Contemplation," a personage. "Prunes," pricks, smooths. Is she an angel or a bird? – "ruffled," rumpled, rugged, uneven, tumbled; – "free soul," not enslaved, unshackled, no bondage, no subjection; "looks down," pities George, Louis, Frederick, Philip, Charles, etc.[3]

Unless we recognize from a case like this how far the eighteenth-

[1] Jean H. Hagstrum, *The Sister Arts. The Tradition of Literacy Pictorialism and English Poetry from Dryden to Gray* (Chicago, 1958).

[2] Chester F. Chapin, *Personification in Eighteenth-Century English Poetry* (New York, 1955).

[3] *The Life and Works of John Adams*, ed. C.F. Adams (Boston, 1850–56), Vol.II, p.132.

century reader would go in collaborating with his authors, in supplementing them, building upon their hints so as to particularize their generalities and incarnate their abstractions, we shall fail to recognize how profoundly pictorial or statuesque the Augustan imagination was: Pope, himself a painter, who structured, for instance, his 'Moral Epistle. On the Characters of Women' on allusions to specific admired paintings by Titian, Guido Reni, Correggio, and others, is merely an extreme case. Only a trained habit of visualizing on the part of the reader, along with an admiration for paintings and statuary significantly different from those we most admire today, could have made possible the new idiosyncratic kind of poem written by William Collins in the 1740s, the allegorical ode. To be sure, Collins transcends himself, and draws upon more senses than the one sense of sight in order to create his distinctively moist and cold and pallid universe; yet it was through the eye – an eye habituated, for instance, to the elaborately allegorical statuary of the funeral monuments of the period – that the eighteenth-century reader gained access to Collins's extremely rarefied world of imagined sense-impressions.

In other words, much eighteenth-century English poetry was essentially picturesque, long before 'the picturesque', as opposed to or combined with 'the sublime', became a preoccupation of psychological aesthetics toward the end of the century. As regards landscape this is generally recognized, and it is commonplace to remark that Thomson describes his prospects from a fixed and elevated vantage-point identical with that from which Claude painted. But poetry that has nothing to do with landscape may be no less picturesque. Marshall McLuhan has argued powerfully that the picturesque perspective from a fixed point of view was a necessary and ultimately inhibiting consequence of a culture, such as eighteenth-century culture, dependent upon the linear arrangements of the printed page as its principal medium of communication. And in the perspective of European cultural history as a whole, this may well be true. Yet, as I have suggested, there were particular reasons why the English eighteenth century, committed to conservation while other eighteenth-century cultures were yearning for a breakthrough, should have been drawn to working within the secure rigidity of the square picture-frame. Tumultuous, dynamic, and Baroque poetry like Derzhavin's in Russia was inconceivable in eighteenth-century England.

More strikingly, whereas in eighteenth-century France one may plot a movement through the century from a language of art to a language of realism, in England the movement is precisely the reverse. In the first decades of the century one perceives, in verse and prose alike, an uninhibited shifting up and down among the levels of style, and a busy traffic between the spoken and the written language; as the century wears on, the literary language becomes rapidly more oratorical and elaborately artful, colloquialism is distrusted and discouraged, and writers apply themselves more and more to heightening and dignifying the reality that they transform into art. It is as if English society, in the faithful mirror-image of the English language, marshalled itself ever more strictly, and defined its own hierarchies ever more sharply, as it girded itself against the shock of the revolutionary upheaval that thinking Englishmen could see in the offing across the Channel. An Edmund Burke, of course, was not a last-ditch defender of the status-quo at all costs and in every particular. On the contrary, the England that thus closed its ranks was preparing to go on the march into the future, but only at its own pace. Burke himself had learnt from Montesquieu – as Gray had with his *Education and Government* in the 1750s and Goldsmith with *The Traveller* in the 1760s – that climate and terrain conditioned different nations in different ways, so that forms of society and of art fitted to one people's needs were not appropriate to another's. Once historical and geographical circumstances were thus seen to alter cultural cases, the Augustan myth could not be so unequivocally potent for the English imagination as when Pope composed his imitations of Horace, or Johnson his imitations of Juvenal. By the time of *The Decline and Fall of the Roman Empire* (1776–88), the richly ambiguous ironies that Gibbon found in the spectacle of Rome tell their own tale. But when, for instance, the underpinning of the Horatian precedent for colloquialism in verse was thus knocked away or at any rate shaken, there was all the more reason for colloquialism to be proscribed except within explicit and narrow limits. As the Augustan myth is questioned and the Augustan precedents challenged, the erectness of the poet's stance before experience may cease to be the vibrant rectitude of the walker on the high wire and become the ramrod stiffness of a footman or a grenadier, observing the absolute dictates of a prescribed decorum. But by that time many of the best spirits are no longer holding themselves erect, but leaning into the wind or flying before it.

The exemplary career from this point of view is Thomas Gray's: he was profoundly Augustan in the 1740s, Pindaric in the 1750s, and in the 1760s producing versions from the Welsh and Old Norse of poems and self-styled 'fragments' that lean urgently out of their frame, out of just that frame (we might say) that the quatrains of the famous 'Elegy' (1749) had fixed four-square. And yet to the very end of the century there were poetic conservatives – Cowper, pre-eminently – who framed their poems as vibrantly as ever. For this reason it can never be satisfactory to acknowledge the classical precedents behind English eighteenth-century poems, and the continuous allusion that they make to Greek and Latin originals, merely as an extra dimension that we must, however reluctantly, forgo.

Accordingly I am ready to accept the reprimand of Albert Cook,[1] and to think that I was at fault on an earlier occasion when I found the distinction of this poetry chiefly in the use it made of metaphor, submerged or overt.[2] It will not do, for instance, to explain the characteristic use of 'grove' for any assemblage of trees as a submerged metaphor of the natural Creation made into the park of a planter God – though it is surely true that this is how the usage must affect readers who are poor Latinists, as most readers now are. Cook is surely right to object: 'More appositely, grove is the most general word for a group of trees that carries with it an implication of order in the group, as well as the closest translation for the Latin word *nemus*, itself somewhat more general than the handful of English words by which it could also be translated.'[3] And Cook's essay on 'The Refined Style' allows us to define more exactly what the Augustan myth was for eighteenth-century England, at the point where it informed poetic diction and style:

> There is a kind of lyric poetry . . . which, like epic poetry, tends to be direct and normative in style . . . to eschew metaphor or else to use it for mere rhetorical condensation instead of Blake's apocalyptic overtones or Baudelaire's correspondences. This "direct" kind of lyric poetry . . . does not attempt to embrace or suggest as much as possible of some apprehended whole; instead it contents itself with trying to set forth some understood part with maximum objectivity and control, and in such a moderate way that it comes to seem like stylized prose. A speech so controlled in manner gives an impression that is cultivated and purified: refined.

In the ancient world, Cook suggests, this style is to be found in *The Greek Anthology* and the Alexandrian poets; in Catullus; in Horace and Virgil, who learned it from the Alexandrians; in Ovid, though with a difference; and in the Latin elegists. It is, of course, quite foreign to the Homeric style, the Pindaric, or (in Latin) the Lucretian. Cook exemplifies the style in English with quotations from Chaucer

1 Albert Cook, *The Classic Line. A Study in Epic Poetry* (Bloomington & London, 1966), p.159.

2 Donald Davie, *Purity of Diction in English Verse* (London, 1952).

3 Cook, *op. cit.*

and Samuel Daniel, Herrick and Herbert, Dryden and Tennyson, Robert Frost and Edwin Arlington Robinson; also, with particular relevance to the present discussion, from both Denham and Edmund Waller, the two seventeenth-century forerunners whom the English Augustans revered in a manner that most later readers have found excessive. The quality of this style depends, Cook suggests, on 'a tendency to logical play in word-repetition, a certain predilection for monosyllables and abstract or generic words, and a perhaps unconscious care *not* to follow the Romantic injunction "load every rift with ore," so that the statements carry a large breathing space around them.' And, he says, 'Pope gets this quality as an echo from Horace; Horace from the Alexandrians.'

This is certainly excessive. For one thing, Pope held so far as he could by the Renaissance principle of decorum, and adjusted his style according as he essayed each of the traditional poetic kinds, even to the desperate expedient of using the heroic style for mock-heroic poems because only mock-heroic subjects seemed to present themselves; and this means that Pope has not one style but several.[1] In some of those styles he surely does 'load every rift'. In the second place, although Pope in the 1690s was certainly trained by Sir Samuel Garth and William Walsh in a consciously Horatianizing climate of opinion, and although his and Swift's Horatian allegiance can hardly be over-estimated because it was to a style of life as well as to a style of writing (suburban in the Horatian sense, with Bolingbroke and Harley playing Augustus and Maecenas), yet a close inspection of the *Imitations of Horace* shows Pope fairly consistently broadening and corrugating the urbanity of the Horatian *sermo*, never for long staying clear of the more burly and shagged Juvenalian style that in English satire had a longer history than the Horatian.[2] And indeed the presence of the non-Augustan and non-refined Juvenal, in Dryden and pre-eminently in Johnson even more than in Pope, is left unexplained by Cook's contention that the 'refined style' was what all the English Augustans aimed at. Nevertheless the way in which 'balance', self-correcting and self-cancelling, is the nerve of the antithetical syntax of the couplet – whether decasyllabic as with Pope and Johnson or octosyllabic as in Swift and Gay – certainly fits with what Cook says of the refined style, that it 'is always more remarkable for the exquisite balance it achieves among its elements than for the predominance of any one of them', and that 'poetry, for the refined style, lies in the balance.' Probably the solution is to bear heavily on the proposition that this is what the earlier Augustans

[1] Reuben A. Brower, *Alexander Pope. The Poetry of Allusion* (Oxford, 1959).

[2] See Rachel Trickett, *The Honest Muse* (Oxford, 1967).

aimed at, rather than achieved; with the proviso that we may admire Pope more for falling passionately short of his aim than we should if he had achieved it. Another way of putting this is that whereas Pope's syntax and metric are always beautifully balanced, his tone rather often is not.

This has the further advantage of explaining how it is that the English reader feels that a landmark of imperturbable refinement has been reached by Gray's 'Elegy' as late as 1749, and not before:

> But knowledge to their eyes her ample page
> Rich with the spoils of time did ne'er unroll;
> Chill Penury repress'd their noble rage,
> And froze the genial current of the soul.
>
> Full many a gem of purest ray serene,
> The dark unfathom'd caves of ocean bear:
> Full many a flower is born to blush unseen,
> And waste its sweetness on the desert air.

Chapin quotes from John Scott's *Critical Essays* of 1785 to show an eighteenth-century reader visualizing Gray's personifications in the first of these stanzas as strenuously as John Adams visualized Pope's personifications in the example given earlier.[1] But Chapin rightly points out that in general in the 'Elegy' Gray's personifications, unlike those of Collins, do not invite or sustain this sort of attention. If they had done so, Gray would have departed from the refined style by disturbing 'the exquisite balance it achieves among its elements.' For in the refined style at its strictest, personification, like metaphor, is simply a means to rhetorical condensation, and must not exert disproportionate power over the reader's imagination. In the second stanza quoted, the self-cancelling balance is achieved in a way that some readers may regard as cheating. In William Empson's words, 'a gem does not mind being in a cave and a flower prefers not to be picked; we feel that the man is like the flower, as short-lived, natural and valuable, and this tricks us into feeling that he is better off without opportunities.' If we compare this with an earlier, much balder treatment of the same theme by Thomas Parnell in his 'Night-Piece on Death' (published 1722),[2] altogether less refined but quite unambiguous, we see very clearly how the balance achieved by the refined style, when applied to a subject potentially so disruptive to society as that of a career open to the talents, can mask tensions and contradictions in social life, enforcing social and political stasis or

1 Chapin, *op. cit.*, p.34.

2 See Davie, *op. cit.*, pp.197-8.

stability by persuading us of a self-correcting equilibrium that in fact does not exist. The refined style, although it creates a continuous illusion of absolute perspicuity, allows for and masks much obscurity; consider only the commentators' ink that has been spilt on determining the career, in Gray's poem, of the stone-cutter.

A more obvious example of obscurity in the refined style is Christopher Smart's *Song to David* (1763). This will be contested. The legendary disorder of Smart's life, his intermittent insanity, his great and idiosyncratic learning, his fragmentary and insanely great *Rejoice in the Lamb* (*c.* 1760), and above all the fervent militancy of his Anglicanism have persuaded us that Smart is a great exception and a special case, and that his poetry is indeed tumultuous and dynamic in just the way that we denied was possible to the English eighteenth century. But this is an error; and it was fatuous for San Francisco beatniks some years ago to couple Smart's name with Blake's as an exemplar of the tumultuous poetry they themselves sought to write. Smart, who translated Horace, was a profoundly Horatian poet, although what he sought was the *curiosa felicitas* of the *carmina*, not the urbanely conversational style of the *sermones*, which Pope and Swift had emulated.[1] His *Odes*, his *Hymns and Spiritual Songs*, his convivial and amorous and humorous occasional poems, even his metrical Psalms, – they are all triumphs of the refined style. And so is *A Song to David*:

> The pheasant shows his pompous neck;
> And ermine, jealous of a speck,
> With fear eludes offence;
> The sable, with his glossy pride,
> For ADORATION is descried
> Where frosts the waves condense.
>
> The chearful holly, pensive yew,
> And holy thorn, their trim renew;
> The squirrel hoards his nuts;
> All creatures batten o'er their stores,
> And careful nature all her doors
> For ADORATION shuts.
>
> For ADORATION David's psalms
> Lift up the heart to deeds of alms;
> And he, who kneels and chants,
> Prevails his passions to controul,
> Finds meat and med'cine to the soul,
> Which for translation pants.

[1] See R. Brittain (ed.), *Poems by Christopher Smart* (Princeton, 1950).

The use of 'translation' in its Latinate sense, and the self-delighting artifice of the locution for the protective coloration of the ermine, but no less the ambiguity (is 'prevails' a main verb, or is it not?), reveal here the Horatian refinement at its most intense. The symmetrically regular rhyming in each stanza is part of a larger symmetry by which, in this section of the poem, the key phrase 'For ADORATION' slips, stanza by stanza, from the first line to the sixth twice over; and this in turn is locked into a larger structure based on the numbers three and seven, which makes the *Song* perhaps the most intricately rigid and self-balancing poem in the language.[1] There is even, in this poem of rapt religious devotion, a hint of how once again the balance of the art enforces a more precarious balance in society; for the epithet 'chearful' stood for a social attitude that had been recommended as allegedly a Christian duty ever since *The Spectator*, an attitude that has obvious connections with contentment in the lot and the social station to which each reader has been called.

Cook's example of the refined style from the latter half of the eighteenth century is audacious and fascinating. For he finds it in Burns:

> We twae hae paidl'd in the burn,
> Frae morning sun till dine;
> But seas between us braid hae roar'd,
> Sin auld lang syne.

He comments:

> The traditional lyric meditation here is quite alien to the ballad; diction and tone are kept in a refined balance. And only the powerful admixture of the ballad stanza itself keeps the refined note from being as pure as in Horace. The Scotch dialect alone, in this style, attains a well-nigh Tuscan normalcy when handled thus, though not always in Burns.[2]

This is not the place to test this contention against other poems by Burns. But at first sight it is, though surprising, plausible. And if it could be sustained, it might suggest that only in his poems in English is Burns a voice of the Scottish Enlightenment, whereas in his greater poems in Scots he is an Augustan.

I shall play safe, however, by continuing to take my examples from English. Here is a stanza from Cowper's 'The Castaway' (1799):

1 See R.D. Havens, *Review of English Studies* 14 (April 1938), pp.178–82.

2 Cook, *op. cit.*, pp.148–9.

At length, his transient respite past,
  His comrades, who before
Had heard his voice in every blast,
  Could catch the sound no more:
For then, by toil subdued, he drank
The stifling wave, and then he sank.

There is nothing I wish to retract from an account I have already given of these verses, and I must be allowed to quote that earlier account:

> 'Stifling' is a characteristic use of the participial adjective. It generalizes the fact of drowning, because 'stifling' is equally applicable to all the ways of dying; and so it affects us as dry, chastening and logical. More powerful still, in the same way, is 'drank'. For drinking we think of as a wilful imbibing for pleasure, whereas Cowper generalizes it to mean all drawings in of liquid to the throat. This is horrible, and strikes to the heart of Cowper's view of human life. For Cowper the Calvinist maintained that, even in a world of rigid predestination, the salvation or damnation of the soul was still the responsibility of the individual. He had cried out, in 'Truth',
>
> Charge not, with light sufficient and left free,
> Your wilful suicide on God's decree.
>
> By presenting the rush of water into the drowning throat as a voluntary act of 'drinking', Cowper brings this idea to appalling life. The death of the castaway is 'wilful suicide'. And the one word 'drank', in this places takes up all the Calvinist arguments of free-will and fate.[1]

What this account does not sufficiently stress is how Cowper gets an effect thus piercingly specific not by departing from an accepted style or breaking through its limits, but on the contrary by adhering strictly to the accepted norm, pushing the style to its limits but not an inch beyond them. For, as Albert Cook says, 'the normative style in poetry, of which the classical refined style is the clearest example, tends to select normative words, a diction that quietly, at every step, insists on its generality....'[2] Cowper's 'stifling' and his 'drank', although they serve his special meaning so momentously, seem to have been chosen less to serve that end than because the style that he shared with others demanded them. And this compels one to applaud all over again a remark made long ago by Arthur

[1] Davie, *op. cit.*, p.53.

[2] Cook, *op. cit.*, p.162.

Quiller-Couch: 'What is salt in Cowper you can taste only when you have detected that by a stroke of madness he missed, or barely missed, being our true English Horace, that almost more nearly than the rest he hit what the rest had been seeking.'[1] This, we now realize, applies not only to the ruminative or conversational poems such as *The Task* (1785) or 'Table Talk', nor to the Horatian style of Cowper's life, very deliberately provincial, cultivating the small and gentle pleasures of civilized retirement. It applies perhaps more challengingly to poems such as 'The Castaway' and 'The Loss of the Royal George' (1782). In particular, now that Kenneth Maclean has shown[2] how often Cowper's poems about pet animals mirror his own appalling predicament as the victim of an intermittent madness that no mode of life, however retired, could guard against, we recognize as Horatian such a poem as 'On the Death of Mrs Throckmorton's Bullfinch', where horror and hysterical merriment are only just controlled by the generalized diction and by being sunk deep inside a symmetrical frame of classical mythology and allusion.

If, as Cook suggests, the generality of the diction determines the refined style more than any other feature, one may take the risk of quoting an undistinguished eighteenth-century poem, so as to clinch the issue by seeing how a twentieth-century poet adapts it. Goldsmith's song, in *The Vicar of Wakefield* (1766), goes thus:

> When lovely woman stoops to folly,
> And finds too late that men betray,
> What charm can soothe her melancholy,
> What art can wash her guilt away?
>
> The only art her guilt to cover,
> To hide her shame from every eye,
> To give repentance to her lover,
> And wring his bosom – is to die.

And this becomes, in T.S. Eliot's *The Waste Land* (1922):

> When lovely woman stoops to folly and
> Paces about her room again, alone,
> She smoothes her hair with automatic hand,
> And puts a record on the gramophone.

As with other calculated discords in Eliot's poem, we can easily be mistaken about how this works upon us. It is not at all the case, for

1 Sir Arthur Quiller-Couch, *On the Art of Writing* (London, 1916), p.127.

2 Kenneth Maclean, 'William Cowper', in F.W. Hilles (ed.), *The Age of Johnson. Essays Presented to Chauncey Brewster Tinker* (New Haven & London, 1949).

instance, that an allegedly depleted or disorderly present is being held up against a richer or more ordered past. For Goldsmith's 'guilt', 'shame' and 'repentance' do not belong to any finer or firmer scheme of moral discrimination than what the twentieth-century lady can appeal to; and there is nothing particularly squalid about a gramophone, or about the lady's abstracted gesture, automatic though it is. The dissonance is effected not at all by way of content but wholly within style: by the painfully asymmetrical rhyme of 'and' with 'hand', and especially by the abrupt descent from the generality of 'folly' to the particularity of 'gramophone'. 'Gramophone' is unrefined, not because it is modern or mechanical or connotes squalor, but simply because it is particular; hearing the generality of Augustan diction thus jarred upon, we are made unusually aware of how powerfully a sustained generality of diction may work upon us.

On the other hand, it is also plain from this example that the symmetry of rhyme (in Goldsmith, alternately feminine and masculine) and the regularity of metre, not to speak of the more ambitious and constricting symmetries of *A Song to David*, are not optional features of the refined style, but necessary accompaniments to a linguistic feature such as the generality of the diction. This is where rigidity comes back into the discussion, as arguably the principle that in the first place attracted the English Augustans to the refined style. We can say of English poems in this style what Albert Cook says of Greek and Latin poems:

> Within their restrictive diction and tightness of metre, within the delicate superstructure of syntax, each of these refined poems attains a sort of fixity – so much so that it seems fitting for the epigram to have begun as an epitaph, a last word in which the personal must by the nature of the utterance be fully incorporated into the summary, and graven on stone. Nor is it surprising that a whole book of *The Greek Anthology* consists of poems about statues: the stone fixity of the subject occasioning the small, fixed poem.[1]

Indeed, the lapidary rigidity of the English Augustan poem – one need hardly go further than the symmetrical look on the page of every stanza I have quoted – goes far beyond some of the classical originals. For a Horatian ode is musical, in the sense that we move through it and end far from where we began,[2] in a way that no

1 Cook, *op. cit.*, p.171

2 See J.V. Cunningham, *The Quest of the Opal* (San Francisco, 1942), and *Tradition and Poetic Structure* (Denver, 1960), pp.47-9.

English Augustan poem, however euphonious, can afford to be. That musical dynamic and impetus could return to English poetry, with Blake and Coleridge, only when English society had ceased to hold itself taut and rigid, in fear of the tumult unleashed by the Enlightenment abroad.

Literature and Western Civilization, vol. 3, eds David Daiches and Anthony Thorlby (London: Aldus, 1974).

12 Two Reviews

I

The Social Milieu of Alexander Pope: Lives, Example, and the Poetic Response. By Howard Erskine-Hill. New Haven and London: Yale University Press, 1975.

This is one of those very rare books which truly deserve the description: *humane* scholarship. It is very learned indeed, the product of what must have been many years of patient and meticulous research, nearly all of it among MSS in the British Museum, the archives of the Historical Manuscripts Commission, the Birmingham Reference Library, the Dorset and Herefordshire and Staffordshire Record Offices, and so on, not to mention family papers still in private hands. In England, I am afraid, we have become unused to literary scholars undertaking and carrying through original researches on this scale, especially when the scholar is a full-time teacher, as Dr Erskine-Hill is. Such 'grubbing', we tend to suppose, can be left to the historian and the biographer. But Howard Erskine-Hill has acted on the principle that I dare say we would all uphold in theory: that not just literary history but literary *criticism* involves us in the labours of the historian and the biographer, and not solely or chiefly with printed sources. How to do the grubbing while not losing sight of what the grubbing is for (that is to say, the incontrovertible illumination of great works of the imagination) is something so difficult that we are tempted to think it impossible, and to think we can get round it by division of labour, Dryasdust painstakingly turning up materials which Bright Critic can then polish and put into patterns. Perhaps that two-stage process really can extend our knowledge and our understanding at times; but the gains are never so firmly secured, never so conclusively established, as when it is one and the same mind that has carried the project through from first to last, that first grubbed and then reflected on what his grubbings had brought him, that proceeded as historian, as biographer, and as critic, each in due order. This is what Howard Erskine-Hill has done; his book is a great achievement, and also a great pleasure. It is even in its sober way entertaining as well as instructive. I do not know when literary scholarship in England came up with anything so deeply satisfying.

The plan of the investigation was extremely ambitious, and yet massively straightforward. It proceeds towards a rereading of some of Pope's greatest poems by way of biographical sketches of six men named in those poems: John Kyrle, the 'Man of Ross' of the *Epistle to Bathurst*; John Caryll, the Roman Catholic nobleman with Jacobite connexions and sympathies; Peter Walter, the unsavoury attorney and estate agent who made a fortune out of speculating in land, driving tenants hard, and negotiating marriage settlements for his employers; William, fifth Baron Digby, whose outlook and activities (says Dr Erskine-Hill finely) 'were moulded in that remarkably earnest and evangelical phase of Anglicanism, at the end of the seventeenth century and beginning of the eighteenth, which fostered the rise of the charity schools, and in which so many of the Non-Jurors were involved'; Sir John Blunt, the Baptist London financier who was largely responsible for the South Sea Bubble, and was made almost *solely* responsible, once the bubble had burst; and Ralph Allen of Bath, who made his name and his fortune by reorganizing the postal service, and thereafter by quarrying and building.

These names did not choose themselves. On the contrary, Howard Erskine-Hill's gallery is assembled with great imagination, and very sensitively arranged: two peers of the realm, one Catholic, the other Protestant; three self-made men (Walter, Blunt, and Allen); and Kyrle, of good family but modest means, in his country town. Or else, to look down the gallery from another vantage-point; three men of the landed interest (Caryll, Walter, Digby); one of the City interest (Blunt); one man of trade (Allen, though he bought himself into a landed property later); and Kyrle, the odd one out, once again. Finally, though this perspective is the least interesting: four men of whom Pope vigorously approved (Caryll, Digby, Allen, Kyrle), and two whom he condemns (Walter, however, condemned much more emphatically than Blunt). This is the least interesting perspective, not because moral judgement is not what Pope is interested in (on the contrary, it is his prime interest, and one of Dr Erskine-Hill's main concerns is to establish Pope's moral 'positives', how firm they are, and yet how flexible and how *nuanced*); but because through each of these small biographies, Dr Erskine-Hill's focus is precisely and purely the biographer's, an imaginative entering into the mode of being of the man he is examining. Even Peter Walter is recreated therefore with sympathy, that being indeed the only way possible. This is what one means by saying that scholarship here is *humane*.

After more than two hundred pages devoted to these biographies, only eighty or so are given to 'Part Three: The Poetry'. But this does not argue any disproportion, still less does it mean that the author's concern for the poetry is in any way perfunctory; for the truth is that the examination of the poems can be compact and rapid precisely because the relevant points have been established with a fine tact, unobtrusively, in the biographical pages. The poems in question (mostly the Epistles to Bathurst, to Burlington, and to Bethel, together with the Second Satire of Donne Versified, and the 'Epilogue to the Satires') are considered under three heads: 'The Betrayal of Society', which identifies Peter Walter with Robert Walpole, and clears both Pope and Bolingbroke from the imputation that their protests against 'corruption' were no more than partisan name-calling; 'The Country House Ideal', which decorously refuses to go all the way with Raymond Williams in his argument that this ideal, in poems of the seventeenth and eighteenth centuries, was the appealing fiction of a backward-looking nostalgia; and 'Imperial Works', which brings the whole splendid arc of argument to rest on a restatement of Pope's Augustanism, to be seen not just in what he explicitly evokes as models of civic virtue (especially Ralph Allen, putting his self-made wealth back into public service both architectural and philanthropic, as Kyrle did also on his necessarily smaller scale) but also in how Pope articulates the architecture of his own Epistles.

Howard Erskine-Hill does not need to be polemical, or to do more than register an occasional disagreement with other commentators. But the rethinking to which he continually incites us can be illustrated from a passage I have quoted already, 'that remarkable earnest and evangelical phase of Anglicanism, at the end of the seventeenth century and beginning of the eighteenth'. Of course scholars of the period know what Dr Erskine-Hill means, and will know better than to cavil. Yet is 'earnest and evangelical' what we normally say of the England of William and Mary, and Anne, of the dissenters of that period, any more than of the Anglicans? We all know that on the contrary apathy and torpor, lethargy, and Erastianism, are the words that spring not just to the lips of our bright students but to our own lips, also. The gravity and, yes, earnestness of the greatest poet of the age will never be recognized, I fear, until we get it into our heads that his was the age of William Law and Isaac Watts, Bishop Ken and Bishop Butler and Bishop Berkeley.

II

The Works of John Wesley. Volume XI. *The Appeals to Men of Reason and Religion and Certain Related Open Letters.* Edited by Gerald R. Cragg. Oxford: Clarendon Press; London: Oxford University Press, 1976.

This is the first volume to appear of a massive edition of Wesley's *Works* which has been in preparation since 1960, originally on the joint initiative of the theological schools of four Methodist-related universities in the United States: Drew, Duke, Emory, and Southern Methodist. For some years now the editor-in-chief has been Frank Baker of Duke University. The need for such an edition cannot be questioned, since otherwise we still have to use the 'standard' edition of 1872, conveniently available in a lithographically produced reprint (14 volumes) by the Zondervan Publishing House of Grand Rapids, Michigan (1958-59). The task, however, is daunting, because of the peculiar nature of Wesley's writings over and above their sheer bulk. The bibliographical and editorial difficulties are great, and it is no wonder that the enterprise is proceeding at such a deliberate pace.

Professor Cragg's volume gives us *An Earnest Appeal to Men of Reason and Religion* (1743); the *Farther Appeal to Men of Reason and Religion* (1744-45); the *Letter to the Right Reverend the Lord Bishop of London* (1747); three open letters to Lavington, Bishop of Exeter (1750-52); *A Letter to the Rev. Mr Horne* (1762); and Wesley's rejoinder to Warburton, *A Letter to the Right Reverend the Lord Bishop of Gloucester* (1763). It cannot have been easy to decide what items should go together in the same volume, and Wesley's reply to Josiah Tucker, *The Principles of a Methodist* (1740), is not the only work that one would ideally have liked to see in this volume, rather than held over for another.

The importance of the *Appeals* is manifest in their title: they are addressed to 'men of reason' as well as to 'men of religion' – two distinct categories, though certain men (and women) belong in both. From 1740 to 1978 Wesley has been charged with (at some times, more deplorably, extolled for) advocating a sort of Christian belief which bypasses the exercise of discursive reason. From the first, and repeatedly, he denied this and argued vehemently that on the contrary, as he conceived and experienced Christianity, it was an eminently *reasonable* religion. Even today, whenever Wesley and the Wesleyans are taken account of in our understanding of eighteenth-century England (they are more often passed over in silence, or acknowledged only in footnotes), the emphasis is likely to be the same: they, and with them the whole of eighteenth-century evangelicalism, are presented as appealing to heart rather than head, to 'feeling' rather than rationality. Yet it is plain, not just from Wesley's passionately explicit repudiations, but also from the tenor of his prose style (harshly, stubbornly, and impatiently commonsensical) that this was not in the least how he saw his own endeavours, nor those of his followers. If he was right about this, it is important to get one of these texts into the hands of 'the general reader', for instance the student of literature, so that this hoary misunderstanding may be rooted out. But one is forced to recognize, with dismay, that none of the *Appeals* lends itself to this purpose. Even the first and by any account the best of them, the original *Earnest Appeal*, could be represented in any anthology of eighteenth-century literature only by excerpts, and, as the editor acknowledges, the three hefty parts of the *Further Appeal* are quite hopeless from this point of view. The point is not merely that the conventions of eighteenth-century theological polemic (the closeness and slow pace of its arguments, the quoting at length in order to rebut in detail, the insistent and principled interlarding of scriptural texts) are wholly foreign to the experience of the modern reader, and also (so many will feel, understandably) not worth recovering. On top of this, as Gerald Cragg reminds us, in these writings Wesley had his back to the wall, and felt compelled to establish his intellectual and scholarly credentials, in particular by the logic-chopping that he knew inside out from tutoring in logic as a Fellow of Lincoln. This means that, despite the colloquial and already old-fashioned vividness of Wesley's prose ('I cannot conceive how that harmless word "immediate" came to be such a bugbear in the world'), the conduct of his arguments is altogether too slow and too congested for modern taste.

Unfortunately the same considerations apply *a fortiori* when Wesley replies to such princes of the church (that church which he always asserted was also *his*) as the dangerous buffoon Lavington of Exeter, author of *The Enthusiasm of Methodists and Papists Compared* (1750), or the more dangerous bully, Warburton of Gloucester. With these antagonists Wesley was even more compelled, as he saw it, to the closest in-fighting, and though the editorial head-notes quite admirably point us to the different tone that Wesley adopted according to whether he was addressing Lavington or Warburton or (a man he respected) George Horne of Magdalen, still this interest is not enough to sustain us through the texts of the Open Letters which, however sympathetically we may reconstruct the context for each of them, nevertheless in the long run have to strike us as arid.

To this, however, there is one splendid exception. Edmund Gibson, Lord Bishop of London, was built on altogether more generous and admirable lines than a Lavington or a Warburton: a man of learning, of principle, even of sanctity. Wesley recognized this, and addressed him accordingly. The last paragraph of Wesley's open letter to Gibson has been often quoted, yet is not so well known that it will not bear repetition:

> But I must draw to a conclusion. Your lordship has without doubt had some success in *opposing* this doctrine. Very many have, by your lordship's unwearied endeavours, been deterred from hearing it at all, and have thereby probably escaped the being *seduced* into holiness, have lived and died in their sins. My lord, the time is short, I am past the noon of life, and my remaining years flee away as a shadow. Your lordship is old and full of days, having passed the usual age of man. It cannot therefore be long before we shall both drop this house of earth, and stand naked before God; no, nor before we shall 'see the great white throne coming down from heaven, and him that sitteth thereon'. On his left hand shall be those who are shortly to dwell in 'everlasting fire, prepared for the devil and his angels'. In that number will be all who died in their sins. And among the rest, those whom you *preserved* from repentance. Will you then rejoice in your success? The Lord God grant it may not be said in that hour: 'These have perished in their inquity; but their blood I require at thy hands.'

One wants to believe the old Methodist tradition that this closing appeal 'had a profound effect' on Edmund Gibson; he was dead within the year.

Moreover, within the body of Wesley's letter there are passages in their way no less fine. Because the immediate occasion of Wesley's piece was Gibson's charge to his diocese in 1746–47, in which he warned against the Methodists, Wesley exclaims: 'How awful a thing is this! The very occasion carries in it a solemnity not to be expressed. Here is an angel of the church of Christ, one of the stars in God's right hand, calling together all the subordinate pastors for whom he is to give an account to God.' And from this he proceeds to protest: 'Is it possible! Could your lordship discern no other enemies of the gospel of Christ? Are there no other heretics or schismatics on earth? Or even within the four seas? Are there no Papists, no deists left in the land? Or are their errors of less importance?... Have the Methodists (so called) already monopolized all the sins, as well as errors, in the nation? Is Methodism the only sin, or the only fatal or spreading sin, to be found within the Bills of Mortality?' The *Letter to the Right Reverend the Lord Bishop of London* could, and surely should, be something that every student of our eighteenth-century literature is required to come to terms with.

It may be said that, since this document is now available in a reliable text, with admirably judged and self-effacing editorial commentary, nothing more need be asked for. But alas, though the intention was no doubt sincere 'to enable Wesley to be read with maximum ease and understanding, and with minimal intrusion by the editors', it was in the nature of the case that this intention should not be fulfilled. Partly from the character of the texts themselves, and partly from the very nature of 'a scholarly edition', these writings by Wesley cannot be read in this format 'with maximum ease and understanding'. A scholarly edition was abundantly called for, and it is ungrateful to protest, as some have done, that the top-hamper of erudition is excessive. The scholars are doing their proper work; it remains for the responsible *vulgarisateur* to profit, and enable others to profit, by their labours.

Modern Language Review 73: 2 (April 1978); 74: 4 (October 1979).

13 Christopher Smart: Some Neglected Poems

Smart's translations of the Psalms do not constitute one of his main claims to fame or to our attention. And Father Devlin is right when he says of this work that 'its main interest lies in its being an unintentional rehearsal for the *Song to David*.'[1] But this in itself is a notable claim on our attentions, and we sharpen it if we say that the Psalm versions make a bridge to the *Song to David* from *Rejoice in the Lamb*. For this is the chronology – *Rejoice in the Lamb* was begun and pushed forward in the first half of 1759, when Smart, having been discharged as incurable from one madhouse, enjoyed an interval at liberty before being committed to another about August of that year; the further fragments which Bond calls B_1 and B_2 were written in confinement once again, up to about August 1760; fragment C belongs to March, April, and May 1761; and fragment D, the latest section, runs from July 1762 through to the end of January 1763, the eve of his release.[2] But these later sections of *Rejoice in the Lamb* are not much more than Smart's therapeutic device for keeping himself occupied, and for counting off on the calendar the days remaining before the release which he knew was being negotiated. The grandiose liturgical design which Smart had in mind when he composed the A and B fragments of *Rejoice in the Lamb* has quite disappeared from the later sections of that manuscript; for its place had been taken by the work on the Psalms, to which Smart refers excitedly in the later parts of the other poem. Moreover, since Smart set about as soon as he was released to solicit subscribers and arrange publication for his Psalms, it appears that not only the bulk of the voluminous *Rejoice in the Lamb* but also most of the more than 50,000 words of his Psalter derive from the period 1759 to 1763 – that is, to the second and longer stretch of his confinement, in which he was allowed pen and paper (which on his first stretch had been denied him). In other words, the work on the Psalms went on concurrently

1 Christopher Devlin, *Poor Kit Smart* (London, 1961), p.139.

2 W.H. Bond (ed.), *Jubilate Agno* (London, 1954), Introduction.

with the writing of at least the D fragment of *Rejoice in the Lamb*; but because so much of this later work on *Rejoice in the Lamb* is perfunctory or private, it is legitimate to regard the Psalms as having to all intents and purposes *succeeded Rejoice in the Lamb*. For it seems clear that not later than 1762 the energy of Smart's principal concern and dedication shifted from the one to the other.

The psalms in Smart's version are not true translations of the Hebrew poems, but rather quite loose paraphrases. One likes them a great deal less, once one compares them with any true translation, such as those in the Authorized Version, in the Prayer Book, or even among the freer versions of the Sidney Psalter made by Philip Sidney and his sister Mary and members of their circle. And yet every time that Smart departs from his original, as he does frequently and widely, this departure was intended to *tell* – and to tell not as a matter of literary decorum, but as a matter of doctrine.

In the first place, like many sincere Christians since his own day but like few of his own time, Smart was disturbed and shocked by the barbarous ferocity of many of the Hebrew psalms, especially those which are martial exhortations or morale-builders for the ancient Jewish nation in its struggle to survive among the heathen; and so Smart consistently emasculates the Psalms, converting the often barbarous morality of the Old Testament into the sweeter tone of the New.[1] The name of Christ is invoked as often as possible. Moreover, and more interestingly, Smart exploits to the utmost any chance of connecting Christ with the natural creation – and this, once again, not because he was at bottom 'a nature-poet' (which is what Father Devlin comes near to suggesting), but for reasons of Christian doctrine. Throughout all his sacred poems Smart directs his praise not in the first place to God the Redeemer, nor to God the Judge, nor to God the Protector of His faithful (which last is the characteristic emphasis of the Hebrew psalms), but to God the Creator. God as Christ, as the Son rather than the Father; and yet God as Creator rather than Redeemer – these are the emphases which Smart wants, and his wish to make these emphases is what lies behind nearly all the liberties he takes.

This severely doctrinal and moral purpose cannot be distinguished from a purpose which may be called liturgical. The particular form which religious mania took with Smart was a fervent wish that the Church of England should supplant the Church of Rome as the

[1] Brittain points out that precedents for such 'evangelical interpretation' are Archbishop Parker's versions of 1557(?), John Patrick's of 1679, Isaac Watts's of 1719. Brittain's example from Smart is Psalm 7, where God's bow bent to shoot the arrow of vengeance becomes the rainbow, emblem and pledge of God's mercy. See *Poems by Christopher Smart*, ed. R. Brittain (Princeton, 1950), pp.279-80.

cardinal and catholic church of Christendom. This is a wish which many Anglicans have entertained and doubtless still entertain. But they held by it, or they hold by it, only as a pious hope; Smart espoused it as a deliberate programme, and one which might be speedily implemented, since he believed that God had called him to implement it. Apparently he thought it quite feasible that St Paul's in London might supplant St Peter's as the metropolitan cathedral of international Christendom – hence the line in his 'Hymn for the Day of St Philip and St James', 'In the choir of Christ and WREN'. And certainly when he planned first *Rejoice in the Lamb*, and later the Psalms along with the Spiritual Songs, as a form of liturgy for Anglicanism rejuvenated and thus made supreme, he thought there was a real possibility that the Church of England might accept a form of service built around these compositions of his.[1] Smart's hopes crashed about him in 1765 when so far was the Church of England from recognizing him that Anglican opinion solidly preferred before his version of the Psalms the paraphrases of an old rival, James Merrick. Merrick's versions got into print before Smart's, and it was particularly galling that Merrick's publisher was John Newbery, Smart's father-in-law. (Smart's marriage is an enigma; Robert Brittain blames Smart's wife and his father-in-law for a great deal that went wrong with Smart's life, whereas Father Devlin pleads strenuously that they be acquitted.) What is important is to realize that in his paraphrase of the Psalms Smart had invested a great deal; it was not intended merely to take its place among the many metrical versions of the Psalter (such as Merrick's), but on the contrary to equip the Church of England for the vastly enhanced role which Smart unrealistically thought that she was to play. The motives behind it are not in any usual sense literary; and if we describe it instead as a work of piety, we must understand that what informs it is something far more ambitious and urgent than what is usually connoted by that word.

And yet there is no hope of our reading Smart's psalms in this way, in the spirit and with the sort of attention which he hoped for. We owe it to him to know what his intentions were. But the way to read these pieces with enjoyment is to take them as eighteenth-century devotional poems in their own right, pausing to check them by other versions only when, as often happens, they seem so wholly of the eighteenth century that one cannot conceive how they have

[1] At least he may have hoped for such recognition as George Wither received for his *Hymns and Songs of the Church* (1623), for which Wither got a royal patent directing that these original poems be bound up with Wither's *Metrical Psalter* for the use of the Church. See Brittain, p.286.

any relation to the world of ancient Israel; there is much instructive amusement to be got from comparing Smart's versions at such points with the Prayer Book or the Authorized Version. Often one will be disappointed; in Psalm 147 for instance, such splendidly quaint expressions as 'The blessings of a social mess', or the ice 'Like vitreous fragments o'er the field', turn out to have little or no warrant from the original. But it is not always so. In Psalm 78, while enumerating the mercies of God to the Children of Israel in the wilderness, Smart writes:

He rained flesh upon them thick
    As dust upon the ground,
And fowls he lavish'd, quill'd and quick,
    Like sand beside the sound

Unless we have the Scripture at our fingertips we may well think that the idea of 'raining flesh', when God sent fowls falling on the Israelite tents, was possible only to the witty and bizarre imagination of eighteenth-century rococo. But it is there in the Prayer Book: 'He rained flesh upon them as thick as dust: and feathered fowls like as the sand of the sea.' Even the typically unsubtle but splendid alliteration of 'quill'd and quick' is only half redundant to the original; for Smart's delightful discovery 'quill'd' corresponds exactly to the Prayer Book's 'feathered'. If we care to compare the Sidney Psalter version we find that it is the seventeenth-century wit which is quaint and cumbrous, and elaborates on the original, for it speaks here about 'rain of admirable kind', about 'The dainty quails that freely wont to fly', and later (delightfully but redundantly) of how the Israelite encampment 'With feath'red rain was wat'red every way.'

For my next example, three verses from Psalm 139, it will be confusing if I do not give the Prayer Book version first:

14. My bones are not hid from thee: though I be made secretly, and fashioned beneath in the earth.
15. Thine eyes did see my substance, yet being imperfect: and in thy book were all my members written;
16. Which day by day were fashioned: when as yet there was none of them.

This is an astonishing penetration by the imagination of the psalmist into the mysteries of embryology. Smart's version runs tamely at first but rises to a fine concentration:

The substance of each nerve and bone
To thee are intimately known,
    And at my hour of birth

Thou didst thy quick'ning spirit breathe,
Though I be taken from beneath,
And but refin'd from earth.

Thine eyes review'd th' imperfect sketch
Ere yet my limbs began to stretch
And were for action ripe;
Before my members were of age
For birth, thou wrote them in thy page,
And with the fairest type,

Which day by day assay'd to live,
And as thou didst conception give,
Were warm'd with gradual heat;
When flesh and vital moisture both
Slept in the burial of their growth,
And none were yet compleat.

Smart, as it seems at first, gives, for 'though I be made secretly, and fashioned beneath the earth', 'Though I be taken from beneath, / And but refin'd from earth'. And this is disappointing: 'taken from beneath' has a disconcertingly constrictive literal sense to it; and for 'refin'd' ('refin'd from earth') there is no warrant in the original's 'fashioned beneath in the earth'. But Smart like all great translators disperses his effects, and this is no more than a stop-gap measure; the translation of 'fashioned beneath in the earth' is completed two stanzas later with the splendid expression 'Slept in the burial of their growth'. Again, 'thou wrote them in thy page', which seems at first like the tired use of a stock conceit, turns out to be as close as possible to 'in thy book were all my members written'; as for the redundant elaboration of this, 'And with the fairest type', it is impossible to read this in the context of the Psalms and Spiritual Songs as a whole without seeing a serious pun, on the type set by the printer and on the type which we encounter in words like 'prototype' and 'archetype', for Smart uses the word continually in this latter sense, being vowed to the sort of scriptural exegesis which sees for instance David as a type of Christ.

But now hear what the Sidney Psalter makes of this passage:

Thou, how my back was beam-wise laid,
And raftering of my ribbs dost know:
Know'st ev'ry point
Of bone and joynt,
How to this whole these partes did grow,
In brave embrod'ry faire arraid,
Though wrought in shop both dark and low.

Nay, fashionless, ere form I tooke,
Thy all and more beholding eye
My shapeless shape
Could not escape:
All these tymes fram'd successively
Ere one had being, in the booke
Of thy foresight enrol'd did ly.

'Raftering of my ribbs' and 'wrought in shop both dark and low' – these murky splendours lie outside Smart's range altogether; but they are out of Coverdale's range also, and indeed out of range of the psalmist himself. The original gives no warrant for them. Yet who would wish them away? This I take as evidence that in translation redundancy is not the unforgiveable sin – not if the redundant material is sufficiently splendid.

And this shall be my cue for a last example, from Psalm 118, where 'This is the Lord's doing: and it is marvellous in our eyes' becomes, in Smart:

It is the work of God direct,
For he himself is architect,
So beautiful and bold;
'Tis elevated to surprize,
Beyond our thought, before our eyes.
Believe ye, and behold.

This is redundancy with a vengeance! And yet, given that the image of the architect is not gratuitous (for just before has come the famous image of the corner-stone – 'The same stone which the builders refused: is become the head-stone in the corner'), then the expressions 'beautiful and bold' and 'elevated to surprize' – taken as they are from the vocabulary in which the eighteenth century characteristically appreciated architecture – may very justly be taken as necessary to a fresh and vivid, and therefore true translation of the Prayer Book's single word, 'marvellous'.

I turn now to the *Hymns and Spiritual Songs*, bound up with the Psalms on their first publication in 1765. For these higher claims have been made, and must be made, than for the versions of the Psalms, interesting and often beautiful as those are. Father Devlin says (p.159), 'the best of his hymns have a quality all their own, austerely tender, as if the baroque had developed gently and easily from the medieval, skipping the doubt and the passion and the grandeur that lay between...' This seems to be penetrating and just, and yet it is difficult to make use of this formulation as a starting point for reflections and explorations of our own. For the term 'baroque', though it has proved useful in relation to some of the other arts in England, has never proved itself useful in relation to our literature; and when we look at the confusions it seems to have provoked in the French in relation to French literature, we may well be grateful that it is one category we do not have to deal with. Yet in relation to Smart's *Hymns* it certainly *feels* right. One way of taking it is offered by Brittain when he asks us to see, as a crucial element in the *Hymns*, the influence of English baroque music, as Smart knew it and responded to it in the work of such composers as Arne and Boyce. However Brittain's remarks on this, though they are certainly illuminating about how each of the Hymns requires the context of all the others, being interlinked and interwoven, otherwise leave the analogy with eighteenth-century English music as no more than a tantalizing suggestion.

What we are looking for, in order to make use of Devlin's word 'baroque', is some precedent in English for the sort of thing we find in Smart's *Hymns*. It may be of course that no even partial precedent is to be found. What we have, thanks chiefly to Brittain's very distinguished work, are precedents for Smart's style in foreign languages – in Horace, and also in Hebrew poetry. And Devlin makes the further suggestion that interesting precedents may be found in medieval Latin, a matter which I wish that students of medieval Latin would investigate. But all of this leaves us as far as ever from finding English precedents for Smart. Very early in his career Smart translated into Latin Pope's 'Ode for St Cecilia's Day', and won Pope's approval for it; and undoubtedly that side of Pope's achievement (one to which nowadays we give rather little attention) left its mark on Smart's style of writing in Odes and ceremonial Hymns. Devlin suggests that Smart's first and most influential English model was Marvell, but he does not argue this case nor give any external evidence of it; and in default of such evidence and argument, I am inclined to think that where Smart seems to strike a Marvellian note (as he certainly does) this is because the same qualities in Horace appealed to Smart as to Marvell, and that what looks Marvellian is really Horatian. But one further possibility presents itself, among three works which Brittain (p.286) interestingly notes as partial precedents for at least the *genre* of poetry which the *Hymns and Spiritual Songs* represent. These are Herbert's *The Temple* (1633), Crashaw's *Steps to the Temple* (1646), and Herrick's *Noble Numbers* (1647). One of these names in particular should make us pause, when set beside the word 'baroque' which we take from Father Devlin. This is the name of Crashaw. For Crashaw, as the one notable English poet of the counter-Reformation, is the one poet in English to whom the term 'baroque' can be applied with proper strictness. And it might be instructive to compare the *Hymns and Spiritual Songs* with Richard Crashaw's *Steps to the Temple*.

One interesting thing about both the poets just proposed as furnishing Smart with English precedents of a sort – Crashaw, that is, and Pope – is that they are Roman Catholics. Smart on the other hand is militantly anti-Roman, as was inevitable, given his hope that St Paul's should supplant St Peter's. And yet in order to do this Smart's Protestantism had to take on some of the colouring of that which it hoped to supplant; and not just in Smart's concerns for saints and especially angels does he seem near to Romanism, but also his attempt to conceal some of the ferocity of the Old Testament behind the New seemed to some of his contemporaries, and may seem to us if we think about it, to smack of the Roman Church. It is Father Devlin who has brought this out, and has pointed out also, as no previous biographer has done, that Smart's wife was a Roman Catholic. It is too soon to say that Devlin is right in his theory about the connection between Smart's queer and unsuccessful marriage, and the liturgical and doctrinal implications of his poems; but some connection there must be, and the clue to much that is still baffling about Smart must lie in this area and have to do with his very complicated attitude towards the Roman Church.

As for Richard Crashaw, one of the things characteristic of Crashaw's poetry is a disparity between the complexity of the surface and the simplicity beneath. This is what distinguishes Crashaw from the so-called 'metaphysicals' with whom he is often grouped – the extreme ingenuity of his poetic wit and the elaboration of his poetic structures do not, as with Donne, testify to a divided or tormented, self-doubting or self-questioning attitude in the writer. And the same is true of Smart, particularly in the *Hymns and Spiritual Songs*. Smart's poetry is unsubtle, but this does not mean either that Smart was simple-minded, or that the structure of his poems is straightforward. It is the attitude behind the poems which is simple, impressively simple; naïve in the very best, most valuable sense. For it is the attitude of praise, praise undertaken from a position of unshakeable and unquestioning conviction. On the other hand Smart, like Crashaw, deploys in the service of this single-minded purpose a very elaborate and copious rhetoric indeed. In both poets the local effects are often of a very subtle kind, and the means employed to this end are very subtle means; yet the total effect is not subtle, but simple.

A good example is the Hymn on the Nativity:

Where is this stupendous stranger,
  Swains of Solyma, advise,
Lead me to my Master's manger,
  Shew me where my Saviour lies.

O Most Mighty! O MOST HOLY!
  Far beyond the seraph's thought,
Art thou then so mean and lowly
  As unheeded prophets taught?

O the magnitude of meekness!
  Worth from worth immortal sprung;
O the strength of infant weakness,
  If eternal is so young!

If so young and thus eternal,
  Michael tune the shepherd's reed,
Where the scenes are ever vernal,
  And the loves be love indeed!

See the God blasphem'd and doubted
  In the schools of Greece and Rome;
See the pow'rs of darkness routed,
  Taken at their utmost gloom.

Nature's decorations glisten
  Far above their usual trim;
Birds on box and laurel listen,
  As so near the cherubs hymn.

Boreas now no longer winters
  On the desolated coast;
Oaks no more are riv'n in splinters
  By the whirlwind and his host.

Spinks and ouzles sing sublimely,
  'We too have a Saviour born,'
Whiter blossoms burst untimely
  On the blest Mosaic thorn.

God all-bounteous, all-creative,
  Whom no ills from good dissuade,
Is incarnate, and a native
  Of the very world he made.

Here the total effect is the characteristic Smart effect – a full-throated paean of praise, whole-hearted simple gratitude to God, unconditional, without qualifications or reservations or doubts or questionings. And this full-throatedness, this absence of complications, is faithfully mirrored – as always in Smart, notably in the *Song to David* – in the firmness with which the poem hammers out its metrical beat, in the emphatic alliterations ('stupendous stranger'), and in the reverberating richness of the rhymes, especially the rhymes on two syllables: 'stranger' / 'manger', 'Holy' / 'lowly', 'meekness' / 'weakness', 'eternal' / 'vernal'. It is easy to get so caught up in this resonance that one does not notice how witty the poem is; that is, how strenuous the thinking is. Consider only the third quatrain:

> O the magnitude of meekness!
> Worth from worth eternal sprung;
> O the strength of infant weakness,
> If eternal is so young!

Alliteration binds 'magnitude' with 'meekness', so as to bring out how unusual it is for these two qualities to go together – they are not quite incompatible, yet 'magnitude' usually points one way, 'meekness' another. After a line which lets down the tension, it is screwed up again to 'the strength of... weakness', which is *oxymoron*; that is, the two qualities crammed together *are* in normal usage incompatible, blank opposites indeed – and the implication is that for an occasion so abnormal as the Incarnation of a God normal usage is inadequate, its values are all reversed, its categories confounded. And now, instead of letting down the tension again, it is screwed up further still; and the poem soars – not just into more fervent feeling, but intellectually, into paradox – 'If eternal is so young!' This means, literally, 'if God is a new-born infant'; but it means also, imaginatively, 'if the divine is unchangeable, inexhaustible vigorous and creative'. To take 'eternal', which means by definition 'outside time', and ram it up against 'young', which has meaning only within the dimension of time – this expression ought to be meaningless, nonsensical; but we discover to our astonishment that it isn't meaningless at all, though the mind at full stretch can only just grasp the meaning and can only with great difficulty formulate the meaning to itself.

'If eternal is so young' is deftly re-arranged then into 'If so young and thus eternal' – which is the sort of effect that Brittain would want to analyse by way of analogies from contrapuntal baroque music. And 'young' is not taken away from the human timespan into that of the seasons: 'young' now means 'the youth of the year', i.e. 'spring'. Hence 'vernal', and the identification naturally and wittily follows of the archangel Michael with the pastoral poet piping a spring eclogue. And yet the birth was at Christmas in the depth of winter, when 'the pow'rs of darkness' (Satan of course but also the long nights and short days of December) are 'Taken at their utmost gloom.' With 'Nature's decorations glisten', we hear an aggressively anti-Wordsworthian string such as Smart plucks very often – for instance, in the 'painted beauties' of the Hymn to St Philip and St James. But here the artificiality is even more deliberate and necessary. This is to represent the natural as unnatural? But of course! Spring in midwinter *is* unnatural. How can it not be, since it is supernatural? The language is artificial? But of course! It is speaking of a divine artifice disrupting the natural order.

The whole conceit and paradox of Boreas (who *is* winter) no longer 'wintering' (the use of the verb is masterly) is clinched in the penultimate stanza. Here, as Brittain acutely points out, Smart telescopes two legendary stories – the story of the Glastonbury thorn which is supposed to bloom at Christmas, being sprung from the staff of Joseph of Arimathea; and the rod of Aaron, which in Numbers XVII bloomed in the tabernacle to approve the elevation of the Levites to the status of a hereditary priestly caste. By thus telescoping a story of the apostle in Britain with a story of divine sanction for a chosen priesthood, Smart implies the possibility and the rightness of regarding the Church of England (rather than of Rome) as God's chosen church.

And one paradox remains, the most astonishing and profound of all – the gloss on the word 'incarnate' by which, in a way that ought to be nonsensical but astoundingly isn't, God who created the world is said to be himself a creature of that world – 'a native / Of the very world he made.'

Smart's translations from Horace should be better known. There are two of them: a prose translation of the 1750s and a verse translation which appeared in 1767. Whereas the painstaking prose-crib was often reprinted and used by generations of schoolboys, the verse-translations have never been reprinted after the first edition; not only are they almost unknown, but copies are very hard to find. And yet the Preface which Smart wrote for these translations is the only document we have in which Smart explains, or hints at explaining, his own poetic practice.

Unfortunately, this is not so useful as it sounds. For it is hard to agree with Christopher Devlin that the Preface, no less than the translations themselves, shows 'his complete sanity and urbanity in everything that did not probe the one secret obsession.' On the contrary, it seems to me that the Preface, though it is certainly not the product of a deranged mind, no less certainly comes from a mind that is seriously disoriented – a mind which, to say the least, has lost its sense of proportion. (See for instance Smart's gratuitous footnote to the effect that Stonehenge was the work of giants.) The Preface touches in disconnected fashion on three topics, and two of these – Smart's remarks on the 'curious felicity' of Horace, and his observations on what he calls 'impression' – are of immediate importance; but Smart's treatment of both these matters is glancing and general, and the most we can make of them is tantalizing and tentative, not solidly helpful.

Smart begins his Preface by speaking of 'the lucky risk of the Horatian boldness'. And he elaborates:

> Horace is by no means so much an original in respect to his matter and sentiments (which are rather too frequently borrowed) as with regard to that unrivalled peculiarity of expression, which has excited the admiration of all succeeding ages.

Then, after some distracting digressions, he returns to the topic:

> Mr. *Pope* himself, however happy in taking off the spirit and music of *Horace*, has left us no remarkable instance, to the best of my memory, of this kind. In truth this is a beauty, that occurs rather in the Odes, than the other parts of Horace's works; where the aiming at familiarity of style excluded the curiosity of choice diction.

Robert Brittain, who alone has wrestled so far with the problem of what Smart meant by this, has some enlightening and sensible pages, suggesting how, not just in these translations but in all his poems, Smart strove for the Horatian 'curious felicity' by following the instructions given in the *De Arte Poetica* about the tactful use of archaic words and neologisms. I think Brittain is right about this, though he does not sufficiently recognize how much which he presents as peculiar to Smart was common to eighteenth-century poets in general: for example, the use of English words in the sense of their Latin roots, as when Smart uses 'vague' to mean 'wandering'. But I suspect that curious felicity in Smart has less to do with artful choice of words than with artful arrangement of them: Smart goes on to specify those of his translations of the Odes in which he believes he has attained to this felicity, and very few of those he specifies exemplify the curiosities of vocabulary to which Brittain draws attention. Moreover, my own experience has been that in the Second Book of the Odes, for instance, those by which Smart on this basis lays most store are by and large those which are least to my taste.

It seems important, therefore, to consider the possibility that often when Smart essays 'the curiosity of choice diction', he is striving for something which we would rather he had never achieved. A little thought will reveal how this may well be so. For from the remarks by Smart which I have quoted already, meagre as they are, we gather at least one thing quite definitely – that Horace's 'curious felicity', as Smart sees it, is attainable only in an elevated style. This is implied when Smart says that in Horace's poems other than the Odes this felicity should not be looked for since 'the aiming at familiarity of style' excluded it. And there is a footnote which tells the same story, in which Smart concedes that in the first Ode of the first book (in which he believes that he has managed curious felicity in many places) he has made the style more lofty and less conversational than in the Latin. Because twentieth-century taste is for the most part still Wordsworthian enough to prefer eighteenth-century poetry at its least ornate, when it is most conversational, it may well be that we shall prefer Smart's less ornate versions of the epodes and satires to his version of the Odes, though he laid most store by these.

It is worth dwelling on this for a little, for it affects Smart's poetry as a whole. Except for his youthful and admirable *vers-de-société*, and the poems which he wrote for children, Smart's diction is characteristically very ornate indeed, and his tone is very lofty. Moreover one effect which is peculiar to him, which is very valuable and moving, the effect which one commentator has called his 'piercing naïveté', is possible only because his style is thus choice and elevated. The naïveté pierces only because it strikes at us suddenly out of a body of language which in general is not naïve at all, but on the contrary very sophisticated and polished. The Hymn on the Nativity provides an example:

Boreas now no longer winters
    On the desolated coast;
Oaks no more are riv'n in splinters
    By the whirlwind and his host.

Spinks and ouzles sing sublimely,
    'We too have a Saviour born,'
Whiter blossoms burst untimely
    On the blest Mosaic thorn.

When the spinks and ouzles are made to speak with childlike simplicity, the effect is indeed piercingly childlike and not childish, infantile or mawkish, only because they speak to us out of a context defined by the stilted artifice of 'Boreas', and the no less deliberate grandeur of 'the blest Mosaic thorn.' The effect is earned, it is not at all a cheap gimmick which loses its value as soon as we see through it. For the naïveté of language in the one case witnesses to a real directness of apprehension, just as the elaboration of language in the other cases reflects a genuine complexity. Smart's distinction is in the rapidity and lack of fuss with which he can switch from extreme indirectness to extreme directness and back again. It is probably impossible to say whether this characteristic effect is part of what Smart intended by 'curious felicity', or whether it came about as a lucky by-product of Smart's striving after something else.

However that may be, in Smart's translations of Horace's Odes the efforts at 'curious felicity' rather often end unhappily. Book I Ode 4 is a fair example:

> Solvitur acris hiems grata vice veris et Favoni:
> Trahuntque siccas machinae carinas.
> Ae neque iam stabulis gaudet pecus, aut arator igni;
> Nec prata canis albicant pruinis.
> Iam Cytherea choros ducit Venus, imminente Luna:
> Iunctaeque Nymphis Gratiae decentes
> Alterno terram quatiunt pede: dum graves Cyclopium
> Vulcanus ardens urit officinas.
> Nunc decet aut viridi nitidum caput impedire myrto
> Aut flore, terrae quem ferunt solutae.
> Nunc et in umbrosis Fauno decet immolare lucis,
> Seu poscat agnam, sive malit haedum.
> Pallida mors aequo pulsat pede pauperum tabernas,
> Regumque turres, ô beate Sexti,
> Vitae summa brevis spem nos vetat incohare longam.
> Iam te premet nox, fabulaque manes,
> Et domus exilis Plutonia, quo simul mearis,
> Non regna vini fortiere talis,
> Nec tenerem Lycidam mirabere, quo calet juventus
> Nunc omnis, et mox virgines tepebunt.

> A grateful change! Favonius, and the spring
> To the sharp winter's keener blasts succeed,
> Along the beach, with ropes, the ships they bring,
> And launch again, their watry way to speed.
> No more the plowmen in their cots delight,
> Nor cattle are contented in the stall;
> No more the fields with hoary frosts are white,
> But Cytherean Venus leads the ball.
> She, while the moon attends upon the scene,

> The Nymphs and decent Graces in the set,
> Shakes with alternate foot the shaven green.
> While Vulcan's Cyclops at the anvil sweat,
> Now we with myrtle shou'd adorn our brows,
> Or any flow'r that decks the loosen'd sod;
> In shady groves to Faunus pay our vows,
> Whether a lamb or kid delight the God.
> Pale death alike knocks at the poor man's door,
> O happy Sextius, and the royal dome.
> The whole of life forbids our hope to soar,
> Death and the shades anon shall press thee home.
> And when into the shallow grave you run,
> You cannot win the monarchy of wine,
> Nor doat on Lycidas, as on a son,
> Whom for their spouse all little maids design.

It is not just an unreasoning preference for the colloquial which makes us (surely) pick out as the best things in Smart's verse translation the two points where he is most conversational – that is to say, the exclamatory opening, 'A grateful change, Favonius!', and, at the close (corresponding to lines now rejected from the Latin text), the delightful discovery of the 'little maids', 'Whom for their spouse all little maids design.' In between, we are repeatedly aware of loss if we look from Smart's prose translation to his verse. There is a loss in moving from the sturdy word 'hale' in Smart's prose ('hale from shore the dry ships') to the weak alternative 'bring'; the single word 'dry' in the prose is worth infinitely more than the redundant 'their watry way to speed'; 'the royal dome' is similarly more stilted for the Latin *turres* than is 'towers of kings'; and 'forbids our hope to soar' quite loses the suggestion of a balance-sheet which there is in the original and, faintly, in Smart's prose. And when we turn from these matters of choice of words, to the question of their arrangement, the case is even clearer. It will be recalled that this is the ode with which in a famous essay T.S. Eliot compares Marvell's 'To His Coy Mistress', in respect of the introduction of death into both poems. J.V. Cunningham has argued, persuasively I think, that the comparison Eliot proposes does justice to neither poem. And Cunningham remarks, of Horace's poem:

> Death occurs in this poem with that suddenness and lack of preparation with which it sometimes occurs in life. The structure of the poem is an imitation of the structure of such experiences in life. And as we draw from such experiences often a generalization, so Horace from the sudden realization of the abruptness and impartiality of death, reflects

> vitae summa brevis spem nos vetat incohare longam
> The brief sum of life forbids our opening a long account with hope
>
> But the proposition is subsequent to the experience; it does not rule and direct the poem from the outset. And the experience in Horace *is* surprising and furnishes the fulcrum on which the poem turns.[1]

Cunningham's point is that in Marvell's poem the experience is *not* surprising and does *not* provide a fulcrum; because it isn't that kind of poem. But if Horace's poem is the sort that does have a fulcrum, then Smart's treatment of it will be crucial. And Cunningham indicates what the fulcrum is; it is the famous line and a half,

> Pallida mors aequo pulsat pede pauperum tabernas,
> Regumque turres...

What does Smart make of this? –

> Pale death alike knocks at the poor man's door,
> O happy Sextius, and the royal dome

He pulls back the renewed address to Sextius from the succeeding sentence where it belongs (as his own prose acknowledges), and rams it in as an interjection between 'poor man's door' and 'royal palace', where it is crucially important that these two should go closely together. The rearrangement only weakens and distracts because the run of the line persuades us to look, at first reading, for a connection between Sextius and 'royal dome', as if the latter too were being addressed. Unhappy re-arrangements of this kind, producing pointless ambiguities and obscurities, are not uncommon in Smart's versions; and if these, as I suspect, came about by his efforts after 'curious felicity', so much the worse for him and for that principle which he espoused. For another example I take four lines from Ode 10 of the first book, addressing Mercury:

> Thee when a boy, with threads injoin'd
> To bring the steers you had withdrawn,
> Apollo laugh'd aloud to find
> His quiver also gone.

These lines are incomprehensible until we turn to Smart's prose translation, where we find: 'While Apollo in threatening voice terrified you, then but a boy, unless you should restore the oxen conveyed away by your artifice, he laughed, being deprived of his quiver

[1] J.V. Cunningham, *Tradition and Poetic Structure* (Denver, 1960).

into the bargain.' And even when we have thus learned what Smart's verses mean, or are intended to mean, we still cannot make sense of the grammar of his lines. What we have in a case like this is English being treated, particularly in the matter of word-order, as if it were a highly inflected language like the Latin Smart is translating from. This is a charge which is habitually levelled at the Milton of *Paradise Lost*, but the charge sticks on Milton much less than on a later Latinist, Walter Savage Landor; and such unfortunate effects as this recall nothing more insistently than some of the more congested passages of Landor.

In all of this I am not suggesting that these forgotten translations of Horace are deservedly forgotten; on the contrary they are frequently delightful. And I put before you the example of Ode XI from Book I, to show how graceful and surprising Smart's versions can be:

> Seek not, what we're forbid to know,
> The date the Gods decree
> To you, my fair Leuconoe,
> Or what they fix for me.
> Nor your Chaldean books consult,
> But chearfully submit,
> (How much a better thought it is?)
> To what the Gods think fit.
> Whether more winters on our head
> They shall command to low'r,
> Or this the very last of all,
> Shall bring our final hour.
> E'en this, whose rough tempestuous rage
> Makes yon Tyrrhenian roar,
> And all his foamy breakers dash
> Upon the rocky shore.
> Be wise and broach your mellow wine,
> Which carefully decant,
> And your desires proportionate
> To life's compendious grant.
> E'en while we speak the moments fly,
> Be greedy of to-day;
> Nor trust another for those pranks
> Which we may never play.

Here we must applaud the wholly eighteenth-century and yet compact and accurate lines – 'And your desires proportionate / To life's compendious grant.' But it remains true that Brittain's claims for this part of Smart's work, just and generous as those claims are, have to be treated with caution.

As for the other principle which Smart enunciates in his Preface – the principle of 'impression' – his remarks on this unfortunately are even more cryptic and elusive than his treatment of the Horatian *curiosa felicitas*. He speaks of:

> another poetical excellence, which tho' possessed in a degree by every great genius, is exceeding in our Lyric to surpass; I mean the beauty, force and vehemence of *Impression*: which leads me to a rare and entertaining subject, not (I think) any where much insisted on by others.
>
> *Impression* then, is a talent or gift of Almighty God, by which a Genius is impowered to throw an emphasis upon a word or sentence in such wise, that it cannot escape any reader of sheer good sense, and true critical sagacity. This power will sometimes keep it up thro' the *medium* of a prose translation; especially in scripture, for in justice to truth and everlasting pre-eminence, we must confess this virtue to be far more powerful and abundant in the sacred writings.

That last sentence necessarily brings to mind Longinus on the Sublime; for 'Longinus' not only makes a point of praising Hebrew poetry for its sublimity (and, of the confusingly many examples which Smart proceeds to give, the first three are in Hebrew), but 'Longinus' also, by implication, indicates that sublimity can persist through translation. Moreover Smart himself, introducing a later example from Homer, speaks of how the lines he quotes from Homer 'are worked up to . . . a pitch of sublimity.' Out of 'Longinus' the passage which seems most nearly to correspond to Smart's idea of 'impression' comes in Section X when the ancient critic is commenting on some lines from (again) Homer, and on lines moreover which, like the lines in Smart's example, describe a storm at sea. 'Longinus' says that Homer in this place 'has stamped, I had almost said, upon the language the form and features of the peril' (A.O. Prickard's translation). Unfortunately we look in vain in Smart's remarks for what the ancient critic so remarkably gives us – an analysis of the sublime effect in terms of particular use of particular words:

> Yet again, by forcing together prepositions naturally inconsistent, and compelling them to combine [and 'Longinus' then quotes the specific Homeric phrase he has in mind], he has so strained the verse as to match the trouble which fell upon them; has so pressed it together as to give the very presentment of that trouble; has stamped, I had almost said, upon the language the form and features of the peril . . .

This passage of ancient criticism suggests quite precisely, as a modern analogue to the ancient effect he so much admires, something like some passages from Hopkins's 'Wreck of the Deutschland'. And only some of the passages which Smart cites as examples seem to be passages in which Hopkinsian or Homeric liberties are taken. All the same, as has been remarked by others, the principle of 'impression' was for Smart an important one, a constantly guiding principle – as one sees from *Rejoice in the Lamb* several years before: 'For my talent is to give an impression upon words by punching, that when the reader casts his eye upon 'em, he takes up the image from the mould wch I have made.' Plainly 'impression' is not used by Smart loosely, but is a word which seems to draw behind it a complicated metaphor from die-casting, a metaphor which indicates what Smart consceived himself to be doing when he wrote. And yet this metaphor is not to be found in 'Longinus', (whose treatise Smart studied when attending Bishop Lowth's lectures on Hebrew poetry), but in Horace's *Ars Poetica* (I.59). It is a puzzling business, and deserves further study.

If anything has emerged from this consideration of Smart, I hope it is this – that whether he writes poems of ecstasy and wonder, or poems of a more worldly cast, he does not fit into the category that is sometimes called 'pre-Romantic'; he is not 'a Romantic precursor', but wholly a poet of the eighteenth century. This appears in nothing so clearly as in his verse for children, to which I now turn all too briefly; to the *Hymns for the Amusement of Children*, Smart's last work, not published until 1775.

It may seem, from a point made earlier, that since in these poems Smart abandoned 'the high style', he might here have fallen into that mawkishness from which in general his lofty tone and style rescued him even when he was dealing in effects of piercing simplicity. This is not so, however. In the first place, though the Hymns for Children may be said to be in a low style, this is true only relative to the unusually high style which Smart employed in his other devotional poems; the style is not so low as what Wordsworth and Blake after him were to employ in children's verse, or what Isaac Watts had employed before him in writing for children. In fact, our first impression is likely to be of surprise at how few concessions Smart made to his audience of children, how much he demands of his young readers, in width of vocabulary particularly. The matter to which Brittain draws attention, Smart's artifice of *recherché* archaism in diction, can be illustrated from these poems as from the poems Smart wrote for adults. For example, in Hymn V:

And still peculiar on my side,
Keep me from rigour free;
Make me forgive, in manly pride,
All that exact on me.

Here the use of 'peculiar' is by no means a straightforward one. It is so much a favourite word of Smart that it becomes an idiosyncratic mannerism. As Father Devlin says (p.173), '"Peculiar" is Smart's favourite adjective for subtleties..., as "stupendous" is for mysteries.' The children who have wrestled with this special meaning in the first line of the quatrain are faced in the last line with the archaic oddity of 'exact on' instead of 'exact from'. Or there is Hymn XXVIII:

Then pray with David, that the Lord
Wou'd keep himself the door;
And all things from the lips award,
That make thy brother sore

(where 'award' is used in the strictly Latinate sense of 'ward off'). Thus Smart is not 'coming down to the child's level' at all so much as most writers for children think they have to do. And this in itself saves him from seeming either mawkish or patronizing.

But more important is the fact that behind these poems there lies a wholly non-Romantic idea of what a child is. Smart is as far as possible from seeing the child in the Wordsworthian way as 'mighty prophet, seer blest'; there is no sign of the Romantic conviction which lies behind some of Blake's *Songs of Innocence* as well as behind Wordsworth's 'We are Seven' – the conviction that the child has access to sources of wisdom and insight which are closed to the adult. Smart on the contrary seems to believe, as perhaps all centuries before the nineteenth believed, that the child is a small and incomplete adult; that his lack of adulthood is a misfortune, though an inevitable one – a privation, which must be remedied as soon as possible, in his own interests; that the duty of the adult towards the child was to feel compassion for him in his incompleteness, to protect him from the perils which this brought upon him, and to assist him to complete himself. The best thing an adult can do for a child is to help him to grow up as quickly as possible – hence the awesome precocity of many children in earlier literature, which we as post-Romantic readers find disconcerting and unpleasant though the writers plainly felt nothing of the sort. Smart's *Hymns for the Amusement of Children* are meant to help the children to stop being children. When they are set in the mouth of a child (many of them are not spoken by the child but addressed to him by an adult), we are not to take it that the child is speaking out of his own resources but is repeating back words which the adult has put into his mouth, and made him learn. Since we are all more or less like children in our imperfect grasp of eighteenth-century values, many of these poems are highly instructive for the twentieth-century reader – especially those many hymns which have for title a single word, like Taste, Learning, Elegance, Honesty, Moderation, Temperance, Prudence; for these are in effect versified definitions of what these crucial terms meant for an eighteenth-century adult mind. Here is Hymn XV, 'Taste':

I

O guide my judgment and my taste,
Sweet SPIRIT, author of the book
Of wonders, told in language chaste
And plainness, not to be mistook.

II

O let me muse, and yet at sight
The page admire, the page believe;
'Let there be light, and there was light,
Let there be Paradise and Eve!'

III

Who his soul's rapture can refrain?
At Joseph's ever-pleasing tale,
Of marvels, the prodigious train,
To Sinai's hill from Goshen's vale.

IV

The Psalmist and proverbial Seer,
And all the prophets sons of song,
Make all things precious, all things dear,
And bear the brilliant word along.

V

O take the book from off the shelf,
And con it meekly on thy knees;
Best panegyric on itself,
And self-avouch'd to teach and please.

VI

Respect, adore it heart and mind.
How greatly sweet, how sweetly grand,
Who reads the most, is most refin'd,
And polish'd by the Master's hand.

What this is about is 'immediacy' – a matter which is clearly very much to the point of what Smart meant by that cardinal principle of his, 'Impression'. 'Taste', he implies, is the capacity to recognize immediacy; not an ability to weigh pros and cons, but the capacity to bypass or anticipate that process of reasoned judgement by responding vividly and at once to the artistic experience. It is astonishing and melancholy that the only poem by Smart which has evoked that vivid response at all generally is the *Song to David*; I am convinced that this happens only because so few readers ever look at Smart's other poems.

Eighteenth Century Studies III: 2 (winter 1969).

14 *Goldsmith as Monarchist*

In 1771, in his preface to *The History of England, from the Earliest Times to the Death of George II*, Oliver Goldsmith wrote:

> It is not yet decided in politics, whether the diminution of kingly power in England tends to encrease the happiness, or the freedom of the people. For my own part, from seeing the bad effects of the tyranny of the great in those republican states that pretend to be free, I cannot help wishing that our monarchs may still be allowed to enjoy the power of controlling the encroachments of the great at home. A king may easily be restrained from doing wrong, as he is but one man; but if a number of the great are permitted to divide all authority, who can punish them if they abuse it? Upon this principle, therefore, and not from any empty notion of divine or hereditary right, some may think I have leaned towards monarchy.[1]

This had indeed been consistently Goldsmith's principle. But he had not always avowed it so guardedly and suavely as he does here. Eight years before, in *The Traveller*, he had been much more vehement:

> Yes, brother, curse with me that baleful hour
> When first ambition struck at regal power;
> And thus, polluting honour in its source,
> Gave wealth to sway the mind with double force.
> Have we not seen, round Britain's peopled shore,
> Her useful sons exchang'd for useless ore?
> Seen all her triumphs but destruction haste,
> Like flaring tapers brightening as they waste;
> Seen opulence, her grandeur to maintain,
> Lead stern depopulation in her train,
> And over fields, where scatter'd hamlets rose,

I have anticipated some of my arguments as 'Notes on Goldsmith's Politics', in *The Art of Oliver Goldsmith*, ed. Andrew Swarbrick (London, 1984).

[1] Oliver Goldsmith, *Collected Works*, ed. Arthur Friedman, 5 vols. (Oxford, 1966), 5:339–40. Further references to this edition, including volume and page numbers, will be included in the text.

In barren solitary pomp repose?
Have we not seen, at pleasure's lordly call,
The smiling long-frequented village fall?
Beheld the duteous son, the sire decay'd,
The modest matron, and the blushing maid,
Forc'd from their homes, a melancholy train,
To traverse climes beyond the western main;
Where wild Oswego spreads her swamps around,
And Niagara stuns with thund'ring sound?
(4:267-68, ll. 393-412)

This passage is generally remembered, because it contains in embryo what was to become *The Deserted Village*. But if that later treatment surpasses this one, as is usually but not universally supposed, Goldsmith (and we also) have to pay a price. For *The Deserted Village* is in important ways much less specific than *The Traveller*. Nothing in the later poem is so uncompromising as 'Her useful sons exchang'd for useless ore...' Indeed it is notoriously unclear why in *The Deserted Village* the villagers have been expropriated. And this vagueness permits of the time-honoured debate whether the village, Auburn, is to be understood as in England or in Ireland. The debate of course is misconceived, since the poetic imagination surely transforms disparate experiences by amalgamating and compounding them, often enough. It remains true that agricultural distress in the 1760s took different forms in England and in Ireland; and our inability to determine which kingdom is meant shows how far the poem is from specifying the cause of the calamity. In both poems mercantile interests expropriate the villagers, but in reading *The Deserted Village* we notice this only if we are very attentive. Indeed, we may go further. If we identify 'the man of wealth and pride' who drives the villagers out as a nouveau-riche 'nabob', returned with a fortune from the East or West Indies, this is only a plausible conjecture; the poem itself does not identify him in that way, nor in any other. And it is reasonable to wonder if this lack of specificity is not one of the features that have always made *The Deserted Village* more appealing than *The Traveller*. If so, that appeal is suspect. For instance:

But a bold peasantry, their country's pride,
When once destroyed, can never be supplied.
(4:289, ll. 55-56)

Who would not agree? What bosom does not return an echo? Whom does the couplet put out of countenance? But in *The Traveller*, where the expropriation is emphatically and unequivocally laid at the door of commercial imperialism, the sentiment would embarrass anyone who practised, or profited from, the import of raw material ('ore') from overseas.

Moreover *The Deserted Village* prescribes no remedy for the state of affairs that it deplores, and so puts no reader under any obligation to do anything about it. *The Traveller* however does prescribe a remedy: enhanced power for George III. And that prescription is even less palatable for the modern reader than for Goldsmith's contemporaries. For it flies in the face of the Whig Interpretation of History – an interpretation which, though in theory we recognize its partiality, most of us are bound by more than we realize. It is one thing to exculpate George III from the charges thrown at him by Tom Paine and others; it is something else to believe, as Goldsmith would have us do, that in the contention between the king and demagogues like Paine or John Wilkes, the right (and also the *freedom*) was with the king. For that is undoubtedly what Goldsmith means when he calls on his brother to join him in cursing the inroads made on 'regal power'. *The Traveller* is a fervent apologia for the monarchical form of government, taking the time-honoured ground that, since the unprivileged need a power to appeal to above the power of local and financial privilege, the only such power conceivable is the power of the monarch, elevated above all sectional interests. *The Deserted Village* may be the more seductive poem; it is *The Traveller* that is clearer and more challenging.

However, Goldsmith's thinking about the monarchy had gone through an earlier phase before he wrote *The Traveller*. In 1759 in *The Bee* had appeared 'Custom and Laws Compared'. Here Goldsmith (for I follow Arthur Friedman in supposing him the author) finds Tacitus, with his *Corruptissima republica, plurimae leges*, at odds with 'the great Montesquieu, who asserts that every nation is free in proportion to the number of its written laws.' Forced to choose, Goldsmith plumps for Tacitus, and for 'custom' against 'laws', in this anticipating that other Irish political thinker of his day, Edmund Burke. Goldsmith concludes:

> From hence we see how much greater benefit it would be to the state rather to abridge than encrease its laws. We every day find them encreasing; acts and reports, which may be termed the acts of judges, are every day becoming more voluminous, and loading the subject with new penalties. (1:486)

In the next year we find him harping on the same string. This is in a charming paper in *The British Magazine*, 'A Reverie at the Boar's-head-tavern in Eastcheap', where Mr Rigmarole (Goldsmith himself) tells the ghost of Mistress Quickly: 'I rather fancy, madam, that the times then were pretty much like our own; where a multiplicity of laws give a judge as much power as a want of law, since he is ever sure to find among the number some to countenance his partiality' (3.104)

And yet Goldsmith at once sets about reversing this judgement, or rather standing it on its head. According to his new argument, the plethora of legislation in eighteenth-century England, so far from being a sickness in the state, was a sign of its health – but only, he insists, because England was a monarchy. This argument appears first, so far as I can see, already in 1760, in an essay in *The Royal Magazine*:

> Examine every state in Europe, and you will find the people either enjoying a precarious freedom under monarchical government, or what is worse, actually slaves in a republic, to laws of their own contriving. What constitutes the peculiar happiness of Britain, is, that laws may be overlooked without endangering the state. In a mere republic, which pretends to equal freedom, every infringement upon law is a dissolution of government, and must consequently be punished with the most unremitting severity; but in England, laws may be sometimes overlooked without danger. A King who has it in his power to pardon, gives the government at once the strength of the oak, and the flexibility of the yew. (3:68)

However, Goldsmith's fullest exposition of this paradoxical position (which surely again anticipates in its tenor Burke's hostility to written constitutions) had appeared less than two weeks before in the important Letter L of *The Citizen of the World*:

> In all those governments, where laws derive their sanction from the *people alone*, transgressions cannot be overlooked without bringing the constitution into danger. They who transgress the law in such a case, are those who prescribe it, by which means it loses not only its influence but its sanction. In every republic the laws must be strong, because the constitution is feeble: they must resemble an Asiatic husband who is justly jealous, because he knows himself impotent. Thus in Holland, Switzerland, and Genoa, new laws are not frequently enacted, but the old ones are observed with unremitting severity. In such republics therefore the people are slaves to laws of their own making, little less than in unmix'd monarchies where they are slaves to the will of one subject to frailties like themselves.
>
> In England, from a variety of happy accidents, their constitution is just strong enough, or if you will, monarchical enough,

> to permit a relaxation of the severity of laws, and yet those laws still remain sufficiently strong to govern the people. This is the most perfect state of civil liberty, of which we can form any idea; here we see a greater number of laws than in any other country, while the people at the same time obey only such as are immediately conducive to the interests of society; several are unnoticed, many unknown; some kept to be revived and enforced upon proper occasions, others left to grow obsolete, even without the necessity of abrogation. (2:211)

And Goldsmith expatiates:

> Scarce an Englishman who does not almost every day of his life, offend with impunity against some express law, and for which in a certain conjuncture of circumstances he would not receive punishment. Gaming houses, preaching at prohibited places, assembled crowds, nocturnal amusements, public shews, and an hundred other instances are forbid and frequented. These prohibitions are useful; though it be prudent in their magistrates, and happy for their people, that they are not enforced, and none but the venal or mercenary attempt to enforce them.
>
> The law in this case, like an indulgent parent, still keeps the rod, though the child is seldom corrected. Were those pardoned offences to rise into enormity, were they likely to obstruct the happiness of society, or endanger the state, it is then that justice would resume her terrors, and punish those faults she had so often overlooked with indulgence. It is to this ductility of the laws that an Englishman owes the freedom he enjoys superior to others in a more popular government; every step therefore the constitution takes towards a Democratic form, every diminution of the regal authority is, in fact a diminution of the subjects freedom; but every attempt to render the government more popular, not only impairs natural liberty, but even will at last, dissolve the political constitution. (2:211-12)

Thus the Englishman of Goldsmith's time is persuaded that he lives under the rule of law by the assurance that the laws will be enforced only capriciously!

At first sight, this is one of those quixotic, 'Irish' arguments that Goldsmith was famous for in conversation, which made it so difficult for his English friends, even his great champion Johnson, to take him seriously. Yet in fact Goldsmith has here put his finger on an anomaly in eighteenth-century England that recent historians have found exceptionally significant: the anomaly that 'the number of capital statutes grew from about 50 to over 200 between the years

1688 and 1820,' and yet 'the available evidence suggests that, compared to some earlier periods, the eighteenth-century criminal law claimed few lives.' What has to be explained is 'the coexistence of bloodier laws and increased convictions with a declining proportion of death sentences that were actually carried out.'[1] I am quoting from an essay of capital importance, Douglas Hay's 'Property, Authority and the Criminal Law'. What Hay shows is that the commuting or pardoning of severe sentences was, at least outside the commercial centres of London and perhaps Bristol, a principal way of knitting English society together, in a way that was hierarchical indeed and inequitable, yet effective and even in a deep sense humane. As in other perspectives, what has been denounced in English eighteenth-century society as 'corrupt' (and was even so denounced at the time) turns out to be the margin of humanity – of humane feelings and human relationships – that that society provided for. Intercession on behalf of inferiors and dependents was taken for granted as an essential part of the mechanism of society, alike by those who needed such help and those who (on conditions, of course) extended it. Without this 'corrupt' play between the majesty of the law and the acknowledgement of special interests, the society would have been less flexible and less stable than it proved to be. And to this extent modern scholarship may be thought to vindicate Goldsmith's speculations, which thus turn out to have been remarkably astute. Moreover, in a curious and devious way Goldsmith may be thought to vindicate his earlier preference for 'custom' over 'laws', since the very multiplicity of laws ensured that their severity would be *customarily* alleviated.

What remains to be justified is Goldsmith's conviction that things could work out this way only under a monarchy. Readers of Hay's essay will be tempted to think that Goldsmith was wrong and starry-eyed about this (if nothing worse). For Hay shows that the system worked so as to put life and death in the hands of those local tyrants, justices of the peace and their cronies, from whom, on Goldsmith's understanding of the matter, the Crown was supposed to liberate the unprivileged. That pardons came from the king was a legal and ideological fiction, masking the fact that they were handed down as a result of interplaying interests in the ruling class. However, this fiction – that all clemency is the king's – has far more power than the more or less squalid or whimsical fact of letters written on behalf of this or that convicted person at this or that level of influence. For

[1] Douglas Hay, 'Property, Authority and the Criminal Law', in *Albion's Fatal Tree: Crime and Society in Eighteenth-century England*, ed. Hay et al. (London, 1975), pp. 18, 22; further references to this essay, abbreviated 'P', will be included in the text.

it is of the nature of an ideology to be a tissue of fictions, that is to say in the most serious sense a *myth*. Hay abjures this word. And one can hardly blame him. For too often in these contexts 'myth' seems at once facile and pretentious, pretending to explain what in effect it only consigns to the ineffable. Yet where 'monarchy' is in question, though the word itself may be dispensed with, the sense of it hardly can be:

> Where authority is embodied in direct personal relationships, men will often accept power, even enormous, despotic power, when it comes from the 'good King', the father of his people, who tempers justice with mercy. A form of this powerful psychic configuration was one of the most distinctive aspects of the unreformed criminal law. Bentham could not understand it, but it was the law's greatest strength as an ideological system, especially among the poor, and in the countryside. ('P', p.39)

'Powerful psychic configuration' is certainly a drier expression than 'myth', but it surely means much the same thing. And indeed whenever Hay invokes 'paternalism', as he is compelled to do, he acknowledges the same mythic dimension. For under a monarchical dispensation the fatherliness of a squire to his tenant is thought to mirror in microcosm the fatherliness of the king towards the entire realm.

It is notable moreover that Hay is forced to explain how 'the criminal law, more than any other social institution, made it possible to govern eighteenth-century England without a police force and without a large army' ('P', p.56), by following through the same logic which, when we first encountered it in Letter L of *The Citizen of the World*, struck us as quixotic:

> An ideology endures not by being wholly enforced and rigidly defined. Its effectiveness lies first in its very elasticity, the fact that men are not required to make it a credo, that it seems to them the product of their own minds and their own experience. And the law did not enforce uniform obedience, did not seek total control; indeed, it sacrificed punishment when necessary to preserve the belief in justice. ('P', p.55)

This is the same logic that governs the policy of the English monarch even today. The monarch has powers which he or she retains on the tacit understanding that except in barely conceivable circumstances he or she will never exercise them. According to this understanding, the theory of monarchism is analogous to what naval strategists understand by the principle of 'the fleet in being'. So long as the fleet is never hazarded in combat (but only detached units or squadrons), it remains, as a menacing potency, an important pawn in grand strategy and in diplomacy. So too with the unreformed criminal law, as both Hay and Goldsmith understand it.

None of this intricate and perhaps special pleading enters into *The Traveller*. For this poem Goldsmith reverts to the not unconnected but bolder argument of 'The Revolution in Low Life' (*Lloyd's Evening Post*, 1762):

> Wherever we turn we shall find those governments that have pursued foreign commerce with too much assiduity at length becoming Aristocratical; and the immense property, thus necessarily acquired by some, has swallowed up the liberties of all. Venice, Genoa, and Holland, are little better at present than retreats for tyrants and prisons for slaves. The Great, indeed, boast of their liberties there, and they have liberty. The poor boast of liberty too; but, alas, they groan under the most rigorous oppression. (3.197-98)

Goldsmith protested – and coming from Samuel Johnson's very insular England, the protestation should be attended to – that when he spoke in this lordly fashion of Venice, Genoa, Holland, he drew on the experience of one who had travelled, needy and on foot, through their territories. What poetic capital Goldsmith could make of these experiences appears in a passage where he makes a smooth and yet momentous transition from considering the Netherlands to considering Great Britain:

> Heavens! how unlike their Belgic sires of old!
> Rough, poor, content, ungovernably bold;
> War in each breast, and freedom on each brow;
> How much unlike the sons of Britain now!
>
> Fir'd at the sound, my genius spreads her wing,
> And flies where Britain courts the western spring;
> Where laws extend that scorn Arcadian pride,
> And brighter streams than fam'd Hydaspis glide.
> There all around the gentlest breezes stray,
> There gentle music melts on every spray;
> Creation's mildest charms are there combin'd,
> Extremes are only in the master's mind;
> Stern o'er each bosom reason holds her state.
> With daring aims, irregularly great,
> Pride in their port, defiance in their eye,
> I see the lords of human kind pass by
> Intent on high designs, a thoughtful band,

By forms unfashion'd, fresh from Nature's hand:
Fierce in their native hardiness of soul,
True to imagin'd right above controul,
While even the peasant boasts these rights to scan,
And learns to venerate himself as man.
(4:262-63, ll. 313-34)

The diction is very stilted. Modern prejudices in favour of the colloquial will prompt us to say that the language is at no point in touch with spoken usage. But this is plainly untrue: 'I see the lords of human kind pass by' could certainly be *said* (sarcastically). And that drop in the level of the diction has a force that depends on the level in the preceding lines having been pitched so high. A more 'natural' idiom could not make the point with such economy. The panegyric is keyed so high, and the diction is so fulsome ('courts the western spring'... 'Arcadian pride'... 'fam'd Hydaspis'), precisely so that the sentiment conveyed can be undermined so soon, and so insidiously. The effect is that when this florid oratorical voice begins to drop into its discourse words like 'extremes' and 'irregularly' and 'pride', our first recation is to ask ourselves: 'Does he understand what he is *saying*?' We begin to think that he does when we reach 'the lords of human kind', but we are not wholly sure of it until 'True to imagin'd right above controul'. We see the claims of English complacency advanced, acceded to, and then denied, all inside twenty lines. The elevated diction is crucial for the achievement of masterly economy.

The verses that bite and drive most fiercely are yet to come:

That independence Britons prize too high
Keeps man from man, and breaks the social tie;
The self dependent lordlings stand alone,
All claims that bind and sweeten life unknown;
Here by the bond of nature feebly held,
Minds combat minds, repelling and repell'd;
Ferments arise, imprison'd factions roar,
Represt ambition struggles round her shore,
Till over-wrought, the general system feels
Its motions stopt, or phrenzy fire the wheels.
(4:263-64, ll. 339-48)

The metaphors that flame in the last two couplets – from chemistry, from the sea, from medicine, from mechanics – seem 'mixed' only because in a positively Shakespearean way the imagination is whirling so rapidly from one analogy to the next. And 'factions' here means something more inclusive than power-blocs vying and shouldering at court, in parliament, or in Whitehall offices. It is *minds* that are factious, and more than minds; personalities and sensibilities, human beings, are locked into this prison of unending combat, 'repelling and repell'd'. We have here in fact what may be the earliest and also the most caustic indictment of the world of 'free enterprise', unstructured and unrestricted competitiveness, the morality of the marketplace – in ideas, in status, and in feelings, as well as commodities. Nothing can save us from this, or alleviate it, except – Goldsmith insists – the institution of monarchy. Why is a passage so memorable seldom remembered or extolled? It is easy to see why. For most of us the indictment is launched from the wrong end of what we conceive of as the political spectrum. These sentiments and insights are thought to be the monopoly of the liberal democratic left, and we refuse to acknowledge them when they come to us from conservative monarchists like Goldsmith and Johnson. The Whig Interpretation is at work once again.

At least once more, before he submerged his analsysis in the indulgent haze of *The Deserted Village*, Goldsmith restated it. This was in chapter 19 of *The Vicar of Wakefield* (1766):

> 'No, Sir,' replied I, 'I am for liberty, that attribute of Gods! Glorious liberty! that theme of modern declamation. I would have all men kings. I would be a king myself. We have all naturally an equal right to the throne: we are all originally equal. This is my opinion, and was once the opinion of a set of honest men who were called Levellers. They tried to erect themselves into a community, where all should be equally free. But, alas! it would never answer; for there were some among them stronger, and some more cunning than others, and these became masters of the rest; for as sure as your groom rides your horses, because he is a cunninger animal than they, so surely will the animal that is cunninger or stronger than he, sit upon his shoulders in turn.' (4:99)

The speaker is Dr Primrose, the vicar, who here shows that he knows about primitive communism and anticipates George Orwell's *Animal Farm* in discrediting it by way of a bestial fable. The vicar goes on:

> 'Since then it is entailed upon humanity to submit, and some are born to command, and others to obey, the question is, as there must be tyrants, whether it is better to have them in the same house with us, or in the same village, or still farther off, in the metropolis. Now, Sir, for my own part, as I naturally hate the face of a tyrant, the farther off he is removed from me, the better

> pleased am I. The generality of mankind also are of my way of thinking, and have unanimously created one king, whose election at once diminishes the number of tyrants, and puts tyranny at the greatest distance from the greatest number of people. Now the great who were tyrants themselves before the election of one tyrant, are naturally averse to a power raised over them, and whose weight must ever lean heaviest on the subordinate orders. It is the interest of the great, therefore, to diminish kingly power as much as possible; because whatever they take from that is naturally restored to themselves; and all they have to do in the state, is to undermine the single tyrant, by which they resume their primaeval authority.' (4:99–100)

Dr Primrose may here seem to be more tough-minded than Dr Goldsmith, since he asserts that the power of the king is of its nature tyrannical; however, we may suppose that both the learned doctors know, and rely on their hearers to know, that *tyrannos* in ancient Greek is a term morally neutral, as 'tyrant' in English is not.

Since wealth is power (thus the argument develops), and since 'an accumulation of wealth...must necessarily be the consequence, when as at present more riches flow in from external commerce, than arise from internal industry' (4:100), it follows that in proportion as fortunes are made by international trading more and more attempts will be made to abridge the power of the monarch. The speaker, whom we may as well call Goldsmith as Primrose, accordingly declares his allegiance to 'people without the sphere of the opulent man's influence', a 'middle order of mankind' in whom 'are generally to be found all the arts, wisdom, and virtues of society' (4:101, 102). Indeed, he does not scruple to say, 'This order alone is known to be the true preserver of freedom, and may be called the People' (4:102). Here, it might reasonably be proposed, we see the sharp-sightedness of the Irishman, the outsider, detecting what now we take for granted though for observers at the time it was obscured by the conspicuousness of the landed grandees: the truth that eighteenth-century England was essentially a *bourgeois* civilization.

If the historical circumstances are such as he has described, what then, the speaker asks, is in the interest of that 'middle order' with which he has declared himself in sympathy? And he answers, '"to preserve the prerogative and privileges of the one principal governor with the most sacred circumspection. For he divides the power of the rich, and calls off the great from falling with tenfold weight on the middle order placed beneath them"' (4:102). But what began as protestation and proceeded as exposition has by this time become, as the speaker apologetically recognizes, a *harangue*. Accordingly it ends with a peroration:

> 'I am then for, and would die for, monarchy, sacred monarchy; for if there be any thing sacred amongst men, it must be the anointed sovereign of his people, and every diminution of his power in war, or in peace, is an infringement upon the real liberties of the subject. The sounds of liberty, patriotism, and Britons, have already done *much*, it is to be hoped that the true sons of freedom will prevent their ever doing more. I have known many of those pretended champions for liberty in my time, yet do I not remember one that was not in his heart and in his family a tyrant.' (4:102-3)

But it is plain that the alleged sacredness and anointedness of the monarch belong in a quite different dimension of discourse from the hard-nosed calculations of interest that have made the case for monarchy up to this point. That extra dimension can only be called 'mythological'.

Dr Primrose, the vicar, is of course a ninny; an endearingly foolish and unworldly man – as was, so we are assured by numerous but always controvertible witnesses, Oliver Goldsmith himself. But at no point are we invited to make fun of him in his capacity as priest and pastor, spiritual guide to his flock. Nor do we see him as easily deluded by catch-phrases – on the contrary his unworldliness often consists in his taking seriously and literally what other people say only as a matter of form. Accordingly, when he speaks of 'the *anointed* sovereign', we are in duty bound to suppose him in earnest. And indeed to a Christian nation like the eighteenth-century English (not nominally but deeply Christian), the figure of David, shepherd-king and warrior-psalmist of ancient Israel, could not fail to loom behind, and to transfigure, the image of any king whom they knew or knew about. The myth of kingship was for them underpinned by scriptural reading and religious observance. This is surely a main part of that 'powerful psychic configuration' which Hay postulates.

It has been argued that, in creating Dr Primrose, Goldsmith miscalculated. When the Whig Addison had created the lovable but foolish Tory figure of Sir Roger de Coverley, he had taken care not to put in Sir Roger's mouth any arguments that he, Addison, could take seriously; whereas Goldsmith took no such precautions. I now think this is wrong. Addison's Coverley papers are remarkably inventive and insidious political polemic, whereas *The Vicar of Wakefield* is, as Goethe admiringly and astutely recognized, an *idyll*. Within the conventions of the idyll – and the myth of kingship is itself, one might argue, idyllic – Goldsmith could safely expound doctrines that he took in all seriousness. Accordingly Donald Greene was surely right to quote from this chapter 19 and to present it as 'the view of Goldsmith... one of the most vigorous rebuttals of the Whig contention that what was good for Russells and Cavendishes was good for England.'[1] About politics this Irish zany was more levelheaded and penetrating than has ever been acknowledged.

[1] Donald J. Greene, *The Politics of Samuel Johnson* (New Haven, Conn., 1960), p.185.

Politics and Poetic Value, ed. R. Von Hallberg (University of Chicago Press, 1987).

15 *John Ledyard: the American Traveller and his Sentimental Journeys*

It is not much to our credit if, as students of the eighteenth century, we seldom accord more than a footnote, if indeed that much, to the field of eighteenth-century accomplishment that is represented by names like Anson and Commodore Byron, Bligh and Carteret and Wallis, Bougainville and La Pérouse, Kerguelen and Marion du Fresne. There are signs that a generation which has learned to concern itself, however superficially, with ecology may redress this balance, and teach us that we cannot know the European Enlightenment unless we know its navigators and hydrographers, who are necessarily also its first 'experimental' ethnologists and zoologists. It is high time. And the consequences may be extraordinary and astonishing. What happens, for instance, to our image of 'the age of sensibility', if we try to accommodate, as a massive and defining enterprise of that age, the most momentous and heroically sustained navigations of all, the three voyages of Captain James Cook? What does Cook amount to, in the image that we make for ourselves of that Europe of the 1760s and 1770s which Cook departed from, and returned to? So far as I am aware, the question has been put, and a tentative answer to it has been ventured, by only one scholar – by J.C. Beaglehole, whose magnificent erudition on everything that concerns the great hydrographer is monumentally summed up in his great editions of Cook's Journals. Beaglehole, more than any one else, has the right to put the question:

> He was not a tortured Titan, like Dr. Johnson; or charming, like Goldsmith; or witty, like Sheridan; or profound, like Henry Cavendish or Burke; or dashing, like Wolfe; he did not build an empire, like Warren Hastings, or maintain a vast correspondence, like Horace Walpole. Shall we then say he had a plain heroic magnitude, and let it go at that? Or shall we give a list of the virtues taught by the sea, and picture him as a character out of a Conrad novel, a serious sailor, a survivor of typhoons, a large-scale rendering of Fidelity? No; because although he had that

> sort of mind, and was serious, and faithful, and came through if not typhoons, at least a great deal of very bad weather, it is possible to be all that, and do all that, and yet be rather stupid; and Cook was by no means stupid. He had, in fact, a first-class brain, a really powerful intellect. He had some originality. I doubt whether he had subtlety. But I don't know. He was a late developer, and he was killed when he was fifty.[1]

Where Professor Beaglehole doesn't know, we can safely assert that no one else will. Cook's reticence and reserve will preserve him as an enigma. But after all, he did not sail alone. And no one can think of the Royal Navy in the eighteenth century as a closed corporation, pursuing a way of life and of the mind sealed off, by special tradition, from life and ideas in that England and that Europe which Cook and his shipmates conceived themselves to be serving and enlightening. We cannot think this if we note, as the most obvious instance out of several that could be cited, the presence on Cook's last and fatal journey of Lieutenant James Burney, Charles Burney's son and Fanny Burney's brother. New Zealand and Polynesia and Antarctica, Nootka Sound and the Bering Straits – these were exciting new additions to the map of the world which the Age of Sensibility conceived itself as inhabiting, as much in Versailles or St Petersburg as in London.

Here I shall be concerned with one in particular of Cook's shipmates on the third voyage, Corporal of Marines John Ledyard. Ledyard's account of Cook's third voyage is notable in the first place as the only one written by an American. Ledyard indeed appears to have been the only American to sail with Cook on his last voyage, with the notable exception of the Virginian John Gore, who in 1780, at the height of the Revolutionary War, commanded the entire expedition on its way back to London, after the death in Kamchatka (hardly less heroic than Cook's own) of Captain Charles Clerke, on whom the command had devolved after Cook's assassination by the Hawaiians the year before.

Ledyard, writing for his fellow Americans at a time when they were at war with England, was perhaps anxious to show his American loyalties by dissociating himself from the English captain he had served under. So much, at least, has been supposed ever since Jefferson, in his *Autobiography* (1821) credited Ledyard with having vouchsafed 'details unfavorable to Cook's deportment towards the savages, and lessening our regrets at his fate'. And accordingly

[1] See J.C. Beaglehole, 'On the Character of Captain James Cook', *The Geographical Journal* CXXII: 4 (December 1956), pp.417-29.

British hagiographers of Cook, in so far as they notice Ledyard's account at all, are hostile towards it and him. Alan Villiers, for instance, (*Captain James Cook*, New York, 1967), is comically vituperative in a footnote: 'The family papers of the Ledyards, now at the University of Syracuse, indicate that the corporal was not highly thought of by anyone. Apart from having been once with Cook, his chief claim to fame seems to be the fact that he was probably the first American citizen deported from Russia for spying.' What Villiers alludes to here is Ledyard's later exploit in 1787 and 1788 when, having failed to raise the funds that would have taken him back by sea to the Northwestern America he had glimpsed with Cook, Ledyard, under the characteristically guarded patronage of Jefferson and with funds supplied largely by Sir Joseph Banks and others in London, got two-thirds of the way back to the American North-West the long way round, by land through the Siberian provinces of Catherine the Great. Balked by Catherine, whose police picked him up in Yakutsk and rushed him through Asiatic and European Russia to dump him in Poland, Ledyard found his way back to London and perished the next year in Cairo, on the eve of a new expedition, funded once again by Banks and his associates, to find the headwaters of the Niger.

Such a bare outline of Ledyard's inconclusive career suggests that, more than any other of Cook's shipmates except perhaps William Bligh, Ledyard may be taken as a surrogate for the great navigator himself, by students who apply themselves to the question why and how the Age of Sensibility could also have been a great age of global exploration. In this respect, his importance is enhanced when we recognize that Ledyard is as articulate, or at all events as garrulous, about the imaginative significance of his travelling as Cook was reticent. And yet not Villiers alone but almost any student of the great Cook will be affronted by this suggestion that Captain Cook and Corporal Ledyard had anything in common, imaginatively. And it is hard not to sympathize with them, in the face of any one of the many passages of singular fatuity that Ledyard perpetrated, in his account of Cook's last voyage. From among several beguiling and hilarious instances, I select one, which tells of a night's stay by Ledyard, in June 1777, in the home of a Tongan chief whom he calls Polahow:

> As soon as Polahow had lain down, the girl approached him and spread the cloth over him after which she sat down behind him as he lay upon his side and began one of the most extraordinary operations I ever before had seen or heard of, which was pating [*sic*] him on the posteriors with the palms and back of her hands

> alternately in a constant and quick succession of gentle strokes which she continued with unremitted uniformity and celerity until she found her lord fast a sleep when she gently rose and went off. This performance lasted about three quarters of an hour and both the novelty of it and the situation I was in respecting a variety of objects and sentiments left me in a kind of listless reverie. Whether this ceremony respected Polahow merely as a mark of distinction, or whether the operation was applied as a provocative to certain passions – as a lulaby [*sic*] to sleep, or to assuage the embarrassments he was under in that altitude from his asthmatic complains I cannot determine. It is true said I, rising from my reverie and walking out into the middle of the green in the full moonshine, where I could extend my prospects and where the sounds that preceded from the circumventulating flutes would more regularly pass the ear. – It is true, that of all the animals from the polypus to man, the latter is the most happy and the most wretched, dancing through life between these two extremes, he sticks his head among the stars, or his nose in the earth, or suspended by a cobweb in some middle altitude he hangs like a being indigenous to no sphere or unfit for any, or like these Indians he is happy because he is insensible of it or takes no pains to be so.[1]

Full moonshine, indeed! No wonder if, faced with such passages, a commentator like Alan Villiers is provoked into playing the bluff seaman and into dismissing Ledyard as an unstable character. A further example may show how 'unstable' is indeed the word for Ledyard's precariously veering rhetoric. This concerns one of Polahow's Tongan peers, Phenow:

> If we lost any goods, and they were carried either in land upon Tongotaboo or to any of the detached islands our only confidential resource was Phenow; or if any other emergency required dispatch, policy, courage or force, Phenow was the man to advice [*sic*] and act. In short, without his particular assistance joined to that of Polahow our visit at this large populous island would have been one continual broil proceeding from the pilfering disposition of the inhabitants, our methods of obtaining satisfaction and their tumultuous and factious dispositions: But that my accounts of these two noble Indians may be entirely true and impartial. [*sic*] I must observe that notwithstanding this general attachment to our interest and friendship, which did them so

[1] J.K. Mumford (ed.) *John Ledyard's Journal of Captain Cook's Last Voyage* (Corvallis, Oregon, 1963), pp.32–3. All subsequent quotations from Ledyard's Journal of Cook's voyage are from this edition.

> much honor, and us so much essential service, they sometimes fell into temptation themselves and did as the others did. How often, Phenow, have I felt for thee, the embarrassments of these involuntary offences against a people thou didst as well love and wouldst as soon have befriended when thou wast accused and stood condemned as when not, and at that instant would most willingly have shared with thee those distresses which resulted only from imputed guilt and a theory of moral virtue thou couldst be no farther acquainted with, than from the dictates of uncultivated nature or imagine from the countenance of strangers – more savage themselves with all their improvements than thou wert without a single one of them.[1]

The literary ancestry of this sort of writing is manifest. And if we want supporting evidence, it was supplied as long ago as 1946, by Helen Augur, telling of Ledyard's return to his native Connecticut in 1782:

> He had escaped from the British at Huntington Bay, on the strength of a week's leave. Most of his books were left behind on the frigate, but he managed to bring along Sterne's works. *Tristram Shandy* and the rest were about all he had to show for nearly six years in the Royal Navy, and Sterne for a time was to demoralize his unformed style and encourage him to use dashes whenever syntax failed him – which was all too often.[2]

On the evidence of Ledyard's style, if *Tristram Shandy* was indeed among his books, it may have been less well-thumbed than *A Sentimental Journey*. But equally on that evidence his manual of style could have been a volume which by 1782 had reached a fourth edition, *THE BEAUTIES OF STERNE: including all his Pathetic Tales, and most distinguished OBSERVATIONS on LIFE. Selected for the Heart of Sensibility*.

In a challenging and too little regarded passage of modern criticism, Q.D. Leavis has remarked of this production that 'it proves how much easier it was found to read Sterne for the wrong reasons than for the right ones – that is, to make a partial instead of a complete response.' Mrs Leavis quotes from the preface by the compiler: 'I intended to have arranged them alphabetically, till I found the stories of *Le Fever*, the *Monk*, and *Maria*, would be too closely connected for the *feeling reader*, and would wound the bosom of *sensibility* too

[1] *Ibid.*, pp.28-9.

[2] Helen Augur, *Passage to Glory. John Ledyard's America* (New York, 1946), p.115.

deeply: I therefore placed them at a proper distance from each other.'[1] And she points out acutely that whereas in the originals 'Sterne requires careful and persevering reading,' of such an anthology of excerpts this is not true: 'The heart of sensibility could be as satisfactorily catered for by Henry Mackenzie, who separated out of Sterne's balanced whole the most popular elements. In consequence, whereas to read *Tristram Shandy* is a bracing mental exercise, *The Man of Feeling* represents only a refined form of emotional self-indulgence.'[2] Just and properly astringent as that distinction is, a case such as Ledyard's shows that it is necessary, when thus using evidence of reading habits and literary influence to diagnose the emotional hygiene of a society, to allow for special circumstances. For habits of 'emotional self-indulgence' would surely have sapped and destroyed both the shrewdness of judgement, and the perseverance in resolute action, which Ledyard displayed both on the expedition with Cook and on his later astonishing journey through Siberia.

Of course the shrewdness, and perhaps the resolution also, are just what students like Alan Villiers will deny. And although this is not the place to attempt a full-scale vindication of Ledyard's treatment of Cook, I must digress far enough to touch on the main bones of contention. To begin with, Jefferson's observation of 'details unfavorable to Cook's deportment towards the savages' fits at least one other first-hand account as well as Ledyard's. This is the anonymous *Journal of Captain Cook's Last Voyage to the Pacific Ocean on Discovery; Performed in the Years 1776, 1777, 1778, 1779.* (Ld. 1781, Philadelphia 1783). As late as 1930 this was still being attributed to Ledyard, though in 1921 F.W. Howay had conclusively identified the author as John Rickman, 2nd Lieutenant of Cook's sister-ship *Discovery*.[3] Of Cook's behaviour towards the natives in Tonga, whereas Ledyard says that 'perhaps no considerations will excuse the severity which he sometimes used' (p.38), Rickman, after citing particular cases, speaks of 'wanton acts of cruelty'. Again, Ledyard passes over in silence some discontents that we know of from other sources – for instance from Zimmermann, recording the reaction of the crewmen to a scare that all had in the Aleutians on 27/28 June 1778. A rather different complaint is the allegation that Ledyard alone of the commentators presents Cook as jealous of his predecessor

1 See Q.D. Leavis, *Fiction and the Reading Public* (London, 1939), pp.134–5.

2 *Ibid.*

3 F.W. Howay, 'Authorship of Anonymous Account of Captain Cook's Last Voyage', *Washington Historical Quarterly* XII (January 1921), pp.51 ff. For Rickman's text, see *Journal of Captain Cook's Last Voyage to the Pacific Ocean by John Rickman* (Ann Arbor, University Microfilms Inc., 1966).

in exploring the North-West, the Danish navigator in the Russian service, Vitus Behring; this will not survive a reading of the passage in question (pp.99-100), where Ledyard is taking 'envy' in its eighteenth-century sense of 'grudging captiousness', and so far from attributing this to Cook, Ledyard is at pains to clear any taint of it from himself.

Indeed it may be argued very plausibly that Ledyard's admiration of Cook emerges vividly and consistently. For instance, far more than Rickman or any other of the chroniclers, Ledyard (pp.61-4) conveys the war of nerves which Cook sustained with the Society Islanders of Raiatea, in order to get back his deserters, Harrison, Shaw and Midshipman Mouat; he graphically records (pp.72-3) Cook's admiring compliance with the Nootka Sound Indians, when he found they were not to be bullied out of a jealous sense of the sanctity of property, their own and others'; and Cook's hold upon the loyalties of the lower deck is nowhere instanced so compellingly as where Ledyard (pp.87-8) shows him insisting, in the Arctic Ocean, on a diet of walrus-meat:

> On the 19th we lay to among the ice, and sent the boats on the ice to hunt the sea-horse. Killed several and brought them on board, but it was thought an ill reward for their labor by the people when they understood that the short pittance of European food was to be withheld from them, and this substituted in its room. But Cook was determined upon the point, and set the example himself by making it his constant food while it lasted. The people at first murmered, and at last eat it through mere vexation; and trying to see who would eat most of it in order to consume it the sooner, some of the people rather overdid the matter, which producing some laughable circumstances, the Tars swore they would eat it or any thing else that Cook did, for they were certain that nothing would kill him in the heavens above or the earth beneath or in the waters under the earth.

This shows how unassumingly direct and racy Ledyard can be when he forgets his Sternean pretensions. Moreover, the blasphemously Scriptural allusion in the last sentence – reported by Ledyard without reprobation – will seem odd only to those who have made much of his brief and unsuccessful spell as a theological student. There is no evidence that this had been at all momentous for Ledyard; still less, that the New Englander's Christianity was in any way fanatical, or even notably pious. Equally there is no hint in Ledyard's narrative of the opinion, subsequently common among the pious (and first announced, so far as I am aware, in a letter of 1784 from Cowper to John Newton), that Cook invited his own destruction by a jealous

God when he presumptuously permitted the Hawaiians to treat him as divine.

These are the main heads of a defence of Ledyard against the allegations that in his treatment of Cook he was mean-minded or spiteful. To prove that he was shrewd and perceptive, we need only look again at the second of two passages quoted earlier, where behind the incongruous rhetoric ('How often, Phenow, have I felt for thee...') there is quite plainly a strenuous attempt to do justice to all the conflicting claims upon the Tongan chieftains as they try to co-operate with the Englishmen against the grain of an inherited scheme of values in which property was something less than sacred. Ledyard's punctuation and syntax break apart precisely because, as a pioneer anthropologist in the field, he is trying to think in terms of a cultural relativism which involves more variables than the eighteenth-century periodic sentence is equipped to allow for, at least in such unpractised hands as his. But in any case Ledyard's shrewdness appears in his treatment of the crucial question of Cook's behaviour towards the Hawaiians. On this matter, where Ledyard's narrative differs most crucially from all others is in the account he gives (pp. 136-7) of how Cook secured for firewood the fence and idols from the *morai*, the sacred or ceremonial enclosure. King and Ellis, Zimmermann and Rickman,[1] all maintain that this removal was a matter of indifference to the Hawaiians, or at least that Cook struck an amicable bargain with them. Ledyard's allegation, that on the contrary Cook was high-handed and contemptuously over-rode the Hawaiians' religious misgivings, was taken up from Jared Sparks's biography of Ledyard (1828) by the nineteenth-century American missionaries in the islands, who discredited Cook as a matter of policy. Ledyard's testimony being so much at odds with all others is certainly a suspicious circumstance, and our confidence in him is not strengthened when we find him (pp. 137-9) discrediting the other commander, Clerke, with a story that is similarly absent from all other accounts. On the other hand we cannot rule out the possibility of a benevolent conspiracy among the other writers, perhaps tacit and unformulated, to whitewash in retrospect both their martyred heroes. Moreover, as James King himself realized, it is inherently improbable that the Hawaiians should have been so indifferent to the desecration of their sanctuary as the received British account requires them to have been. As all the impartial historians

[1] Cook and King, *A Voyage to the Pacific Ocean*... Vol. III (London, 1784); William Ellis, *An Authentic Narrative of a Voyage Performed by Captain Cooke and Captain Clerke* (2nd edn, London, 1783); F.W. Howay (ed.), *Zimmermann's Captain Cook* (Toronto, 1930); Rickman, *op. cit.*

have realized, there is a large blur of dubiety about this whole episode, a mystery which at this distance in time is not going to be cleared up. Ledyard, however, does throw important light on the tangle, in a way which has gone unnoticed. Very shrewdly he explains (p.136) one reason why Cook's judgement about the Hawaiians should have been at fault, as in the event it too plainly and tragically was: because of the ceremoniousness with which the commanders were entertained throughout their stay, and the rigid stratification of Hawaiian feudal society, Cook, moving exclusively in the circles of the native aristocracy and priesthood, was unable to gauge the increasingly resentful temper of the Hawaiian populace at large – a resentment which Corporal Ledyard, assigned to working parties ashore which were increasingly molested, was very well aware of. If true this is a very important circumstance, which clears up otherwise inexplicable contradictions among the various accounts. (Incidentally, the one man who bridged the gap between quarterdeck and foc's'le on this issue was Lieutenant King, as Ledyard's narrative acknowledges – and King's conduct, though certainly honourable, may not have been altogether responsible: either he didn't warn Cook of the popular resentment growing, or else he did and Cook pooh-poohed it.)

Thus throughout the pages dealing with the return to Hawaii and with Cook's death there, Ledyard gives the impression of being remarkably judicious and level-headed. And before reaching the point (p.170) at which he virtually abandons composition and begins to reproduce Rickman's account without acknowledgement, Ledyard gives conclusive proof of his astuteness and good sense in a remarkably enlightened and scrupulous discussion (pp.157–63) of the question whether Polynesia was peopled from Asia or from America – precisely the problem nowadays much canvassed afresh because of the writings and explorations of Thor Heyerdahl.

The puzzle remains, of the rhetorical flights of singular silliness. For instance (p.55):

> If the system of transmigration forms any part of the Otaheitean religion, it is likly [*sic*] to compose a considerable part, if not the whole of it; if it can be reduced to any system at all. One argument is its universality and strict observance among the people, and another is, that all of the customs of mankind appear to be derivative and traditionary, and that this system in religion exists in Asia, from whence it is probable it emigrated with the people, and that this sentiment, where it does exist, and originally did exist, does, and originally did form a system as materially distinct from any other as systems generally are and perhaps more so as

> the combination of those sentiments which form it were when primarily promulgated the most wild fanciful, innocent, mischievous, subtile, and therefore the most curious opinions that ever entered the head of that child of contradictions, so well known by the name of Man to conceive of: Why what amazing quantities of beef, mutton, port, and fowl hath it saved in Indostan; and on the other hand how hath it increased the prolific generation of flies, musquetos, batts, tarantulas, toads and snakes: Are not the plains of Siam, Pegu and Aracan rendered the most delectable spots on earth by it?

Disconcerted as we are by the ponderous pointlessness of a passage such as this, at least it becomes clear, after reviewing Ledyard's *Journal* as a whole, that Mrs Leavis's diagnosis – 'emotional self-indulgence' – is not the only one possible. A better explanation would be that these passages occur because the writer is trying, needlessly, to compensate for what he believes to be his provincialism, congestedly heaping together irrelevant information to show that he has it, making qualifications merely to show that he can do so, and trying for ponderous ironies in the interests of an urbanity he does not possess and does not need. From this point of view we may say that Ledyard drew upon this decadent and ultimately fatuous idiom, not because he deliberately chose it from among others but because it was the only idiom he knew of that would serve his purpose, however imperfectly. This is to endorse, not just as graceful and generous, but as the only statement which takes account of all the facts, Burney's remarks on how Ledyard, and his literary style, were regarded by his shipmates:

> His ideas were thought too sentimental, and his language too florid. No one, however, doubted that his feelings were in accord with his expressions; and the same is to be said of the little which remains of what he has since written more worthy of being preserved, and which its worthiness will preserve, and particularly of his celebrated commendation of women in his Siberian Tour.[1]

The admirable Burney even allows for Ledyard's provincialism, or his sense of himself as provincial, when he starts his account: '*With what education I know not*, but with an ardent disposition...' (my italics).

As Burney points out, Sternean eloquence is to be found also in Ledyard's journals of his later travels through Siberia, though these

[1] Captain James Burney, *A Chronological History of North-Eastern Voyages of Discovery; and of the Early Eastern Navigations of the Russians* (London, 1819) – quoted by Munford, *op. cit.*, p.xxxi.

survive only imperfectly. At one point indeed a Sternean apostrophe invokes the master by name: 'Sherlock! Tillotson! Sterne! what a Revolution would your sermons produce among such a people.'[1] And Ledyard employs a more audacious and distinctive Sternean device when (p.192), having commented intelligently on Siberian shamanism and its affinities with priestcraft in more advanced societies, he leaves a sentence incomplete, and goes on:

> I leave this Blank for him to fill up that can do it without blushing: & the following vacant Page I leave a blank for the animadversions of an honest Man on the religious sentiment above-mentioned informing such at the same time that the sentiment affects immediately all the Religions of savage America & savage Asia, and collaterally that of every untutored human being.

Ledyard's sharpness towards the shamans will serve as an instance of how far he is from idealizing the primitive peoples that he studies. Though his addiction to the idiom of 'sensibility' sometimes traps him into the vocabulary of those who extolled the noble savage, in fact he never endorses that uncritical and unscientific attitude towards primitive societies. On the contrary, as an ethnologist and anthropologist Ledyard's record is distinguished;[2] detecting the ethnic unity of the Siberian peoples with the Amerindians, he contends that the migration was from Asia to America, not the other way round – a contention which is of course borne out by subsequent opinion, though in Ledyard's time it involved contradicting the massive authority of Buffon (as Jefferson had had to do, in *Notes on the State of Virginia*).

In the Siberian journals the Sternean passages are less obtrusive and therefore less foolish. It may be that Ledyard, if he had lived to polish these writings for publication, would have 'worked them up' offensively. And yet the commendation of women to which Burney refers (pp.182-3) is written in a much more sober and affecting style, Wordsworthian (almost) rather than Sternean.[3] But in broader terms (and far more significantly as regards literary judgements in general), such passages of Sternean eloquence as *do* appear in the Siberian journals are comparatively inoffensive, precisely

[1] Stephen D. Watrous, *John Ledyard's Journey through Russia and Siberia 1787-1788. The Journal and Selected Letters* (Madison, Milwaukee & London, 1966), p.182. All subsequent references to the Siberian Journal are to this edition.

[2] See Sanford H. Bederman, *The Ethnological Contributions of John Ledyard* (Atlanta, 1964).

[3] It is odd that Burney in 1819 could describe this passage as 'celebrated'. So far as I can determine it could be read at that date only in the MS journal, since lost, which Ledyard sent back to Sir Joseph Banks and his other sponsors in London.

because we as sympathetic readers come to share Ledyard's desperations, which accordingly validate the fever-pitch which the Sternean rhetoric requires. After a while, as we sympathize with Ledyard's disappointments and admire his perseverance through them, the apostrophes and exclamations come to seem less and less conventional.

Even before the Empress has countermanded her in any case tacit permission for Ledyard to travel through her realms, we – doubtless because we know in advance that this final blow is impending – find that we can tolerate, and even be moved by, a passage so rhetorically heightened as to be more than half-way into rhymed verse. This comes (pp.167–8) when Ledyard, at Yakutsk in September 1787, learns that he has no hope of pressing forward to the Pacific that season:

> My funds! I have but two long frozen stages more and I shall be beyond the want or aid of money, until emerging from her deep deserts I gain the American Atlantic States and then thy glowing Climates.* Africa explored, I lay me down and claim a little portion of the Globe I've viewed – may it not be before. How many of the noble minded have been subsidiary to me or to my enterprizes: and yet that meagre devil POVERTY who hand in hand has travelled with me o'r half the globe – and witnessed what Oh ye feeling Souls! – the tale I'll not unfold – 'twould break the fibrils of your gentle hearts. Ye sons of enervating Luxury ye Children of wealth and idleness! what profitable Commerce might be made between us, had you the will, and I the power to enter on the trade. A little of my toil might better brace your nerves. [*sic*] give spring to mind, and zest to your enjoyments and a very little of that wealth you scatter round you, would put it beyond the powers of any thing but death to oppose my kindred greetings with all on earth that bear the stamp of man. This is the third time I have been overtaken and arrested by winter and in both the others by giving time for my *evil genius* to rally her hosts about me have defeated the Enterprize. Fortune thou hast humbled me at length, for I am at this moment the slave of cowardly solicitude, least in the womb of this dread winter, there lurks the seeds of disappointment to my ardent desire of gaining the opposite Continent. I submit and proceed with my remarks . . .

After the blow has fallen, and Ledyard has been carried back across Russia, and dumped in Poland to make his own way westward, there is something heroic about his attempting that dubiously useful

* The word 'Africa' seems to be needed here to make sense of this sentence.

but curious and distinctive effect of Sterne's *Sentimental Journey* – the union of elevated humanitarian sentiment with erotic suggestiveness. This seems to have been Ledyard's intention in a passage (pp.209-10) about the Jewish women in Poland:

> ... The Jewish Women have beautiful Complexions. A fine Skin and as happy a mixture of Colour as ever I saw; long black Hair which among the Demoiselles hangs down behind in one and sometimes two plaits, the rest is hid, as the Married Women do all theirs under one or more Handkerchiefs. They have large full Jet black Eyes which like all others of that Sort rather surprize than convince me into the Idea of Beauty. They have good Teeth and some very pretty Features. But I am disgusted the Moment I view a horrid clumsy, large coarse dirty Hand; this added to their uniform filth, and now and then the Itch – I know nothing of their shapes; I regret it, but they are disguized under a vile Eastern Dress. The Child of damned Jealousy or damned Superstition called into existence expressly to turn the Eyes of Man from viewing a Work of Nature as expressly formed to attract Attention, Admiration Esteem & Love.

The questionable value of such a psychological manoeuvre, and even the silliness of it, morally and emotionally – these seem irrelevant matters in the context of a life so *driven* as Ledyard's was by this time.

And there comes a moment of the strangest, most piercing pathos, at Vilno in 1788. It is quite without parallel, I think. At this point (p.212) Ledyard discovers that the *persona* of the capriciously egotistical narrator – a crucial convention for the narration of *Tristram Shandy* or *A Sentimental Journey* – is necessary to him, Ledyard, not just as a writer but as a man, if he is to persist in his chosen destiny. Deflected time and again – by circumstances, by misfortune, and by the fickleness of men and women in power – from pursuing his chosen role as philosophical traveller, he finds that only a capricious wilfulness in himself can sustain it:

> I am constantly thinking about Hills, or something else of the Kind and as my thoughts are all my own I write what I think without knowing whether it is of Importance or not & leave others to judge of it being convinced only of this that I ought to write if I think so, and that it is better to write many pages in vain than that one of Service to Mankind should not be written. – I make this remark once for all to inform my Friends that I am sensible of my humble Genius but not ashamed of it, & to intimate to them that I wish them to deal with me with the same honest careless freedom I do with them. to be damned is no torment

> to the Guilty, & to enjoy fame is no happiness to him who is not convinced he merits it.

This I take to be a poignant example of how a literary convention, in itself and in its origins only dubiously respectable, can become, in the case of a life lived through with unnatural consistency, a sustaining style or idiom for *living*.

A poet of our own day has seen a little further still into Ledyard's case. In his poem, 'Ledyard. The Exhaustion of Sheer Distance', Edward Dorn says to the shade of Ledyard, 'Mystic sheer distance was in thine eye'.[1] And as I read Dorn's poem he means by this that in the end Ledyard was not exploring any terrain except that of his own human nature; that what drew him was travelling as such, travelling as one possible human condition which, if explored with imagination, would reveal something about what the human condition is, necessarily and in general. We are indebted to Watrous for printing a document which indeed appears to substantiate Edward Dorn's sympathetic perception. This is a letter from Yakutsk dated 22 October 1787, to one of Ledyard's sponsors, the American Colonel William S. Smith. And the crucial passage (Watrous, pp.137-8) is one in which Ledyard writes 'to be traveling is to be in error'.[2] The passage is confused, for by this point Ledyard's travelling answers to Bernard de Voto's description, 'Ledyard's frenzied, tragic, and the truth is half-mad, journey.'[3] But is clear that Ledyard is teasing out the puns which link 'error' through 'errant' with 'wandering', and that the landscape through which he errs is no longer Siberia but the epistemological landscape through which one seeks for certain knowledge and self-knowledge. If one accepts Harold Bloom's persuasive idea that we can properly speak of Romanticism in literature as the stage at which the traditional motif of 'the quest' is internalized, then we are able to say that when Ledyard reached these perceptions he had pushed 'sensibility' to the point at which it turns into Romanticism; the point where the self is displayed, no longer for approbation or self-approbation, nor as a model to be

[1] See Edward Dorn, *Hands Up!* (New York, 1964).

[2] '. . . & I will declare that I never was so totaly at loss how to accommodate myself to my situation. The only consolation I have of the argumentative kind is to reflect that him who travels for information must be supposed to want it, and though a little enigmatical it is I think equaly true that to be traveling is to be in error: that this must more or less necessarily anticede the other, and that an error in judgment only, is always to be forgiven.'

[3] Bernard de Voto, *The Course of Empire* (Boston, 1952), p.299.

followed, but wonderingly, as an enigmatic terrain to be explored. Ledyard was a manifestly incompetent writer; but behind the disorder of his writing we perceive, indubitably, an intelligent, intensely serious and responsible individual. He deserves the epitaph which Edward Dorn finds for him:

> Mystic sheer distance was in thine eye,
> that beautiful abstract reckoning,
> the feet, walking: for no other reason
> the world.

No one can gainsay us if we speculate that the epitaph might have fitted James Cook no less.

Eighteenth Century Studies IV: 1 (fall 1970).

16 *The Critical Principles of William Cowper*

After Ben Jonson, Cowper is the most neglected of our poets. It was Hayley's *Life and Letters* that set the fashion; ever since, no poet has been surrendered so frequently, and with so little compunction, to the tender mercies of the biographer. Such criticism as there is has labelled Cowper 'Romantic precursor'; and it seems that we read his poems only to discover in them things that have been done better since, by Wordsworth or some other. No one will deny that the Wordsworthian and other potentialities are there, but they are surely not the most important things in Cowper's poetry. His work is far more the consummation of one tradition than the prelude to another. 'What is salt in Cowper you can taste only when you have detected that by a stroke of madness he missed, or barely missed, being our true English Horace, that almost more nearly than the rest he hit what the rest had been seeking.'[1] He was very consciously and deliberately a neo-classical poet.

He was, if anything, a defiant rearguard. Already, by the time he wrote, the neo-classical austerity was rare, and the taste was all for florid diction, the sublime, a syrupy metrical smoothness, and melting sensibility. His critical conservatism is apparent enough in the poems that are not read, such as 'Truth', 'Table-talk' and 'Retirement'. It is also apparent in the letters, along with the famous (and genuine) charm; but criticism in the letters is sparse and scattered, and it is only when a number of random judgements are put together, that one sees the consistency of Cowper's conservatism:

For a first exhibit, we may take the lines on Johnson:

> Here Johnson lies – a sage by all allow'd,
> Whom to have bred may well make England proud;
> Whose prose was eloquence, by wisdom taught,
> The graceful vehicle of virtuous thought;

[1] Sir Arthur Quiller-Couch, 'On the Lineage of English Literature'. *On the Art of Writing*, (London, 1916), p.127.

Whose verse may claim – grave, masculine, and strong,
Superior praise to the mere poet's song;

The word 'strong' is not there just for the rhyme; it means something exact. Jeffreys was to say, of some 'very sweet verses' by Rogers, 'They do not, indeed, stir the spirit like the strong lines of Byron'. Going along with 'grave' and 'masculine', Cowper's 'strong' cannot mean anything like that; it means, in fact, 'the strength of Denham', which Johnson had himself described, writing of that poet. By way of proof, one need only point to another complimentary poem, Cowper's stanzas 'To Dr. Darwin, author of *The Botanic Garden*':

We, therefore, pleas'd, extol thy song,
  Though various, yet complete,
Rich in embellishment as strong,
  And learn'd, as it is sweet.

For here, very neatly, Darwin is complimented on his 'strength' in lines which echo most plainly just those hackneyed lines from 'Cooper's Hill' which were taken by Johnson, and indeed by the whole eighteenth century, as the model of that strength.

If there is a master-key to the principles of Augustan poetry (still so little understood), it is Johnson's 'Life of Denham'. There Johnson's description and illustration of 'strength' is masterly; and it would be presumptuous to offer a paraphrase. 'Strength' is a name given to a certain quality of 'compactness' in expression. 'Compactness' is Cowper's word, and we do well to adopt it instead of 'concentration', which is more familiar. Concentration of expression is a form of words which we commonly use when meanings lie one upon another in layers, or sail one above another on different planes. This is the world of William Empson's ambiguities and Cleanth Brooks's ironies. Their characteristic metaphors – meanings in 'layers', meanings on 'levels' – are valuable. But they are not much use when we deal with the Augustans. 'The Castaway' is probably the only poem by Cowper which will respond to treatment in these terms; and it is no coincidence that 'The Castaway' is probably read today far more than any other poem by Cowper, except perhaps 'John Gilpin'. It is a great poem; but it stands alone in Cowper's work. It is in 'a class by itself', but not because it shows Cowper excelling himself, only because it shows him writing in an unusual mode. Layers and levels are not much use, in reading the rest of Cowper; there are only two layers ('tenor' and 'vehicle'), and only one level. His poetry like Denham's is uni-vocal. Its characteristic virtue is the saying one thing at a time as succinctly as possible; not the saying of many things at once. The metaphor here is of a more or less rigid metrical box, into which, by syntactical expertness, an astonishing number of things can be lodged – all of them distinct, all inter-locking. This is the meaning of 'strength'.

By showing that Cowper appeals to 'the strength of Denham', we place him in the tradition not of Johnson alone, but of Pope and Dryden, both of whom appealed back to Denham in the same way. In fact of course the tradition was much older; Carew, long before, had extolled Donne as 'masculine', and Suckling had told Godolphin 'not to write so strong'. Strength did not appear with Denham; he only displayed it precociously, in a form suited for the things Dryden wanted to do. At any rate, for Dryden and for Pope, as is well known, this aspect of their art, represented by Denham, went together with another, represented by Waller, who stood for metrical correctness. In their view, the Denham element was a complement to the Waller element, and vice-versa. Not that the one led naturally into the other; on the contrary, there was tension between them. It was difficult to follow both of them at once, and so, in trying to do so, the poet generated the energy which could give his writing grit and force. Waller stood for the rigidity of the metrical box; the more rigid the metrical frame, the harder it was to pack it as full as Denham did. Conversely it was easy to be as smooth as Waller so long as one was diffuse; the one model counteracted the other.

The lines to Darwin show Cowper taking just these bearings, as Dryden and Pope had done; for 'sweet' stands for Waller, just as 'strong' stands for Denham. It is true, however, that Cowper's view of metre was not Pope's. In passage after passage,[1] he deplored the vicious taste of his time for a cloying smoothness in cadence, and insisted on a certain roughness in metre, a redundant syllable or a reversed foot. So, although no poet (not even Hopkins) was more an admirer of Milton, he deliberately rejected the Miltonic model for his own blank-verse.[2] Similarly, in a well-known passage in 'Table Talk' he censures Pope for reducing English versification to a mechanical technique. On the other hand (what is less often remembered) he has just implied that this worked for Pope precisely because he was so 'compact'. In other words, Pope could afford to be smooth in a rather obvious way, just because he was so 'strong'; Cowper and his contemporaries, he says, have to make their music less obvious because they can't rival Pope in closely packing their matter. The two criteria are always linked together for Cowper, balancing and checking against each other; but his interpretation of

1 Eg., *Letters*, ed. Hayley (1806), IV, 43, III, 279, II, 341.

2 *Ibid.*, II, 279.

the one criterion, the model of Waller, is nearer to Dryden's view than to Pope's – and in fact he admired Dryden the more.[1]

Strength in the sense of compactness and closeness is nearly always the first gauge that Cowper applies; but 'harmony' or 'music' is nearly always the second. The clearest examples of this two-fold standard occur in the many comments on Homer, when Cowper is occupied with his Homeric translations:

> A story-teller, so very circumstantial as Homer, must of necessity present us often with much matter in itself, capable of no other embellishment than purity of diction, and harmony of versification can give to it. *Hic labor, hic opus est.* For our language, unless it be very severely chastised, has not the terseness, nor our measure the music of the Greek. (*Letters*, III, 13)

A critic who sees in poetic diction no more than a 'certain traditional decorum of language, a necessary convention (and a necessarily changing one) about the use of words in poetry',[2] will be at a loss to understand how the purity of such a diction can be associated with 'terseness'. Indeed, the notion of 'purity' in such a case will seem meaningless, unless it means what the Elizabethans called 'decorum', the proper maintaining of a convention once established. That, indeed, is part of what Cowper and Johnson meant by 'purity'; and another part of their meaning, the part associated with terseness, is, as I have suggested, their concern for 'strength'. But neither of these exhausts the meaning of the term in their criticism. To be 'pure' a diction must maintain the decorum of the convention chosen for a given poem (and, beyond that, decorum also dictated what conventions were proper to different kinds). To be pure, a diction must also sustain comparison, in respect of compactness, with Denham and (later) with Pope. But it must satisfy other requirements; and these others were concerned with the relation between the poet's selected language and the language spoken about him in what was agreed to be the best society.

[1] *Ibid.*, II, 289, 290. cf. 'English Bards and Scotch Reviewers' (Dryden compared with Pope).

> Like him great Dryden pour'd the tide of song,
> In stream less smooth, indeed, yet doubly strong.

To Cowper, Pope's excessive smoothness is redeemed by his incomparable 'strength'; to Byron, Pope is smoother but Dryden stronger. But Byron means by 'strength' what Jeffreys means, not what Cowper has in mind. It is a revealing illustration of how Byron's pretensions to belong to the neo-classic tradition are really quite empty gestures, trailings of a coat.

[2] G.S. Fraser, 'Some Notes on Poetic Diction', *Penguin New Writing*, Number 37 (1949), p.116.

This is the aspect of the matter acknowledged by Cowper when he says that English, the spoken language, must be 'severely chastised' before it is equal to the task of reproducing Homer. This too will strike us as strange. It seems to us that the spoken language was not so much chastened as heightened, in order to produce the Augustan diction. In consequence it is inconvenient to find Cowper admiring Homer for his 'majestic plainness':

> I am truly happy, my dear, in having pleased you with what you have seen of my Homer. I wish that all English readers had your unsophisticated, or rather unadulterated taste, and could relish simplicity like you. But I am well aware, that in this respect, I am under a disadvantage, and, that many, especially many ladies, missing many turns and prettinesses of expression, that they have admired in Pope, will account my translation in those particulars defective. But I comfort myself with the thought, that in reality it is no defect, on the contrary that the want of all such embellishments as do not belong to the original will be one of its principal merits with persons indeed capable of relishing Homer. He is the best poet that ever lived for many reasons, but for none more than for that majestic plainness that distinguishes him from all others. As an accomplished person moves gracefully without thinking of it, in like manner the dignity of Homer seems to cost him no labour. It was natural for him to say great things, and to say them well, and little ornaments were beneath his notice. (*Letters*, II, 362)

He strikes this Wordsworthian note more than once:

> Simplicity is become a very rare quality in a writer. In the decline of great kingdoms, and where refinement in all the arts is carried to an excess, I suppose it is always rare. The latter Roman writers are remarkable for false ornament, they were yet no doubt admired by the readers of their own day; and with respect to authors of the present era, the most popular among them appear to be equally censurable on the same account. Swift and Addison were simple. (*Letters*, II, 146)

Yet in calling this Wordsworthian, it is easy to blur distinctions. It is easy to argue that Cowper certainly is plain by comparison with Pope, but ornate by comparison with Wordsworth, that he stands in an interesting half-way house. This is to make him a Romantic precursor all over again, and it is necessary to insist that while Cowper differs from Pope only in degree, he differs radically from Wordsworth. His Homer is compared with 'an accomplished person', whose ease and simplicity seem natural just because they have been so assiduously worked for. There is no question of dignity and simple eloquence being innate. For Wordsworth, on the other hand, to be genuine these things had to be innate.

In this matter Johnson was more Wordsworthian than Cowper, and Cowper took him to task for it. The occasion was Johnson's 'Life of Prior', a poet whom Cowper much admired:

> His reputation as an author, who, with much labour indeed, but with admirable success, has embellished all his poems with the most charming ease, stood unshaken 'till Johnson thrust his head against it. And how does he attack him in this his principal fort? I cannot recollect his very words, but I am much mistaken indeed, if my memory fails me with respect to the purport of them. 'His words', he says, 'appear to be forced into their proper places. There indeed we find them, but find likewise, that their arrangement has been the effect of constraint, and that without violence, they would certainly have stood in a different order.' By your leave, most learned Doctor, this is the most disingenuous remark I ever met with, and would have come with a better grace from Curl, or Dennis. Every man conversant with verse-writing, knows, and knows by painful experience, that the familiar stile, is of all stiles the most difficult to succeed in. To make verse speak the language of prose, without being prosaic, to marshal the words of it in such an order, as they might naturally take in falling from the lips of an extemporary speaker, yet without meanness; harmoniously, elegantly, and without seeming to displace a syllable for the sake of the rhyme, is one of the most arduous tasks a poet can undertake. He that could accomplish this task was Prior; many have imitated his excellence in this particular, but the best copies have fallen far short of the original. And now to tell us, after we and our fathers have admired him for it so long, that he is an easy writer indeed, but that his ease has an air of stiffness in it, in short, that his ease is not ease, but only something like it, what is it but a self contradiction, an observation that grants what it is just going to deny, and denies what it has just granted, in the same sentence, and in the same breath? (*Letters*, I, 294)

There can be little doubt that Cowper is right; the 'Life of Prior' shows Johnson the critic at his least impressive. It seems likely that the critic was put on edge by Prior's charming licentiousness, in 'Henry and Emma', for instance, which shocked the High-Churchman Johnson, as it did not shock Cowper, the evangelical Calvinist. At any rate, it can hardly be doubted that on Prior Johnson was not just severe, in fact not just at all, but querulous. If we agree as to

Prior, with Johnson rather than Cowper, so much the worse for us; it is time we realized that Prior was not just the Austin Dobson-*de-son-jour*, and I think he deserves all Cowper claims for him – but that is by the way.

The passage is of interest in several ways, apart from presenting Johnson in a careless moment as more of a Romantic precursor than ever Cowper was. In the first place, Cowper's admiration of Prior's ease sets him back, once again, in the strictest neo-classical tradition, along with Dryden. As Cowper stands with Dryden in esteeming 'strength' (for Dryden, Denham; for Cowper, Denham and Pope), and 'correctness' (for Dryden, Waller; for Cowper, Dryden himself); so, with him, he values 'ease', and as Dryden admired Suckling, Cowper admires Prior. Ease should not be identified with metrical smoothness, though smoothness is often an aspect of it. At bottom, the 'ease' esteemed by neo-classical writers is as old as Castiglione; it is a sort of urbane *insouciance*, almost insolence, an attribute of tone in addressing the reader. It is something more stable and more discreet than the raffishness of 'Don Juan', which was the best the Romantics could put in its place. And of course it was something for which Wordsworth, that provincial by conviction, could find no room at all.

The Wordsworthian reference is inevitable, for it is another feature of Cowper's comments on Prior that he here comes as near as ever he does to the Wordsworthian principle that 'There neither is, nor can be . . . any essential difference between the language of prose and of metrical composition'. Cowper admires Prior for having shown, among other things, how 'To make verse speak the language of prose, without being prosaic'. This is an aspect of the neo-classical attitude to literature which is hardly ever understood, indeed seldom noticed. Johnson, no less than Cowper – in fact, the Augustans in general – insisted, as Wordsworth insisted, that the poet had a duty to the spoken language. And, again like Wordsworth, they meant, by 'the spoken language', no Audenesque colloquialism, but the sort of speech to be found reflected in informal prose. But for them this requirement, this duty laid upon the poet, was one among many, others being the observance of decorum, the need for compactness, and metrical felicity. Cowper, for instance, takes account of decorum when he congratulates Prior on his prosaicism at the same time as he distinguishes his style as 'familiar'. Wordsworth, in his criticism, elevated the one criterion at the expense of all others, and in so doing broke down, not only for his own readers but for succeeding generations, a critical mechanism of far greater delicacy, attempting and promising a finer discrimination. Perhaps the mechanism was delicate to no end, ingenious, intricate and ineffective.

If so, it is a monument to the pedantry of not the eighteenth century only, but of the sixteenth and seventeenth also. The reader of poetry who is honest with himself must decide, by deduction from his own readings, whether the writing of poetry is an affair of massive simplicity, or a province where nicety of taste and sureness of judgement is as important as integrity of purpose. In any case there can be no question where Cowper stands. He stands for taste and judgement. In his own eyes, at any rate, he was nobody's precursor, but a poet coming late in an old tradition rich in achievement and based on principles tested in the practice of two centuries.

Cambridge Journal VII: 3 (December 1953).

17 *Personification*

Although this is an academic occasion, I think none of us want to see the academic proprieties observed with any sort of prissy austerity. That was never Freddy Bateson's way. And it would be particularly out of keeping with my sense of him, and my memories. For deeply as I was indebted to him for compliments that he paid to me in my capacities as literary historian and literary critic, what has always weighed more with me is the encouragement that I got from him when I was a beginning poet. And there are other poets among my contemporaries who would say the same. Indeed it was Bateson's virtually unique distinction, in his generation, not just that he never divided poetry as an object of study from poetry as a source of pleasure, but that he always moved from considering a poem of the past as a source of information or of intellectual and imaginative stimulus to thinking of it as a poem *we* might have written or one that might have been written yesterday or last week. And it's in that context, of the here and now, that I want to consider the matter of personification.

Bateson himself characteristically, on that very page of *A Guide to English Literature* which supplies me with a text for my sermon, turns from considering the diction of our eighteenth-century poetry to deliver the mordant aside: 'Such effects have not been possible in more recent poetry, when the poet has all the words in the English dictionary at his beck and call and is allowed to be as long-winded as he likes'. However that may be, the sentences from Bateson that I want to remind you of are these:

> ... the specifically Augustan personifications simply exploit – at their best with great force and economy – a grammatical characteristic of the English language, viz. that a single noun, however abstract or general, must be followed by a verb in the third person singular. The present indicative tense, simply because it distinguishes between its singular and plural forms, inevitably imposes a degree of personification on the single abstract word. (Compare 'war begins' with 'hostilities commence'.) Horace Walpole's comment on Gray's speech compared with the slovenly

> conversation of the London drawing rooms of the time was that 'Mr Gray was so circumspect in his usual language that it seemed unnatural, though it was only pure English'. The case for Augustan personifications could be put in precisely those terms; they may at first seem unnatural, but they are really pure English.

What is particularly valuable here, I think, is Bateson's point, thrown out in passing, that there are *degrees* of personification. This means that we cannot always be sure, and will not always agree among ourselves, when we have a personification and when we haven't. This is necessarily obscured whenever we go for a definition to the Dictionary, for instance to Dr Johnson's of 1755:

> *Personification*, prosopopoeia; the change of things to persons: as, "Confusion heard his voice".

This cannot help but suggest, especially with the help of Johnson's characteristically unequivocal example, that what we have to do with, in 'personification', is a detachable and clearly recognizable *device*, a rhetorical 'figure'. But Bateson's treatment of it goes all the other way, towards recognizing that on the contrary personification is inherent in the very grammatical structure of our language, hence that we 'personify' when we're not aware of doing anything of the sort. Accordingly for our present purposes we may ignore Johnson's offer of 'prosopopoeia', which if we followed it up would reveal that whereas the word 'personification' goes back only to the eighteenth century, the thing it signifies was known under a different name as early as 1578, and of course in other languages than English known also by the Ancients. Whether the grammatical structures of ancient Greek and Latin engendered personification just as the structure of English does – this is an interesting question, and doubtless not hard to answer, but it is not our business. Whatever the classical precedents and models that might be cited, our concern like Bateson's is with personification as a potentiality innate in the structure of English.

Another way of saying this is that if prosopopoeia is indeed a figure of rhetoric, then there is no way for us to use our language, however artless and unpremeditated, that is not *rhetorical*. And if this is so, then our common practice of calling some usages 'rhetorical', as against others that aren't, is wholly unreasonable. H.W. Fowler bears us out in this. In his *Dictionary of Modern English Usage* we read of 'ill-advised personification', with as one example the sentence: 'Just now the world wants all that America can give her in shipping' – where to call the world 'her' rather than 'it' is a personification of the sort that Fowler calls 'ill-advised'. And he says magisterially that to do this 'is to be frigid – the epithet proper to those who make futile attempts at decoration'. Clearly, in Fowler's manual of rhetoric for our times, if there can be ill-advised personification, it follows that there is other personification that is well-advised; as also, that if there is decoration which is 'futile', there must be other decoration which is effectual. And yet, in the language that we use for describing poetry, 'decoration' and 'decorative' are words of very ill omen indeed. This shows how far our sense of poetry has diverged from our sense of rhetoric. And yet frigidity, 'to be frigid', is an expression we surely need to define one sort of poetic fault – an expression we need, yet can hardly use any longer because of its association with rhetoric, though we have fashioned no other word or form of words to do for us what 'frigidity' in this sense once did.

No one needs to be told who got us into this bind. It was Wordsworth and Coleridge 180 years ago who tried to separate poetry from rhetoric; and their endeavour throws a long shadow over the Romantic and post-Romantic generations up to the present day. It is possible to admire them for trying, even as we recognize they were trying to do the impossible.

A few years ago there was a great deal of what was called 'Protest Poetry'. And I was often asked, when I read or lectured, whether Protest Poetry was 'real' poetry. The people who asked were, whether they knew it or not, worrying about whether poetry can be *rhetorical*, and still remain poetry. For rhetoric is the art of persuasion – persuading the audience to adopt some course of action. And plainly this is what protest poetry tries to do, as does propagandist poetry (of which indeed protest poetry is only one not very special variant). Obviously a lot of people think, and have thought for a long time, that this is the responsibility of the public speaker and the journalist and the priest or pastor in his pulpit, not the job of the poet any more than it's the job of the musician or the architect or the painter. We may be ready to agree. But we ought to be quite clear – when we say that people have been thinking like this 'for a long time', we mean: for 150 or 170 years. And in the history of poetry that's a very short time indeed. Earlier than 150 years ago, only very exceptional and eccentric people thought that poetry was 'above' propaganda: to put it bluntly (and over-simplify only a little) for 2000 years before 1800 nobody would have had any trouble with 'protest poetry' as somehow not 'real' poetry. It's only in the last 200 years that this has troubled people. And it's not at all clear that in this matter the last 200 years is wiser than the preceding 2000. In particular we should always beware of contracting still further poetry's sphere of operations, in the interests of some hypothetical 'purity'. To purify and to emasculate can amount to pretty much the same thing.

Moreover (and to come back to our business today) supposedly 'real' poetry and supposedly 'half-real' (protest or propagandist) poetry turn out to use the same tricks of language. As we have seen, personification or prosopopoeia is the name of one such trick of language used by orators and poets alike. In the case of the orator or the protest-poet this is very plain: 'Justice demands that we...' do something, march on the White House perhaps; 'mere Humanity calls upon us to...' do something, perhaps refuse to buy South African oranges. In sentences like these, an abstract quality, 'Justice' or 'Humanity', is made to 'demand' or to 'call upon' us to do something or other; that is to say, these abstractions are made to act in a way which, as a matter of literal fact, only persons can act in. And thus, when we respond to declarations like these (whether we go along with them or repudiate them), at the edge of our consciousness there is a hazy image of a sort of person called Justice or called Humanity – perhaps a stately and bigbreasted lady in a Roman toga, such as we can in fact find sculpted on some of our public buildings, often enough with a helpful label carved beneath her – JUSTITIA or HUMANITAS. For personification (or, prosopopoeia) is found in other arts besides poetry – in sculpture, and sometimes in painting.

Certainly it crops up in poetry that no one would think of as propagandist or protest poetry. Here are three examples, chosen (I assure you) at random and in a matter of minutes:

> So in the failing Life when Death and Dread
> With axe and mongrel stalk the withering wood:...
> (Masefield);

> Most wounds can Time repair;
> But some are mortal... (de la Mare);

> Nor dread nor hope attend
> A dying animal;
> A man awaits his end
> Dreading and hoping all;... (Yeats)

'Death' and 'Dread' in Masefield, 'Time' in de la Mare, 'dread' and 'hope' in Yeats, are surely personifications no less than the propagandist's 'Justice' or 'Humanity'. It so happens that in the not specially authoritative text from which I've culled these examples (*The Chatto Book of Modern Poetry*, 1956) Masefield's and de la Mare's personifications are capitalized, whereas Yeats's 'dread' and 'hope' aren't. But of course personification cannot depend merely on the printer's choice of upper or lower case. In cases like these the degree of personification depends surely on the verb that these nouns govern. In Yeats that verb is 'attend', and it is surely true that the degree of personification will be felt as slight or emphatic according as the reader is or is not apt at recognizing in a Latinate word like 'attend' the vivid image of 'waiting upon'; and so the degree of personification varies not just from one text to another, but from one reader to the next. Thus 'a sneaky wind' and 'inclement weather' will be experienced by one reader as equally personifications, whereas to another reader less apt at construing Latinisms the first expression will seem to involve personification, the second not.

These examples, turning on epithets, show how personification can occur in other figurations of language besides that one which Bateson emphasized, that of noun-plus-verb. Yet that case is the most instructive; and, staying with it, it seems we must say that personification happens whenever an abstract noun is made to govern an active verb such as we normally associate only with a human agent. And thus 'Time will tell' is as much an instance of personification as Johnson's 'Confusion heard his voice'.

'An *abstract* noun', I have said; and here of course we run into another of our hang-ups, one so often exposed that I haven't the patience to spend much time with it. Poetry, we have been told, flies abstractions; its business is with the concrete and the particular. As a rule of thumb for beginning or inexperienced writers this dubious axiom has its usefulness. But of course it won't stand up as soon as we start looking at poems. Literary people can't any longer get away with opposing *concrete* (a good thing) to *abstract* (a bad one). We abstract *from* experience, and if we didn't continually do this, we couldn't master or order our experience at all; an unremitting barrage of unrelated particular experiences would simply overmaster us. Thus abstraction has to operate in poetry because it operates continually in our life from one moment to the next. And so there can be no objection to personification on the grounds that it is the product of a process of abstraction. It is; but so is virtually every word that we ever use. For twenty years, for instance, I have admired the elegance of four sentences in T.C. Pollock's *The Nature of Literature*:

> If an abstract term is the sign of an abstraction from an individual experience (E) or a group of individual experiences (E), a non-abstract or a concrete term would be the sign of that from which the abstraction was drawn, the non-abstract individual experience (E) in the group of experiences (E). The opposite of an abstract term would therefore be, not the name of a specific or 'concrete'

> object, but the sign of a total or concrete *experience* (E). The error arises because of the assumption that the abstraction is from objects, instead of from *experiences* (E). (On the contrary, what we call 'objects' are psychologically abstractions from *experiences* (E).)

The implications of this are explosive indeed. In a tediously famous programmatic poem, 'The Red Wheelbarrow', William Carlos Williams wrote: 'so much depends / upon // a red wheel / barrow // glazed with rain / water // beside the white / chickens'. And what T.C. Pollock shows (since 'what we call "objects" are psychologically abstractions from experiences') is that whatever may be the case with other words in Williams's little poem, the words 'wheelbarrow' and 'chickens' are, properly or psychologically speaking, *abstractions.* And so, when we turn to Williams's famous slogan, 'No ideas but in things', if by 'things' Williams meant objects like wheelbarrows and chickens (and there's every reason to suppose he did), then his slogan is the prescription not for a highly *concrete* poetry, but for a poetry that is full of abstractions.

This may seem to be mere logic-chopping. Moreover poetic theory is one thing, writing poems is something else. A silly theory can work out well in practice, as it did through several years for Wordsworth. And so it needn't surprise us that some of the best poems of our century have been written under a swirling banner which reads: 'Concrete and particular always! Abstract and general, never!' This, or something very like it, was the legend on the banner of the Imagist movement, unfurled nearly 70 years ago in London; and for perhaps fifty years the Imagist movement surely exerted a fertile and salutary influence on both British and American poetry, including the poetry of Williams.

All the same a false poetic theory does take its toll in the long run. We have to believe this if we hold it as an act of faith that muddle is worse than clarity. (Not all poets and readers of poetry do hold this – some will explicitly prefer a warm damp muddle to a hard dry clarity; and to them I have nothing to say.) In any case I believe observation confirms that there comes a point at which the modicum of error in a theory does more harm than the modicum of truth does good. And my guess is that we reached that point, and passed it, quite some time ago.

Meanwhile how do we, snarled in our late-Romantic muddles about abstraction and concreteness, and about the relation between rhetoric and poetry, deal with the pre-Romantic poetry that on the contrary was clear-headed about these matters? If we believe that rhetoric is the enemy of poetry, what access can we have to the eighteenth-century poetry of Dr Johnson or William Cowper or Christopher Smart, who wrote in the contrary belief that rhetoric and poetry were closely allied? I look back on thirty years of teaching and criticism and polemic, here and in America, when I give it as my opinion that most of us have no real access to such poetry at all, except as documentation for the history of ideas. Despite many passionate and conclusively argued advocacies of this poetry (like Bateson's, which I began by quoting) the common reader is as unpersuaded as he was forty years ago, still stubbornly experiences this poetry as – if he is honest – *boring*. Well, but (it may be said) the common reader can still respond to poetry of yet earlier centuries, to Shakespeare and to Donne. But *can* he? If he can, it is very odd. For as we saw when we traced 'personification' through the Dictionary back to 'prosopopoeia', the sixteenth and seventeenth centuries wrote a rhetorical poetry no less than the eighteenth. And so we may harbour the suspicion that many of us have the illusion of getting access to the poetry of Donne only because we have transformed the Renaissance rhetorician that Donne was into a late-Romantic confessional poet that he was not. And indeed it has been demonstrated that this is what we do, or what we used to do not long ago.

How much does this matter? It matters not at all to the quality of our poetry today, if we define our poetry as 'modern', and then define 'the modern' (as some do) as the product of a clean break with the inherited past, the throwing overboard of so much useless lumber. If on the other hand we believe with T.S. Eliot no less than Joshua Reynolds that the modern in art in any period consists of adding to the inherited corpus of art-works, *in such a way as to review the whole of that inheritance and alter the proportions within it*, then the lack or impossibility of creative access to whole centuries of our past cannot fail to be immediately and drastically constricting, impoverishing, in the present. And the impoverishment shows up just where it can least be alleviated – in the very medium of our art, in our *language*. *Either* the English that we write in is the English of Chaucer, Shakespeare and Dryden no less than the English of Blake and Whitman, *or else* it is not. A drastically foreshortened perspective on the historical past cannot help but be an equally drastic impoverishment of the very medium out of which we carve or orchestrate our poems. *Either* the past of our art in our own language is a dead weight that we have lugged along with us for too long, *or else* it is a repertoire of resources which, if we turn our back on it, shows us to be not big enough to face the (admittedly awesome) competition.

So far have I come, or been carried, from the comfortably restricted topic that I announced at the outset. And yet I think I have not digressed. However, I am aware of Bateson's impish presence warning me to moderate a tone that has become *hortatory*. And so I must – if only to acknowledge the chastening fact that the state of affairs that I have been sketching is not to be put right by any act of will by any of us. If you do not feel ('on the pulses', as John Keats said) that John Dryden is at least as great a poet as William Blake, no private regimen of imaginative push-ups is going to remedy that state. You may know that received opinion ranks these two poets on a level, you may know the arguments which buttress this received opinion, you may see the force of them and defer to them. You may even concur in the received opinion, tacitly or otherwise, on many occasions; and no shame to you if you do. But your prejudice against the one poet in favour of the other, though it may in time be lessened and even eroded altogether, cannot be made to do so by any steely resolve on your part. The reader is not his own master, and cannot command his own responses. So too with the poet – the poet of our time who is convinced by the arguments I have been advancing, as of course I am convinced by them. What will be the outcome? Will he henceforth write as if he were a contemporary or near-contemporary of John Dryden or Fulke Greville, not of W.H. Auden and William Carlos Williams? Among my younger contemporaries I seem to detect some who have taken that fearless option. In this they are like my honoured late friend Yvor Winters, by whom indeed some of them seem to have been influenced. But the plain fact is that we *are* nearer being contemporaries of Auden than of Dryden; and that historical fact determines not just the themes to which we should address ourselves, but also the language we should use. Certain historical developments – notably in the present context what we may call with the broadest possible application 'the Romantic Movement' – have irreversibly taken place; and no act of will, no stroke of the pen, no resolute fiat will rule them out of a record imprinted as indelibly on our individual sensibilities as on the pages of written history. Accordingly Blake and Wordsworth and Whitman *do* stand between us and the eighteenth and earlier centuries; we can negotiate around them, but negotiation is certainly what is called for, and when we win through or round them the landscape that we get to is not the landscape known to Joshua Reynolds, but rather that landscape as transformed by a subsequent landslide. And thus at the present day a verse-style that acknowledges no precedents later than say William Collins, which employs for instance personification with the unblinking confidence of Collins and his contemporaries, reveals itself as a product of perverse resolution, and therefore sterile.

Moreover, if we approach this matter by another road, we find ourselves coming into the world of rhetoric by another door. Yvor Winters wrote proudly and on principle in a certain way, an unfashionable way and challenging way, and waited for his readers to come round to him. A few came, but not many. It's to be hoped that more will come, for Winters was a fine and devoted poet. But not enough came, and Winters's writing suffers from the writer's knowledge that he would be read by only an unrepresentative few. In other words, if we are to accept the impurities that come as soon as we recognize that poetry and rhetoric are inextricably intermingled, we must accept, along with other impurities, the presence of a potential reader, with all the doubtless wrongheaded and muddled assumptions that we can ascribe to him with some confidence. Like rhetoric, though for nobler and purer motives, poetry seeks to persuade. And it cannot persuade if it cannot get a hearing; to get a hearing it must make what will look like concessions and compromises though in fact they are only acknowledgements by the poet that he is historically conditioned, like every one else. (And this is true even though, at any given moment, there are of course more poets who will gladly compromise than poets who won't.) We may wish that the Romantic Movement had never happened; but it did, and we must live with the consequences.

So far, my defence of personification in poetry has been just that – defensive. I have tried to show, or to suggest, that personifications are abstractions no doubt; but so are most of the other words we use, including words like 'wheelbarrow' and 'chicken'. (If it should be proposed that a poem in its totality re-constitutes the original non-abstract experience from which most of its constituent words are abstractions, I should be eager to be persuaded; but that would be another argument.) Secondly, I have followed Bateson in arguing that personification, so far from being a detachable and recognizable rhetorical manoeuvre, is inherent in the grammatical structure of English. It is therefore, as a few minutes' unprejudiced eavesdropping will bear out, as much a feature of spoken English as of written. This is the point surely of Bateson's quoting Horace Walpole on Gray's conversation, which has incidentally the merit of insisting (as eighteenth-century enthusiasts often forget to do) that in that century as in any other the distinguished individual Thomas Gray was swimming against a tide of usage that was, then as now, for the most part 'slovenly'. This as I think self-evident contention that personification is a potentiality in *all* of our language, colloquial as well as literary, ought to stop in their tracks those opinion-makers, through many decades as vociferous on one side the Atlantic as on the other, who would have it that English-speakers and writers are presented with a choice between an English that is true, honest, direct and innocent (the language of children or of the uneducated, a language that is spoken); and another English that is untrue, dishonest, manipulative and rhetorical (the language of adults, of public life as against private, a language that is written). Unless I am mistaken, we have found reason for thinking that we are presented with no such choice: the language of our poets is the language of our advertisers, our media-merchants and our politicians – the distinction between poets and the others is not in their eschewing some rhetorical manoeuvres that the others make play with, still less in any greater *skill* on the poets' part, but simply (nowhere else) in a greater purity of motive.

But I don't want to close without going on the offensive, and proposing a *positive* virtue in personification. To do this I have to mount into metaphysics – a realm where I feel very unsure of myself, and a dimension that I think in general critics should stay well clear of, or stop short of. But at least my example is firm enough. It is the young Christopher Smart writing about 1750 'A Morning Piece, Or an Hymn for the hay-makers':

> Strong Labour got up. – With his pipe in his mouth
> He stoutly strode over the dale.
> He lent new perfumes to the breath of the south,
> On his back hung his wallet and flail.
> Behind him came Health from her cottage of thatch,
> Where never physician had lifted the latch.

'Strong Labour got up with his pipe in his mouth / And stoutly strode over the dale' – so misread, in his excitement, Oliver Goldsmith, adding, 'There is not a man now living who could write such a line'. And what did Goldsmith mean, if not that the real labourer smoking real tobacco in a real pipe ('He lent new perfume to the breath of the south') is also, by this way of putting it, an instance and a proof of the energies altogether more generally alive in the waking world – for example the labour of bees in the flower or the hive – of which the perfume might be as readily sweat or honey as tobacco?

This seems to me a profoundly imaginative and exciting perception rendered with a compact vividness that only personification could make possible. But there is more to it (I can't help thinking) than the compactness of phrasing, splendid as that is. The conception of the universe which personification at this level of intensity enforces, is quite definite and exclusive; this is a universe, a 'Nature', driven through and determined by impalpable forces. These forces, these energies, are called 'Labour' or 'Health', 'Death' or 'Dread' or 'Time' or 'Hope'. Some of these energies appear to originate in the human psyche ('Dread'), others ('Hope') may seem to originate there but have long been thought to operate also in a sphere outside the human, yet others ('Time', 'Death', 'Health') seem active quite outside the reach of human control or perhaps of human consciousness. We may in our considered opinion reject a view of Nature thus at the mercy of largely inscrutable energies running wild; but my point is that not just our poetry, but our very language, impels us to a 'Nature' conceived in this way. Wretchedly aware of my incompetence in this area, I am forced to the conclusion that a whole-heartedly nominalist or mechanistic view of Nature, if it tries to express itself in our language, will find itself obstructed by the ingrained bent of that language and will have to turn instead to other 'languages': algebriac equations, or computer-talk. From this point of view 'personification', far from being a device that we may or may not avail ourselves of as we please, implies one rather alarming image of what sort of world it is that we live in. Either that world is by and large 'up to us'; or else it is not. And personification implies that it is not.

Of course Romantic poets also personified, though usually with a much less clear idea than Christopher Smart of just what it was they were doing. And 'energy' and 'Nature' have been for nearly two centuries so much part of the stock in trade of enthusiasts for Romanticism that Romanticism may think it has established a prescriptive right to them – to the terms, and to the concepts. I am aware too that in indulging what begins to look like a diatribe against Romanticism, as the source of all the muddles about Art and Nature which now bedevil us, I am conveying a sort of quaintly 'period' flavour to these proceedings. It smacks of Irving Babbitt and a period when F.W. Bateson was still a very young man. Certainly, as I have conceded, we can no longer entertain that notion which some of us seem to have imbibed in our youth (I think of Kingsley Amis's good poem, 'Against Romanticism') – the notion, that is, that Romanticism was an aberration in our cultural past which we have the ability and the duty to expunge from our consciousness. And hence we long ago got rid of that idea which now seems so undeniably quaint – the idea that T.S. Eliot wrote an anti-Romantic poetry, rather than poetry which is the product of what is in important ways a late-Romantic sensibility (as it could not help but be, Eliot living when he did). All this is true. Yet Bateson was not a young man when he wrote the masterly pages of Chapter VIII in *A Guide to English Literature*; and in that chapter, which he called 'The Approach to Romanticism', though he stays at all points scrupulously far from anything that could be construed as 'diatribe', yet I detect dismay and impatience never far below the surface, especially when he compares the Romantics with their successors whom he calls enthusiastically 'the great Edwardians'. We need not deny that Bateson, like any one else, had his blind spots; yet I think it is a pity that the case against Romanticism which in that chapter he presents by implication is now heard and attended to much less than it used to be. One reason for this, I suspect, is that momentous development in Bateson's lifetime, the institution of schools of American Studies and the strenuous promotion of American literature as in important ways distinct from English-speaking literature generally. For the plain fact is that a distinctively American literature has no historical existence before Romanticism; and so, although Irving Babbitt and Yvor Winters and Arthur O. Lovejoy were all Americans, yet our American colleagues today are almost inevitably much less critical of Romanticism (theirs, as well as ours) than we can afford to be. This is reflected in their poetry, particularly in that poetry which some of them are now calling 'post-modernist', of which the emergence can be dated with unusual exactness, in the year 1955. This American poetry has influenced our poetry also – very properly, since great and dedicated talents as well as flamboyant personalities have been associated with it. What vitiates it, I dare to suggest, is a renewed effort to surprise English into acting unrhetorically, the revival of a categorical distinction between the poet and the rhetorician. I have tried to suggest that if we attend to a feature of our language such as personification we are forced to think that all such attempts are doomed to failure because based on untenable notions about the relation between our human nature and our human arts.

This, the first F.W. Bateson Memorial lecture, was given in Oxford on 25 February 1981 and published in *Essays in Criticism* XXXI: 2 (April 1981).

18 Politics and Literature: John Adams and Doctor Johnson

Professor Oakeshott has argued that poetry makes an irreplaceable contribution to the conversation of mankind; but that it can be seen to be irreplaceable only if the conversation of mankind is understood as something distinct from, because more comprehensive than, the sustained enquiry of the human mind into 'ourselves and the world we inhabit'.[1] Poetry, he argues, is irreplaceable in the conversation of mankind to just the degree that it does *not* contribute to that enquiry.

Although Professor Oakeshott conducts this argument with wonderful grace and amenity, and although his essay is directed mainly against the crass philistine who believes that poetry is ultimately (or sooner) replaceable, yet in my view no serious devotee of the poetic can afford to accept his civil compromise. For such a devotee of poetry (a term which, as Professor Oakeshott uses it, comprehends all literature and all the finer arts), it is essential to maintain that the poetic activity contributes not just to the conversation of mankind but to its enquiry also, that the poetic is a mode of that enquiry, and that a devotion to poetry entails 'a belief in the pre-eminence of enquiry, and of the categories of "truth" and "reality"'.[2]

In respect of this disagreement, a crucial case is the large class of writers who conceived of themselves, and are conceived by others, as contributing to an established field of enquiry; who nevertheless can be seen to be 'making images of a certain kind and moving about among them in a manner appropriate to their characters'[3] – that is to say, acting poetically in the very course of their enquiries. Certain enquirers into politics are particularly interesting from this point of view, if only because, as Professor Oakeshott reminds us, 'in ancient Greece... "politics" was understood as a "poetic" activity in which

[1] Michael Oakeshott, *The Voice of Poetry in the Conversation of Mankind*, (London, 1959).

[2] *Ibid.* p.35.

[3] *Ibid.* p.31.

speaking (not merely to persuade but chiefly to compose memorable verbal images) was pre-eminent, and in which action was for the achievement of "glory" and "greatness" – a view of things which is reflected in the pages of Machiavelli.'[1]

I propose to consider, as a political writer of this kind, John Adams, the second President of the United States. And I shall suggest, first, that Adams indeed combines perceptiveness in politics with poetic activity, in the same way, if not to the same degree, as a Bacon or a Burke; secondly, and more immediately to the point, that there is a limit to his political sagacity as to his poetic capacity, a limit which appears when we compare him with Doctor Johnson, an author who (it turns out) meant more to him than he ever cared to acknowledge; and thirdly that his fallings short in political sagacity and in poetry are related, so that we may vindicate common sense and common usage, and speak simply of a single failure of imagination. By this stage of my argument I shall be suggesting that properly to read John Adams as an ornament of American literature is not different from reading him as a shrewd observer of the political arena; and this is to reject, as untrue to the experience of reading John Adams vigilantly and with sympathy, the distinction which Professor Oakeshott asks us to make between 'conversation' and 'enquiry'.

The work by Adams which I shall consider is his *Discourses on Davila*. These appeared at intervals through the year 1790, in the *Gazette of the United States*, a federalist periodical published in Philadelphia. They appeared between hard covers in Boston in 1805, and when C.F. Adams a half-century later reproduced them in Volume VI of the *Life and Works* of Adams, he incorporated some valuable marginalia, dating from as late as 1812-13, found in John Adams's library copy. The Davila whom Adams is discoursing upon is Enrico Caterino Davila, whose *Historia delle guerre civili di Francia*, published in Venice in 1630, was known to Adams not in the English translation by W. Aylesbury (1647), though that folio was in Adams's library, but in the French translation of 1757 by the Abbé Mallet. Adams may well have been led to the work in the first place by Bolingbroke's commendation of it in the fifth of his *Letters on the Study and Use of History*.

Zoltan Haraszti, in his invaluable *John Adams and the Prophets of Progress*,[2] says of those parts of the *Discourses* which are not straight translations from Davila (as are eighteen out of the thirty-two papers), 'The papers are striking, and reading them one has at first

1 *Ibid.* p.15 n.

2 Cambridge, Mass., 1952, p.168.

the feeling of having discovered a literary treasure.' Unfortunately, he goes on, this feeling cannot be trusted, since 'the entire group is based upon a single chapter of Adam Smith's *Theory of Moral Sentiments*'. The logic of this is unacceptable unless we have very simple-minded and mechanical ideas of plagiarism on the one hand, originality on the other. Shakespeare himself would not scape whipping if we counted all his borrowings against him. And Mr Haraszti allows that Adams's phrasing is often more powerful than Smith's, and that 'his passion for stringing together epithets and metaphors makes his presentation particularly vivid'.

However, it is worth examining in some detail Haraszti's case that Adams is heavily indebted to Adam Smith, if only because this will bring us to what interests us more – Adams's indebtedness to Dr Johnson. We find to begin with that Section II of the *Discourses*, with epigraph from Voltaire, though it is not at odds with anything that Smith says, is a genuine elaboration of it – and in a direction (hence in a tone) quite alien from Smith's:

> Of what avail are all these histories, pedigrees, traditions? What foundation has the whole science of genealogy and heraldry? Are there differences in the breeds of men, as there are in those of horses? If there are not, these sciences have no foundation in reason; in prejudice they have a very solid one.

There is nothing in Smith's chapter to approach this implication that if the philosopher's reason permits him to do nothing with such a deep-rooted prejudice but merely deplore it, *so much the worse for him, and especially for his politics*. (This section quotes Young's 'Love of Fame', and aptly.)

Section III, with epigraph from Voltaire, begins with a passage which, as Haraszti shows, has a parallel on the first page of Smith's Chapter. But it soon changes. One may usefully compare a passage about the poor man in Adams (a passage, incidentally, which is much wrenched by Hannah Arendt in her *On Revolution*)[1] with the no less good but quite different development by Smith. And what follows, beginning, 'Is there in science and letters a reward for the labor they require?' has no source in Smith; it recalls rather Dr Johnson's

> When first the college rolls receive his name,
> The young enthusiast quits his ease for fame;

[1] New York, 1963. Miss Arendt quotes the passage with long *lacunae*, and this alters the force of it, since Adams allows as Miss Arendt does not that the emulous appetite can be satisfied *socially* (e.g. by the man who keeps a dog to 'look up to him') as well as *politically*. Miss Arendt ignores the source in Adam Smith.

> Through all his veins the fever of renown
> Burns from the strong contagion of the gown;
> (*Vanity of Human Wishes*, ll. 135-8.)

At the end Adams shifts from the learned profession to the military, just as Johnson does in his poem.

And sure enough, Section IV has an epigraph from the *Vanity of Human Wishes* about martial glory (of which Smith says nothing):

> Such bribes the rapid Greek o'er Asia whirl'd,
> For such the steady Romans shook the world

Compare Johnson's versions of these 'bribes' ('The festal blazes, the triumphal show') with Adams's taunting interrogations: 'A ribbon? a garter? a star? a golden key? a marshal's staff? or a white hickory stick?' After a remarkable passage on death-beds, and a grandly eloquent paragraph on marks of distinction in the Roman republic (entirely his own), Adams approaches Smith only in his last paragraph, with the example of the triumph of Paulus Aemilius.

Section V has a four-line epigraph from *The Vanity of Human Wishes*, ll. 177-8 conjoined with ll. 183-4 (with no acknowledgement of a *lacuna*). But it is in respect of this paper that comparison with Smith is most in order, and most damaging to Adams. Smith writes:

> To those who have been accustomed to the possession or even to the hope, of public admiration, all other pleasures sicken and decay. Of all the discarded statemen who, for their own ease, have studied to get the better of ambition, and to despise those honours which they could no longer arrive at, how few have been able to succeed! The greater part have spent their time in the most listless and insipid indolence, chagrined at the thoughts of their own insignificancy, incapable of being interested in the occupations of private life, without enjoyment, except when they talked of their former greatness, and without satisfaction, except when they were employed in some vain project to recover it. Are you in earnest resolved never to barter your liberty from the lordly servitude of a court, but to live free, fearless, and independent? There seems to be one way to continue in that virtuous resolution; and perhaps but one. Never enter the place from whence so few have been able to return; never come within the circle of ambition; nor ever bring yourself into comparison with those masters of the earth who have already engrossed the attention of half mankind before you.

And Adams:

> Ministers of state are frequently displaced in all countries; and what is the consequence? Are they seen happy in a calm resignation

> to their fate? Do they turn their thoughts from their former employments, to private studies or business? Are they men of pleasant humor, and engaging conversation? Are their hearts at ease? Or is their conversation a constant effusion of complaints and murmurs, and their breast the residence of resentment and indignation, of grief and sorrow, of malice and revenge? Is it common to see a man get the better of his ambition, and despise the honors he once possessed; or is he commonly employed in projects, intrigues after intrigues, and manoeuvres on manoeuvres, to recover them? So sweet and delightful to the human heart is that complacency and admiration, which attends public offices, whether they are conferred by the favor of a prince, derived from hereditary descent, or obtained by election of the people, that a mind must be sunk below the feelings of humanity, or exalted by religion or philosophy far above the common character of men, to be insensible, or conquer its sensibility. Pretensions to such conquests are not uncommon; but the sincerity of such pretenders is often rendered suspicious, by their constant conversation and conduct, and even by their countenances.

Adam Smith is much superior to Adams here, for Adams, once he has committed himself to rhetorical questions, seems unable to break the habit; and Johnson is not in the picture at all. He can be brought into it if we recall that the disappointed statesman probably in Smith's mind as well as in Adams's was *Bolingbroke*, whom Jefferson and Adams both admired (though not uncritically). Johnson had written, in his review of Soame Jenyns's *Free Enquiry*, of 'the contemptible arrogance, or the impious licentiousness of Bolingbroke'.

Section VI has an epigraph from Juvenal and also from Johnson's imitation of him, in a couplet from *London* that was never far from Adams's lips, nor from the tip of his pen:

> This mournful truth is everywhere confess'd,
> Slow rises Worth, by Poverty depressed.

This section owes nothing to Smith (if only because it is wholly and specifically *political*) and it owes nothing to Johnson, though it has one curious parallel with him:

> The Romans allowed none, but those who had possessed curule offices, to have statues or portraits. He who had images or pictures of his ancestors, was called noble. He who had no statue or pictures but his own, was called a new man. Those who had none at all, were ignoble.

Compare Johnson, *The Vanity of Human Wishes*, ll. 83-90.

From every room descends the painted face,
That hung the bright Palladium of the place,
And smoak'd in kitches, or in auctions sold,
To better features yields the frame of gold;
For now no more we trace in ev'ry line
Heroic worth, benevolence divine:
The form distorted justifies the fall,
And detestation rids th' indignant wall.

The similarity here is presumably a matter of Johnson and Adams having a common source in Juvenal.

Section VII appears to owe little to Smith and nothing to Johnson. It has an epigraph from Pope's Moral Essays:

Tis from high life high characters are drawn,
A saint in *crape* is twice a saint in *lawn*.

And in Section VIII, which is given up almost entirely to a barely acknowledged verbatim quotation from Smith, the epigraph is again from Pope:

Wise, if a minister; but if a King,
More wise, more learn'd, more just, more everything

Section IX however has an epigraph from Johnson:

Heroes, proceed! what bounds your pride shall hold?
What check restrain your thirst of pow'r and gold?
(*London*, ll. 61-2)

Adams begins: 'The answer to the question in the motto...' And this prepares us for the Section to stay quite close to Johnson. So it does, in a curious way; when Adams says, 'Consider the story of the ambition and the fall of Cardinal Wolsey and Archbishop Laud; the indignation of the world against their tyranny has been very faint; the sympathy with their fall has been very strong', he can hardly *not* be reproaching Johnson, or urbanely sneering at him, for treating both these characters in just this way – not in *London* however, but in *The Vanity of Human Wishes*:

For why did Wolsey near the steeps of fate,
On weak foundations raise th' enormous weight?
Why but to sink beneath misfortune's blow,
With louder ruin to the gulphs below?
(ll. 125-128)

and

Rebellion's vengeful talons seize on Laud.
(l. 168)

And Adams indeed could claim, when he goes on to quote and praise from Juvenal's Satire III and from Johnson's imitation of it in *London* ('Although the verse, both of the Roman and Briton, is satire, its keenest severity consists in its truth'), that the poet of *London* castigates in others just that thoughtless veneration for eminence which the poet of *The Vanity of Human Wishes* fell into himself when he wrote so mournfully of Wolsey and of Laud. It would be no more than natural for Adams to applaud the young firebrand Johnson, friend of the reprobate Richard Savage, who wrote *London* against the establishment of Walpole, and to deplore the older and mellower or perhaps more politically timorous Johnson who write *The Vanity of Human Wishes*.

In the four papers which remain of the *Discourses on Davila* I detect no traces of Doctor Johnson, unless indeed it was Johnson, in his capacity as editor and commentator on Shakespeare, who brought to Adams's attention the passages from Shakespeare's *Troilus and Cressida* which make up Section X of the *Discourses*. It is at any rate quite impossible to accept Zoltan Haraszti's insinuation that the 70 lines of Shakespeare, to which of course there is no parallel in Adam Smith, are merely 'padding', an embellishment or amplification of the source only in this discreditable sense. On the contrary Adams's citation of Ulysses' speech on Degree is perhaps the most astonishing and admirable thing in all the *Discourses*. It is common form nowadays to take this as the key passage in the understanding of Shakespeare's political philosophy (the understanding in particular of how undemocratic Shakespeare is); but the passage was first given this central importance only thirty years ago, by the late E.M.W. Tillyard and the late Theodore Spencer. Adams's citation of it thus has the force of a startling anticipation of modern opinion, which that opinion has vindicated.

And yet this ought not to startle us. Twenty-five years ago Alfred Van Rensselaer Westfall in his *American Shakespearean Criticism 1607-1865*,[1] quoted an entry in Adams's Diary for 1772, which consists of a comment on some lines from *The Merry Wives of Windsor*, and declared: 'What may be called the first American Shakespearean comment, if not criticism, began with this man who became the second president of the United States.' Adams in fact was quite exceptional among men of affairs of his age, not just in the United States but in Britain also, in having a mind stocked with literary experience, and in drawing upon that experience not just for flowery embellishments but as a repository of moral and political wisdom. We are accustomed to think of the Founding Fathers as representing,

[1] New York, 1939, pp.193–5.

not just a high level of social responsibility and political astuteness, but as representing also, more generally, a high level of civilization. And this is surely right. But when we think in this way we think pre-eminently of Jefferson, and of his sensibility to pictures, statuary, music, architecture. Jefferson read widely in the classical literatures, and undoubtedly he had the best library of all the early Presidents. But of all the Presidents, with the possible exception of Lincoln, the only one to outstrip John Adams as a Shakespearean was his son John Quincy Adams, 'who read the plays on his mother's table when he was twelve years old'. The conclusive evidence of the literary civilization of the elder Adams is not after all in such a full-dress instance as this use of Shakespeare in the *Discourse on Davila* but in the extent to which Shakespeare and Milton, Prior and Pope, Swift and Young, are ever present in his prose on whatever subject, in the fully assimilated aspect of submerged and unacknowledged quotation and allusion. And Johnson is there too, in just the same way.

In this matter, as in much else, John Adams was at pains to obscure his own tracks. In his old age at least he was ready to blow many a blast on a Philistine trumpet. To Jefferson in 1816 he declared:

> Style has governed the Empire. Swift, Pope and Hume have disgraced all the honest Historians. Rapin and Burnet Oldmixon and Coke, contain more honest truth than Hume and Clarendon and all their disciples and Imitators. But who reads any of them at this day? Every one of the fine Arts from the earliest times has been inlisted in the service of Superstition and Despotism. The whole World at this day Gazes with Astonishment at the grossest Fictions because they have been immortalized by the most exquisite Artists, Homer and Milton, Phidias and Raphael. The Rabble of the Classic Skies and the Hosts of Roman Catholic Saints and Angells are still adored in Paint and Marble, and verse.[1]

In the next year he is still haranguing Jefferson on the same score:

> Eustace is a Supplement to Dupuis; and both together contain a compleat draught of the Superstition, Credulity and Despotism of our terrestrial Universe. They show how Science, Litteratur, Mechanic Arts, and those fine Arts of Architecture, Painting, Statuary, Poetry, Musick and Eloquence: which you love so well and taste so exquisitely, have been subservient to Priests and Kings Nobles and commons Monarchies and Republicks. For they have all Used them when they could, but as the rich had

[1] *The Adams-Jefferson Letters*, ed. Lester J. Cappon (Chapel Hill, 1959), II, 502-3.

> then oftener than the poor, in their power, the latter have always gone to the Wall.[1]

And less than three weeks later he asks another correspondent:

> Is it possible to inlist the 'Fine Arts', on the side of Truth, of Virtue, of Piety, or even of Honour? From the dawn of History they have been prostituted to the Service of Superstition and despotism. Read Herodotus, Pausanias, Plutarch, Lucian, and twenty others, not forgetting several of the Christian Fathers and see how the fine Arts have been employed. Read Eustace's classical Tour of Italy.[2]

But this is rather different, is it not? The question is neither rhetorical nor frivolous; and we know the answer to it no better than Adams did. Certainly I cannot answer it, who would never have read Adams at all, nor Jefferson either, but for the recommendations of that frequently exquisite and always honest poet, Ezra Pound, Fascist and anti-Semite. *Is* it possible to enlist the Fine Arts? We know how to do so no more than Doctor Johnson when he deplored, in the finest of all tributes to Shakespeare, that Shakespeare's plays did not uniformly punish wicked characters and reward the virtuous.

And this is Adams's dilemma. It is not that he does not know what the arts are about, or that he cannot respond to them; what puzzles him, as it puzzled Johnson and puzzles all of us in some degree, is how to square with his conscience the fact that he does respond to them, intensely. This is very clear from another letter written to Waterhouse twelve years earlier:

> I have heard, as you insinuate, that Sterne was a wicked man; and there are traits of a false Character, in his Writings: yet Benevolence, Generosity, Simpathy and Humanity that fill the Eyes and bosoms of the readers of his Works, will plead forever for their immortality. Virtues and Vices, Wisdom and Folly, Talents and imbecility, Services and demerits are so blended in most of the distinguished Sons of Men, that there is no knowing what Judgment to form of them, or what to do with them. Julian, in that ingenious Fable, The Caesars, throws headlong into the gulph of Tartarus, all the Tyrants; Alexander, Caesar, Augustus, Trajan and Constantine, are made to acknowledge that Fame, Power, or Pleasure were their Objects; Marcus Aurelius alone was confessed to have aimed Singly at the good of the People.

1 *Ibid.* p.507.

2 *Statesman and Friend. Correspondence of John Adams with Benjamin Waterhouse, 1784-1822,* ed. W.C. Ford (Boston, 1927).

> I know not whether the number of pure Characters among Mankind in general will bear a greater proportion. The Number of unexceptionable Romances is not greater. Most of the fashionable ones, deserve to be slighted more than Sterne. Yet I own myself to be childish enough to be amused with their fictions. . . .[1]

'Virtues and Vices, Wisdom and Folly, Talents and imbecility, Services and Demerits are so blended in most of the distinguished Sons of Men, that there is no knowing what Judgment to form of them' – because Adams believed this, we need not be surprised to find that Johnson, some of whose writings were never far from the surface of Adams's mind, should nevertheless never be spoken of by Adams except with marked hostility.

For instance, in Mr Cappon's admirable edition of the *Jefferson-Adams Letters* there are two entries in the index under 'Johnson, Samuel, lexicographer'. One of them sends us to Adams declaring in 1815, 'Johnson and Burke were more of Catholicks than Protestants at Heart and Gibbon became an Advocate for the Inquisition'. The other, no more amiable, of date 1813, is much more interesting:

> The fundamental Principle of all Phylosophy and all Christianity is REJOICE ALWAYS IN ALL THINGS. Be thankfull at all times for all good and all that We call evil.' Will it not follow, that I ought to rejoice and be thankful that Priestley has lived? Aye! that Voltaire has lived? That Gibbon has lived? That Hume has lived, though a conceited Scotchman? That Bolingbroke has lived, tho' a haughty arrogant supercilious Dogmatist? that Burke and Johnson have lived, though superstitious Slaves or self-deceiving Hypocrites both. Is it not laughable to hear Burke call Bolingbroke a superficial Writer? To hear him ask 'Who ever read him through?' Had I been present I would have answered him 'I, I, myself, I have read him through, more than fifty Years ago, and more than five times in my Life, and once within five Years past. And in my Opinion, the epithet "Superficial" belongs to you and your Friend Johnson more than to him.' I might say much more. But I believe Burke and Johnson to have been as political Christians, as Leo 10th.

The interesting name here is that of Bolingbroke. For Mr Haraszti has confirmed that the influence of Bolingbroke on Adams was as great as it is here asserted to be. (It was even greater on Jefferson.) Yet Adams finds no inconsistency – nor, given his view of human nature, is there any – in declaring Bolingbroke 'a haughty arrogant

[1] *Ibid.* pp.29-30.

supercilious Dogmatist'. But the letter goes on to more interesting matters:

> I return to Priestley, though I have great Complaints against him for personal Injuries and Persecution, at the same time that I forgive it all, and hope and pray that he may be pardoned for it all, above. Dr. Broklesby an intimate Friend and convivial Companion of Johnson told me, that Johnson died in Agonies of Horror of Annihilation, and all the Accounts We have of his death corroborate this Account of Broklesby. Dread of Annihilation! Dread of Nothing? A dread of Nothing I should think would be no dread at all. Can there be any real substantial rational fear of nothing? Were you on your deathbed, and in your last moments informed by demonstration or Revelation that you would cease to think and to feel at your dissolution, should you be terrified? You might be ashamed of yourself for having lived so long to bear the proud Mans Contumely.

('The proud man's contumely' – a good example of how intimately Adams's mind is impregnated with Shakespeare.)

> You might be ashamed of your Maker, and compare him to a little Girl amusing herself her Brothers and Sisters by blowing Bubbles in Soap Sudds. You might compare him to Boys sporting with Crakers and Rocketts: or to Men employed in making more artificial Fire Works; or to Men and Women at Farces and Operas, or Sadlers Wells Exploits; or to Politicians in their Intrigues; or to Heroes in their Butcheries; or to Popes in their Devilisms. But what should you fear? Nothing. E mori nolo Sed me mortuum esse nihil estimo.

'I have no wish to die, but that I be dead I consider as nothing.' Brave words! But what have they to do with the piously barbed hope in the same paragraph that Joseph Priestley, for his injuries to Adams, 'be pardoned for it all, above'? At any rate, one of several other places where Johnson figures in Adams's letters (but unnamed and unacknowledged in the index), reveals Adams not quite so stoical at the approach of death. This is in 1814:

> I am sometimes afraid that my 'Machine' will not 'surcease motion' soon enough; for I dread nothing so much as 'dying at top' and expiring like Dean Swift 'a driveller and a Show' or like Sam. Adams, a Grief and distress to his Family, a weeping helpless Object of Compassion for Years.[1]

[1] *The Adams-Jefferson Letters*, II, 435.

Swift comes into Adams's head out of Johnson's *Vanity of Human Wishes*:

> In life's last scene what prodigies surprise,
> Fears of the brave, and follies of the wise?
> From Marlb'rough's eyes the streams of dotage flow,
> And Swift expires a driv'ler and a show.

As the latest editors austerely explain, 'Swift was intermittently insane before his death in 1745. Servants are said to have shown him to tourists for a fee.'

At this point we have reached the inflammatory question of how far either Adams or Jefferson died a Christian. There seems to be little doubt that the two old men conceived themselves to be in some sort Christians, though aware that their Christianity was too sceptical and conditional for them to afford to be frank about it, except to each other. But Adams at least, with his ferocious anti-clericalism, was quite incapable of understanding how Johnson, particularly in such a work as *The Vanity of Human Wishes*, rested his whole view of life on a very bleak and agitated but unshakeable faith in the Christian God. Adams and Jefferson, in their letters, are still locked into historical time – Adams like his later admirer Pound convinced that only sinister destruction of records has lost the clue which lies somewhere in the historical past; Jefferson, more sanguine and with a more successful career behind him, looking still, though with chastened eyes, for fulfilment in the future. In each case the deistic approval of the Christian ethic simply overlooks the great claim of Christianity – to have redeemed history, and made it meaningful once and for all, by the historical event of the Incarnation. No unitarianism, not any Jeffersonian admiration for Jesus as a great moral teacher, could come near to satisfying what a mind like Johnson's in *The Vanity of Human Wishes*, weary of mere historical process and iteration, looked for in Christian faith.

And this is why, to speak for myself, Adams in his Letters pleases more after a hundred pages than after five hundred. At first one is delighted by his tough-minded and humorous cordiality, his unflagging curiosity, the strong savour as well as the flexibility of his writing. But the suspicion grows that Adams's scepticism is not after all tough-mindedness but the product of a conspiracy theory of history (whence, too plainly alas, some of Ezra Pound's liking for him); the curiosity is (Adams almost admits as much) the running wild of a still hungry intelligence, operating irresponsibly because his conspiracy theory has got him to the stage where every speculation has as much and as little point as any other; and the humour even is irresponsible and after a while leaves a bad taste. A scepticism so thorough as Adams's was by 1812, even if it had firmer bases than it has, leaves a man nothing with which to face the future; and of course Adams was so old by this time that, as he acknowledges, he has really no future to face. It is his age – that is, the age he grew up in, which formed him, the age of the Enlightenment – which gives to all this the unexpected, and undoubtedly quite genuine, good humour.

The Discourses on Davila are another matter. And I hope I have shown that when Zoltan Haraszti had 'the feeling of having discovered a literary treasure', he ought to have trusted that feeling. His discovery that the *Discourses*, when they depart from Davila, rest on a chapter of Adam Smith which Adams amplifies out of Johnson and Shakespeare and others – this, which Haraszti thinks reveals the treasure as fool's gold, in fact does nothing of the kind. He is misled by a mistaken and out-dated notion of what originality is, in literature. The *Discourses on Davila*, at least the fourteen essays of useful reflections embedded in them, are a literary masterpiece. One is tempted to enforce this judgement by quoting a sustained passage, for instance the paragraph from Section IV beginning, 'Has there ever been a nation who understood the human heart better than the Romans. . . ?' But it is better to avoid giving any impression that great literature is a matter of detachable purple passages. On the contrary, what makes the *Discourses* an achievement of the literary imagination is something much more nearly connected with what makes them also a penetrating and perennially relevant examination of political behaviour.

Accordingly, Adams's limitations as an observer of politics are also his limitations as a writer; for in both cases what we have is a failure of imagination. If we now define the place where that failure comes, it is by no means to deny that the *Discourses* are a great imaginative achievement; it is on the contrary to define that achievement by setting bounds to it.

In the *Discourses* Adams is arguing for political institutions as a way of harnessing the allegedly universal passion of emulation. In fact I believe we have to deny that this passion *is* universal: for there are cultures of the unprivileged which elevate 'solidarity' as the highest value, and condemn as betrayals of that principle the distinctions achieved by individuals. Such is the culture of the Trade Unionist, which Adams had no opportunity to observe. But I find that his argument fails in another way, for instance in Section V:

> Emulation really seems to produce genius, and the desire of superiority to create talents. Either this, or the reverse of it must be true; and genius produces emulation, and natural talents, the

> desire of superiority; for they are always found together, and what God and nature have united, let no audacious legislator presume to put asunder.

The concession which Adams makes here – when he envisages 'the reverse' proposition – reaches much farther than he seems aware of. For if it is only talented men who are emulous, then emulation and the desire for distinction are not such universal appetites as he elsewhere in his treatise supposes. But in any case there is a more horrifying possibility, which Adams does not envisage. What if the *un*talented are emulous? An apparition like Lee Oswald, or other pathetic killers who seem to kill only so as to be caught and 'get their names in the papers' – these suggest that the wish to be distinguished, while not universal, is distributed at random, among talented and untalented alike.

Adams is saved from envisaging this because he still confides in a providentially determined harmony between the desire for distinction and the deserving of distinction – 'what God and nature have united'. And this is characteristic. Although it seems to be true that for Adams 'nature' as a providentially ordained order is less tightly organized than for Jefferson,[1] still he shares with him the conviction that there is such a providential order in nature, and that human reason can discern it. This is indeed the force of the epigraphs he takes from Pope, particularly the motto on Section XIII:

> First follow nature; and your judgment frame
> By her just standard, which is still the same.

For Adams as we might expect seeks authority from the Pope of *Essay on Man* and *Moral Essays*, from the poet whose horizons are bounded by the precepts of Bolingbroke, not from the greater poet who in *The Dunciad* envisaged all providential order swept away and chaos come again.

Now Johnson on the other hand could share the experience behind the last lines of *The Dunciad* no less than the experience behind the *Essay on Man*. It is Johnson the devout Christian of Augustinian temper (also Pope the Roman Catholic) who can envisage that God moves in mysterious ways, above and perhaps athwart the natural order which He ordained; it is Adams the sceptic who cannot afford not to believe that God guarantees a beneficent harmony in Nature and human nature. There is one more place where Johnson appears in the *Discourses on Davila*, which brings this out clearly. In section XV, where Adams is in effect denying the contention of the Declaration of Independence that 'all men are created equal', he declares:

[1] See Daniel J. Boorstin, *The Lost World of Thomas Jefferson* (New York, 1948).

> Nature, which has established in the universe a chain of being and universal order, descending from archangels to microscopic animalcules, has ordained that no two objects shall be perfectly equal.

And in the marginalia which Adams subsequently wrote to his own work, he notes against this passage:

> This is not a chain of being from God to nothing; *ergo*, not liable to Dr Johnson's criticism, nor to the reviewer's.

The reviewer is identified by Zoltan Haraszti as Arthur Maynard Walter (1780–1807), and his review appeared in the *Monthly Anthology*. Johnson's criticism of the alleged 'great chain of being' appeared in his review in 1757 of Soame Jenyns's 'Free Enquiry into the Nature and Origin of Evil' – a review which is one of Johnson's greatest works:

> The scale of existence from infinity to nothing, cannot possibly have being. The highest being not infinite must be, as has often been observed, at an infinite distance below infinity...
>
> Between the lowest positive existence and nothing, wherever we suppose positive existence to cease, is another chasm infinitely deep; where there is room again for endless orders of subordinate nature, continued for ever and for ever, and yet infinitely superior to non-existence.
>
> To these meditations humanity is unequal. But yet we may ask, not of our Maker, but of each other, since on the one side creation, wherever it stops, must stop infinitely below infinity, and on the other infinitely above nothing, what necessity there is that it should proceed so far either way, that beings so high or so low should ever have existed? We may ask; but I believe no created wisdom can give an adequate answer.

Adams, it may be, *does* just escape by the skin of his teeth from Johnson's unanswerable objection. But Johnson goes on to explode the whole image of 'the great chain'. In famous words, which have been vindicated by A.O. Lovejoy in his standard work on this topic, Johnson declares:

> This scale of being I have demonstrated to be raised by presumptuous imagination, to rest on nothing at the bottom, to lean on nothing at the top, and to have vacuities from step to step through which any order of being may sink into nihility without any inconvenience, so far as we can judge, to the next rank above or below it.

And Adams cannot escape the charge of 'presumptuous imagination'. In the *Discourses on Davila* Adams is a very great writer. But Johnson is greater – not by virtue of greater facility in the management of language but simply because Johnson's imagination could comprehend abysses and exaltations beyond the compass of that Enlightenment culture which Johnson transcended whereas Adams, restive and sceptical though he was, remained in the end bounded by its assumptions.

Politics and Experience. Essays presented to Professor Michael Oakeshott on the occasion of his retirement (Cambridge: CUP, 1968).

19 *Dionysus in* Lyrical Ballads

1

'I am myself,' said Wordsworth, 'one of the happiest of men; and no man who does not partake of that happiness, who lives a life of constant bustle, and whose felicity depends on the opinions of others, can possibly comprehend the best of my poems.' It was thus that he delivered himself on 8 May 1812, to Henry Crabb Robinson: and it is a good example of the frightening and repellent self-assurance with which Wordsworth contemplated the fact and the nature of his own genius, and communicated his sense of these to others. But this need not mean that Wordsworth was self-deluded, that there was nothing to contemplate, or that what was there was something different from what Wordsworth saw. It will be the contention of this essay that Wordsworth knew the facts of his own genius better than anyone.

It is remarkable, to begin with, how readily Wordsworth proceeds to oppose his happiness, or his own sense of it, to 'a life of constant bustle'. Did it not occur to him that many men experience a quite genuine happiness precisely in 'bustle', in a sense of purposeful activity around them, in the changing spectacles of energetic life? Apparently not; and this from the first tells us something about Wordsworth's sort of happiness. It expressed itself in stillness and silence:

> I was glad to accompany the Wordsworths to the British Museum. I had to wait for them in the ante-room, and we had at last but a hurried survey of the antiquities. I did not perceive that Wordsworth much enjoyed the Elgin Marbles; but he is a still man when he does enjoy himself, and by no means ready to talk of his pleasure, except to his sister.[1]

[1] Crabb Robinson, *Diary* (20 Nov. 1820). Compare Robinson's description (5 Apr. 1823) of Wordsworth at a musical party: '(he) declared himself perfectly delighted and satisfied, but he sat alone, silent, and with his face covered, and was generally supposed to be asleep.'

'He is a still man when he does enjoy himself'. And so are the people in his poems, like the Idiot Boy, who was 'idle all for very joy'. We shall go some way towards understanding how Wordsworth's personal happiness goes into his poems, as he asserted it did, if we begin by noticing, as many have done already, how often silence and immobility are the distinguishing features of the personages he introduces into his poems. This connection is forced upon the attentive reader with particular vividness by what is the profoundest response to this aspect of Wordsworth the man as he was known to his contemporaries. This is Benjamin Haydon's account of how he took a cast of Wordsworth's face:

> I had a cast made yesterday of Wordsworth's face. He bore it like a philosopher. John Scott was to meet him at breakfast, and just as he came in the plaster was put on. Wordsworth was sitting in the other room in my dressing-gown, with his hands folded, sedate, solemn and still. I stepped in to Scott and told him as a curiosity to take a peep, that he might say the first sight he ever had of so great a poet was in this stage towards immortality.
>
> I opened the door slowly, and there he sat innocent and unconscious of our plot, in mysterious stillness and silence.[1]

'Solemn and still...', 'mysterious stillness and silence...': these are the very terms in which Wordsworth himself characteristically offers for contemplation his own most important human figures, such as the Idiot Boy, Michael, the Leech-Gatherer. And Haydon's prose, here bringing out the symbolic reverberations of a commonplace and accidental situation, is already half-way to poetry.

But Haydon goes on:

> When he was relieved he came in to breakfast with his usual cheerfulness and delighted us with his bursts of inspiration. At one time he shook us both in explaining the principles of his system, his views of man, and his object in writing.
>
> Wordsworth's faculty is in describing those far-reaching and intense feelings and glimmerings and doubts and fears and hopes of man, as referring to what he might be before he was born or what he may be hereafter.
>
> He is a great being and will hereafter be ranked as one who had a portion of the spirit of the mighty ones, especially Milton, but who did not possess the power of using that spirit otherwise than with reference to himself and so as to excite a reflex action only: this is, in my opinion, his great characteristic.

[1] Haydon's *Autobiography*, ed. M. Elwin (London, 1950), p.245. Journal entry for 13 Apr. 1825.

Haydon's testimony is uniquely valuable in thus proceeding though by an associative rather than logical link, from the stillness of Wordsworth the man to the stillness of his poetry. For that is what it amounts to, this 'reflex action only': the conspicuous lack in Wordsworth of any dramatic feeling, the way his insights never express themselves in terms of energetic action or of steadily suspenseful events developing out of an initial situation. It is clear that this feature of Wordsworth's work, whether we interpret it as a limitation or merely a distinguishing characteristic, was a commonplace in the circles which Haydon and Robinson and (less constantly) Wordsworth himself frequented. It is what lies behind Keats's famous judgement about 'the egotistical sublime',[1] and there is obviously a close relationship between this and Hazlitt's remarks in *The Spirit of the Age*:

> Those persons who look upon Mr Wordsworth as a merely puerile writer, must be rather at a loss to account for his strong predilection for such geniuses as Dante and Michelangelo. We do not think our author has any very cordial sympathy with Shakespear. How should he? Shakespear was the least of an egotist of any body in the world.[2]

Plainly, in this curiously left-handed compliment, the word 'egotist' is meant to convey a sense of Wordsworth's incapacity for the dramatist's feat of sinking his own personality in those of his creations. And this is one of the places where the relationship is clearest between Hazlitt and Keats, who in his letters expatiated on the judgements here passed by implication on both Wordsworth and Shakespeare. Similarly, the whole Keatsian doctrine of 'negative capability', as exemplified especially by Shakespeare, must be related to what Hazlitt says of the latter in his *Lectures on the English Poets*.

Less obviously related but more arresting is a Shelleyan judgement which puts him in the same camp. This is expressed in four acute and crucial stanzas from *Peter Bell the Third* (Part the Fourth):

> He had a mind which was somehow
> At once circumference and centre
> Of all he might or feel or know;

1 Keats, *Letters*, ed. Forman (3rd edn), p.227, Oct. 1818, to Richard Woodhouse: 'As to the poetical Character itself (I mean that sort of which, if I am any thing, I am a Member; that sort distinguished from the Wordsworthian or egotistical sublime; which is a thing *per se* and stands alone) it is not itself – it has no self – it is everything and nothing – It has no character – it enjoys light and shade;...'

2 Hazlitt, *The Spirit of the Age*, ed. A.R. Waller (London, 1910, Everyman Edition), p.258.

Nothing went ever out, although
  Something did ever enter.

He had as much imagination
  As a pint-pot; – he never could
Fancy another situation,
From which to dart his contemplation,
  Than that wherein he stood.

Yet his was individual mind,
  And new-created all he saw
In a new manner, and refined
Those new creations, and combined
Them, by a master-spirit's law.

Thus – though unimaginative –
  An apprehension clear, intense,
Of his mind's work, had made alive
The things it wrought on; I believe
  Wakening a sort of thought in sense.[1]

The imagination which Shelley here denies to Wordsworth is specifically the dramatic imagination. 'Nothing went ever out although / Something did ever enter' – this limiting judgement is as just as the wonderful compliment, 'Wakening a sort of thought in sense'. And it is worth pondering. It is not just that *The Borderers*, while it has an interesting and important theme and contains distinguished writing, is yet, by common consent, an unsuccessful drama. Whenever Wordsworth essays the dramatic monologue, writing in character, as in the notorious case of 'The Thorn', the effect, as Coleridge pointed out, is disastrous. And to go further again, to that loose sense of 'dramatic' which covers the contrivance of tense situations and logical development of plot in narrative, it will be generally allowed that here too Wordsworth is deficient. The plot of 'The Idiot Boy', for instance, is illogical and arbitrary – unforgivably so, were it not that Wordsworth, humorously and arrogantly, makes it clear that his perfunctory handling of it is deliberate. For Wordsworth was aware of this peculiarity in himself, and as usual stood over it without apology. Admitting the absence from his poetry of the interest, for the reader or spectator, of dramatic conflict and crisis, he throws down the gauntlet: 'then let him see if there are no victories in the world of spirit, no changes, no commotions, no

[1] *The Complete Poetical Works*, ed. Thomas Hutchinson (London, 1945), pp. 293-312.

revolutions there, no fluxes and refluxes of the thoughts which may be made interesting by modest combination with the stiller actions of the bodily frame.'[1] Let Wordsworth's own word 'stiller', applied with characteristic arrogance to the eventful world of dramatic action, stand as one more proof that the peculiarity of Wordsworth's imagination, the way it resists dramatic embodiment, is related to his being 'a still man when he does enjoy himself'. And it is a real peculiarity, for of no earlier poet of comparable stature by common consent (Chaucer, Dante, Milton, not to speak of Shakespeare) is it true to anything like the same extent. Presumably it does not seem so odd to later generations of Wordsworthians as to the first one, simply because we have ceased since then to expect the great poetic imagination to express itself dramatically, and hence objectively. Perhaps one way to define the Romantic movement would be to call it that change in artistic sensibility which substituted the reflective or the ruminative for the dramatic imagination.

2

De Quincey shows one way of getting into Wordsworth's poems by way of the avenue he himself indicated: his happiness, his capacity for joy. De Quincey says finely:

> Whoever looks searchingly into the characteristic genius of Wordsworth, will see that he does not willingly deal with a passion in its direct aspect, or presenting an unmodified contour, but in forms more complex and oblique, and when passing under the shadow of some secondary passion. Joy, for instance, that wells up from constitutional sources, joy that is ebullient from youth to age, and cannot cease to sparkle, he yet exhibits in the person of Matthew, the village schoolmaster, as touched and overgloomed by memories of sorrow. In the poem of *We are Seven*, which brings into day for the first time a profound fact in the abysses of human nature – viz. that the mind of an infant cannot admit the idea of death, cannot comprehend it, any more than the fountain of light can comprehend the aboriginal darkness... – the little mountaineer, who furnishes the text for this lovely strain, she whose fullness of life could not brook the gloomy faith in a grave, is yet (for the effect upon the reader) brought into connexion with the reflex shadows of the grave;

1 *The Letters of William and Dorothy Wordsworth: The Middle Years*, ed. E. de Selincourt, 2 vols. (Oxford, 1937), p.198.

> and if she herself has *not*, the reader *has*, and through this very child, the gloom of that contemplation obliquely irradiated, as raised in relief upon his imagination, even by *her*. That same infant, which subjectively could not tolerate death, being by the reader contemplated objectively, flashes upon us the tenderest images of death. Death and its sunny antipole are forced into connexion.[1]

This account of 'We are Seven' is just, and central to my argument. But as De Quincey says, it is only a particular instance of something that is generally true of Wordsworth's Lyrical Ballads, in which 'joy that is ebullient' is constantly being 'overgloomed by memories of sorrow'. The necessity of this for Wordsworth, and its attraction for him, is well but teasingly expressed (to take a further instance) in a stanza from his 'Anecdote for Fathers':

> A day it was when I could bear
> Some fond regrets to entertain;
> With so much happiness to spare,
> I could not feel a pain.
>
> (13–16)

The poem tells how Wordsworth walked out with a five-year-old boy at Liswyn farm, and found himself, while relishing to the full the attractions of that place, regretting that it had not also the beauties of a seaside-place which he calls 'Kilve'.[2] It is most important to take the force of Wordsworth's explanation of this. It is not the trite observation that joy unalloyed is no part of man's lot. Nor is it that man necessarily manipulates his emotions to bring about a more piquant taste, as for instance the enervated enthusiasts of the sensibility cult would roll their feelings on the tongue, to produce 'grateful tears, delicious sorrow'. No; it is, as De Quincey saw, the very 'ebullience' of natural joy which brims over into regret. The phenomenon is of superabundant feeling, not enervation; as the quoted stanza says.

And this, too, is what the poem says. The poet presses the boy to admit that he shares the same sort of ambiguous feeling; and, when he admits it, he badgers him to know how he explains it. The boy resists, until at last:

1 *De Quincey's Literary Criticism*, ed. H. Darbishire (London, 1909), pp.227–8.

2 The poem was written at Alfoxden, and the names, though the names of real places, were chosen for euphony; the boy was Wordsworth's ward, son of his friend Basil Montagu.

His head he raised – there was in sight,
It caught his eye, he saw it plain –
Upon the house-top, glittering bright,
A broad and gilded vane.

Then did the boy his tongue unlock,
And eased his mind with this reply:
'At Kilve there was no weather-cock;
And that's the reason why.'

(49-56)

If we have not taken the point of the earlier stanza, we shall miss the poignancy in the boy's artlessness. The point is not the child's inability to see things in adult perspective, so that to him the presence or absence of a weather-vane over-rides all other considerations. Wordsworth precluded this by making the boy say he preferred the other place because it hadn't a weather-vane, not because it had. Wordsworth does not invite us to adult condescension. We are not to say, 'Oh, how sweet!' On the contrary, we have to see that the adult and the child are at one; that the boy, like the man, is enjoying himself so much that he can afford, and deliberately seeks out, some regret for which there is no objective reason. Pressed by the grown-up to find a reason, he fobs him off with a weather-vane: but he does not deceive himself, and as it happens he does not deceive the poet, though he deceives some readers. The pathos in the close derives from our compassionate realization that the child feels the same complex emotion as the man, and is even less able to explain it to himself. And yet that's not right either; for, left to himself, the boy would feel no need to account for it. Hence:

O dearest, dearest boy! my heart
For better lore would seldom yearn,
Could I but teach the hundredth part
Of what from thee I learn.

(57-60)

What the poet has learned is not to badger other people, and still more not to badger himself, to find reasons for feeling as he does; what he has to do is to feel thus and thus, and trust the feeling.

On no other reading is there justification for those lines which seem at first so deplorable:

His head he raised – there was in sight,
It caught his eye, he saw it plain –

This is not inexcusable padding-out, saying one simple thing three ways; it is daring. Pressed and fussed by the probing elder, the boy's eyes have a hunted look; and casting about in desperation, his eye lights upon the weather-cock. The lines convey brilliantly how his eye flits across the weather-cock, returns to it, and then, seeing it will do for a pretext, focuses on it.

Even so, Wordsworth had more in hand than the evoking of a pathos, however poignant. De Quincey in another fine passage emphasizes that the best of the Lyrical Ballads are genuine *discoveries* about human sentiment. Wordsworth was exploring unmapped territories, and coming home with treasure-trove. The realization that in the child's mind, as in the man's, abundant elation could express itself in illogical regret – this was such a discovery. Its importance, for Wordsworth as perhaps for us, can be brought home if we see it in the context of the cult of sensibility in the late eighteenth century, and the special sort of sentimentality it produced. One most marked feature of that cult, perhaps the central motive behind it, was a consuming interest in ambiguous emotional states. Sterne and Richardson, who had more important matters on hand, nevertheless could be (and were) excerpted and bowdlerized in order to nourish this appetite. One finds it everywhere in the minor poetry of Wordsworth's time and a little earlier. It is for instance the point of Samuel Rogers' verses 'On a Tear'. It is in the very title of James Montgomery's appallingly vulgar poem, 'The Joy of Grief':

'Tis the solemn feast of feeling,
  'Tis the Sabbath of the soul.

Or else we recognize it very readily in the elegiac form, as with John Logan:

Nor will I court Lethean streams,
  The sorrowing sense to steep;
Nor drink oblivion of the themes
  On which I love to weep.

We are accustomed to regard this sort of thing as vicious, and there can be little doubt that Wordsworth would have agreed. The ambiguous feeling that concerns him in 'Anecdote for Fathers' is something different, though it looks the same. As De Quincey noticed, Wordsworth himself defined the difference, insisting that the one sort of ambiguity is the effect of ebullience, the other, of enervation. The same distinction had to be made, in the same situation, by a writer concerned with ancient Greek literature:

> Is pessimism inevitably a sign of decadence, warp, weakened instincts, as it was once with the ancient Hindus, as it is now with us modern Europeans? Or is there such a thing as a *strong*

> pessimism?...Could it be, perhaps, that the very feeling of superabundance created its own kind of suffering: a temerity of penetration, hankering for the enemy...so as to prove its strength...?[1]

The same strange attitude is defined, with equal precision, in the 'Lines written in Early Spring':

> I heard a thousand blended notes,
> While in a grove I sate reclined,
> In that sweet mood when pleasant thoughts
> Bring sad thoughts to the mind.
>
> (1-4)

Again we misread if we think that the joy and peace of 'nature' remind the poet by contrast of the turbulence of man. This is not a scene, 'Where every prospect pleases and only man is vile.' For both 'pleasant thoughts' and 'sad thoughts' are comprised in 'that sweet mood'. It is a case, once again, of joy brimming over from its first motive into thoughts which, to the reason, are joyless. This is not, I think, forced quite home in this poem, but we need it to explain the jaunty movement, which seems so much at odds with the poet's assertion that he has 'reason to lament / What man has made of man.' This jaunty movement is characteristic of the Lyrical Ballads and, more than any peculiarities in the diction, is what unsettles the reader in 'Simon Lee' and 'The Last of the Flock'. It is in any case easy to point out the faults in both diction and metre which ruin these poems (though both, incidentally, have fine moments). And when we seek to generalize these failures, we usually do so by reference to Wordsworth's theory of diction. But that, it may be, is a red herring which Wordsworth drew across Coleridge's path and ours. And in any case to lay the blame there is not to generalize far enough. These failures among the Lyrical Ballads could be explained by supposing that in these poems Wordsworth tried for, and failed to achieve, this same tone of almost lunatic elation in which 'pleasant thoughts / Bring sad thoughts to the mind'. Wordsworth's word for this state, or one of his words, is 'glee'; and it is possible to regard all the Lyrical Ballads as experiments in expressing glee and/or investigations of that state.

Wordsworth said of 'The Idiot Boy', 'I never wrote anything with so much glee'. And in fact, for the effect of this splendid poem,

[1] Nietzsche, *A Critical Backward Glance* (1886) to *The Birth of Tragedy* (1871). *The Birth of Tragedy* and *The Genealogy of Morals*, tr. Francis Golffing (Garden City, N.Y., 1956), p.4.

'glee' is the exact word. The poet writes with glee, and the principal figure is the incarnation of glee:

> But when the Pony moved his legs,
> Oh! then for the poor Idiot Boy!
> For joy he cannot hold the bridle,
> For joy his head and heels are idle,
> He's idle all for very joy.
>
> And, while the Pony moves his legs,
> In Johnny's left hand you may see
> The green bough motionless and dead:
> The Moon that shines above his head
> Is not more still and mute than he.
>
> His heart it was so full of glee
> That, till full fifty yards were gone,
> He quite forgot his holly whip,
> And all his skill in horsemanship:
> Oh! happy, happy, happy John.
>
> (72-86)

And yet the subject is one that is, or ought to be, extremely painful – an idiot boy is not normally a pleasant or reassuring spectacle. What redeems the image, for the poet and for the reader, is the stillness, the muteness, the idleness.

The idleness should send us back to 'Expostulation and Reply' and 'The Tables Turned', where the poet is accused of idleness by the old schoolmaster, Matthew. He replies:

> The eye – it cannot choose but see;
> We cannot bid the ear be still;
> Our bodies feel, where'er they be,
> Against or with our will.
>
> Nor less I deem that there are Powers
> Which of themselves our minds impress;
> That we can feed this mind of ours
> In a wise passiveness. . . . ;[1]

and in the second poem:

> One impulse from a vernal wood
> May teach you more of man,

[1] 'Expostulation and Reply', 17-24.

Of moral evil and of good,
Than all the sages can.[1]

These are famous lines which we try to read with due solemnity, however their doctrine may outrage us. But perhaps we give them more solemnity than is due. For put them back in their contexts, and willy-nilly they read jauntily, trippingly. It will not do to decide that these stanzas are saying in another way what is said in 'Tintern Abbey'. It is the other way of saying that is important. The bearing and sense of these lines, when abstracted from them, may be identical with the bearing of some lines in 'Tintern Abbey', but these differ from those in being informed with glee, carried on the back of that lunatic elation which Wordsworth was at some pains to define, if only by rhythm – and never better than by the helter-skelter stumbling rhythms of 'The Idiot Boy'.

Wordsworth *was* the Idiot Boy. Consider these lines given to the idiot, lines from which, so Wordsworth says, the whole poem evolved:

The cocks did crow to-whoo, to-whoo,
And the sun did shine so cold![2]

This piercing shrillness can be described only by repeating what Matthew, in 'Expostulation and Reply', is made to say to Wordsworth:

You look round on your Mother Earth,
As if she for no purpose bore you;
As if you were her first-born birth,
And none had lived before you!
(9-12)

The idiot, seeing the moon and hearing the owls, is Adam on the first night after Creation.

It is the same with the other lunatic of the Lyrical Ballads, the mad mother of 'Her Eyes are Wild':

'Sweet babe! they say that I am mad,
But nay, my heart is far too glad;
And I am happy when I sing
Full many a sad and doleful thing;...'
(11-14)

What sort of sad things could thus be sung in high glee? What, but 'The Idiot Boy' or 'Goody Blake and Harry Gill'? Except for the

[1] 'The Tables Turned', 21-4.

[2] 'The Idiot Boy', 450-1.

Tintern Abbey lines, all Wordsworth's Lyrical Ballads are either analyses of the state of glee (as are 'Expostulation and Reply' and 'Anecdote for Fathers') or else expressions of that glee (as are 'Goody Blake and Harry Gill' and 'The Idiot Boy').

To be sure, it should now be clear that the sort of enjoyment called glee, no less the 'happiness' to which Wordsworth laid prescriptive claim, are something different from what normally goes under those names. If a definition is required beyond that furnished by Wordsworth's poems, one may go to S.T. Coleridge as recorded by E.H. Coleridge: 'He (Coleridge) called it joy, meaning thereby not mirth or high spirits, or even happiness, but a consciousness of entire and therefore well being when the emotional and intellectual faculties are in equipoise.' This carries special weight as the contribution of a poet, who, in *Dejection: An Ode*, showed himself ready to put as high a price on this state as Wordsworth did. It was because Coleridge thought it impossible he would ever experience this state anew, that he seems to have thought that his career as a poet was over.

The ass, the idiot, the moon, the owls – these motifs from 'The Idiot Boy' recur in Wordsworth's poems of 1799. There is the ass in *Peter Bell*; there are owls in the lines beginning, 'There was a Boy; ye knew him well, ye cliffs'; the moon figures with appalling effect in the 'Lucy' poem, 'Strange fits of passion have I known'; and Ruth, deserted by her lover, becomes a harmless lunatic. What is more, it is clear that all these images retain, for Wordsworth, the symbolic force he gave them in 'The Idiot Boy'. Wordsworth says comically that he studied the habits of asses before he wrote *Peter Bell*; but it was a sort of study which strove to learn what was the *meaning* of the ass, not what it looked like or how it behaved. In the same way, the owls:

And they would shout
Across the watery vale, and shout again,
Responsive to his call, – with quivering peals,
And long halloos, and screams, and echoes loud
Redoubled and redoubled; concourse wild
Of jocund din![1]

This 'jocund din' is what no one else, no previous poet and surely no reader, has ever heard in the calling of owls. It is not one of Wordsworth's discoveries, which we can corroborate, once the fact has been pointed out. The owls have a symbolic force, or none. Surely, then, the 'jocund din' is another version of that lunatic glee with which, stock-still in silence, the Idiot Boy heard the owls, and with which Wordsworth conceived him doing so.

[1] 'There was a Boy', 11-16.

In the 'Lucy' poem, the symbolic function of the moon is insisted on:

> My horse moved on; hoof after hoof
> He raised, and never stopped:
> When down behind the cottage roof,
> At once, the bright moon dropped.
>
> What fond and wayward thoughts will slide
> Into a Lover's head!
> 'O Mercy!' to myself I cried,
> 'If Lucy should be dead!'[1]

The connection between the obscuring of the moon and the death of a girl remains mysterious. The irrationality of it is pressed upon our attention.

But it can be rationalized without much trouble. Coleridge, in Germany with the Wordsworths at the time this poem was written, wrote to Thomas Poole: 'There are moments in which I have such power of life in me, such a *conceit* of it, I mean, that I lay the blame of my child's death on my absence.'[2] Coleridge was just emerging from his Berkeleyan phase, and the brilliant Berkeleyan paradox, *esse est percipi*, had led him to wonder how we could know that anything existed except in those moments when the mind perceived it. In his letter he takes the further step of speculating why, if the movements of the mind can thus annihilate whatever is out of mind, the movements of the body (from England to Germany, for instance) should not have the same power. Similarly, in Wordsworth's marvellous poem, the movements of the poet's body astride his horse make the moon drop out of sight and therefore (by Berkeleyan logic) out of existence; and if the movements of the body are thus capable of snuffing out the moon, why should they not snuff out a life, or, if the body has this power, must we not suppose the mind has equal power, such that, if you cease to think of a person, that person dies? We know from the famous note which Wordsworth dictated to the Immortality *Ode*, that he was capable of such an 'abyss of idealism'. Moreover, if we recall Coleridge's definition of joy ('a consciousness of entire and therefore well being'), or Wordsworth's definition of the poet ('a man pleased with his own passions and volitions, and who rejoices more than other men in the spirit of life that is in him'), we realize that when Coleridge writes of 'such power of life in me, such a *conceit* of it', he is talking of joy or glee. And thus, Wordsworth's

[1] 'Strange fits of passion have I known', 21–8.

[2] Coleridge, *Letters*, ed. E.H. Coleridge (London, 1895), p.295 (6 May 1799).

poem about Lucy turns once again upon the central theme of joy, and expresses in fact one of those 'fond regrets' which, 'with so much happiness to spare', the mind can bear, and delights, to entertain.

Common to all the treatments of glee is the silence and immobility of the chief actor. The Idiot Boy goes 'Burr-burr' and the teeth of Harry Gill 'chatter-chatter', but these sounds seem even further from human speech than silence would be. They only define the inhuman silence into which erupt, with piercing effect, the hooting of owls and the braying of donkeys. As for immobility, Charles Williams noticed long ago its mysterious attraction for Wordsworth in such later poems as 'Resolution and Independence' and 'Michael'. It is already present, as a potent force, in 1798; the Idiot Boy throughout, and Peter Bell after his criminal fury with the ass, and the horseman of the 'Lucy' poem, are immobile without being statuesque. None of them ride their mounts, for they do not guide them: they sit idle and immobile upon the animal's back, rapt in glee. 'Idle' is one of Wordsworth's words in this period, and he seems to see it, not as in reality it most commonly appears, as an aimless toying and fussing, but as a state of relaxed immobility.

3

The reader who has noticed this, though subconsciously, will not be surprised at a new feature of the poems of 1799, a recurrent concern with the fact of death. A corpse is silent and motionless, as Peter Bell was, and the Idiot Boy. What more natural than for Wordsworth to start wondering where the difference was, between this life and this death? It is as if Wordsworth, having repeatedly demanded a specially high value for rapt and silent immobility, should have a voice protest: 'Why, this that you value so highly – what is it but being half-dead?' 'Half-dead' is precise; for idiots are only half-alive. And Wordsworth turns to deal with the heckler. In the passive absorption of glee, a man is rapt out of time as the dead are out of time.

Wordsworth answers his heckler in two ways. On the one hand he seems to say: 'Yes, death is a state of permanent glee. And death therefore is good.' And he says the same thing, but subjectively, when he seems to say: 'Yes, my glee is so abundant that I can regard even death with joy.' The joy that spills over and transforms sad thoughts can now transform even thoughts of death. When Wordsworth's expression is at its most concentrated and masterly, he says both these things together:

A slumber did my spirit seal;
I had no human fears:
She seemed a thing that could not feel
The touch of earthly years.

No motion has she now, no force;
She neither hears nor sees;
Rolled round in earth's diurnal course,
With rocks, and stones, and trees.

The boy who called to the owls died young, but there is no implication that this was cause for sorrow, any more than the death of Lucy:

Thus Nature spake – The work was done –
How soon my Lucy's race was run!
She died, and left to me
The memory of what has been,
And never more will be.[1]

This is much truer to the experience (to judge from the appropriately trance-like melody, as from the logic of the situation) than is that other version of Lucy's death:

But she is in her grave, and, oh,
  The difference to me![2]

It is possible to hear the rhythm in these lines as gleeful, tripping. If we hear it in this way, we can hardly believe what the verses say. And we shall prefer to believe other, more honest poems, which seem to say that it makes next to no difference at all. Wordsworth is indifferent, since death and life can be equally gleeful, as in 'The Danish Boy':

For calm and gentle is his mien;
Like a dead Boy he is serene.
(54-5)

Wordsworth does not care whether the Danish Boy is a live boy or a dead ghost; in either case, he is '*glee*'. Nor does he care about 'Lucy Gray':

Yet some maintain that to this day
She is a living child;
That you may see sweet Lucy Gray
Upon the lonesome wild.

[1] 'Three years she grew', 37-42.

[2] 'She dwelt among the untrodden ways', 11-12.

O'er rough and smooth she trips along,
And never looks behind;
And sings a solitary song
That whistles in the wind.

(57-64)

Are the boy and girl both ghosts? The possibility is not brought in as a piece of fabulous machinery. It is to that suggestion Wordsworth conducts us, just to emphasize how little the possibility disturbs him. Alive or dead, their existence is joy. They represent a mode of being to which the question of life or death as normally conceived is irrelevant.

At the same time as Wordsworth probes this new vein, of the connection between glee, or natural joy, and death, he probes and extends an old vein, trying to define what this 'glee' is, to establish the conditions most favourable for it, and to distinguish it from perversions or vicious imitations.

Wordsworth repeats the definition he gave in 'Anecdote for Fathers'; glee is a state in which abundant joy spills over and transforms trains of feeling normally not joyful at all. In the fragment 'Nutting', the objects on to which joy spills over are merely 'indifferent':

In that sweet mood when pleasure loves to pay
Tribute to ease; and, of its joy secure,
The heart luxuriates with indifferent things,
Wasting its kindliness on stocks and stones,
And on the vacant air.

(39-43)

But the old ambiguity re-appears in its original form, with 'The Danish Boy':

The lovely Danish Boy is blest
And happy in his flowery cove:
From bloody deeds his thoughts are far;
And yet he warbles songs of war,
That seem like songs of love,
For calm and gentle is his mien;
Like a dead Boy he is serene.

(49-55)

If we ask why, when 'from bloody deeds his thoughts are far', the boy none the less 'warbles songs of war', and why, when warbled, they 'seem like songs of love', the only answer is the one we gave when the mad mother unaccountably found happiness singing 'many a sad and doleful thing'. Their consciousness of the richness of their own being is such that they deliberately seek out what is inimical to it, so as to transform it out of their own resources.

On the other hand, Wordsworth greatly extends his conception of 'glee', for it now seems elastic enough to include the state of mind of the Old Cumberland Beggar, or that defined in the related fragment, 'Animal Tranquillity and Decay'. The connection is in the term 'tranquillity', but it is brought home in a stanza of 'Three years she grew in sun and shower':

> She shall be sportive as the fawn
> That wild with glee across the lawn,
> Or up the mountain springs;
> And her's shall be the breathing balm,
> And her's the silence and the calm
> Of mute insensate things.
>
> (13-18)

The wildly sportive and the mutely insensate are alike manifestations of a glee which expresses itself as readily in a breathing silence as in wild activity. Or again, the connection is made in the fine poem on Matthew, 'The grey-haired man of glee'. For if glee is a state in which joy spills over into thoughts of sadness, we observe from Matthew's case that old age is naturally gleetful; for the joy of animal tranquillity in Matthew turns to sad thoughts of those near to him whom he has out-lived. To survive contemporaries and juniors is sad, and yet few will consider it a matter of regret to have that evidence of the power of life in one's self. (It is a fine stroke, incidentally, to make Matthew rebuff the poet's offer to take the place of his dead sons; for he is in a state of *animal* tranquillity, in which there can be no substitute for the animal passions of the blood-tie.)

Of course the state of mind of the principal figure is not the centre of interest in 'The Old Cumberland Beggar'. This is the first of the poems which asks, in respect of glee, what are the conditions in which glee can flourish; and the conditions in question are social conditions. This poem, therefore, like the other long narratives ('The Brothers' and, in its way, 'Michael'), expresses Wordsworth's view of the good society, the right social philosophy. In fact, it was occasioned by specific enactments for the relief of the indigent, and was sent to Charles James Fox, with a very bold and reasoned letter on the state of the poor laws.

Wordsworth's originality is not in choosing a subject such as a country beggar, but in making the light fall on him from an unforeseen angle. For he is concerned with acts and habits of charity not as they affect the recipient of alms, but as they affect the alms-giver –

a concern foreshadowed in the last stanza of 'Simon Lee'.[1] The 'moral' of 'The Old Cumberland Beggar' (our squeamishness demands the quotation-marks round 'moral', though Wordsworth would have seen no need for them) is that the old beggar was invaluable for cementing together in a common responsibility a community otherwise loosely knit. As Martin Buber has said, 'A community is where community happens.' And Wordsworth's poem has the effect of stressing that proper use of the word as denoting a spiritual fellowship, bound together in habitual disciplines of usage and unwritten law. This Burkean view of society as bound together by unwritten law and not by paper constitutions, coming so early in Wordsworth and so plainly in keeping with the whole tenor of his thought, serves to show how, despite his generous fellow-feeling with the French revolutionaries, his political outlook was innately conservative; and accordingly the charge that he was a political renegade loses most of its point. These habitual disciplines of custom and unformulated precedent are part of what Wordsworth was later to praise and examine as 'natural piety'.

Both 'The Brothers' and 'Michael' look rather different from this point of view. In the former poem, the younger brother, James, personifies glee: 'And many, many happy days were his...' (346). (The line as it stands is commonplace, but in the context, not just of this poem but of others, the 'happiness' carries weight.) Glee is possible to James Ewbank because, no less than the Cumberland Beggar, he is the responsibility of the whole rural community:

> He was the child of all the dale – he lived
> Three months with one, and six months with another,
> And wanted neither food, nor clothes, nor love;...
> (342-5)

The poem revolves around the uncertainty of Leonard, the elder brother, whether James is alive or dead. With him, as with the other personifications of glee, it is hard to tell. And it is magnificently appropriate that in the end it should appear that James died while sleep-walking, for this narrows still further the gap between life and death in the case of existences so fortunate as his. Equally ingenious and masterly is the device by which Leonard's uncertainty is made plausible, that is, the habit in the dale-village community of burying the dead without headstones or other means of identification. The

[1]'I've heard of hearts unkind, kind deeds
With coldness still returning;
Alas! the gratitude of men
Hath oftener left me mourning.'

whole community partakes of the idyllic life of glee, and the community's refusal to identify their dead exemplifies this people's difficulty in separating the dead from the living, and their indifference about it. (It is 'We are Seven' all over again.) The wandering brother, outside the community and *déraciné*, cannot share this indifference. He is shut out from glee and its concomitant, animal tranquillity. So in the end, oppressed and sorrowful, he leaves the dale for a second and final time. Those who regard Wordsworth as a proto-Victorian figure would do well to ponder this figure of Leonard Ewbank, and the doom that Wordsworth reserves for him. He has all the virtues of Smiles's self-help: independence, pride, resourcefulness, energy, courage. Not for him the solution that his weaker brother embraces – of living on charity. Yet it is the weak who inherit Wordsworth's earth. And indeed the praise of idleness, of idleness as a duty, should have prepared us: if the early Wordsworth is a Tory, he is a Tory anarchist. But all this was changed after the 'Ode to Duty'.

Wordsworth's blank-verse in 'The Brothers' is quite undistinguished, and barely adequate: but the poem is a great one because of the invention, the masterly conduct and disposition of the fable.[1] If this is bitter medicine to swallow in an age which believes that poetry exists in diction and nowhere else, this is not Wordsworth's fault.

The same is true of 'Michael', even though the verse as such is a little better, and in particular gets off to a better start. (At this period, Wordsworth's attempts to 'lead in' to his subject are lamentable, and the first lines of 'The Brothers' are especially disastrous; this is a particular case of Wordsworth's lack of dramatic imagination in even the loosest sense.) 'The Brothers' and 'Michael' are really very similar. In the first poem, one brother stays in the dale and benefits from the communcal discipline of glee, while the other leaves the dale and the community, thereafter unable to return; in the second poem, a father stays in the dale and within the community, exhibiting the animal tranquillity which is glee's counterpart or other aspect, while his son leaves never to return. If in these broad terms the poems treat of an identical situation, within this frame occur other situations which are identical:

[1] *Cf.* Wordsworth's definition of 'invention' (as one of five 'powers requisite for the production of poetry') in the Preface of 1815: 'Invention, – by which characters are composed out of materials supplied by observation; whether of the Poet's own heart and mind, or of external life and nature; and such incidents produced as are most impressive to the imagination and most fitted to do justice to the characters, sentiments and passions, which the poet undertakes to illustrate.'

They had an uncle; – he was at that time
A thriving man, and trafficked on the seas:
And, but for that same uncle, to this hour
Leonard had never handled rope or shroud;
For the boy loved the life which we lead here;
And though of unripe years, a stripling only,
His soul was knit to this his native soil...[1]

...We have, thou know'st,
Another kinsman – he will be our friend
In this distress. He is a prosperous man,
Thriving in trade – and Luke to him shall go,
And with his kinsman's help and his own thrift
He quickly will repair this loss, and then
He may return to us. If here he stay,
What can be done?....[2]

To be sure, in an age of agricultural depression and industrial expansion, this situation – of the beggared agriculturalist sending one or more of his family to be set up by an urban and mercantile relative – was being repeated in villages all over England (though incidentally Cumberland and Westmorland constituted rather a special case).[3] And of course Wordsworth was cognizant of this, and had something to say about it, more obviously in 'Michael' than in 'The Brothers'. But all the same, once we detect the identical situation in the two poems, the fact that Luke, Michael's son, turns out to be a bad lot, is hardly important. His bad behaviour, after leaving the dale, seems at first to be the pivot on which everything turns: but when we compare 'Michael' with 'The Brothers', we see that the crux of the story is Luke's departure in the first place. In the same way, Michael's inability to complete his sheepfold is often taken to mean that he has no will to continue, once his son has failed him. Undoubtedly this implication is present and throws a beam of pathos on the famous line, 'And never lifted up a single stone' (466). But once again, the attainment of pathos is not the end of Wordsworth's intention; and this is not the last line of the poem.

Michael, as has been pointed out, belongs with the other great figures which loom, in Wordsworth's poems, immobile through the mist upon the fells. He belongs with the Leech-gatherer, and with that other who is

[1] 'The Brothers', 292-8.

[2] 'Michael', 247-54.

[3] See Kenneth Maclean, *Agrarian Age. A Background for Wordsworth*. New Haven, 1950.

insensibly subdued
To settled quiet; he is one by whom
All effort seems forgotten; one to whom
Long patience hath such mild composure given,
That patience now doth seem a thing of which
He hath no need.[1]

Michael at the unfinished sheepfold is, in fact, another instance of animal tranquillity. Tranquillity may seem out of the question in respect of one so grievously wounded in the one relationship that was his life; and if we remember the close connection between this tranquillity and 'glee', we may seem to make of Wordsworth a monster of inhumanity. But in the quite special senses of tranquillity and of glee which Wordsworth's other poems have established, the idea becomes more acceptable. For instance, he has insisted from the first that *his* tranquillity and *his* glee in no way exclude sorrow and regret. If he still seems inhuman, this is because any insight carried relentlessly through to its conclusion looks what it is, relentless. And Wordsworth is inhuman only as the fact and presence of genius is inhuman.

4

If Wordsworth's central interests in *Lyrical Ballads* are such as I have expounded, if the connections he makes are indeed such as I have seen, the first response of the humane and intelligent reader must be to exclaim at his originality. And this is just. But in a period like ours when originality does not command such respect in and for itself as it did in the age succeeding Young's *Conjectures on Original Composition*, this perception can be made into a limitation; we are often asked to see Wordsworth, on whatever terms we present him, as a special case, and to dismiss him from our minds accordingly whenever we think of poetry in general and of poetry at the present time in particular. In these circumstances, at a time when (thanks to Eliot) we never use the concept of originality without at once passing nervously to the supposedly complementary notion of tradition, it is worth pointing out that Wordsworth's concerns, and his attitudes, were not unprecedented; that he had a tradition, and an ancient one, to which he could have appealed if he had chosen. It is characteristic of him that he didn't choose, and for the most part disdained to invoke the authority of Aristotle and Longinus. Nevertheless, such authority is available.

[1] 'Animal Tranquillity and Decay', 7-12.

Wordsworth's emphasis on the poet's pleasure in perception as the central and distinguishing feature of poetry – a pleasure even in perception of what is painful, indeed especially in such perceptions[1] – goes back to the classical and originally Aristotelian commonplace, *admiratio*, which was, in classical and again in scholastic and Renaissance times, particularly of moment in respect of the painful subjects of tragedy. *Admiratio* in these contexts is normally translated as 'wonder'; and this does not help matters, since Watts-Dunton's definition of the Romantic movement as 'The renascence of wonder' is now a very unfashionable idea. At the risk of rehabilitating a much-disliked Victorian, the point must be made; and we find the root of the tradition of poetic wonder in Aristotle's *Metaphysics*:

> For it is owing to their wonder that men both now
> begin and at first began to philosophize....

As Albert the Great, commenting on this passage, remarks, 'Wonder is something like fear in its effect on the heart.' And this may serve to show the connection between Aristotle on this point and Longinus, whose treatise on the elevated style, *On the Sublime*, is centrally concerned with the rhetorical concept of *admiratio*. For most readers will be aware of how eighteenth-century commentators on Longinus, such as Burke, spent a great deal of time with the apparently nonsensical proposition, which was however validated by experience as well as by Longinus' authority, that the pleasurable effect of sublime art was hardly distinguishable from the usually very unpleasurable emotion of fear. While Burke and others revived and explored this ancient connexion between wonder (*admiratio*) and fear, Wordsworth can by seen in Lyrical Ballads to be exploring its connection with joy. This too was a traditional connexion, though it was always secondary to the connexion with fear. J.V. Cunningham, for instance (to whom I am indebted for all these citations) defines *admiratio* as 'the shocked limit of feeling', and, summing up the implications for an understanding of Shakespeare of his use of the marvellous in his latest plays, decides: 'Wonder, then, is associated not only with extreme fear but also with extreme joy, and is marked by silence and immobility.'[2] As has been seen, states of silence and immobility occur in nearly every one of the Lyrical Ballads,

[1] Henry Crabb Robinson, *Diary* (9 May 1815): 'Wordsworth, in answer to the common reproach that his sensibility is excited by objects which produce no effect on others, admits the fact, and is proud of it.... The poet himself, as Hazlitt has well observed, has a pride in deriving no aid from his subject. It is the mere power which he is conscious of exerting in which he delights, not the production of a work in which men rejoice on account of the sympathies and sensibilities it excites in them.'

[2] J.V. Cunningham, *Woe or Wonder* (Denver, 1951), p.92.

and these features are explained in the poems as the effects of joy.

It is with deliberation that I describe what these poems do by the homely word, 'explaining'; for it is characteristic both of Wordsworth's practice in his poems and of his theory in his *Preface*, that he is quite unembarrassed by any wish to distinguish between knowing the human mind through poetry and knowing it in other ways, through the case-book of the field researcher or the rationally controlled introspection of the philosophical psychologist. It is therefore not only appropriate but necessary to point out, as J. V. Cunningham does for his purposes, that for Aristotle 'wonder' is a concept which straddles the gap between logic and rhetoric, or, as we might say, between conceptual and aesthetic experience. This is the point of citing Aristotle's reference in the *Metaphysics*, and it is taken up in the *Rhetoric*:

> Again, since learning and wondering are pleasant, it follows that such things as acts of imitation must be pleasant – for instance, painting, sculpture, poetry – and every product of skilful imitation: this latter, even if the object imitated is not in itself pleasant; for it is not the object itself which here gives delight; the spectator draws inferences ('That is a so-and-so') and thus learns something fresh.

Cunningham comments on this passage very justly,[1] 'What we call aesthetic experience is for Aristotle substantially the experience of inferring.' This is true of Wordsworth also, and this is the pleasurable experience he gave to a reader such as De Quincey. Poetry for Wordsworth is a means of knowing the world, not a means of self-expression or self-adjustment.

Again, on the point that 'it is natural for all to delight in works of imitation', Aristotle writes in the *Poetics*:

> The truth of this second point is shown by experience: though the objects themselves may be painful to see, we delight to view the most realistic representations of them in art, the forms for example of the lowest animals and of dead bodies. The explanation is to be found in a further fact: to be learning something is the greatest of pleasures not only to the philosopher but also the rest of mankind, however small their capacity for it; the reason of the delight in seeing the picture is that one is at the same time learning – gathering the meaning of things, e.g. that the man there is a so-and-so;...

[1] *Op. cit.*, p.65.

St Thomas makes the same connection. 'Wonder,' he says, 'is a kind of desire for knowledge'; and he goes on:

> For this reason, everything wonderful is pleasurable: for example, anything that is infrequent, as well as any representation of things, even of those that are not in themselves pleasant. For the soul delights in comparing one thing with another, since this is a proper and connatural activity of reason, as Aristotle says in his *Poetics*.

If we can rid ourselves of the notion that Wordsworth's *Preface* is exclusively or even chiefly the expression of an extreme and unbalanced theory of poetic diction, and read it again looking for other things, it will appear that what chiefly interests Wordsworth about poetry is that which interested Aristotle, Longinus, Aquinas and Albertus Magnus, and that in speculating about it Wordsworth follows, whether he knows it or not, in paths trodden by those great predecessors. Moreover, all this element in the *Preface* is far more immediately and fruitfully relevant to the poems thus introduced, than is the theory of diction.

Wordsworth's theory of metre, for instance, is, as expounded in the *Preface*, generally and rightly thought to be inadequate – chiefly for the reason that Wordsworth lights upon an adequate rationale for metre only after he has already advanced several inadequate justifications, which he was then too careless or too idle to expunge. And so, when Elisabeth Schneider decides, 'The conclusion is inescapable... that in theory at least, he did not get beyond the conception of metre as something "superadded" to poetry, not an organic part of it,'[1] we can hardly blame her, for Wordsworth appears to have lit upon such a conception without realizing it or else without caring for what he had come upon. Nevertheless, the passage exists to prove that at least the discovery was made, even if nothing was to be made of it; and the conception of metre there expressed is superior to either Hazlitt's or Coleridge's (those with which Miss Schneider compares it), superior because it sees metre as far more organic to poetry than on either Coleridge's or Hazlitt's showing. Metre in this conception is more organic to poetry because it is derived immediately from the principle which Wordsworth saw as central to all poetry whatever – the principle of delight, of the mind taking pleasure in the exercise of its own powers:

> If I had undertaken a SYSTEMATIC defence of the theory here maintained, it would have been my duty to develope the various causes upon which the pleasure received from metrical language

[1] Elisabeth Schneider, *The Aesthetics of William Hazlitt* (Philadelphia, 1933).

> depends. Among the chief of these causes is to be reckoned a principle which must be well known to those who have made any of the Arts the object of accurate reflection; namely, the pleasure which the mind derives from the perception of similitude in dissimilitude.

It is easy to see Aquinas ('For the soul delights in comparing one thing with another') in this pleasurable 'perception of similitude in dissimilitude,' which is, as Wordsworth goes on to say, 'the great spring of the activity of our minds, and their chief feeder'. Moreover, this view of what metre does locks in with the rest of Wordsworth's thought as do none of his alternative cases for metre, which he develops earlier and at greater length. For just as St Thomas's perception of the pleasure of comparing is based on a perception of how knowing is pleasure and pleasure is in knowing, so Wordsworth's recognition that the pleasure in metre consists in the perception of similitude in dissimilitude is based upon the same realization: knowing is pleasure, and pleasure is in knowing.

> We have no sympathy but what is propagated by pleasure: I would not be misunderstood; but wherever we sympathise with pain, it will be found that the sympathy is produced and carried on by subtle combinations with pleasure. We have no knowledge, that is, no general principles drawn from the contemplation of particular fact, but what has been built up by pleasure, and exists in us by pleasure alone.

And if it is still required to be proved that this pleasure without which 'we have no knowledge' is the pleasure which Aristotle perceived when he wrote how 'learning and wondering are pleasant', the proof is in the poems themselves, which concern themselves continually with those features of immobility and silence which are, as we have seen, traditionally connected with the rapt delight of the state of wonder.

5

It may still be unclear where the connection is between the central concern of Wordsworth's poetry and the forms that poetry took. In particular, why were those forms, as Wordsworth's contemporaries noticed, so consistently undramatic? What is the connection, if any, between this habit of Wordsworth's imagination and the central importance, for that imagination, of the fact of happiness, of joy? I can only venture a reply, and that reply in such general terms as perhaps to be useless. But Nietzsche has been cited already as one who was struck, as Wordsworth was, by the way in which health seeks out morbidity, by (to use Nietzsche's own terms) 'A penchant of the mind for what is hard, terrible, evil, dubious in existence, arising from a plethora of health, plenitude of being.' And this 'penchant of the mind' Nietzsche identifies with the Dionysiac temper or the Dionysiac principle. Now, in some exceptionally close and difficult passages of *The Birth of Tragedy*, Nietzsche explains how the Dionysiac dithyramb evolved into dramatic presentation, by the necessity for the Dionysiac to relate itself to (and in part assuage itself by) the sunny objective images of the Apollonian. Thus it becomes possible to conceive that in Wordsworth his contemporaries were struck by the Dionysiac spirit operating without any Apollonian admixture or complement; and if so, Wordsworth's Romanticism manifests itself very exactly as the rejection of the classical and neo-classical tradition, as the rejection of the supposedly necessary harmony between these two principles – a harmony continuously maintained or aimed at from ancient Greece through Rome to Augustan England. And is this, after all, to say any more than that Wordsworth witnesses to the conquering by the subjective of the objective world, of a reality bodied over against the perceiver? This after all is no new diagnosis of Romanticism. All that we gain, perhaps, from putting it in Nietzschean terms, is the realization that in pre-history men had lived in those 'abysses of idealism' into which Wordsworth plunges anew, with all the excitement and assurance of a man who treads where none have trod for centuries.

Wordsworth's Mind and Art, ed. A.W. Thomson (Edinburgh: Oliver and Boyd, 1969).

20 *The Poetry of Sir Walter Scott*

Lockhart tells a story of how Scott, in the midst of writing *The Lady of the Lake*, decided to measure his own fiction by the facts. He threw himself on horseback and, in Lockhart's words, 'put to the test the practicability of riding from the banks of Loch Vennachar to the Castle of Stirling within the brief space which he had assigned to Fitz-James's Grey Bayard, after the battle with Roderick Dhu'.

It is the sort of anecdote which delighted those many admirers of Scott throughout the nineteenth century who applauded in such episodes of Scott's life, as in the poems themselves, Scott's robust and virile, extroverted attitude to the business of writing. The most authoritative expression of this was Byron's, in *Beppo*:

> One hates an author that's *all author*, fellows
> In foolscap uniforms turn'd up with ink,
> So very anxious, clever, fine and jealous,
> One don't know what to say to them, or think,
> Unless to puff them with a pair of bellows;
> Of coxcombry's worst coxcombs e'en the pink
> Are preferable to these shreds of paper,
> These unquench'd snuffings of the midnight taper.
>
> Of these same we see several, and of others,
> Men of the world, who know the world like men,
> Scott, Rogers, Moore, and all the better brothers,
> Who think of something else besides the pen;

This account of Scott, which ranges him, if with Byron himself, also with Samuel Rogers and Tom Moore as against Coleridge and Wordsworth, is in line, so far as I can see, with our current estimate of Scott as poet. In the present century the case often goes by default; Scott's poetry is quite simply overlooked. But I dare say if challenged, the instructed reader today would agree with Byron, though not in Byron's spirit nor on his grounds, that Scott as poet stands nearer to Rogers than to Wordsworth. However, anyone who thinks it worth while talking about Scott's poetry at all cannot be satisfied with this estimate of Scott as just a representative Regency versifier, and of his poetry as having therefore, by and large, only historical importance.

The reader who on the other hand endorses this estimate will think he finds confirmation if he turns to the passage in question, the account of Fitz-James's ride:

> Along thy banks, swift Teith! they ride,
> And in the race they mock'd their tide;
> Torry and Lendrick now are past,
> And Deanstown lies behind them cast:
> They rise, the banner'd towers of Doune,
> They sink in distant woodland soon;
> Blair-Drummond sees the hoof strike fire,
> They sweep like breeze through Ochtertyre;
> They mark just glance and disappear
> The lofty brow of ancient Keir;
> They bathe their coursers' sweltering sides,
> Dark Forth! amid thy sluggish tides.
> And on the opposing shore take ground,
> With plash, with scramble, and with bound.
> Right-hand they leave thy cliffs, Craig-Forth!
> And soon the bulwark of the North,
> Grey Stirling, with her towers and town,
> Upon their fleet career look'd down.

We may relish the exultation of this, the swing and fire of the rhythm, and still find ourselves thinking that it is essentially, necessarily trivial. One way to disturb this impression is to read on in Lockhart, who remarks, 'the principal landmarks in the description of that fiery progress are so many hospitable mansions all familiar to him at the same period – Blair-drummond, the residence of Lord Kaimes; Ochtertyre, that of John Ramsay, the scholar and antiquary . . . and "the lofty brow of ancient Keir", the splendid seat of the chief family of the name of Stirling . . .'. The names then were not chosen at random, not just for euphony and rhyme. And if we read the passage again with this information to assist us, we can indeed envisage the possibility – that the litany of place-names has such pace and stir, not only because they mark the stages in a furious ride against time, but also because of the fellow-feeling and the patriotic excitement which their associations awake in the poet. However, this remains only a possibility. The example is not at all conclusive. And no doubt the passage cannot count for much one way or the other.

But perhaps the unsympathetic reader will object to more in this passage than what he sees as its triviality. One can imagine the objection, 'But how wasteful this is! so many ways of saying simply that they galloped past or galloped through!' This seems to me a more profound misunderstanding. At their least considered such objections reveal a misunderstanding not just of Scott's poetry but of all poetry; they strike at and strike down not just the habit of Scott's imagination, but the act of the poetic imagination as such. I should like to dwell on this.

The ride to Stirling comes in Canto V of *The Lady of the Lake*; what follows is from Canto III, which as a whole is a good deal finer. It is a description of an ancient battlefield; or rather, more precisely, a meditation upon it –

> The Knot-grass fettered there the hand,
> Which once could burst an iron band;
> Beneath the broad and ample bone,
> That buckler'd heart to fear unknown,
> A feeble and a timorous guest,
> The field-fare framed her lowly nest;
> There the slow blind-worm left his slime
> On the fleet limbs that mock'd at time;
> And there, too, lay the leader's skull,
> Still wreath'd with chaplet flush'd and full,
> For heath-bell with her purple bloom
> Supplied the bonnet and the plume.

Clearly the reader who complained, 'So many ways of saying only that they galloped!' could complain of this, 'So many ways of saying only that they are dead and gone!' And yet I think he would be more reluctant in this case, would feel uneasily that to complain on these grounds might be to miss the point of poetic perception altogether.

For the way in which syntax and word-order in this passage are continually varied so as to mask, and yet to assert, the identity of the relationships – as knot-grass is to the hand, so field-fare to the heart, blind-worm to the limbs, and heath-bell to the head – this is an example of what may be called 'elegant variation', simply the saying of one thing many ways. And such variation is a constant and governing feature of Scott's style. Another name for it, perhaps a better one, was found by Roman Jakobson when he spoke of the 'poetry of grammar'. Following Sapir, Jakobson would say that grammatically each of the clauses in this passage is identical with all the others. They differ not grammatically but lexically; an identical grammatical structure is differently 'filled out', but the difference is only in the trappings as it were, and in the disposition.[1] In much

[1] I am here reproducing almost verbatim a passage from Jakobson's paper to an International Conference of Linguistics and Poetics in Warsaw, 1960. It seems to me

ancient poetry such grammatical parallelism, often in a more elementary form, serves as a self-sufficient principle of poetic ordering – as it does once again in some modern *vers-libre*. By Scott, of course, it is used only in conjunction with other ordering principles, the traditional ones of rhyme and imagery and metre. But Scott seldom uses these traditional devices with real power; by the time he wrote *The Lady of the Lake* Scott was, for instance, a dexterous but also a very unsubtle metrist. In any case it is when the traditional principles of order are reinforced by grammatical patterning and parallels that we recognize a poetry thoroughly achieved, structured through and through; and elegant variation, the saying of one thing many ways, brings with it for Scott this additional source of order.

When we speak of such variation as 'elegant', we should not seem to imply that it is peculiarly characteristic of late sophisticated styles. On the contrary, repetition with variation, riddles, and grammatical parallels are staple features of primitive forms like the ballad and the lay and the song; indeed the device of the refrain has meaning and power only in relationship to this principle. And so the distinction of this passage about the battlefield is the same in principle as that of the incomparable 'Proud Maisie', or of a much more relaxed but still wonderfully achieved song, the exquisite 'Brignall Banks are wild and fair' in Canto Third of the otherwise tedious *Rokeby*. The augmented and diverted significance with which on each repetition the refrain is endowed – this is, in poems of this kind, a stroke of the highest art.

Poetry of grammar enters also into rhyme, for the rhyming of a verb with a noun has a more striking and normally a more artistic effect than the rhyming of verb with verb or (but this is different again) of noun with noun.[1] And thus elegant variation or the poetry of grammar is present in the sophisticated rhyming poetry of Pope as in the riddle and the kenning or those other ancient poetic forms which Scott encountered in the ballad-collections of Ritson and Bishop Percy, which he encountered at first hand for himself when he compiled *Minstrelsy of the Scottish Border*. On the other hand, rhyme is rather a special case, since it involves direct repetition only of sound, not of sense. And the good poets of the eighteenth century,

[1] See W.K. Wimsatt, 'One Relation of Rhyme to Reason', in *The Verbal Ikon* (University of Kentucky Press, 1954).

one case in which linguistics has had something to say which literary criticism cannot afford to ignore. I think the same position was approached out of *criticism*, by R.P. Blackmur in his use of the idea of 'ad-libbing' in an essay on Yeats – a passage which once shocked me into incredulity, which now, however, I am disposed to accept.

Scott's predecessors, tended to look askance at manoeuvres which involved repetitions of sense, for the sufficient and admirable reason that they valued very highly the qualities of terseness, rapidity, and compactness. Modern poetic theory, because it similarly places a high premium on these qualities, is ill placed to acknowledge as legitimate, still less to enjoy and admire, the sort of talent in Scott which produces his meditation on the ancient battlefield. And Scott himself appears to have held that the terseness and compactness of *The Vanity of Human Wishes* made it poetry of a higher order than any he wrote himself. What needs to be insisted on, however, when we notice the lack of these qualities in Scott's poetry, is that Scott's leisurely and expansive narration can achieve effects which are as foreign to Johnson's style as Johnson's pithiness is foreign to the style of Scott. These are the effects of that gift which seems to figure in our older criticism as 'copiousness of invention'. Not only has this expression disappeared from our criticism, but I do not see what other expression has taken its place. And it puzzles me how we manage without it, or something like it, except by growing blind to that range of poetic effects which it used to denote, ancient and universal as those are. Certainly this, the copiousness of his invention, is the greatest thing in Scott, in poetry and prose alike; and so when we find him saying 'they rode on' in seven different ways, one after the other, we should not suppose that this is wasteful superfluity, but direct creative energy revelling in its own fecundity. If any one protests that this is Art for Art's sake, I would retort that it is rather Nature for Nature's sake; Pasternak has a profound passage in his autobiography, *Safe Conduct*, where he says that just as a physicist plots upon squared paper the track followed by a unit of physical energy such as an electrical charge, so the poet plots in a poem the track followed among images by that psychic energy which we call 'feeling'.

This answer is effective, if only because it is the same copiousness of invention in Scott which elaborates sentiments through variation and contrives one grammatical pattern after another, which elaborates his plots and contrives episode after episode. But the argument is not quite fair, still less conclusive. For the fact is, of course, that very little of *The Lady of the Lake* is so well written as the passages I have so far considered. George Ellis, in his *Quarterly* review of *The Lady of the Lake*, noted, as new developments since *Marmion* and *The Lay of the Last Minstrel*, 'a profusion of incident, and a shifting brilliancy of colouring that reminds us of the witchery of Ariosto'.[1]

[1] I take it that this reference to Ariosto was what gave the cue to those admirers of Scott who brought it about that a few years later Scott was being advertised all over the Continent as 'the Ariosto of the North'.

That 'shifting brilliancy' can be illustrated, more literally perhaps than Ellis intended, by a passage such as this, from the first Canto:

> The western waves of ebbing day
> Roll'd o'er the glen their level way;
> Each purple peak, each flinty spire,
> Was bathed in floods of living fire,
> But not a setting beam could glow
> Within the dark ravines below,
> Where twined the path in shadow hid
> Round many a rocky pyramid,
> Shooting abruptly from the dell
> Its thunder-splinter'd pinnacle;
> Round many an insulated mass,
> The native bulwarks of the pass,
> Huge as the tower which builders vain
> Presumptuous piled on Shinar's plain.
> The rocky summits, split and rent,
> Form'd turret, dome, or battlement,
> Or seemed fantastically set
> With cupola or minaret,
> Wild crests as pagod ever deck'd,
> Or mosque of Eastern architect.
> Nor were these earth-born castles bare,
> Nor lacked they many a banner fair;
> For, from their shiver'd brows display'd
> Far o'er the unfathomable glade,
> All twinkling with the dew-drops sheen,
> The brier-rose fell in streamers green,
> And creeping shrubs, of thousand dyes,
> Waved in the west-wind's summer sighs.

This is wretched work. It is no good asking the affronted reader not to look in a long poem for a compactness of sentiment, for a weight and also a polish in the expression, which only the short poem can give him. He may be thus outflanked, he is not convinced. And he is right. Such verse as this is not to be excused by any talk of energetic invention, or of bluff appetite and gusto too caught up in its own narrative to pause for effeminate niceties. On the contrary, what is disastrously lacking to this writing is precisely masculinity, masculinity as Pater defined it when he spoke of 'manliness' in art as 'a full consciousness of what one does, of art itself in the work of art, tenacity of intuition and of consequent purpose'. It lacks that 'masterly execution' which, to Hopkins too, as Pater's pupil, 'is a kind of male gift'. It lacks precisely that structuring through and through which appears in the passage about the battlefield. It is this, an energy of apprehension which, so far from running wild, seeks out of itself the structures to control it, which makes a piece of writing masculine or manly, as Pater and Hopkins understood those terms. And I hope it is plain that their understanding of masculinity is more serious, more ancient (for it goes back, I think, to 'Longinus'), and also far more relevant to poetry as poetry, than Byron's liking for 'men of the world, who know the world like men' or, to take another example, the 'virility' which W.M. Rossetti in 1870 allowed to Scott, as something implied by calling him 'spirited'. And if Scott always has Byron's and Rossetti's kind of masculinity, only seldom does he rise to the manliness demanded by Hopkins and Pater.

The effeminacy of this last passage, the absence from it of the truly masculine, the *truly* robust, appears in nothing so clearly as in the handling of the metre. It was Ellis again, reviewing the poem on its first appearance, who was sorry to see it cast into octosyllabic couplets. If one speaks, in a time-honoured phrase, of the 'fatal fluency' of this metre, one ought to mean, I think, that the metrical norm asserts itself so insistently as to iron out any play of spoken stress against that norm. Thus in the case of 'The brier-rose fell in streamers green', the interesting rhythm of that line in isolation, with its hesitation on the very weak second syllable of 'brier', and the breath-pause that must intervene between the stressed syllables 'rose' and 'fell', is subjugated entirely when the line is read in the context, so that we read Thē bríēr-rōse féll; the stressed syllable 'rose' being crammed into the weak supposedly unstressed place in an iambic foot, while the frailty of the second syllable of 'brier' is drowned out completely. (This is a good example, incidentally, of how delicacy with metre assists diction also, for if Scott had respected the innate rhythm of his words he would have noticed how 'rose' and 'fell' lived awkwardly together because of the other 'rose' that comes from 'to rise'.) 'Earth-born castles' and 'the west-wind's summer sighs' are two other phrases whose rhythms are stunned by the metre. And in fact, scansion reveals that, throughout, the disposition of stress against the syllables is insensitive, arbitrary, slipshod, and improvised.

And yet this is the poet who wrote 'Proud Maisie'; who wrote also this –

From the sound of Teviot's tide,
Chafing with the mountain's side,

From the groan of the wind-swung oak,
From the sullen echo of the rock,
From the voice of the coming storm,

The Ladye knew it well!
It was the Spirit of the Flood that spoke,
And he called on the Spirit of the Fell
. . . 'Sleep'st thou, Brother?' . . .

The shock which this gives us (it is from *The Lay of the Last Minstrel*) is almost entirely a matter of rippling, resilient movement; it has to do with the accentual, rather than accentual-syllabic, metre. Not only is it more resilient and sprightly; the rhythms are given more margin to gather power before being reined back. Then too, the wandering of the stress keeps us alert so as to find it, never in each new line quite where it was in the line before. Scott, we are told, took the hint for this from Coleridge; but he deserves credit for having of himself a sufficiently inward aliveness to verse-movement to be able to profit from Coleridge's rediscovery of this ancient music. And in any case, to some extent this new alertness and unpredictability of rhythm were characteristic of all the good verse from the first phase of the English Romantic Movement, when it was still close to Percy's *Reliques*. Professor Josephine Miles in her very instructive and learned *Eras and Modes of English Poetry*, sets these lines from the *Lay* along with stanzas from Blake, from Burns, and from Tom Moore, to recreate very challengingly our sense of what a new departure was inaugurated when these poets and others began writing in this way at various dates in the 1790s. We are so aware of the confusingly many things that Romanticism later became, that we are in every danger of forgetting what a simple and salient thing it must have appeared to start with; and most of our difficulties with, for instance, the masterpiece of this first phase, *The Rime of the Ancient Mariner*, come when we try to read that poem as if it belonged to a later Romanticism which trafficked in allegory. But this is to stray from considerations simply of metre. And as to this, I am glad to borrow Professor Miles's authoritative account, when she speaks of 'a varied and broken line pattern, the constant remission of four stresses to three, with consequent effects of easy repetition or wordlessness, the lightness of masculine endings, shadings of echo and progression from stanza to stanza, and indeed in every new form of modification in sound, the quality of shadow, echo, or answer, rather than the massed and cumulative forces of the old pentameters'. This is a description of the musical dimensions of *The Lay* and, not so exactly but still substantially, of *Marmion* also. Such fineness in the texture of sound is absent from *The Lady of the Lake*; and in fact it may well be maintained that by the time Scott wrote *The Lady*, the third of his narrative poems, his most original work was already behind him. Certainly, although there are interesting things, in later narratives such as *The Lord of the Isles* and *Harold the Dauntless*, there are the clearest indications in his long poems after *The Lady of the Lake* that the resources of the author's most vivid imaginative life were already being husbanded against the time when he would draw upon them for his novels. And equally certainly some of the most impressive characteristics of *Minstrelsy of the Scottish Border*, of *The Lay of the Last Minstrel* and *Marmion*, have already disappeared from *The Lady of the Lake*.

We see this in another way, at the level of diction rather than metre, if we go back for a moment to what Ellis said of 'the shifting brilliancy of colouring' in *The Lady of the Lake*. In the passage I quoted from this poem it is indeed the 'purple peak', the brier-rose which is '*twinkling* with the dew-drops' sheen', and the 'creeping shrubs, *of thousand dyes*', which are the clearest symptoms of the loss by Scott of his initial vision and impetus. It is not that these notations are inaccurate or imprecise. For neither an Imagist exactitude nor a Keatsian full vividness of sensuous register was at any time part of Scott's purpose. In his earlier poems, as in the ballads which inspired them and (what should give us pause) in the heroic poetry of the ancient world, colours for instance have a function as much emblematic or heraldic as descriptive. Quite simply, in *The Lay* and in *Marmion* as opposed to *The Lady of the Lake* or *Rokeby*, Scott used a far more restricted palette of bold primary colours, and so achieved a more severe effect:

> When red hath set the beamless sun,
> Through heavy vapours dark and dun;

or:

> Till, dark above, and white below
> Decided drives the flaky snow,...

(where 'Decided', I think, is very fine); or else (Flodden field seen from afar):

> And, first, the ridge of mingled spears
> Above the brightening cloud appears;
> And in the smoke the pennons flew,
> As in the storm the white sea-mew...,

where the diverse colours of the pennons are strangely and emblematically bleached to a uniform white.

Ruskin in volume III of *Modern Painters* takes another example from the description of Flodden:

> The white pavilions made a show
> Like remnants of the winter snow
>   Along the dusky ridge.

And Ruskin makes a great deal of Scott's use of colour:

> in general, if he does not mean to say much about things, the *one* character which he will give is colour, using it with the most perfect mastery and faithfulness, up to the point of possible modern perception. For instance, if he has a sea-storm to paint in a single line, he does not, as a feebler poet would probably have done, use any expression about the temper or form of the waves; does not call them angry or mountainous. He is content to strike them out with two dashes of Tintoret's favourite colours:
>
> '*The blackening wave is edged with white,*
> To inch and rock the sea-mews fly.'

And –

> Again: where he has to describe tents mingled among oaks, he says nothing about the form of either tent or tree, but only gives the two strokes of colour:
>
> 'Thousand pavilions, *white as snow,*
> *Chequered* the borough moor below,
> Oft giving way, where still there stood
> Some relics of the old oak wood,
> That darkly huge did intervene,
> *And tamed the glaring white with green.*'

But this last example is something different, as Ruskin should have acknowledged. 'And tamed the glaring white with green' – this is too painterly, too precious I had almost said, for comfort.

There are other places where Scott shows this sort of preciousness in stylized patterning of colour. A place where it causes no discomfort is the first stanza of Canto Second of *The Lay*:

> If thou would'st view fair Melrose aright,
> Go visit it by the pale moonlight;
> For the gay beams of lightsome day
> Gild, but to flout, the ruins grey.
> When the broken arches are black in night,
> And each shafted oriel glimmers white;
> When the cold light's uncertain shower
> Streams on the ruin'd central tower;
> When buttress and buttress, alternately,
> Seem fram'd of ebon and ivory;...

This domino pattern of black and white, with the painterly perception of 'cold light' in the fine line, 'When the cold light's uncertain shower', has not at all the severe effect of the whites and blacks at Flodden. On the contrary this is plainly a perception of the Regency man of letters, not of any belated harpist of the Scottish border. It is none the worse for that; indeed it comes conveniently to remind us that *The Lay* for all its loving re-creation of the conventions of late medieval romance, is by no means a simple pastiche, however expert, like some of Scott's art-ballads. The distinction of the poem is precisely that its author, while not pretending to be other than he is, a man of the Regency, can nevertheless assimilate into that modern posture habits of thought and feeling from an older and very different age.

The quite different colour-effect which Scott brings over from the ballads appears at its most impressive, as I think, in the introduction to the third Canto of *Marmion*. Here, in an epistle to William Erskine, Scott excuses himself for having deserted classical precedents of form, of genre, and of subject ('Brunswick's venerable hearse'). The emphasis falls on structure, as Scott vindicates the rambling development of 'the romance' against the classical requirement of a single unified great action. But the verse comes to life when the alternative unclassical inspiration is seen in terms not of structure but of *hue*:

> Yet was poetic impulse given
> By the green hill and clear blue heaven.

And the other example which Scott gives, besides the green and blue of his native Scotland, of how early environment moulds the poet beyond what precept can later correct, is similarly seen in terms of primary colour:

> Look east, and ask the Belgian why,
> Beneath Batavia's sultry sky,
> He seeks not eager to inhale
> The freshness of the mountain gale,
> Content to rear his whiten'd wall
> Beside the dank and dull canal?
> He'll say, from youth he loved to see
> The white sail gliding by the tree.

The surely unpremeditated repetition here – 'whiten'd' and 'white' – has a mysterious purity and force which imprint it on the mind as the metrical resilience and eagerness imprint 'By the green hill and clear blue heaven'. What both passages have is a simplicity which is not Wordsworth's simplicity, though related to his. For it is a definitive characteristic of English Romanticism as the literary historian knows it in its earliest phase, when it is the deliberate revival, not just in subject and mood, vocabulary and metre, but also in *morality*, of the poetic style of the ballad.

When I speak of morality, I have not in mind codes or habits of morality between man and man, such as the code of chivalry to which Scott pays tribute when William of Deloraine stands over the body of his enemy Richard Musgrave. Rather I mean the sort of morality which particularly concerned Ruskin, the morality of man's relation to the non-human Creation. Accordingly I return to Ruskin for a statement of the morality implicit in Scott's way of seeing and Scott's way of writing:

> Scott is able to conquer all tendencies to the pathetic fallacy, and instead of making Nature anywise subordinate to himself, he makes himself subordinate to *her* – follows her lead simply – does not venture to bring his own cares and thoughts into her pure and quiet presence – paints her in her simple and universal truth, adding no result of momentary passion or fancy, and appears, therefore, at first shallower than other poets, being in reality wider and healthier.

It is generally held, I suppose, that 'the pathetic fallacy' is a bee which never buzzed in any bonnet but Ruskin's. And for my part I have no wish to bring back the days when the first thing to do with any poet was to inquire after his 'feeling for nature'. Yet ours is an age when we are invited to see the non-human world for purposes of poetry as merely a repertoire of 'objective correlatives', of potential symbols ready to 'stand in' for the human reality which, on this showing, alone deserves the poet's attention. In such a period we may indeed dismiss as shallow what is simply sane and truly robust.

For here I believe 'manliness' appears again, with yet another meaning. When Byron said of Keats, 'Such writing is a sort of mental masturbation... I don't mean he is indecent, but viciously soliciting his own ideas', he was surely defending his own practice as the author of such lines as these:

> It was the cooling hour, just when the rounded
> Red sun sinks down behind the azure hill,
> Which then seems as if the whole earth it bounded,
> Circling all nature, hush'd, and dim, and still,
> With the far mountain-crescent half surrounded
> On one side, and the deep sea calm and chill,
> Upon the other, and the rosy sky,
> With one star sparkling through it like an eye.

This stanza from *Don Juan* is, as usual with Byron, extremely careless. But 'the deep sea calm and chill' represents a strength which Byron shares with Scott and with no one else among his contemporaries.

The bold and simple epithets – 'deep', 'calm', 'chill' – are like Scott's greens and blues, whites and reds and blacks, his bright and dark and cold. They represent a morality in respect of the natural world which is incompatible with the Keatsian morality, but not necessarily inferior. Such a brave risking of the obvious which issues for both Scott and Byron (notably in *Don Juan*) in simple naming of objects and their appearances, seems to testify to a straightforward gratitude for the pleasures of sense, and a fear that to probe them too nearly, on the one hand so far from heightening will tarnish them, on the other hand will seem ungrateful. There are several reasons for calling this refusal to fuss and probe a masculine attitude. For one thing such a casual registering of only the broad appearance is appropriate to the horseman or the traveller, the man in active life; whereas the more sedulous analysis and enumeration of Keats, of Coleridge, Tennyson, Hopkins (different as these are) is plainly, by contrast, sedentary. The modern writer who at his best shares this attitude is a self-consciously masculine author, Ernest Hemingway.

It may have appeared perverse in me to dwell so long on what must be called, however loosely, the descriptive element, in what are after all narrative poems. But Scott himself, in a headnote to *The Lay of the Last Minstrel*, declared that 'the description of scenery and manners was more the object of the author than a combined and regular narrative'. For narrative in the narrow sense of an unpredictable but probable story suspensefully told, *The Lady of the Lake* is the best of the poems; but then it is also the poem of which one feels that the story would do better as a Waverley novel, in prose. On the other hand, the clumsy and improbable plot of *Marmion*, though it is irritating, is less so in verse than it would have been in prose. In *The Lay of the Last Minstrel* the story is so slight and simple, so patently only the vehicle for other matters, that it does not get in the way. This is as much as we ask, and it is what we get; though particular episodes, such as Deloraine's visit, in Canto II, to the tomb of Michael Scott in Melrose Abbey, are well and suspensefully handled. In none of the poems is the plot itself the symbol of the issues being debated, as it is, for instance, in *Waverley*. But this would be to ask of Scott what neither he nor any other poet in English has provided, the novel in verse such as Pushkin provided with *Eugene Onegin*, and Mickiewicz in Poland with *Pan Tadeusz*. If we did have such works in English poetry, we should be hard pressed to know what to do with them, so readily do we assume that plot is trivial, so eagerly do we probe behind the literal meaning, and the subject overtly offered, to the 'theme' which we suppose lies behind it. It is this which makes us treat *The Ancient Mariner* as if it were a poem *about* the alientation of the artist from society, or *about* Christian redemption, or *about* neurosis and its cure; so far are we from seeing it as about a mariner and the strange voyage he took. Only if we recover the conviction that the meaning at the literal level is at any rate part, and a principal part, of the total meaning of a poem, only then shall we be in a position to appreciate a poem like *The Lay of the Last Minstrel*, the literal meaning of which is all the meaning there is (and quite sufficient too), a poem which is 'about' no more than what it is overtly about, that is, a foray into the Scottish lowlands in the sixteenth century. It is true, moreover, that in *The Lay of the Last Minstrel* Scott did aim at what has come to be accepted as a principal function of the European novel – the substantiation of a whole provincial society. And I think he succeeded, for we do indeed realize an image, convincing to the imagination, of the society of the Border in the sixteenth century, at every social level from the brutalized smallholder Watt Tinlinn, through the man at arms William of Deloraine, and the monk of Melrose, to the nobility. If I have said little of this, where Scott (it is clear) laid great store by it, it is partly because it is difficult to illustrate in any way that illuminates equally matters of diction, syntax, and metre. Moreover, this delineation of manners is something which the Waverley novels do sometimes better and nearly always equally well; whereas my object has been to show that Scott is a poet, not merely a novelist who also wrote verse.

Chatterton Lecture to the British Academy, read on 8 March 1961.

21 *William Cullen Bryant's 'To a Waterfowl'*

Whither, 'midst falling dew,
While glow the heavens with the last steps of day,
Far, through their rosy depths, dost thou pursue
Thy solitary way?

Vainly the fowler's eye
Might mark thy distant flight to do thee wrong,
As, darkly seen against the crimson sky,
Thy figure floats along.

Seek'st thou the plashy brink
Of weedy lake, or marge of river wide,
Or where the rocking billows rise and sink
On the chafed ocean side?

There is a Power whose care
Teaches thy way along that pathless coast, –
The desert and illimitable air, –
Lone wandering, but not lost.

All day thy wings have fanned
At that far height, the cold thin atmosphere,
Yet stoop not, weary, to the welcome land,
Though the dark night is near.

And soon that toil shall end;
Soon shalt thou find a summer home and rest,
And scream among thy fellows; reeds shall bend,
Soon, o'er thy sheltered nest.

Thou'rt gone, the abyss of heaven
Hath swallowed up thy form; yet, on my heart
Deeply hath sunk the lesson thou hast given,
And shall not soon depart.

He who, from zone to zone,
Guides through the boundless sky thy certain flight,
In the long way that I must tread alone,
Will lead my steps aright.

It is convenient to point to the sixth stanza as the point at which we feel a more than usual honesty in the poet. 'And scream among thy fellows...' Screaming, with its connotations of rage and terror, seems not at all appropriate to Bryant's intention in this place, where 'rest' in the line before, and 'sheltered' in the following line, carry the idea of earned repose, wings folding, and the fall to rest. But the moment is beautifully controlled; for the implications of earned repose are there, but qualified and sharpened by the word 'scream'. We are only too ready to lapse with the bird into shelter, into the arms of a comfortable Providence; but Bryant will not allow it, demanding that we remain alert, aware of the bird in itself as a foreign creation, not only as a text for the poet's discourse. How easy, and how dishonest, would have been the word 'cry', falling fitly into place with the tired lapse upon the lap of nature. But in that case it would have been a tired child that lapsed upon a mother's lap, the lap of 'mother Nature' or a maternal God. And the cry would not have been what it purports to be, the cry of a bird, but a human cry, or a bird's cry treated as if human. Water-fowl *do* scream. Yet it is not true that the word denotes only. It carries connotations, though not the ones expected. It connotes the bird's 'beastliness', its otherness, its existence in and for itself, as well as in the eyes of man. There is no question of our entering into this otherness by an effort of sympathy. We are only to remember that a bird is not a man. So we are not invited to identify ourselves with the bird, only, while keeping our distance, to take it for a sign. 'Summer home' has the same effect.

This is enough to show Bryant disowning the indulgence of the neo-Georgian poet. It is just as important to notice how he avoids the self-indulgence of another kind of poet, how the surprising word draws no attention to itself, how the temptingly *recherché* epithet is avoided, so that the momentary pungency does not halt the exposition. So I said that it is convenient to regard this point as the one at which our attention is forced to be close. It is convenient so to regard it. But in fact there is no forcing here or anywhere else. The demand for attention does not assert itself. It is easy to read this poem carelessly and pass it off as merely creditable or even dull.

One could for instance equally well take the last line of the fourth stanza, 'Lone wandering, but not lost'. If we look back on this from the end of the poem, we perceive that 'lost' is something not far short of a pun. Here the word has the homely tang of 'Lost in a wood'; but after the rest of the poem has been read, it takes on also the other meanings or the other shades of meaning represented by 'the lost tribes', or even by 'lost' = 'damned'. For the moment what is pleasing is the approach to popular idiom in a poem up to this point couched in rather literary diction. The word demands once again an alertness in the reader, a keeping of one's wits about one, a refusal to go all the way after the easily cheapened emotional appeal of 'lone'. And on the other hand the pun or near-pun is submerged, refusing the opposite temptation to stand and preen upon a slick smartness. The poet can have it both ways.

It may be here, then, that the careful reader first becomes aware of having to deal with something more than a didactic set-piece. Certainly the first stanzas seem to promise no more, if even so much. 'Rosy depths' is weak, and so is 'crimson sky', while it is only the vagueness of the second line which prevents the reader from asking whether 'steps' is the right word for a progress which leaves a glow. At this point we do not know what we are in for, and later, when we realize that it is no part of the poet's intention to be vivid or 'concrete', our objections to 'rosy depths', for instance, may disappear. (Of course if we are of those readers for whom all poetry must be 'concrete', we shall continue to object; but that is our funeral.) Still, the language of the first two stanzas is no more than tolerable at best. And 'Thy figure floats along' is perhaps unacceptable on any terms. 'Falling dew' may be called artificial, in the sense that it does not appeal to sense-experience (no one sees the dew falling) but to deductions from that experience. 'Thy figure floats along' is artificial in another and less excusable sense. It does not appeal beyond experience to a known fact. It does not appeal to experience, for 'floating' does not adequately represent the experience of seeing a bird in flight; it is as vague as 'figure'. Still less, on the other hand, does it appeal to a known fact, belying experience, about the flight of a bird. The appearance is of ease, the fact is effort. But neither ease nor effort is represented by 'floats'. Moreover there is the disagreeable association of the 'Gothick' heroine seen as a floating form down a perspective of dank arches. This precariousness has its own charm; but it is charming not to the reader of poetry but to the antiquarian amateur. And the image causes discomfort.

What I have called 'precariousness' may deserve a harsher name. At any rate the third stanza explains and confirms it. For this stanza dates the poem and so establishes its convention. It substantiates the Gothick lady. 'Weedy lake' and 'rocking billows' are locutions which show the poet still in touch with the characteristic diction of the eighteenth century; yet 'plashy' and 'marge of river wide', with their Spenserian air, place the poem very late in that tradition, when it was no longer sure of itself. I will play fair here and admit that one of the few things I know about Bryant is that he read and admired Blair and Kirke White, poets in whom the Augustan diction has become corrupted. And of course one of the principal ingredients of that diction, even so early as Dryden, was borrowings from the language of Spenser. Still I think it true that the diction of this third stanza is enough to place the poem at or about the end of the eighteenth century tradition. It could have been written quite a long time after 1800, but only by a poet who was behind the times or out of touch, a sort of provincial. If we were ignorant of the author, I believe we could go so far as this towards dating the piece on internal evidence. But by 'dating' I do not mean so much assigning a period in time. Rather it is a matter of assigning the poem to its appropriate tradition, so that we may know what conventions are being observed, what to look for and what not to expect, what sort of objective the poet is aiming at.

But it is just here that we run into difficulties. For if my analysis holds so far, it appears that this poem appeals clearly to no one tradition, and abides unreservedly by no one system of conventions. It exists in a sort of hiatus between two traditions and in a makeshift convention compounded of elements from both. This is the secret of that precariousness which manifests itself in such uneasy locutions as 'Thy figure floats along'; and it is this that makes the right reading of the poem such an exacting test of taste, difficult but also salutary.

'Weedy lake', for instance, goes along with the 'falling dew' of the first line. It appeals beyond sense-experience in just the same way. 'Rushy' or 'reedy' would have been the Romantic word. And bullrushes are weeds. But to call them so shuts out Sabrina and Midas and their whispering, and places them firmly in the vegetable kingdom, where, for this poet as for the botanist, they belong. 'Chafed' does just the same. The chafing of land by the sea is not an observed fact, but a deduction from many observed facts. 'Chafed' is a dry, merely descriptive word. 'Weedy' and 'chafed', then, belong to one convention, as the appropriate diction of an age concerned not so much with experience as with the lessons to be drawn from it. 'Plashy', on the other hand, and 'marge', familiar archaisms, seem to invite just those legendary and literary associations that the other epithets so sternly suppressed. These are not *dry* words at all; they yearn out at the reader, asking him to colour with inarticulate feeling the things to which they refer. They thus appeal to quite another convention. Some readers may feel this betwixt-and-between air unsettling; others may think the poet deserves credit for bringing the two conventions into harmony. I will say only that the harmony, if it is achieved, is precarious, in the sense that while the poet may sustain it throughout his poem (and the reader feels that it is touch and go with him all the way), his success will not help him with the next poem he writes – he is as far as ever from perfecting a style that he can trust, a reliable tool. He is even further from himself contributing to a tradition in the shape of a heritable body of techniques; no later poet will be able to take his procedure as a model.

One sort of poet works his way to God by learning the lessons of experience, drawing conclusions from it, and so coming upon the moral laws behind it. Another sort of poet leaps up to God by dwelling with a fervent intensity upon experience as it is offered to him, not for the lessons it can give, but for what it is in itself. In the first stanzas of this poem, the reader is uncertain which sort of poet he is dealing with, so uncertain that he wonders if the poet himself knows. But the balance of probability was always towards the first alternative, because of the ceremonious tone and stately movement, and the rigidity of the metrical arrangement. For the leap to God would have to be made in the verse, and so it would demand, not Bryant's stanza, but some larger unit which would provide for a gathering impetus and *élan*.

Poet and reader alike begin to move with more assurance in the fourth stanza. Here, for the first time in the poem, we encounter something in the nature of Empson's ambiguities. For 'teaches thy way' appears as an impurity, an awkward construction forced upon the poet by the exigencies of metre and rhyme, until we remember the usage 'teaching the way to do'. And this, once remembered, gives to the phrase the sense not only of guiding along a navigated track, but of teaching wings how to fly. In the same way, the sea-coast is not pathless, but only the coast imagined as duplicated at the altitude of the bird's flight. And once the idea of altitude is introduced, there is the merest hint, no more, of that other 'coast' which comes with 'coasting', so obviously a better word for the flight of a bird than that 'floating' of six lines before.

Only now can the point of the pun on 'lost' be properly taken. For in the third line of this stanza the equable flow and the subdued tone are abandoned. 'The desert and illimitable air' – a reverberation, a powerful élan; and fine, but at once controlled and valued by the earthy and quaint tang of the colloquial 'lost'. The Miltonic blast has been worked for, and is paid for; at the same time it asserts magnificently the importance and the glory of what the poet has in hand. And so it is possible to talk in a heightened tone, to move into 'that far height, the cold thin atmosphere', and for the wings to grow into sails, into a dragon's vans, 'fanning' the air. So the subsidence is effected upon several different levels. First the movement subsides after the beautiful break at 'weary'. Second, the flight subsides to the nest. Third, the vaulting human thought subsides, to a need for shelter. And finally, with 'scream among thy fellows', the bird subsides, from a dragon or an angel, fanning the wheat from the chaff in lofty speculation, to being, precisely, once more a bird, a brute creature.

Thus, when,

> Thou'rt gone, the abyss of heaven
> Hath swallowed up thy form,

not only is the flying bird lost to sight, but the symbol too is lost to the eye of the mind. The abyss is not only the blue depth, but also the profundity of paradox in which the questions of destiny evade answer. Only so, having realized the incomplete and arbitrary nature of the 'lessons' given, can Bryant's certainty ('And shall not soon depart') appear heroic and admirable, more than a windy gesture. The certainty of conviction impresses the more, not because of the uncertainty of the revelation, but because of the poet's acknowledgement of what in it would seem uncertain to others.

Or so we might have said, were it not for the last stanza. It is difficult to be fair to this. The moral is thumped home very pat indeed, but I think we deceive ourselves if we suppose that this is what offends us. We should not mind the certainty if the moral itself were more acceptable. Perhaps most readers will agree with me in thinking the migratory instinct in birds is no just analogy for the provisions made by divine solicitude for the guidance of the human pilgrim. And Bryant seems to assert something closer than analogy. In fact he seems now, at the end, to approach that identification of himself with the bird, that earlier he took care to avoid. Yet we cannot but think that the human being has a margin of choice for good and evil, that a bird has not. Hence divine guidance in the human soul must work in a way very different from the automatic and undeviating operation of instinct in migratory birds. To think otherwise is to cheapen alike the idea of Providence and the idea of human dignity – a dignity which depends, by the traditional paradox, upon the possibility of human depravity.

All this, however, is quite extraneous to the poem as poem. In raising these objections, we are in fact asking Bryant, not only to write a different poem from the one he has written, but to believe in a different god from the 'Power' that he offers to us. My disappointment with the last stanza is relevant to the poem as poem, only if I can show that the expectations which it disappoints are such as earlier passages have entitled me to entertain. Only then can my objections stand as a valid criticism of the poem.

I think this can be shown. For if the lesson to be drawn is as straightforward as this, if supernatural guidance in human life is no more of a mystery than the migratory instinct in waterfowl (mysterious as that is), then 'the abyss of heaven' is surely not deep enough. It is no longer the profundity of paradox, only those 'rosy depths' of the first stanza, which have grown, in the interim, no ruddier and hardly any deeper. 'Abyss' now comes to seem a pretentious word, too effusive, making promises that cannot be redeemed.

Thus the piece is seriously flawed both first and last. It is not a great poem, it is only just, perhaps, a good one. Just for that reason it demands very careful reading. When a poet's achievement is precarious at best, he requires in especial degree the co-operation of his readers. Not that he should be repeatedly given the benefit of the doubt; that would not be co-operation but indulgence. Rather it is a question of permitting the poem to establish its own convention; and where a poet is himself uncertain about the convention he is writing in (having perhaps to express something for which the established conventions are inadequate, yet lacking the energy to break wholly free of them), the reader has to be patient while the poet feels his way towards the convention he wants. Bryant feels his way through three or four stanzas.

Ultimately every poem establishes its own convention, dictates its own terms. But in a period when certain conventions (of diction, for instance) are shared by almost all the poets of one or more generations, the reader can with ease take his first rough bearings, and the poet can rely upon his doing so. When poets and readers agree, for instance, that certain metres, certain rhetorical figures, a certain vocabulary, go along with elegy, certain others with satire, the poet can expect his reader to understand quite quickly how any one poem he writes is to be 'taken'. But in periods such as our own, or Bryant's, when the genres are being reshuffled so that they are no longer mutually exclusive, the poet finds it much harder, not just to hold, but to direct the reader's attention, so that he shall know what to look for, what not to expect. Even in these cases, however, the poem establishes a convention for itself by, in effect, challenging comparison with certain poems and not with others. We begin to get somewhere with Bryant's poem only when he brings it home to us (and perhaps to himself) that, although this poem could never have been written in the eighteenth century, yet it belongs, and is to be taken, along with an eighteenth century poem such as Gray's 'On the Spring', not with Shelley's 'To a Skylark'.

From this point of view, to offer to read a poem 'in isolation' is really a piece of trickery. For a great part of any careful reading consists in setting the poem among its fellows, that is, with those poems, in that genre, where it belongs. This has the effect, not of multiplying the meanings to be found, but rather of limiting the meanings to those which are really there, excluding those that come from reading it in the wrong way, expecting things that the poem (not the poet) tells us, by implication, not to expect.

Interpretations: Essays on Twelve English Poems, ed. John Wain (London: Routledge & Kegan Paul, 1955).

22 *John Keats: a Genius and his Limitations*

Fifty years ago, when it was widely held that the sort of poetry inaugurated and exemplified by T.S. Eliot was 'anti-Romantic', the poets of the Romantic Movement came in for much harsh and derisive criticism. But from these strictures Keats was always exempted. It was F.R. Leavis, one of the influential voices of that time, who asked us to admire 'To bend with apples the moss'd cottage trees', finding there 'a strength – a native English strength – lying beyond the scope of the poet who aimed to make English as like Italian as possible'. No one seems to have asked whether the phrase 'native English strength', so plainly offered as commendation, did not suggest an insular chauvinism; nor whether making English as like Italian as possible (Leavis imputed this endeavour to Tennyson) was self-evidently a dishonourable intention.

Much water has since flowed under bridges: Tennyson has rightly been rehabilitated; Eliot himself has been found to be in many ways a Tennysonian poet; and Leavis's subsequent writings have shown that 'insular chauvinism' was indeed a true bill. Yet Keats's reputation continues to enjoy a singular immunity. John Bayley, whose 1962 British Academy lecture flew the flag for a post-Leavisite Keats, was to remark in his *Pushkin: A comparative commentary* how the great Russian poet lacked 'the ability of the English Romantic poets to be clumsy with point and power'; and would cite, as an instance of such inspired clumsiness Keats's phrase, 'the feel of not to feel it'. A mostly adulatory reviewer remarked mildly that 'to commiserate with a poet for lacking the ability to be clumsy (however powerfully) seems to be a reach of refinement that would have raised a laugh from either Pushkin or Keats'. But Bayley was impenitent, applauding how Keats in the Odes 'perfected' his clumsiness. Moreover, the grounds for Keats's immunity seemed still to be insular, since his clumsiness was associated with 'that wryly complacent English pleasure', which Bayley discerned and endorsed, 'in things going wrong or never having been right', something which, he observed with obvious satisfaction, 'has become so much a part of English culture and consciousness.' Is this a particular instance of the all too well attested English preference for the amateurish over the professional? Perhaps not. All the same, Bayley's criticism has been credited with showing how 'imperfection, awkwardness, even vulgarity' can 'deepen the expressive power of a work' – a prime instance of such deepening being Keats, whose poetry is thus at once convicted of, and absolved from, imperfection, awkwardness and vulgarity. By latter-day champions of Keats we are asked to prefer imperfection to perfection, awkwardness to ease or grace, vulgarity to refinement. A poet whose place in the canon depends on our so drastically reversing normal expectations can hardly be thought secure in his canonical status.

Thus John Barnard's *John Keats* (Cambridge, 1987) appears at an interesting, ticklish time. The ticklishness is aggravated if we look across the Atlantic, where authorities like Harold Bloom and Helen Vendler have enlisted Keats to vindicate their contention that not Eliot, and certainly not Pound, but Wallace Stevens is the representative great poet of the present century in English. Barnard is aware of them, and quotes from Stevens's 'The Man with the Blue Guitar' to argue that not just Keats, but Wordsworth also, are free of Stevens' 'surety that nearly resembles complacency'. He takes note also of British commentators like Bayley and Christopher Ricks, and follows them in being aware of the chronic instability of Keats's diction, yet is leery of following Bayley's logic by which that instability (productive of 'awkwardness, even vulgarity') is worth more than stability would have been. This means that Barnard's tone is mostly dry, cool, uncommitted – a tone of voice that will disappoint many, yet is surely appropriate to the case of this poet at this time. In 1973 Professor Barnard's edition of *The Complete Poems* notably amended what had been the received text; and he does a great service now in being similarly sharp-eyed about received opinion.

What do we mean in this context by stability and instability of diction? We must readily concede that a calculated indecorum at crucial points in a poem is an expressive resource, and one that the best Romantics exploited more often than their precursors (though Dryden for one had a very sure touch with it). But such incidental indecorums depend for their effect on our being aware of the decorum which they violate. And Barnard shows clearly that, when Keats began writing, no such decorum was any longer available. Francis Jeffrey at the *Edinburgh Review* thought he still had hold of such a decorum, and a stubbornly old-fashioned poet like Crabbe could continue to observe its rules – for his purposes, very profitably. But Keats and his friends perceived that Jeffrey's sort of decorum had been challenged and displaced beyond retrieval by the practice of Wordsworth in particular, but also by socio-economic developments which had produced a new public for poetry, or rather a range of such publics. Prominent among these was a public for poetry among leisured women of the expanding bourgeoisie. Keats was very deliberately determined not to address this woman's public, and the determination may have cost him the chance of a lucrative reputation. His bloody-mindedness on this score is striking, and his intransigence was not liked nor understood. Byron was a lady's man but hardly a lady's poet, and yet Barnard brings out very well how Byron's bafflement before some of Keats's locutions was not wholly a matter of the conscious aristocrat confronting the cockney. When Byron told Leigh Hunt that he found unintelligible the line 'O for a beaker full of the warm South', Hunt reflected comfortably that 'the sort of poetry in which he excelled, was not accustomed to these poetical concentrations'. But Barnard points out that Hunt had grasped only half of the truth; that when the line is returned to its context it does indeed generate uncertainties that validate Byron's bewilderment.

He generalizes from this instance to say that 'Keats's stylistic success exists in an eerie proximity to vulgarity or technical failure'. And this, he insists, is no more true of the earlier poetry than the later. A drier word than 'eerie' would be 'unaccountable'. For no one has yet accounted for it, except on the disreputable grounds that nothing succeeds like success, and familiarity through generations of dozing readers has dulled us to what in fact is going on.

In *Endymion*, Peona dries her tears: 'Hereat Peona, in their silver source / Shut her pure sorrow-drops with glad exclaim' – which is, from any point of view, excruciating. Yet elsewhere in the same poem we read how 'dolphins bob their noses through the brine', where Keats insisted on 'bob' when friends urged on him either 'raise' or 'push'. How could a poet, so right about the latter locution, have perpetrated the other? But in saying so we appeal to a standard of decorum that Keats had no access to, since in his time it had not been formulated. Poets of the 1980s who complain that they write in an age when 'anything goes' should probably recognize that on the contrary they observe a quite strict decorum (populist and therefore, in a looser sense, indecorous); whereas under the Regency it was indeed true that anything – but anything – *went*. In such a situation what could a poet do except what Keats did in *Endymion* – learn to swim by throwing himself in at the deep end? Keats, surely a nightmare to his long-suffering publishers, admitted in his Preface that this was what he had done, conceding further that the sensibility in the poem was adolescent:

> The imagination of a boy is healthy, and mature imagination of a man is healthy; but there is a space of life in between, in which the soul is in a ferment, the character undecided, the way of life uncertain, the ambition thick-sighted: thence proceeds mawkishness...

What author before or since ever thus delivered himself, gagged and bound, to the reviewer? How Lockhart in Blackwood's *Edinburgh Magazine*, and Croker in the *Quarterly*, descended upon and tore the carcass thus offered them, is notorious; and nothing can excuse them. Keats, who disdained a large public, gambled everything on the magnanimity of an élite. Nobody since has taken, or ever will take, such a gamble. The élite is as ungenerous and malevolent as the general public from which it claims to be a saving remnant; and so much for any hopes of 'a minority culture'.

Thus the purity of Keats's intentions in *Endymion* is irrefutable. And as for the execution? It is more accomplished than most people have pretended, including notably the author himself. For Keats spoke of the poem as if it were entirely an exercise in self-education; it is that, but it is also an attempt to educate the reader, to extend and stimulate the public taste. Nevertheless, we cannot be disarmed. For Keats was right: mawkish the poem is, and vulgar, not just in places but essentially. If it extended the public taste, as in the long run it certainly did, it simultaneously depraved it. The best Victorian taste would indeed comprehend 'The mighty ones who have made eternal day / For Greece and England', but at what a cost simply in good sense, let alone good manners! Keats himself counted the cost, as few of his admirers have done from that day to this.

Endymion is a narrative, and although the story-line is so tenuous as to seem no more than a convenience, still it is a necessary convenience, for without the thread of it we should be carried helplessly from one luscious tableau into another, and not many of us could or should tolerate this through 4,000 lines. Keats was persistently a narrative poet, though most of his modern admirers, from F.R. Leavis to Helen Vendler, have scanted this side of him in their rush to focus on his Odes. Some younger poets in the United States have lately been uncovering indignantly a conspiratorial prejudice against narrative poetry on the part of modern critics, both those who declare themselves 'modernist' and those who don't. And this is borne out if we look at how modern criticism has dealt with 'The Eve of St Agnes'. Leigh Hunt, who seldom gets a good press from writers on Keats, thought this was the poet's masterpiece; and it is a judgement worth pondering. As with other narratives like *The Rime of the Ancient Mariner*, modern critics find it hard to take Hunt's judgement seriously because they are hung up on an unwarranted distinction between 'plot' and 'theme', the latter supposed to be something deeper than the plot, which the plot merely shadows and provides for. Hence the question: what is Coleridge's poem, or Keats's poem 'about'? – quite occluding the possibility that these poems are about just what they seem to be about, that the overt and literal meaning (the plot) is all the meaning there is, and quite enough too. So modern commentators have tried to find in 'The Eve of St Agnes' a metaphysical or else a psychological 'meaning', or else with Douglas Bush they find it 'no more than a romantic tapestry of unique richness of colour'. The poem tells a story, which is an interesting story since it turns on the perennially interesting question of the nature of sexual passion; and it renders the circumstances of the story with a vividness almost hallucinatory, except that each recorded circumstance can be vindicated from common sense-experience. Add to this that the diction is surprisingly pure within the archaizing register established by Scott's *Lay of the Last Minstrel* (1805), and what more can we ask? 'Much more' will be the answer only of those who look to poetry to do for them what only religion or more dubiously psychiatry can do. There is nothing specifically or controversially 'romantic' about lines like:

> A chain-drooped lamp was flickering by each door;
> The arras, rich with horseman, hawk, and hound,
> Fluttered in the besieging wind's uproar;
> And the long carpets rose along the gusty floor.

This is simply very good writing, by any standards: a model for verse-writers, perhaps prose-writers too.

Keats persistently miscalculated his effects, and misjudged his own compositions. The reason was that, like many a poet since, he resented and disliked the public which at the same time he tried to win over and outwit. He was only just prevented, by Woodhouse and Taylor, from spoiling 'The Eve of St Agnes', and it is hardly believable that he thought he had surpassed that poem with 'Lamia'. It is common form to acknowledge that the couplets of 'Lamia' were inspired by reading Dryden; what is seldom said is that as soon as Dryden is named Keats is damned by the comparison. Dryden's ability to find a rhyme every ten syllables, without enervating his syntax or disturbing the genial flexibility of his tone, is quite beyond Keats's capacities. Keats wanted here to stop himself identifying with the feelings of his dramatis personae, apparently not realizing that in the St Agnes poem he had triumphantly identified with each of his characters in turn, with the Beadsman and Old Angela as well as with Porphyria and Madeline. 'Lamia' expressed a state of feeling that is plainly in some way morbid, and this will ensure that it will always be 'interesting' – especially to those who are interested in how a poem betrays itself, not in how it masters itself. Astonishingly, at the same time Keats was writing his other narrative masterpiece, *The Fall of Hyperion: A Dream*, in which, unshackled from rhyme, he could allow his diction to purify itself from acquaintance with Dante as mediated through Henry Cary. Through many scores of lines at a time Keats here achieves a severe and poignant majesty such as he attained nowhere else:

> But yet I had a terror of her robes,
> And chiefly of the veils, that from her brow
> Hung pale, and curtained her in mysteries
> That made my heart too small to hold its blood.
> This saw that Goddess, and with sacred hand
> Parted the veils. Then saw I a wan face,
> Not pined by human sorrows, but bright-blanched
> By an immortal sickness which kills not;
> It works a constant change, which happy death
> Can put no end to; deathwards progressing
> To no death was that visage; it had passed
> The lily and the snow; and beyond these
> I must not think now, though I saw that face –
> But for her eyes I should have fled away.

Even now many readers, still heeding the baleful advice 'Load every rift with ore', will fail to recognize what a contribution to the total effect is made by the 'unpoetic' lines, 'And chiefly of the veils, that from her brow', or (more piercingly, of course) 'But for her eyes I should have fled away'. Where the form is so thoroughly achieved, as much in alert metre as in diction, it is proper to take the content seriously; and Barnard is right to stress how the poem is bitterly anti-Christian. This will distress some, though fewer than in the past. They may console themselves by noting that whereas the earlier *Hyperion* had been consciously designed as 'a Fragment', *The Fall of Hyperion* merely breaks off, unfinished – as if the attempt to explain suffering on other than Christian terms proved unsustainable.

Barnard believes that Keats, still misconceiving his own genius, did not recognize the major achievements of the Odes to Psyche, On a Grecian Urn, and to a Nightingale, since he seems to turn upon them with a sort of disgust in the Ode on Indolence. But of course a poet who had set his sights on writing Drydenesque or Chaucerian or Ovidian narratives could not easily recognize the Odes, with their avowed and apparent subjectivity, as anything but aberrant self-indulgences. And in any case a line like 'Pipe to the spirit ditties of no tone' is as outlandish, as little naturalized by spoken or written usage, as anything in *Endymion*. Barnard writes ardently of the 'Ode to a Nightingale' in particular, and yet enthusiasts will still find him provokingly cool when he discusses the Odes. What he has in mind, which precludes for him any notion that Keats had achieved maturity before his death, is the lack of any significant overlap, in tone and diction, between Keats's poems and his letters. And it is surely true that, coming to the poems after the letters, one is provoked to murmur, with Matthew Prior (and Falstaff), 'Let us e'en talk a little like folks of this world'. This will be indignantly repudiated by some as the voice of anti-Romantic prejudice. And who can deny that, whether by temperament or conditioning or both, some readers cleave to the poetry of the Romantic period as the tuning-fork for all poetry whatever, whereas others cannot do so? However that may be, the classic status of Keats's poetry may be thought assured, in the sense that it's hard to imagine a time when numerous readers won't fall in love with it. For others of us, measuring him against his own masters (Dryden has been named, and may serve), this body of poetry will always seem more poignant than masterly. But of course the masterly will always be the last thing sought by those who want to master a text and its author, rather than be mastered by them.

Times Literary Supplement, 1987, p.651.

23 *Attending to Landor*

Walter Savage Landor (1775-1874) was sometimes a bigot, sometimes a bully. But there are many places in his *Imaginary Conversations* where he is neither. In one such place, he has Diogenes maintain:

> There is no mass of sincerity in any place. What there is must be picked up patiently, a grain or two at a time; and the season for it is after a storm, after the overflowing of banks, and bursting of mounds, and sweeping away of landmarks. Men will always hold something back: they must be shaken and loosened a little, to make them let go what is deepest in them, and weightiest and purest.

We can set this beside something that Izaak Walton is made to say, about the love-poems of Donne. (The date is 1829 – so much for the prevalent notion that Donne was unknown or undervalued between Dryden and Rupert Brooke):

> So ingenious are men when the spring torrent of passion shakes up and carries away their thoughts, covering (as it were) the green meadow of still homely life with pebbles and shingle, some colourless and obtuse, some sharp and sparkling.

Taken together, these passages seem to say that the lapidary or 'chiselled' effect, as in the epigram or epitaph, so far from witnessing to lack of feeling, on the contrary is the aftermath and proof of very strong and tumultuous feeling. This is what I have always believed, not on the authority of Landor or any one else (for instance not Yeats nor Pound, who can both be shown to have endorsed Landor on this point), but from my experience of how my own emotional experience was or was not convertible into poetry. And the principal sorrow or frustration of my life in poetry has been my inability to persuade others of this to me self-evident truth. On the contrary, so entrenched among us are the associations between the marmoreal and the cold, between the stony and the dry, between the firm contour and the rigid, between the chisel and the scalpel, that any attempt to envisage poetry by analogy with the sister-art of sculpture at once arouses bristling suspicions.

When early in my writing life I became aware of American poets vowed to the epigrammatic and the lapidary, Yvor Winters principally and J.V. Cunningham, I found that they (Winters at any rate) laid the prejudice against such writing at the door of something called 'Romanticism'. But Landor himself was a Romantic poet; at all events his long life spanned all the years that we ascribe to the Romantic Movement, and he extolled the achievement of his contemporaries both severally and together: Wordsworth and Southey, Shelley and Keats. Indeed what could be more lapidary in intention, if not always in effect, than Wordsworth's 'Poems on the Naming of Places'? This hypostatizing of Romanticism, as something one can take arms either for or against, has become over the years a scandalously unscholarly, divisive, habit of literary sentiment and opinion. For an instance, I will go to so good and independent a critic as Herb Schniedau: 'Only in the post-Romantic era is it necessary, with Ruskin, to disown the pathetic fallacy...'[1] But of course, if we consult Ruskin's famous essay, we find that Ruskin did not 'disown' the pathetic fallacy; he diagnosed it, and defined the limits and the conventions inside which it is tolerable. Similarly with Gerald Graff: 'much Romantic poetry deals explicitly with a yearning that can find no objectification in the material world and which escapes the poet's powers of expression.'[2] Why, to be sure; but did not much pre-Romantic poetry, for instance most famously Virgil's, concern itself with just such 'yearning'? Truly, our pre-Romantic ancestors were not such fools as we take them for: Virgil no less than Shakespeare had discovered something problematic about the relation between words, and the things that words supposedly name. Our preoccupation with Romanticism is only one symptom of a foreshortening of historical perspectives by which we make the unmanageable abundance of the inherited past somehow manageable. Accordingly it should not disconcert us that in the last century the most forceful champion of lapidary poetry (for Edmund Blunden as well as Ezra Pound) was Théophile Gautier, by any of the standard tests as 'romantic' a poet as one can find: 'Sculpte, lime, cisèle' was his injunction. The wish for a sculpted, a lapidary poetry has nothing to do with declaring one's self 'classicist' rather than 'romantic'.

And thus, the compositional habits of poets of the present day in high favour among us, though they are often declared to be 'Romantic' or 'post-Romantic', are very hard to relate to the Romantic

[1] H.N. Schneidau, 'Pound's Poetics of Loss', in Ian F.A. Bell (ed.), *Ezra Pound, Tactics of Reading* (London, 1982), p.104.

[2] Gerald Graff, 'Deconstruction as Dogma' (1980), quoted by Schneidau, *loc. cit.*

Movement as an international phenomenon known to literary history. When people claim to find such a connection, it usually turns out that what they are pointing to is an aversion on the part of the poet to anything predetermined or pre-planned. But as a mode of composition, improvisation, the feeling forward from one verse-line to the next in the presence of an actual or imagined audience, was known to the Ancient World as well as to the nineteenth century. Landor wrote (1828):

> ... No *improvisatore* ever rose above mediocrity; few have reached it. Poetry, like wine, requires a gentle and regular and long fermentation. What is it if it can buoy up no wisdom, no reflection? if we can throw into it none of our experience? if no repository is to be found in it for the gems we have collected, at the price sometimes of our fortunes, of our health, and of our peace? Your *improvisatori* let drop their verses as a string of mules their morning oats, for miles together... The first thing a young person who wishes to be a poet has to do, is, to conquer his volubility; to compress in three verses what he had easily thrown off in twelve; and to be an hour about what had cost him a minute. If he has a *knack* for verses, he must break it and forget it. Both the poet and the painter should acquire facility and frankness; but they must be exercised with discretion; they must be sternly regulated, and in great part suppressed. The young poet will remonstrate, and more often scoff; he will appall you by placing before you the *deep mouth* of Pindar and his mountain-torrents. Tell him, and tell older ones too, that Pindar of all poets is the most accurate and the most laborious.

'Gems', in Landor's usage, is no empty figure; it means *stones*, some precious and some not, 'some colourless and obtuse, some sharp and sparkling.' Only by entering into the metaphor with all seriousness can we regain access to the climate of ideas familiar from past centuries, in which it was high praise of a poet to say that he was 'laborious', and of his poetry that it was 'laboured'. From within that climate of ideas we may recover what Landor intended by 'mediocrity': not something run-of-the-mill, boring, of no account; but rather a standard of accomplishment which, though relatively many attain it, many more never do. I suspect we sell it short by thinking of it as what a devoted and gifted student in an excellent Creative Writing school may attain to. It is not in itself good enough to amount to anything; but it is the serviceable platform from which a few may lift themselves to do something that matters, having learned (the first lesson) to suppress in themselves whatever they may have by way of 'knack', of 'facility'. As for what is needed to lift off further, Landor is quite specific: it is not anything to do with technique, with diligence, with the history of the art – it is 'wisdom', it is 'reflection', it is 'experience', accumulated 'at the price sometimes of our fortunes, of our health, and of our peace.' This is what composition by way of improvisation can never attain to. On the contrary, we are invited to think, wisdom and passionate experience in poetry are often to be apprehended as an effect dryly conclusive, mournful or sardonic, *closed*. It is what I have always hankered after, and reached for; and to just the extent that I have attained it, many readers have been repelled.

It is after the lift-off from mediocrity that rules exist only to be broken. Before that there are good rules, and they should be kept. Edmund White (*The Nation*, 16 April 1983) states them succinctly and well: 'Narrative is by its nature linear (from the past toward the present), economical (a small cast of characters), hierarchical (details subordinated to event), impulsive (the forward motion engendered by suspense or mystery), and causational.' (All poetry, it may be observed, is narrative, in so far as the first word is already past by the time the reader arrives at the second.) But having thus stated the rules, how does Edmund White, who is reviewing Amy Clampitt, proceed? 'What Clampitt writes is circular, diffuse, vertiginous and organized through simultaneity. Her method is the one appropriate to our experience.' That's to say, Amy Clampitt breaks all the rules; from which we may deduce, since White means to praise her, that she's good enough to do so and get away with it. Perhaps she is; certainly White thinks so. But we note that this isn't the justification he puts forward. Rather, 'her method is the one appropriate to our experience.' It isn't necessarily that Amy Clampitt is good enough to break the rules; but that 'we' – all of us, simply by virtue of living in a particular phase of history – deserve and require to have the time-honoured rules broken for us, on our behalf, by any artist whom we are to honour with our approval. White drives the point home: 'In the abundance of her imagination she has reminded at least one critic of Keats, but her anxiety – the anxious *luridness* of her perception – is incomparably modern.' To be good, even as good as Keats, is not enough; what matters is to be *modern* – to nourish the foreshortening of historical perspectives by which we shall be confirmed in our conviction that, horrid as we are, we are at all events unprecedented. This vulgar presumption is as alien to a romantic poet like Wordsworth or Keats or Gautier, as to any classical poet. And of course it is entirely foreign to Landor.

Moreover, though the rules may be broken by genius, they don't have to be. And one sort of genius – Landor's sort – will go to pains not to break them; this not from timidity, but on the contrary out of pride, out of a determination to avoid just that quality which Edmund White so much esteems: *luridness.* The pride, the hauteur, is obvious when Landor gives his version of the second of the traditional requirements as Edmund White lists them: economy – not a word (or image, or episode) too many. Landor is speaking of Ovid: 'Had he written in a negligent and disorderly manner, they would have admired his freedom and copiousness, ignorant that, in literature as in life, the rich and noble are as often frugal as the indigent and obscure.' Which of our currently influential reviewers of poetry is not thus 'ignorant'? And which of them, if not ignorant of this truth, could afford to voice it; since it depends so explicitly on a lordly, an anti-populist sentiment? This sentiment is everywhere in Landor, as when he has Dante remonstrate with his wife:

> Ought I to be indignant that my country has neglected me? Do not men in all countries like those best who most resemble them? And would you wish me to resemble the multitude who are deluded? or would you rather that I were seated among the select who are in a position to delude?

Pondering these unanswerable questions, I am made to recognize that the antagonism to the sort of poetry I most admire – frugal because compact, lapidary and shapely – is rooted in something deeper than literary history or poetic theory; it is rooted in politics or (deeper than that) in feelings of egalitarian solidarity such as I do not trust. And of course I do not forget – who could? – that Yeats not much less than Pound was trapped into that false alternative to social democracy, Mussolini's Fascism. The Landorian poetics – Landor himself being an aristocratic republican – have political overtones that are, in the second half of the twentieth century, highly suspect. Landor says intransigently, through the mouth of Machiavelli:

> ... I would rather any state of social life, than naked and rude democracy; because I have always found it more jealous of merit, more suspicious of wisdom, more proud of riding on great minds, more pleased at raising up little ones above them, more fond of loud talking, more impatient of calm reasoning, more unsteady, more ungrateful, and more ferocious; above all, because it leads to despotism through fraudulence, intemperance and corruption.

Aha, says some one, no wonder Landor was esteemed by both Pound and Yeats, those fascists! But where do we stand if, without being in the least beguiled by false alternatives of the Right or the Left, we all the same find Landor's strictures on mass democracy confirmed by our own experience?

One possible answer, and one that Landor at his best underwrites, is to observe that both social democracy and fascism vindicate themselves by invoking (once again) drastically foreshortened perspectives on the past. Both of them are *modern* ideologies; and we can fly in the face of Edmund White, so as to suggest that that is precisely what is wrong with them.

Thinking of poetry as like sculpture – something that Landor's verse-practice invites us to, more than any of his declarations in prose – can prompt many reflections, some of them profound and a few of them topical. It invites us for instance to envisage the inherited language, the poet's medium as the poet apprehends it in the act of composing, as something no less bleakly confronting, no more negotiable, than the cliff of Carrara marble that faced Michelangelo when he went to the quarry looking for a block that should excite his sculptor's imagination. Nothing could be further from the sense of language that French theorists and their Anglo-American followers have lately pressed upon us: language seen as a band of nebulous haze, infinitely malleable and protean according as the needs or whims of speaker and of auditor impinge upon it. The question is not what language *is* (that question which so delightfully exercises philosophers and semioticians), but what language *is taken to be* by those who use it, either those who carve it or those who respond to the shapes it takes at the carver's hands. If we choose to think of the inherited language as a cliff of Carrara or Parian marble, its veins and lines of fracture imperfectly but still usefully traced by the better lexicographers, no voice out of Paris or Geneva can or should persuade us otherwise. Landor was boringly pedantic, in many of the *Imaginary Conversations*, about the etymology of English words; and he was a crank about how to spell them. But remote as all this rightly seems, in an age when English has become the *lingua franca* of airline-pilots and ground-controllers, still we cannot impugn the principle that Landor proceeded on: English is still an artistic medium, if we choose to think of it so; and indeed nothing but our so thinking of it is needed to ensure that, as an artistic medium, it shall persist.

Nothing more; but equally, nothing less. And something a great deal less is implied by the notion current among us, that the language of poetry is only an extension of the demotic English that we use, and hear used, at a neighbourhood barbecue. This seems to derive – for the serious student of poetry – from Wordsworth's declaration that the language of poetry is a selection from 'the language really used by men'. This I take to be a viable and necessary principle, but only if we remember the qualifications with which Wordsworth hedged it round, and add a few more that Wordsworth didn't pause for. Landor, loyal to his friend Robert Southey, praised whenever he could Southey's old associate, Wordsworth; but it's plain to see that his heart wasn't in it, some of the time. And it is surely true that Wordsworth in practice all too often took over from demotic speech one feature that the language of poetry can *not* tolerate: that's to say, garrulity. (Wordsworth is a great poet, however; though neither Winters nor Pound, Yeats nor Eliot, seems to have thought so, Basil Bunting certainly does. And Bunting, though he never writes in metre as I like to do, is nevertheless for me a great exemplar in our time of truly lapidary poetry.) Garrulity is surely the great vice of most contemporary poetry, as it must be of any poetry that is improvised; for any one who has tried to improvise under pressure knows that the trick is to postpone for as long as possible the moment at which any sentence or string of images has to be clinched. Moreover, at public poetry-readings, the poem that will lose the audience after the first minute is the poem that says one thing fast, then moves on fast to say something else.

We should, when we write, think that we are *sculpting* language. Let no one think that this is only a fancy way of saying what we all painlessly subscribe to: the need for craftsmanship. On the contrary, the verb 'to craft', nowadays much in favour among us, is one that we can do without. The sculptor – whether he works on the small scale of medal, medallion and coin, or on portrait-busts, or else monumentally, and whether 'figurative' or 'abstract' – is not a craftsman nor a technician, but an artist, laying on the line (as Landor says) his fortune, perhaps his health, certainly his peace of mind. In a late *Conversation* (1853) Landor speaks in his own person with a sort of cracked defiance:

> Poetry was always my amusement, prose my study and business. I have published five volumes of *Imaginary Conversations*: cut the worst of them thro the middle, and there will remain in this decimal fraction quite enough to satisfy my appetite for fame. I shall dine late; but the dining-room will be well lighted, the guests few and select.

This passage, or rather the last sentence, was remodelled momentously by Yeats, in a poem of his middle years, 'To a Young Beauty':

> There is not a fool can call me friend,
> And I may dine at journey's end
> With Landor and with Donne.

The coupling of Landor with Donne has seemed unaccountable to some readers; but as we have seen, Yeats had warrant for it. Yeats's confidence in posterity sounds much more ringingly than Landor's, and with good reason, for Yeats enjoyed far more fame and esteem in his lifetime than Landor did. Indeed it's not easy to say whether Landor's gamble on posterity has paid off even now; for he's represented in the standard anthologies but his name is seldom on any one's lips, and *Imaginary Conversations* is one of those works remembered far more often than they are read. The point of these reflections is that, if our perspectives on the past are foreshortened, our perspectives on the future are even more so, and for reasons beyond our control. Under the threat of nuclear Armageddon no poet can appeal to posterity as confidently as Yeats or Landor did. If fame does not come in the poet's lifetime, he can have no confidence that it will come hereafter, from a posterity which, if it exists at all, may well take a form quite unimaginable. This means inevitably that the poet, stubbornly proud as he may be, is in our day dependent on his public in the here and now, compelled to adjust to the public's expectations and preferences, in a way that Landor and Yeats could not envisage.

A little later in the same Conversation with Archdeacon Hare, Landor made another prophecy about his posthumous reputation, and one that events have shown to be more accurate:

> I stand out a rude rock in the middle of a river, with no exotic or parasitical plant on it, and few others. Eddies and dimples and froth and bubbles pass rapidly by, without shaking me. Here indeed is little room for pic-nic and polka.

From this passage too Yeats seems to have taken a hint, if no more, for a poem with the sardonic title, 'Men Improve With The Years':

> I am worn out with dreams;
> A weather-worn, marble triton
> Among the streams;
> And all day long I look
> Upon this lady's beauty
> As though I had found in a book
> A pictured beauty,
> Pleased to have filled the eyes
> Or the discerning ears,
> Delighted to be but wise,
> For men improve with the years;
> And yet, and yet,
> Is this my dream, or the truth?
> O would that we had met
> When I had my burning youth!
> But I grow old among dreams,

A weather-worn, marble triton
Among the streams.

But if indeed there are grounds for comparison of Landor's prose with this specimen of Yeats's verse, Yeats comes poorly out of the comparison. His 'dreams', his 'lady', and his 'burning youth' are stock properties out of Yeats's poetical wardrobe; and it's not clear what it is that ears, however 'discerning', have to do with looking at a picture in a book. More generally, Yeats's eroticizing of the matter diminishes the image so as to fall in with the readily available sympathies of the most casual reader; for no one has difficulty imagining and sympathizing with the envy and dismay of an ageing man who finds his sexual performance limited and failing, whereas the septuagenarian Landor's image of himself is far stranger, and has nothing to do with physical decrepitude. It's particularly notable that, whereas Landor compared himself with a rock 'rude' and unworked by human hands, Yeats images himself as a rock already converted into art as a 'marble triton', though subsequently eroded and defaced. And this is typical: though Yeats from time to time dallied with the lapidary aspirations of poetry, beguiled by them, he is much less firmly committed to those aspirations than Landor is. Because of Landor's constancy to that ideal, these few sentences of his may prompt the reflection that the true immortality of the poet lies in his having become, he and his works, one more stratum in that cliff, the inherited language, which future poets will apprehend as the raw material they have to work, and to work with. This is a sort of immortality which, not quite logically and yet reasonably, we can envisage as more plausibly surviving some future cataclysm than any one poet's life-record and body of work; for we all know that there are languages, long 'dead', which survive in fragmentary texts only dubiously attributed to named individuals. Landor's 'rude rock in the middle of a river', the craggily inscrutable island that the pleasure-craft pass by, makes that sort of sense in the nuclear age, as Yeats's 'marble triton' does not, and doesn't try to.

As every one must remember, the image of the stone in the stream gets from Yeats far more memorable treatment than what he could find for it in 'Men Improve With The Years':

Hearts with one purpose alone
Through summer and winter seem
Enchanted to a stone
To trouble the living stream.
The horse that comes from the road,
The rider, the birds that range
From cloud to tumbling cloud,

Minute by minute they change;
A shadow of cloud on the stream
Changes minute by minute;
A horse-hoof slides on the brim,
And a horse plashes within it;
The long-legged moor-hens dive,
And hens to moor-cocks call;
Minute by minute they live:
The stone's in the midst of all.

In these famous lines from 'Easter 1916' Yeats cleaves faithfully to Landor's perception, at the same time as he vastly enriches it. In saying so, remembering the occasion of Yeats's poem and also the lines that come next ('Too long a sacrifice / Can make a stone of the heart'), are we not forced to concede what we began by denying: that the stony, the lapidary, means the unfeeling? No, we are not; for the work that begins in tumultuous feeling ends as something sealed or embalmed, wherein the feelings are recognized but the tumult is stilled. Poetry after all belongs in Art, not in Nature; it begins with the natural, but commands and coerces the natural into something else. And so there is, quite properly, something inhuman about poetry. A stone, that is a hunk of nature yet resistant to all that in nature is metamorphosis and flux, is thus not one among many but on the contrary the one right analogue for the thoroughly achieved poem.

Ironweed 12: 2 (fall 1984).

24 Browning and Modernism

The Poems of Browning. Vol. I: 1826-1840, Vol. II: 1841-1846, edited by John Woolford and Daniel Karlin (Harlow, 1991)

Browning is in high favour once again, or promises to be. Has not A.S. Byatt, CBE, declared him 'one of the very greatest English poets'? In a switch to fighting talk, she adds that 'his greatness has never been fully acknowledged or described... in part because he is difficult to docket in terms of the usual literary discussions of Victorian poetry.'[1] We are given no example of the literary discussions allegedly 'usual'. However, the author of *Possession* (Booker Prize 1990) speaks on these matters with authority, being herself a Victorian poet, industrious and prolific:

> These things are there. The garden and the tree
> The serpent at its root, the fruit of gold
> The woman in the shadow of the boughs
> The running water and the grassy space.
> They are and were there. At the old world's rim,
> In the Hesperidean grove, the fruit
> Glowed golden on eternal boughs, and there
> The dragon Ladon crisped his jewelled crest
> Scraped a gold claw and sharped a silver tooth
> And dozed and waited through eternity...

These verses stand at the head of the first chapter of *Possession*, fathered on Byatt's alter ego in the novel as an excerpt from his supposed poem dated 1860, 'The Garden of Proserpine'. David West in the *Times Saturday Review* for 24 August 1991, show-casing the piece in a panel headed 'Reading a Poem', invited us to see here 'many of the characteristics of the best Victorian verse: the vivid and disturbing pictures, the rich organ music...', and 'the learning'. Byatt, he says, 'wrote this Victorian poetry because she needed it'. Very true, no doubt. But what sort of curious need is this, that impels an English novelist in 1990 to revel in the verse-idiom of 130 years before? Are those intervening years a nightmare from which

[1] A.S. Byatt, *Passions of the Mind* (London, 1991) p.29.

we are just awaking, or being exhorted to awake? The clock *can* be put back – is that what we are to think? It is what not just Byatt's admirers but at times Byatt herself would seem to persuade us of.

So how does one protest that these verses, like the hundreds more that Byatt will put into her novel, are acoustically boring? Never a caesura that does not fall pat and undemanding, never before or after the caesura a reversed foot, no interplay that isn't rudimentary between vowel and consonant, no memorable cadence, no justification but metrical exigency for 'sharped' rather than 'sharpened'. If this is 'the best Victorian verse', it is verse that disregards Wyatt and Campion and Pope before it as certainly as, after it, it disregards Pound and the young Eliot. Such blank verse – the unrhymed, relentlessly regular pentameter – can be squeezed out like toothpaste, ignoring the audible shape of any one verse-line or run of lines, because we are supposed to be attending to larger and more urgent matters, like the 'mythic' correspondence of the Garden of Eden with the Garden of the Hesperides. An admiring reader of *Possession* has told me that she 'skipped the verse-bits', and who will blame her?

'To break the pentameter,' wrote Pound recalling his confident youth, 'that was the first heave.' He was wrong on two counts: first, the venerable iambic pentameter, when tagged by rhyme into true couplets or true quatrains, had a lot of life left in it; secondly, his convicting the unrhymed pentameter as the source and locus of Victorian poetastry would go largely unnoticed, not acted on except briefly by an unregarded few. And so it comes about that the Victorians – Browning, no less than George Eliot – are back in favour, not just for their undemanding and verbally profligate forms but for their portentous preoccupation: how to lose religious faith and yet preserve all the psychological comforts which that faith had afforded. More than a century after George Eliot's delphic pronouncements in the Fellows Garden of Trinity College, Cambridge, it seems we must still be impaled on her agnostic aphorisms.

Seventy or eighty years ago the exit from these occlusions was signalled and found, formally: in the lean and stenographic forms, exploring the strange beauties of disconnection, that nowadays we call 'Modernist' and are invited to consign to history's dustbin. What survives of them – indestructibly, for those who have ears to hear – is an acoustic shapeliness that bypasses George Eliot's threatening alternatives by exhibiting a transcendental value – a shaping and thereby transcending of passing time – such as that sybil had never experienced, and so had taken no account of. Not such an acoustic shape, but one that foreshadows it, is in Browning's 'Cavalier Tunes' (1842).

'Stirring stuff,' says someone amusedly. But that isn't the point.

Browning's political ideology, so far as he condescended to have one, wasn't Royalist but Cromwellian – as was only proper for a nonconformist reared in affluent Camberwell. The overt themes of Browning's poems, certainly when he was young, were seldom more than pretexts for him to invent or uncover cadences and rhythmical shapes at odds with the blanket orthodoxy of the iambic pentamenter. It's to be feared that later he seldom recognized this himself, dutifully bending his back to 'concerns' that his advisers declared to be pressing, though in truth they pressed on him hardly at all. In his youth he had the courage of his unconcern:

> Nobly Cape Saint Vincent to the north-west died away;
> Sunset ran, one glorious blood-red, reeking into Cadiz Bay;
> Bluish mid the burning water, full in face Trafalgar lay;
> In the dimmest north-east distance, dawned Gibraltar
> grand and gray;
> 'Here and here did England help me, – how can I help
> England?' – say,
> Whoso turns as I, this evening, turn to God to praise & Pray
> Yonder where Jove's planet rises silent over Africa.

Militaristic? Imperialistic? Was Browning really so sold on the Early Victorian ethos? Interesting though unanswerable questions. What matters, it may be thought, is Browning's audacity in denying us, in the closing verse, the full rhyme we've been so emphatically led to expect. Asymmetry, discontinuity – all the mileage that Modernist artists were to get from these principles is foreshadowed in this brief and (as it may seem) tub-thumping piece of perhaps 1844. Whether Admiral Lord Nelson deserved such accolades is a question that belongs in another universe of discourse; what matters for *poetics* is the momentous proof that off-rhyme can supply a more satisfying closure than full rhyme could. This was one Victorian who could speak to the Modernists; this is his importance historically, and perhaps intrinsically also.

Browning had already effected such a closure in 'Count Gismond' (1842), a much longer poem in stanzas:

> And have you brought my tercel back?
> I was just telling Adela
> How many birds it struck since May.

But Woolford and Karlin don't notice that closures are what they are dealing with, confidently telling us that 'Adela' must be 'pronounced to rhyme with "May"', as in the other poem that 'Africa' must be 'pronounced to rhyme with the other end-words'. No asymmetries for them! And of course this is not nit-picking. When Amiens in *As You Like It* strikes up 'Blow blow, thou winter wind, / Thou art not so unkind / As man's ingratitude' our schoolmistresses were doubtless right to tell us to pronounce 'wind' as 'wynde'. But these are the opening, not the closing lines of Amiens's little piece and (more important) the piece is a *song*, whereas both the Browning poems are for the speaking voice. Moreover, we shall seldom recite either poem and in silent reading the asymmetry will register willy-nilly to the eye: for the point is not how we speak either of the disputed words but how we imagine them spoken. The Browning who skewed his rhyme schemes even as he signed off surely did so deliberately; and in doing so he proved himself nearer to a sophisticated Modernist that his editors realize or can approve. Pronouncing 'Africa' 'Afrikay' pushes poetic language away from common usage, and as with 'sharped' for 'sharpened' it seems that some of us still like it that way.

As late as the 1950s, Browning's Kentish Sir Byng reappeared as Ezra Pound's 'Duke Liu':

> Duke Liu, the frank,
> unhoused, unhapped,
> from bound to bourne
> put all barned corn in sacks
> and ration bags
> for glorious use, stretched bow
> showed shield, lance, dagger-axe
> and squared to the open road.

Of course the Browningesque cadences are not replicated; they are a murmur in the background, for those who have ears to hear them – they are a theme on which the later poet plays variations. Consider only his dissolving of full rhyme into assonance and echo. It should be plain that this is a quite different operation on a Victorian poet from producing a pastiche of him – the one is creative re-invention, the other parasitical.

Those who can't trust their ears may latch on to another page of Pound's *Confucian Anthology*, where Pound explicitly pays his dues by way of the parenthetical epigraph: '(King Charles)'. But in this case Pound's adaptation is so inferior that there's no point quoting anything but the Browning original. This is a deeper and more troubling poem than 'Kentish Sir Byng', because it articulates the all but suicidal sentiment of a doomed remnant. We might not unreasonably imagine some SS detachment in 1945. Thus, 'in Hell's despite' is not hyperbole, nor a rhetorical flourish. But poetically the achievement (not subtle, for it is Browning's virtue always to be bold) is in making the strong stresses of 'King Charles' set a tune for coupled strong stresses later: 'right now', 'fight now', 'went since', 'sank once', 'spent since', 'drank once', 'quaff else', 'laugh else'. In the last stanza where 'boy George quaff else' gives us four strong stresses in sequence, the variation to the falling cadence of 'begot him' and 'shot him' is heart-breaking. This is an effect that blank verse could not manage so concisely, if at all.

There is here, for those who care, a pretty case of intertextuality. For Woolford and Karlin are inclined to accept R.L. Lowe's suggestion, in *Notes and Queries* for 1952, that the source for Browning's 'Cavalier Tunes' was in Walter Scott's *Woodstock*. And this raises the possibility – very unlikely, I think – that Pound drew directly on Scott without needing Browning as intermediary. However, Pound was a very bookish poet, as Browning was also. In Browning's case, the proclivity was inherited: for Browning's father was a perhaps compulsive bibliophile. (And if this seems out of character for a pre-Victorian Dissenter, perhaps we should revise our stereotypes of what a Dissenter of that age might be.) Browning's most explicit attempt to cope with that legacy, physical as well as psychological, was in the second half of a two-part poem that he sent to *Hood's Magazine* in 1844. It is called 'Sibrandus Schafnaburgensis' (that title bookish in itself): and it is too delightful not to be considered in full:

> Plague take all pedants, say I!
>   He who wrote what I hold in my hand,
> Centuries back was so good as to die,
>   Leaving this rubbish to bother the land;
> This, that was a book in its time,
>   Printed on paper and bound in leather,
> Last month in the white of a matin-prime
>   Just when the birds sang altogether,
>
> Into the garden I brought it to read;
>   And under these arbutes and laurestine
> Read it, so help me grace in my need,
>   From title-page to closing line.
> Chapter on chapter did I count,
>   As a curious traveller counts Stonehenge;
> Added up the mortal account;
>   And then proceeded to my revenge.
>
> Yonder's a plum-tree, with a crevice
>   An owl would build in, were he but sage;
> For a lap of moss, like a fine point-levis
>   In a castle of the middle age,

Joins to a lip of gum, pure amber;
  When he'd be private, there might he spend
Hours alone in his lady's chamber:
  Into this crevice I dropped our friend.

Splash, went he, as under he ducked.
  – I knew at the bottom rain-droppings stagnate:
Never a handful of blossoms I plucked
  To bury him with, my book-shelf's magnate:
Then I went in-doors, brought out a loaf,
  Half a cheese, and a bottle of Chablis;
Lay on the grass and forgot the oaf
  Over a jolly chapter of Rabelais.

Now, this morning, betwixt the moss
  And gum that locked our friend in limbo,
A spider has spun his web across,
  And sate in the midst with arms a-kimbo:
So I took pity, for learning's sake,
  And, *de profundibus, accentibus laetis*
Cantate, quoth I, as I got a rake,
  And up I fished his delectable treatise.

Here you have it, dry in the sun,
  With all the binding all of a blister,
And great blue spots where the ink has run,
  And reddish streaks that wink and glister
O'er the pages so beautifully yellow –
  Oh, the droppings have played their tricks!
Did he guess how toadstools grew, this fellow?
  Here's one stuck in his chapter six!

How did he like it when the live creatures
  Tickled and toused and browsed him all over,
And worm, slug, eft, with serious features,
  Came in, each one, for his right of trover;
When the water-beetle with great blind dead face
  Made of her eggs the stately deposit,
And the newt borrowed so much of the preface
  As tiled in the top of his black wife's closet.

All that life, and fun, and romping,
  All that frisking, and twisting, and coupling,
While slowly our poor friend's leaves were swamping,
  Clasps cracking, and covers suppling!

As if you had carried sour John Knox
  To the play at Paris, Vienna, or Munich,
Fastened him into a front-row box,
  And danced off the Ballet in trowsers and tunic.

Come, old martyr! What, torment enough is it?
  Back to my room shall you take your sweet self!
Good bye, mother-beetle: husband-eft, *sufficit*!
  See the snug niche I have made on my shelf.
A's book shall prop you up, B's shall cover you,
  Here's C to be grave with, or D to be gay,
And with E on each side, and F right over you,
  Dry-rot at ease till the judgment-day!

This poem has its light-hearted but still mordant contribution to make to up-to-the-minute soul-searchings about 'the canon'. What is modernist about it is the foregrounding (as we have learned to call it) of artifice: Browning's rhymes exultantly draw attention to themselves, there is no pretence that they 'just happened' or 'came naturally'. The trans-lingual rhyme in the fifth stanza – '*accentibus laetis*' with 'treatise' – was obviously a precedent for the Greek/English rhyme on 'tin' that has caused apoplexy in readers of 'Hugh Selwyn Mauberley'; though even more audacious, because of the rhythmical disturbance it makes, is, in the seventh stanza, the rhyme of 'blind dead face' with 'preface'. Perhaps this is not modern but post-modern; unashamedly, in any case, it kicks over the traces of the Horatian maxim that the art is in the concealment of art. True on the contrary to the Rabelaisian authority that it invokes, the poem will not pretend to be anything but what it is: exuberantly an artifact. In such a case it is pointless to complain that the occasion, the overt theme, does not deserve such elaboration. For the discrepancy between the occasion and its elaboration is precisely, as in Rabelais, the point that is being made. The far from Rabelaisian texts that Browning subsequently read – David Strauss's and Renan's Lives of Jesus, for instance – are more to the taste of A.S. Byatt, but they supplied the poet with no comparable occasions for displaying the exuberance of artifice.

Moreover this art, pushed so intransigently under our noses, is not 'for its own sake', it is not Parnassian. For Elizabeth Barrett was on the ball when she applauded the poem: 'it is so new, & full of a creeping crawling grotesque life.' We may have had our fill of creepy-crawlies since: but in 1844 to sympathize with slugs and newts was momentous, and an achievement not just of art but precisely of sympathy – that's to say, of nature.

A.S. Byatt's sensibility is, as she knows and frankly professes, mythopoeic or mythographic: the constant slippage of time is, so far as she's concerned, to be arrested and conquered not by acoustic shapings but by the observed and perpetuated recurrence of certain primordial myths. Accordingly she takes seriously Browning's initial sympathy with Shelley, and she finds among his successors Van Gogh (surprisingly but persuasively) and Wallace Stevens – the Stevens who wrote pentameters, in 'Sunday Morning'. But this case for Browning rests on much later poems than those in these first two volumes. The young Browning was at his best when he was being sportive and audacious, formally restless and inventive. We must wait for later volumes in this exhaustively erudite edition to see whether the sportiveness did not ossify into idiosyncrasy, and whether, as hospitality to myth brought Browning nearer the world of Freud and Sir James Frazer, this enriched his poetry or merely demoted him from the rank of poet to that of earnestly worried, though never *very* worried, thinker.

However, there remains *Sordello*, perhaps the most proto-modernist of all Browning's poems and among his most ambitious ever. Woolford and Karlin say roundly: '*Sordello* is Browning's central and pivotal work.' This is disconcerting, for *Sordello* is a very tiresome poem, and has been found so ever since it first appeared in 1840, when it was almost universally panned, and destroyed Browning's reputation for years after. However, a tiresome poem can also be a great one, as we know from the case of Pound's *Cantos*, a poem which began indeed as an attempt to rewrite *Sordello*.

Accordingly it is Ronald Bush, in a book about Pound (*The Genesis of Ezra Pound's 'Cantos'*, 1976), who has put his finger on the tiresomeness of Browning's poem, speaking of its 'infamously confusing use of parataxis'. Parataxis is the habit of mind, hence of speaking and writing, which distrusts all connectives except 'and': in the *OED* definition, 'the placing of propositions or clauses one after another, without indicating by connecting words the relation (of co-ordination or subordination) between them'. This makes it seem that paratactic grammar is primitive or naive; and so it is, if we believe E.A. Havelock in his *Preface to Plato*, who found Homer paratactic whereas Plato set us on the opposite course, hypotaxis, which has governed us ever since. Citing Homer suggests that parataxis is peculiarly fitted to narrative, and Browning, quite apart from the primitivism that attracted him, made this inference too: unbelievably, he thought that, making *Sordello* a narrative, he would appeal to a more popular audience than he'd reached with his non-narrative and Shelleyan poems of length, 'Pauline' and 'Paracelsus'. What he and many of his modernist successors failed to recognize was that harking back to this primitive or naive grammar did not in any way guarantee limpidity: on the contrary, eliminating all the signs that distinguish co-ordination from subordination creates an obscurity, a proliferation of ambiguities, that is all but impenetrable – in the nature of the case, not just because we have been conditioned through centuries to expect the hypotactic rather than the paratactic. In a later phase of the modernist endeavour this would be recognized, so that Michael Edwards (*Of Making Many Books*, 1990) can say of Charles Tomlinson – in my view, quite rightly: 'Tomlinson's syntax is what makes his poems, linguistically, what they are... in the poetry of our century, Tomlinson enacts the revenge of hypotaxis.'

So, where or how does that leave *Sordello*? An enigmatic fossil that, seventy years too soon, encapsulated a modernist endeavour that was bound in the event to fail? Even on that understanding reading *Sordello* is a sort of duty, a required act of homage to, as it were, a dauntless pioneer. But people do not read poems because they are in duty bound to do so (unless they are unfortunate students). So... is *Sordello*, even now, *readable*?

Certainly it is nearer being so in this edition than ever before, thanks to the notes, which much of the time simply explain to us what the hell is going on. But what are the rewards of this in any case unsettling procedure, switching from text to notes and back again? Pound in *ABC of Reading*, having given sixty lines from Book One of *Sordello* as an exhibit, exhorted us: 'There is here a certain lucidity of sound that I think you will with difficulty find elsewhere in English, and you very well may have to retire as far as the *Divina Commedia* for continued narrative having such clarity of outline without clog and *verbal* impediment.' But we may concede to Pound, if only for argument's sake, that the impediment is not 'verbal': what it is, we may protest, is structural (which is worse). For the paratactic principle can be extended outside the sentence, as it is by both Browning and Pound, to govern the disposition in the poem of much larger units, which we may call 'episodes' or 'scenes'. The scene that Pound picks out for his exhibit, the description of a font with caryatids, comes to us with no indication of how it is either co-ordinated with, or subordinated to, what has gone before. And this is what creates the obscurity of the *Cantos* as of *Sordello* – an obscurity that no consulting of dictionaries or Annotated Indexes can clear up.

The most useful thing that Pound says is the tip that he gives in his last sentence: 'Again as in the case of Golding, the reader must read it as prose, pausing for the sense and not hammering the line-terminations.' This Golding is Arthur Golding, who published in 1567 Ovid's *Metamorphoses* translated into couplet-rhyming fourteeners. Earlier in *ABC of Reading* Pound had enthusiastically exhibited excerpts from this work, and had added: 'The reader will be well advised to read according to sense and syntax, keep from thumping, observe the syntactical pause, and not stop for the line ends save where sense requires or a comma indicates.' Pound's advice that this is also how to read *Sordello* flies in the face of Woolford and Karlin, who declare: '*Sordello* is a narrative in six books, written in heroic couplets.' This is surely wrong: Browning's couplets are not 'heroic', for his couplet is not a compositional unit, as it was for Dryden or Pope, but merely as with Golding a device for 'keeping going'. Accordingly, if we look for acoustic shapes in *Sordello*, we cannot expect anything so ringing and emphatic as we find in 'Cavalier Tunes', nor anything so crisp and compact as in the best of Dryden or Pope, but only the much more relaxed and fugitive music that sounds in Golding's couplets or Chaucer's:

> Then wide
> Opened the great morass, shot every side
> With flashing water through and through; a-shine,
> Thick steaming, all alive. Whose shape divine
> Quivered i' the farthest rainbow-vapour, glanced
> Athwart the flying herons? He advanced,
> But warily; though Mincio leaped no more,
> Each foot-fall burst up in the marish floor
> A diamond jet: and if you stopped to pick
> Rose-lichen, or molest the leeches quick,
> And circling blood-worms, minnow, newt or loach,
> A sudden pond would silently encroach
> This way and that.

But no, it's no good. This passage isn't typical; and anyhow it's no great shakes – 'shape divine', indeed! The rhyme doesn't in the end do anything to stiffen or to disturb (except loutishly) the run of pentameters that might as well be blank verse. *Sordello* is, whatever concessions we make and however we genuflect to Pound, indeed a fossil – evidence, for literary archaeologists, of the prehistory of the Modern Movement. The young Browning that we need to remember and revere is the author not of *Sordello* but of 'Sibrandus Schafnaburgensis'.

London Review of Books, 10 October 1991.

Index of Names